T0262729

Embedded Systems: High Performance Systems, Applied Principles and Practice

Embedded Systems: High Performance Systems, Applied Principles and Practice

Edited by **Alan Moore**

New Jersey

Published by Clanrye International,
55 Van Reypen Street,
Jersey City, NJ 07306, USA
www.clanryeinternational.com

Embedded Systems: High Performance Systems, Applied Principles and Practice
Edited by Alan Moore

International Standard Book Number: 978-1-63240-169-4 (Hardback)

Printed in the United States of America.

Contents

Preface

The purpose of the book is to provide a glimpse into the dynamics and to present opinions and studies of some of the scientists engaged in the development of new ideas in the field from very different standpoints. This book will prove useful to students and researchers owing to its high content quality.

In today's time, embedded systems i.e. computer systems that are embedded in different types of devices play a crucial role in particular control functions and have led to progress of different aspects of industry. Hence, we can hardly discuss our life, or even society, nowadays without referring to embedded systems. A number of high quality fundamental and applied researches are crucial to broaden the range of growth of these embedded systems. This book deals with research topics of various researchers and engineers across the world, which discusses embedded systems along with parallel computing, communication architecture, application-specific systems, and embedded systems projects. Various technologies have been illustrated in this book which will prove to be beneficiary for scientists around the globe.

At the end, I would like to appreciate all the efforts made by the authors in completing their chapters professionally. I express my deepest gratitude to all of them for contributing to this book by sharing their valuable works. A special thanks to my family and friends for their constant support in this journey.

Editor

Part 1

Multiprocessor, Multicore, NoC, and Communication Architecture

1

Parallel Embedded Computing Architectures

Michael Schmidt, Dietmar Fey and Marc Reichenbach
Embedded Systems Institute, Friedrich-Alexander-University Erlangen-Nuremberg Germany

1. Introduction

It was around the years 2003 to 2005 that a dramatic change seized the semiconductor industry and the manufactures of processors. The increasing of computing performance in processors, based on simply screwing up the clock frequency, could not longer be holded. All the years before the clock frequency could be steadily increased by improvements achieved both on technology and on architectural side. Scaling of the technology processes, leading to smaller channel lengths and shorter switching times in the devices, and measures like instruction-level-parallelism and out-of-order processing, leading to high fill rates in the processor pipelines, were the guarantors to meet Moore's law.

However, below the 90 nm scale, the static power dissipation from leakage current surpasses dynamic power dissipation from circuit switching. From now on, the power density had to be limited, and as a consequence the increase of clock frequency came nearly to stagnation. At the same time architecture improvements by extracting parallelism out of serial instruction streams was completely exhausted. Hit rates of more than 99% in branch prediction could not be improved further on without reasonable effort for additional logic circuitry and chip area in the control unit of the processor.

The answer of the industry to that development, in order to still meet Moore's law, was the shifting to real parallelism by doubling the number of processors on one chip die. This was the birth of the multi-core area (Blake et al., 2009). The benefits of multi-core computing, to meet Moore's law and to limit the power density at the same time, at least at the moment this statement holds, are also the reason that parallel computing based on multi-core processors is underway to capture more and more also the world of embedded processing.

2. Task parallelism vs. data parallelism

If we speak about parallelism applied in multi-cores, we have to distinguish very carefully which kind of parallelism we refer to. According to a classical work on design patterns for parallel programming (Mattson et al., 2004), we can define on the algorithmic level two kinds of a decomposition strategy for a serial program in a parallel version, namely *task parallelism* and *data parallelism*. The result of such a decomposition is a number of sub-problems we will call tasks in the following. If these tasks carry out different work among each other, we call this task parallelism. In task parallelism tasks are usually ordered according to their data dependencies. If tasks are independent of each other these tasks can be carried out concurrently, e.g. on the cores of a multi-core processor. If one task produces an output which is an input for another task, these tasks have to be scheduled in a time serial manner.

This situation is different in the case of a given problem which can be decomposed according to geometric principles. That means, we have given a 2D or 3D problem space which is divided in sub regions. In each sub region the same function is carried out. Each sub region is further subdivided in grid points and also on each grid point the same function is applied to. Often this function requires also input from grid points located in the nearest neighbourhood of the grid point. A common parallelization strategy for such problems is to process the grid points of one sub region in a serial manner and to process all sub regions simultaneously, e.g. on different cores. Also this function can be denoted as a task. As mentioned, all these tasks are identical and are applied to different data, whereas the tasks in task parallelism carry out different tasks usually. Furthermore, data parallel tasks can be processed in a complete synchronous way. That means, there are only geometric dependencies between these tasks and no casual time dependencies among the tasks, what is once again contrary to the case of task parallelism. If there are time dependencies then they hold for all tasks. That is why they are synchronous in the sense that all grid points are updated in a time serial loop.

Task parallelism we find e.g. in applications of Computational Science. In molecular biology the positions of molecules are computed depending on electrical and chemical forces. These forces can be calculated independent from each other. An example of a data parallelism problem is the solution of partial differential equations.

2.1 Task parallelism in embedded applications

Where do we find these task parallelism in embedded systems? A good example are automotive applications. The integration of more and more different functionality in a car, e.g. for infotainment, driver assistance, different electronic control units for valves, fuel injection etc. lead to a very complex diversity that offers a lot of potential for parallelization, naturally requiring diverse tasks. The desire why automotive goes to multi-core is based on two reasons. One time there are lot of real-time tasks to fulfill for which a multi-core technology offers in principle the necessary computing power. A further reason is the following one. Today nearly every control unit contains its own single core micro controller or micro processor. Multi-core technology in combination with a broadband efficient network system offers the possibility to save components, too, by migrating functionality that is now distributed among a quite large number of compute devices to fewer cores. Automotive is just one example for an embedded system domain in which task parallelism is the dominant potential for parallelization. Similar scenarios can be found for robotics and automation engineering.

2.2 Data parallelism in embedded applications

As consequence one can state that the main parallelization strategy for embedded applications is task parallelism. However, there is a smaller but not less important application field in which data parallelism occurs. Evaluating and analyzing of data streams in optical, X-ray or ultra sonic 3D metrology requires data parallelism in order to realize fast response times. Mostly image processing tasks, e.g. fast execution of correlations, have to be fulfilled in the mentioned application scenarios. To integrate such a functionality in smart cameras, or even in in the electronics of measuring or drill heads, is a challenge for future embedded system design. In this chapter, we lay a focus in particular to convenient pipeline and data structures for applying data parallelism in embedded systems (see Chapter 4).

3. Principles of embedded multi-core processors

3.1 Multi-core processors in embedded systems

In this subsection, we show briefly a kind of evolutionary development comprising a stepwise integration of processor principles, known from standard processors, into embedded processors. The last step of this development process is the introduction of multi-core technology in embedded processors. Representative for different embedded processors, we select in this chapter the development of the ARM processor family as it is described in (Stallings, 2006). Maybe the most characteristic highlights of ARM processors are their small chip die sizes and their low power requirements. Both features are of course of high importance for applications in embedded environments. ARM is a product of ARM Inc., Cambridge, England. ARM works as a fabless company, that means they don't manufacture chips, moreover they design microprocessors and microcontrollers and sell these designs under license to other companies. Embedded ARM architectures can be found in many handheld and consumer products, like e.g. in Apple's iPod and iPhone devices. Therefore, ARM processors are probably not only one of the most widely used processors in embedded designs but one of the most world wide used processors at all.

The first ARM processor, denoted as ARM1, was a 32-bit RISC (Reduced Instruction Set Computer) processor. It arose in 1985 as product of the company Acorn, which designed the first commercial RISC processor, the Acorn RISC Machine (ARM), as a coprocessor for a computer used at British Broadcasting Corporation (BBC). The ARM1 was expanded towards an integrated memory management unit, a graphics and I/O processor unit and an enhanced instruction set like multiply and swap instructions and released as ARM2 in the same year. Four years later, in 1989, the processor was equipped with a unified data and instruction level one (L1) cache as ARM3. It followed the support of 32-bit addresses and the integration of a floating-point unit in the ARM6, the integration of further components as System-on-Chip (SoC) in the ARM6, and static branch prediction units, deeper pipeline stages and enhanced DSP (Digital Signal Processing) facilities. The design of the ARM6 was also the first product of a new company, formed by Acorn, VLSI and Apple Computer.

In 2009 ARM released with the Cortex-A5 MPCore processor their first multi-core processor intended for usage in mobile devices. The intention was to provide one of the smallest and most power-efficient multi-core processor to achieve both the performance, that is needed in smartphones, and to offer low costs for cheap chip manufacturing. Exactly like the ARM11 MP Core, another multi-core processor from ARM, it can be configured as a device containing up to 4 cores on one processor die.

3.2 Brief overview of selected embedded multi-core architectures

The ARM Cortex A9 processor (ARM, 2007) signifies the second generation of ARM's multi-core processor technology. It was also intended for processing general-purpose computing tasks in computing devices, starting from mobile devices and ending up in netbooks. Each single core of an ARM Cortex A9 processor works as a superscalar out-of-order processor (see Figure 1). That means, the processor consists of multiple parallel operable pipelines. Instructions fetched in these pipelines can outpace each other so that they can be completed contrary to the order they are issued. The cores have a two-level cache system. Each L1 cache can be configured from 16 to 64 KB that is quite large for an embedded processor. Using such a large cache supports the design for a high clock frequency of 2 GHz in order to speed-up the execution of a single thread. In order to maintain the coherency between the cache contents and the memory, a broadcast interconnect system is used. Since the number of cores is still small, the risk is low that the system is running in bottlenecks. Two of such ARM Cortex A9 processors are integrated with a C64x DSP (Digital Signal Processor) core and further controller cores in a heterogeneous multi-core system-on-chip solution called TI OMAP 4430 (Tex, 2009). This system is intended also as general-purpose processor for smart phones and mobile Internet devices (MIDs). Typical data parallel applications do not approve as very efficient for such processors. In this sense, the ARM Cortex A9 and the TI OMAP 4430 processors are more suited for task parallel embedded applications.

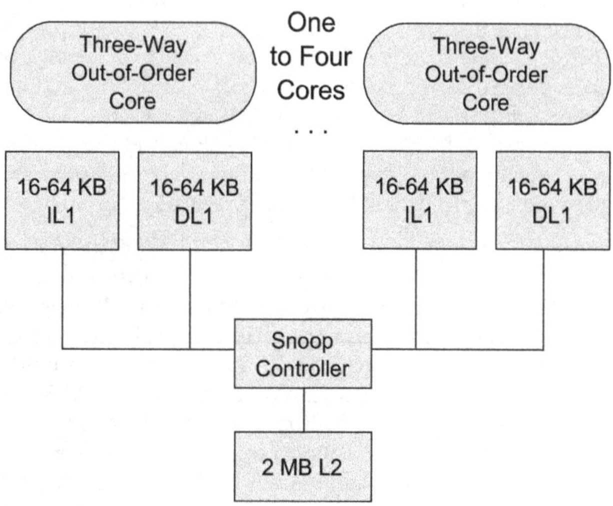

Fig. 1. Block diagram of the ARM Cortex-A9 MP, redrawn from (Blake et al., 2009)

Contrary to those processors, the ECA (Elemental Computing Array) (Ele, 2008) processor family targets to very low power processing of embedded data parallel tasks, e.g. in High Definition Video Processing or Software Defined Signal Conditioning. The architecture concept realized in this solution is very different from the schemes we find in the above described multi-core solutions. Maybe, it points in a direction also HPC systems will pursue in the future (see Chapter 5). The heart of that architecture is an array of fine-grain heterogeneous specialized and programmable processor cores (see Figure 2). The embedded processor ECA-64 consists of four clusters of such cores and each cluster aggregates one processor core operating to RISC principles and further simpler 15 ALUs which are tailored to fulfill specialized tasks. The programming of that ALUs happens similarly as it is done in Field-Programmable-Gate-Arrays (FPGAs).

An important constraint for the low power characteristics of the processors is the data-driven operation mode of the ALUs, i.e. the ALUs are only switched on if data is present at their inputs. Also the memory subsystem is designed to support low power. All processor cores in one cluster share a local memory of 32 kB. The access to the local memory has to be performed completely by software, which avoids to integrate sophisticated and power consuming hardware control resources. This shifts the complexity of coordinating concurrent

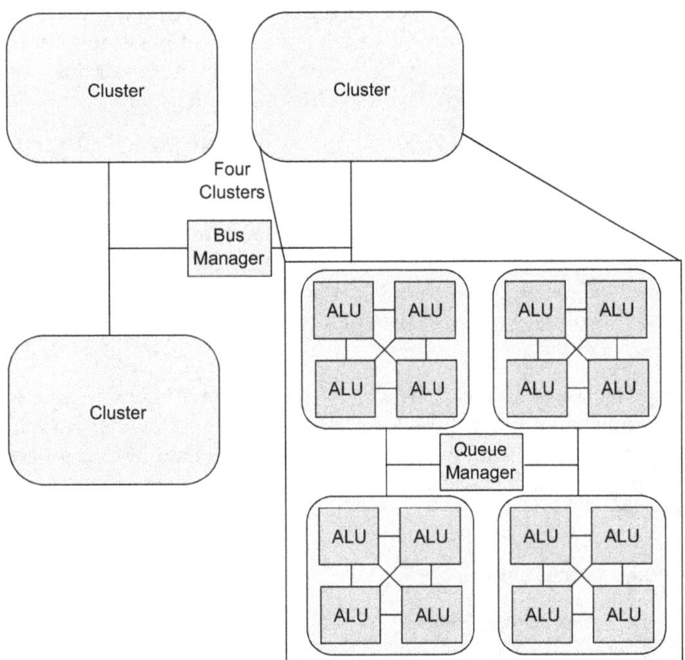

Fig. 2. Element CXI ECA-64 block diagram, redrawn from (Blake et al., 2009)

memory accesses to the software. The interconnect is hierarchical. Following the hierarchical architecture organization of the processor cores also the interconnect system has to be structured hierarchically. Four processor cores are tightly coupled via a crossbar. In one cluster four of these crossbar connected cores are linked in a point-to-point fashion using a queue system. On the highest hierarchical level the four clusters are coupled via a bus and a bus manager arbitrating the accesses of the clusters on the bus.

Hierarchically and heterogeneously organized processor, memory and interconnect systems, as we find it in the ECA processor, are pioneering in our view for future embedded multi-core architectures to achieve both high computing performance and low power processing. However, particular data parallelism applications require additional sophisticated data access patterns that consider the 2D or 3D nature of data streams given in such applications. Furthermore, they must be well-tailored to a hierarchical memory system to exploit the benefits such an organization offers. These are time overlapping of data processing and of data transfer to hide latency and to increase bandwidth by data buffering in pipelined architectures. To achieve that, we developed special data access templates, we will explain in detail in the next section.

4. Memory-management for data parallel applications in embedded systems

The efficient realization of applications with multi-core or many-core processors in an embedded system is a great challenge. With application-specific architectures it is possible to save energy, reduce latency or increase throughput according to the realized operations, in contrast to the usage of standard CPUs. Besides the optimization of the processor architecture, also the integration of the cores in the embedded environment plays an important role. This means, the number of applied cores[1] and their coupling to memories or bus systems has to be chosen carefully, in order to avoid bottlenecks in the processing chain.

The most basic constraints are defined by the application itself. First of all, the amount of data to be processed in a specific time slot is essential. For processor-intensive applications the key task is to find an efficient processing scheme for the cores in combination with integrated hardware accelerators. The main problem in data-intensive applications is the timing of data provision. Commonly, the external memory or bus bandwidth is the main bottleneck in these applications. A load balancing between data memory access and data processing is required. Otherwise, there will be idle processor cores or available data segments cannot be fetched in time for processing.

Image processing is a class of applications which is mainly data-intensive and a clear example of a data parallel application in an embedded system. In the following, we will take a closer look at this special type of application. We assume a SoC with a multi-core processor and a fast but small internal memory (e.g. caches) and a large but slow external memory or alternatively a coupled bus system.

4.1 Embedded image processing

Image processing operations are basically distinguished in pre-processing operations and post-processing operations also known as image recognition (Bräunl, 2001). Image pre-processing operations, like filter operations for noise reduction, require only a local view on the image data. Commonly, an image pixel and its neighbours in a limited environment[2] are required for processing. Image recognition, on the other hand, requires a global view on the image and, therefore, a random access to the image pixels.

Image processing operations with only a local view on the image data allow a much better way of parallelization then post-processing operations, which are less or not parallelizable. Hence, local operations should be prefered, if possible, to ensure an efficient realization on a multi-core architecture in an embedded image processing system. Therefore, we have shown how some global image operations can be solved with only local operators. This concept is called *Marching Pixels* and was first introduced in (Fey & Schmidt, 2005). It allows for example the centroid detection of multiple objects in an image which is required in industrial image processing (Fey et al., 2010). The disadvantage of this approach is that the processing has to be realized iteratively.

To parallelize local image processing operations, there exist several approaches. One possibility is the *partitioning* of the image and the parallel processing of the partitions which will be part of Section 4.2. A further approach is a *streaming* of image data together with an adapted parallelization which is the subject-matter of Section 4.3. Also a combination of both approaches is possible. Which type of parallelization should be established depends strongly on the application, the used multi-core architecture and the available on-chip memory.

---

[1] degree of parallelization

[2] which is called *mask, sliding window* or also *stencil*

4.2 Partitioning

A partitioning of an image can be used, if the internal memory of an embedded multi-core system is not large enough to store the complete image. A problem occurs, if an image is partitioned for calculation. For the processing of an image pixel, a specific number of adjacent neighbours, in dependence of the stencil size, is required. For the processing of a partition boundary, additional pixels have to be loaded in the internal memory. The additional required area of these pixels is called *ghostzone* and is illustrated with waved lines in Figure 3. There are two ways for a parallel processing of partitions (Figures 3(a) and 3(b)).

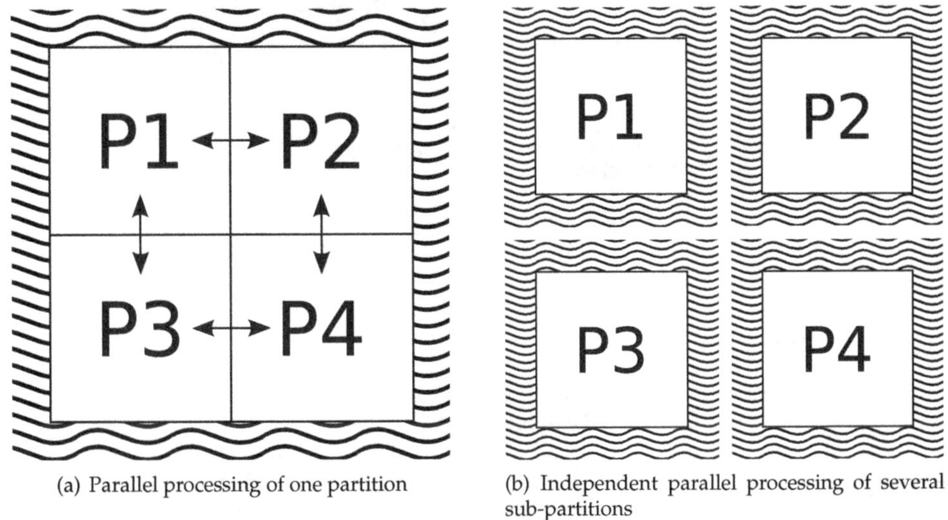

(a) Parallel processing of one partition

(b) Independent parallel processing of several sub-partitions

Fig. 3. Image partitioning approaches

A partition could be loaded in the internal memory, shared for the different cores of a multi-core architecture, and this partition is processed in parallel by several cores as illustrated in Figure 3(a). The disadvantage is, that adjacent cores require image pixels from each other. This can be solved with a shared memory or a communication over a common bus system. In the second approach shown in Figure 3(b), every core gets a sub-partition with its own ghostzone area. Hence, no communication or data sharing is required but the overhead for storing ghostzone pixels is greater and more internal memory is required. If the communication overhead between the processor cores is smaller than the loading overhead for additional ghostzone pixels, then the first approach should be preferred. This is the case in closely coupled cores like fine-granular processor arrays for example.

The partitioning should be realized in squared regions. They are optimal with regard to the relationship between the partition area and the overhead for the ghostzone area. In (Reichenbach et al., 2011), we presented the partitioning schemes in more detail and developed an analytical model. The goal was to find an optimal set of system parameters depending on application constraints, to achieve a load balancing between a multi-core processor and an external memory or bus system. We presented a so called *Adapted Roofline Model* for embedded application-specific multi-core systems which was closely modeled on the *Roofline Model* (Williams et al., 2009) for standard multi-core processors. Our adapted model is illustrated in Figure 4.

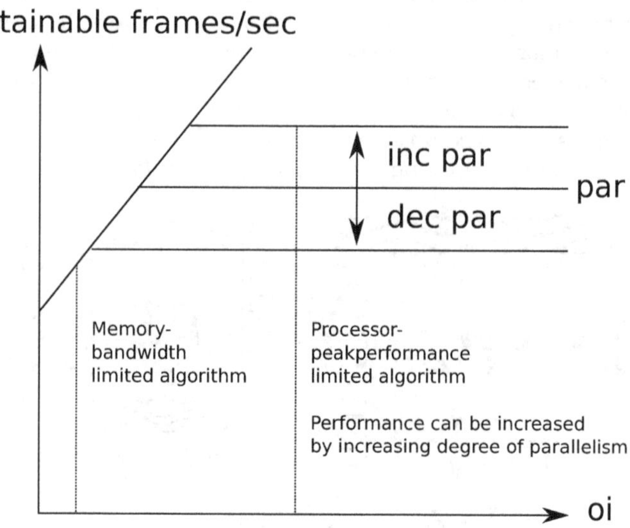

Fig. 4. Adapted roofline model

It shows the relationship between the processor performance and the external memory bandwidth. The horizontal axis reflects the operational intensity *oi* which is the number of operations applied to a loaded byte and is given by the image processing operation. The vertical axis reflects the achievable performance in frames per second. The horizontal curves with parameter *par* represent the multi-core processor performance for a specific degree of parallelization and the diagonal curve represents the limitation by the external memory bandwidth. Algorithms with a low operational intensity are commonly memory bandwidth limited. Only a few operations per loaded byte have to be performed per time slot and so the processor cores are often idle until new data is available. On the other hand, algorithms with a high operational intensity are limited by the peak performance of the processor. This means, there is enough data available per time step but the processor cores are working to capacity. In these cases, the achievable performance depends on the number of cores, i.e. the degree of parallelization. The points of intersection between the diagonal curve and the horizontal curves are optimal because there is an equal load balancing between processor performance and external memory bandwidth.

In a standard multi-core system, the degree of parallelization is fixed and the performance can be only improved with specific architecture features, like SIMD units or by exploitation of cache effects for example. In an application-specific multi-core system this is not necessarily the case. It is possible that the degree of parallelization can be chosen, for example if Soft-IP processors are used for FPGAs or for the development of ASICs. Hence, the degree of parallelization can be chosen optimally, depending on the available external memory bandwidth. In (Reichenbach et al., 2011) we have also shown how the operational intensity of an image processing algorithm can be influenced. As already mentioned, the Marching Pixel algorithms are iterative approaches. There exist also iterative image pre-processing operations like the *skeletonization* for example. All these iterative mask algorithms are known as iterative stencil loops (ISL). By increasing the ghostzone width for these algorithms, it is possible to process several iterations for one loaded partition. This means, the operations per loaded byte can be increased. A higher operational intensity leads to a better utilization of the external memory bandwidth. Hence, the degree of parallelization can be increased until an equal load balancing is achieved which leads to an increased performance.

Such analytical models, like our Adapted Roofline Model, are not only capable for the optimized development of new application-specific architectures. They can also be used to analyze existing systems to find bottlenecks in the processing chain. In previous work, we developed an multi-core SoC for solving ISL algorithms which is called *ParCA* (Reichenbach et al., 2010). With the Adapted Roofline Model, we identified a bottleneck in the processing chain of this architecture, because the ghostzone width was not taken into account during the development of the architecture. By using an analytical model based on the constraints of the application, the system parameters like the degree of parallelization can be determined optimally, before an application-specific architecture is developed.

In conclusion, the partitioning can be used, if an image cannot be stored completely in the internal memory of a multi-core architecture. Because of the ghostzone, a data sharing is required if an image is partitioned for processing. If the cores of a processor are closely coupled, a partition should be processed in parallel by several cores. Otherwise, several sub-partitions with additional ghostzone pixels should be distributed to the processor cores. The partition size has to be chosen by means of the available internal memory and the used partition approach. If an application-specific multi-core system is developed, an analytical model based on the application constraints should be used to determine optimal system parameters like the degree of parallelization in relationship to the external memory bandwidth.

4.3 Streaming

Whenever possible, a streaming of the image data for the processing of local image processing operations should be preferred. The reason is, that a streaming approach is optimal relating to the required external memory accesses. The concept is presented in Figure 5.

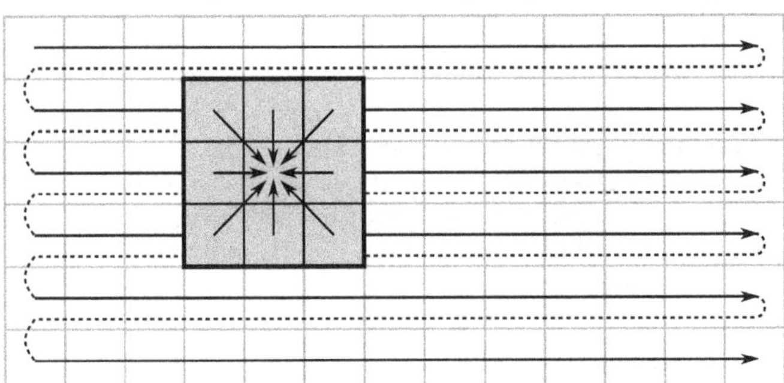

Fig. 5. Streaming approach

The image is processed from the upper left to the lower right corner for example. The internal memory is arranged as a large shift register to store several image lines. A processor core has access to the required pixels of the mask. The size of the shift register depends on the image size and the stencil size. For a 3×3 mask, two complete image lines and three pixels have to be buffered internally. The image pixels are loaded from the external memory and stored in the shift register. If the shift register is filled, then in every clock cycle a pixel can be processed by the stencil operation from a processor core, all pixels are shifted to the next position and the next image pixel is stored in the shift register. Hence, every pixel of the image has to be loaded only once during processing. This concept is also know as *Full Buffering*.

Strictly speaking, the streaming approach is also a kind of partitioning in image lines. But this approach requires a specially arranged internal memory which does not allow a random access to the memory as to the cache of a standard multi-core processor. Furthermore, a strict synchronization between the processor cores is required. Therefore, the streaming is presented separately. Nevertheless, this concept can be emulated with standard multi-core processors by consistent exploitation of cache blocking strategies as used in (Nguyen et al., 2010) for example.

In (Schmidt et al., 2011) we have shown that the Full Buffering can be used efficiently for a parallel processing with a multi-core architecture. We developed a generic VHDL model for the realization of this concept on a FPGA or an application-specific SoC. The architecture is illustrated for a FPGA solution with different degrees of parallelization in Figure 6. The processor cores are designated as *PE*. They have access to all relevant pixel registers required for the stencil operation. The shift registers are realized with internal dual-port Block RAM modules to save common resources of the FPGA. For a parallel processing of the image data stream, the number of shifted pixels per time step depends on the degree of parallelization. It can be adapted depending on the available external memory bandwidth to achieve a load balancing. Besides the degree of parallelization as parameter for the template, the image size, the bits per image pixel and also the pipeline depth can be chosen. The Full Buffering concept allows a pipelining of several Full Buffering stages and can be used for iterative approaches or for the consecutively processing of several image pre-processing operations. The pipelining is illustrated in Figure 7. The result pixels of a stage are not stored back in the external memory, but are fetched by the next stage. This is only possible, because there are no redundant memory accesses to image pixels when Full Buffering is used.

Depending on the stencil size, the required internal memory for a Full Buffering approach can be too large. But instead of using a partitioning, as presented before, a combination of both approaches is also possible. This means, the image is partitioned and a Full Buffering is applied for all partitions consecutively. For this approach, a partitioning of the image in stripes is the most promising. As already mentioned before, the used approach depends on the application constraints, the used multi-core architecture and the available on-chip memory. We currently expand the analytical model from (Reichenbach et al., 2011) in order that all cases are covered. Then it will be possible to predict the optimal processing scheme, for a given set of system parameters.

4.4 Image processing pipeline

In order to realize a complete image processing pipeline, it is possible to combine a streaming approach with an multi-core architecture for image recognition operations. Because the Marching Pixel approaches are highly iterative, we developed an ASIC architecture with a processor array fitted to the requirements of this special class of algorithms. The experiences from the *ParCA* architecture (Reichenbach et al., 2010) has gone into the development process

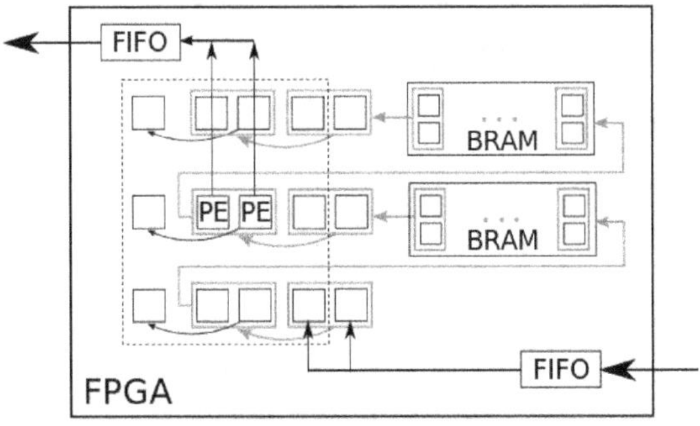

(a) Degree of parallelization p=2

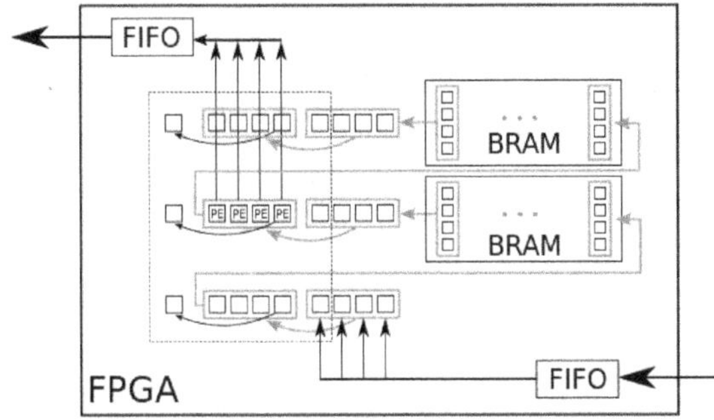

(b) Degree of parallelization p=4

Fig. 6. Generic Full Buffering template for streaming applications

to improve the architecture concept and a new ASIC was developed (Loos et al., 2011). Because an image has to be enhanced, e.g. with a noise reduction, before the Marching Pixel algorithms can be performed efficiently, it is sensible to combine the ASIC with a streaming architecture for image pre-processing operations. An appropriate pipeline architecture was presented in (Schmidt et al., 2011). Instead of a application-specific multi-core architecture for image recognition operations, also a standard multi-core processor like ARM-Cortex A9-MP or the ECE-64 (see Chapter 3) can be used.

In this subchapter we pursued the question which data access patterns can be efficiently used in embedded multi-core processors for memory bound data parallel applications. Since many HPC applications are memory bound, too, the presented schemes can also be profitably used in HPC applications. This leads us to the general question of convergence between embedded computing and HPC which we want to discuss conclusively.

5. Convergence of parallel embedded computing and high performance computing

Currently a lot of people are talking of Green IT. Even if some think this is nothing else like another buzzword, we are convinced that all computer architects have the responsibility for future generations to think of energy-aware processor architectures intensively. In the past

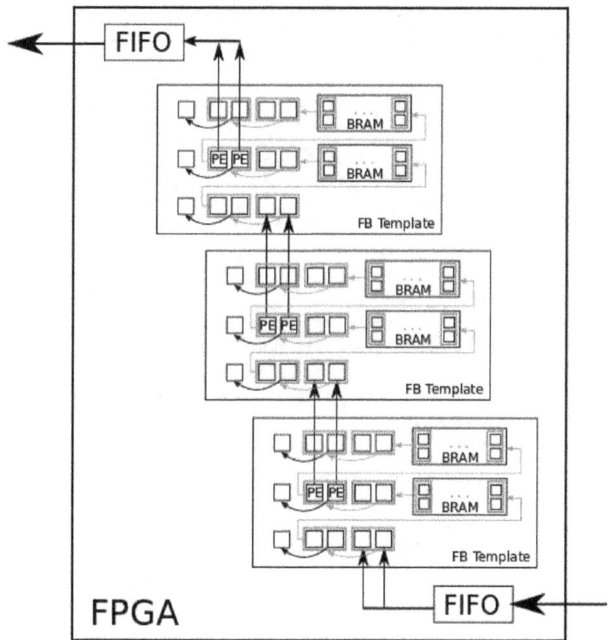

Fig. 7. Pipelining of Full Buffering stages

this was not valid in particular for the HPC community for which achieving the highest performance was the primary goal first of all. However, increasing energy costs, which cannot be ignored anymore, initiated a process of rethinking which could be the beginning of a convergence between methods used in HPC and in embedded computing design.

Therefore, one of the driving forces why such a convergence will probably take place is that the HPC community can learn from the embedded community how to design energy-saving architectures. But this is not only an one-sided process. Vice versa the embedded community can learn from the HPC community how to use efficiently methods and tools for parallel processing since the embedded community requires, besides power efficient solutions, more and more increasing performance. As we have shown above, this leaded to the introduction of multi-core technology in embedded processors. In this section, we want to point out arguments that speak for an adaptation of embedded computing methods in HPC(5.1) and vice versa (5.2). Finally we will take a brief look to the further development in this context (5.3).

5.1 Adaptation of embedded computing methods in HPC

If we consider a simple comparison of the achievable flop per expended watt, we see a clear advantage on the side of embedded processors (see Table 1). Shalf concludes in this context far-reaching consequences (Shalf, 2007). He says considering metrics like performance per power, not multi-core but many-core is even the answer. A moderate switching from single core and serial programs to modestly parallel computing will make programming much more difficult without receiving a corresponding award of a better performance-power ratio for this

- Power5 (server)
  - 389 mm^2
  - 120W@1900MHz
- Intel Core2 sc (laptop)
  - 130 mm^2
  - 15W@1000MHz
- ARM Cortex A8 (automobiles)
  - 5 mm^2
  - 0.8W@800MHz
- Tensilica DP (cell phones / printers)
  - 0.8 mm^2
  - 0.09W@600MHz
- Tensilica Xtensa (Cisco router)
  - 0.32 mm^2
  - 0.05W@600MHz

Table 1. Sizes and power dissipation of different CPU cores (Shalf, 2007)

effort. Instead he propagates the transition to many-core solutions based on simpler cores running at modestly lower clock frequencies. A loss of computational efficiency one suffers by moving from a more complex core to a much simpler core is manifoldly compensated by the enormous benefits one saves in power consumption and chip area. Borkar (Borkar, 2007) supports this statement and supplements that a mid- or maybe long-term shift to many-core can also be justified by an inverse application of Pollack's rule (Pollack, n.d.). This says that cutting a larger processor in halves of smaller processor cores means a decrease in computing performance of 70% in one core compared to the larger processor. However, since we have two cores now, we achieve a performance increase of 40% compared to the larger single core processor.

However, one has to note that shifting to many-core processors will not ease programmer's life in general. Particularly task parallel applications will sometimes not profit from 100s of cores at all due to limited parallelism in their inherent algorithm structure. Amdahl's law (Amdahl, 1967) will limit the speed-up to the serial fraction in the algorithm. The situation is different for data parallel tasks. Applying template and pipeline processing for memory bound applications in embedded computing, as we have shown it in Section 4, supports both ease of programming and exploiting the compute power given in many simpler cores. Doubtless, the embedded community has the most experience concerning power efficient design concepts which are now adapted from the HPC community and it is to expect that this trend will increase further. Examples that prove this statement can be seen already in practice. E.g. we will find processor cores in the design of the BlueGene (Gara et al., 2005) and SiCortex (Goodhue, 2009) supercomputers that are typically for embedded environments.

5.2 Adaptation of HPC methods in embedded computing

In the past the primary goal of the embedded computing industry was to improve the battery life, to reduce design costs and to bring the embedded product as soon as possible to market. It was easier to achieve these goals by designing simpler lower-frequency cores. Nevertheless, in the past the embedded community took over processor technologies like super scalar units and out-of-order processing in their designs. This trend goes on. Massively parallel concepts which are typically for HPC applications are introduced in mainstream embedded applications. Shalf mentions in this context the Metro chip, which is the heart of Cisco's CRS-1 router. This router contains 188 general-purpose Tensilica cores (Ten, 2009). These programmable devices replaced Application Specific Integrated Circuits (ASICs) which were in that router in use before (Eatherton, 2005).

5.3 How the convergence will proceed?

Some experts expect that more and more the CPUs in future HPC systems will consist of embedded-like programmable cores combined with custom circuits, e.g. memory controllers, floating point units, and DSP cores for acceleration of specific tasks. Four years ago, Shalf predicted already that we will realize 2000 cores on one chip in 2011, a number closely to the number of transistors in the first Intel CPU 4004. We know now that this not happened. Possibly the time scaling for that predicted progress is longer than it was expected in the euphoria that came up in the first years when the multi-core/many-core era started. It is still possible that design processes change dramatically in the sense that Tensilica's CTO Chris Rowen is right when he says, "*The processor is the new transistor*". Definitely the two worlds, embedded parallel computing and HPC, which had been separated in the past, converged and it is exciting to see in the future where the journey will exactly end.

6. Conclusion

In this chapter we emphasized the importance of multi-core processing in embedded computing systems. We distinguished parallel applications between task vs. data parallel applications. Even if more task parallel applications can be found in embedded systems, data parallelism is a quite valuable application field as well if we think of image processing tasks. We pointed out by the development of the embedded ARM processor families and the ECA-64 architecture, which is in particular appropriate for data-parallel applications, that hierarchical and heterogeneous processors are pioneering for future parallel embedded processors. Heterogeneous processors will rule the future since they combine well-tailored performance cores for specific application with energy-aware computing.

However, it is a challenge to support data parallel applications for embedded systems by an efficient memory management. On the one side, standard multi-core architectures can be used. But they are not necessarily optimal in relationship to the available external memory bandwidth and, therefore, to the achievable throughput. By using application-specific architectures, an embedded multi-core system can be optimized, e.g. for throughput. The drawback of this is the increased development time for the system. As shown for image processing as field of application, a lot of constraints must be considered. The system parameters have to be chosen carefully, in order to avoid bottlenecks in the processing chain. A model for a specific class of applications, like presented in (Reichenbach et al., 2011), can help to optimize the set of parameters for the embedded system.

In addition the presented memory management system can also be exploited for memory bound data parallel applications in HPC. Anyway there is to observe that both worlds have learned from each other and we expect that this trend will continue. To strengthen this statement we pointed out different examples.

7. References

Amdahl, G. M. (1967). Validity of the single processor approach to achieving large scale computing capabilities, *Proceedings of the April 18-20, 1967, spring joint computer conference*, AFIPS '67 (Spring), ACM, New York, NY, USA, pp. 483–485. URL: *http://doi.acm.org/10.1145/1465482.1465560*

ARM (2007). *The ARM Cortex-A9 Processors*. URL: *http://www.arm.com/pdfs/ARMCortexA-9Processor.pdf*

Blake, G., Dreslinski, R. G. & Mudge, T. (2009). A survey of multicore processors, *Signal Processing Magazine, IEEE* 26(6): 26–37. URL: *http://dx.doi.org/10.1109/MSP.2009.934110*

Borkar, S. (2007). Thousand core chips: a technology perspective, *Proceedings of the 44th annual Design Automation Conference*, DAC '07, ACM, New York, NY, USA, pp. 746–749. URL: *http://doi.acm.org/10.1145/1278480.1278667*

Bräunl, T. (2001). *Parallel Image Processing*, Springer-Verlag Berlin Heidelberg New York.

Eatherton, W. (2005). The push of network processing to the top of the pyramid, *in: Keynote Presentation at Proceedings ACM/IEEE Symposium on Architectures for Networking and Communication Systems (ANCS)*, Princeton, NJ.

Ele (2008). *Element CXI Product Brief ECA-64 elemental computing array*. URL: *http://www.elementcxi.com/downloads/ECA64ProductBrief.doc*

Fey, D. & Schmidt, D. (2005). Marching pixels: A new organic computing principle for high speed cmos camera chips, *Proceeding of the ACM*, pp. 1–9.

Fey et al., D. (2010). Realizing real-time centroid detection of multiple objects with marching pixels algorithms, *IEEE International Symposium on Object/Component/Service-Oriented Real-Time Distributed Computing Workshops* pp. 98–107.

Gara, A., Blumrich, M. A., Chen, D., Chiu, G. L. T., Coteus, P., Giampapa, M. E., Haring, R. A., Heidelberger, P., Hoenicke, D., Kopcsay, G. V. & et al. (2005). Overview of the blue gene/l system architecture, *IBM Journal of Research and Development* 49(2): 195–212. URL: *http://ieeexplore.ieee.org/lpdocs/epic03/wrapper.htm?arnumber=5388794*

Goodhue, J. (2009). Sicortex high-productivity, low-power computers, *Proceedings of the 2009 IEEE International Symposium on Parallel&Distributed Processing*, IEEE Computer Society, Washington, DC, USA, pp. 1–. URL: *http://dl.acm.org/citation.cfm?id=1586640.1587482*

Loos, A., Reichenbach, M. & Fey, D. (2011). Asic architecture to determine object centroids from gray-scale images using marching pixels, *Processings of the International Conference for Advances in Wireless, Mobile Networks and Applications*, Dubai, pp. 234–249.

Mattson, T., Sanders, B. & Massingill, B. (2004). *Patterns for Parallel Programming*, 1st edn, Addison-Wesley Professional.

Nguyen, A., Satish, N., Chhugani, J., Kim, C. & Dubey, P. (2010). 3.5-d blocking optimization for stencil computations on modern cpus and gpus, *Proceedings of the 2010 ACM/IEEE International Conference for High Performance Computing, Networking, Storage and Analysis*, SC '10, IEEE Computer Society, Washington, DC, USA, pp. 1–13.

Pollack, F. (n.d.). Pollack's Rule of Thumb for Microprocessor Performance and Area. URL: *http://en.wikipedia.org/wiki/Pollack's_Rule*

Reichenbach et al., M. (2010). Design of a programmable architecture for cellular automata based image processing for smart camera chips, *Proceedings of the ADPC*, pp. A58–A63.

Reichenbach, M., Schmidt, M. & Fey, D. (2011). Analytical model for the optimization of self-organizing image processing systems utilizing cellular automata, *SORT 2011: 2nd IEEE Workshop on Self-Organizing Real-Time Systems*, Newport Beach, pp. 162–171.

Schmidt, M., Reichenbach, M., Loos, A. & Fey, D. (2011). A smart camera processing pipeline for image applications utilizing marching pixels, *Signal & Image Processing: An International Journal (SIPIJ)* Vol. 2(No. 3): 137–156.
URL: *http://airccse.org/journal/sipij/sipij.html*

Shalf, J. (2007). The new landscape of parallel computer architecture, *Journal of Physics: Conference Series* 78(1): 012066.
URL: *http://stacks.iop.org/1742-6596/78/i=1/a=012066*

Stallings, W. (2006). *Computer Organization and Architecture - Designing for Performance (7. ed.)*, Pearson / Prentice Hall.

Ten (2009). *Configurable processors: What, why, how?, Tensilica Xtensa LX2 White Papers*. URL: *http://www.tensilica.com/products/literature-docs/white-papers/configurable-processors.htm*

Tex (2009). *OMAP4: Mobile applications plattform*.
URL: *http://focus.ti.com/lit/ml/swpt034/swpt034.pdf*

Williams, S., Waterman, A. & Patterson, D. (2009). Roofline: an insightful visual performance model for multicore architectures, *Commun. ACM* 52(4): 65–76.

2

Software Development for Parallel and Multi-Core Processing

Kenn R. Luecke
The Boeing Company
USA

1. Introduction

The embedded software industry wants microprocessors with increased computing functionality that maintains or reduces space, weight, and power (SWaP). Single core processors were the key embedded industry solution between 1980 and 2000 when large performance increases were being achieved on a yearly basis and were fulfilling the prophecy of Moore's Law. Moore's Law states that "the number of transistors that can be placed inexpensively on an integrated circuit doubles approximately every two years."[1] With the increased transistors, came microprocessors with greater computing throughput while space, weight and power were decreasing. However, this 'free lunch' did not last forever.[2] The additional power required for greater performance improvements became too great starting in 2000. Hence, single core microprocessors are no longer an optimal solution. Although, distributed and parallel programming solutions provide greater throughput, these solutions unfortunately increase SWaP. The most likely solution is multi-core processors which have been introduced into the embedded processor markets. Most microprocessor manufacturers have converted from developing single core processors to multi-core processors. With this conversion, the prophecy of Moore's Law is still being achieved. See Figure 1 and notice how the single core processors are not keeping pace with the multi-core processors. Multi-core processors increase throughput while maintaining or reducing SWaP for embedded environments which make them a good hardware solution for the aerospace industry. Intel, in particular, has estimated that by 2011, 95% of all the processors it ships will contain a multi-core design. However, the software market shows less optimism with multi-core processors. For instance, only 40% of software vendors thought their tools would be ready for multi-core processing by 2011. The reasons for software engineering's lack of excitement with multi-core processors include the following drawbacks:

- Lack and immaturity of multi-core specific development and debug software tools.
- Lack of multi-core processor standards.
- Lack and immaturity of multi-core enabled system software.

---

[1] http://en.wikipedia.org/wiki/Moore's_law

[2] Sutter, H., (March, 2005). "The free lunch is over. A fundamental turn toward concurrency in software," *Dr. Dobb's Journal, Volume 30, Number 3.*

- Lack of parallel programming experience by the software community.
- Lack of parallel programming models to support these multi-core processors.
- An abundance of differentiated multi-core processors from multiple suppliers. Greater differentiation with inexperience can be problematic for software developers converting applications for multi-core processors.

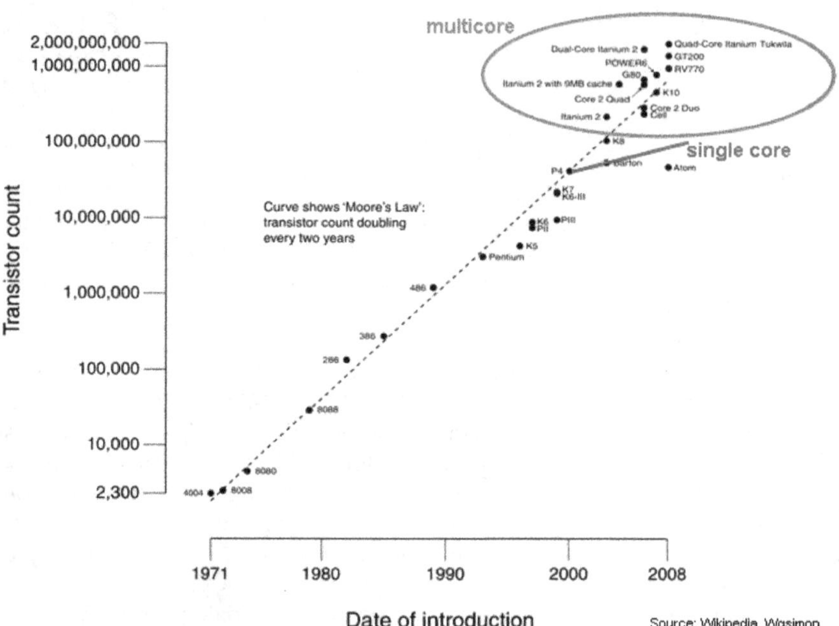

Fig. 1. Processor Transistor Counts and Moore's Law[3].

These problems led Chuck Moore, a Senior Fellow at AMD, to state "To make effective use of Multi-core hardware today, you need a PhD in computer science."[4] Therefore, multi-core software development has fallen behind multi-core hardware development. This chapter will provide information on the current best technologies, tools, methodologies, programming languages, models, and frameworks for software development on multi-core processors. Where different software development options exist, comparisons and recommendations will be provided to the reader.

2. Multicore definition

Previous multiprocessing, as opposed to multi-core processing, solutions, such as parallel and distributed programming, involved two or more processors, which doubled, tripled, or

---

[3] Fittes, Dale, (October 30, 2009) Using Multicore Processors in Embedded Systems - Part 1, *EE Times*.

[4] Moore, Chuck, (May 12, 2008) "Solving the Multi-core Programming Problem", *Dr. Dobbs Journal*.

even quadrupled the board space, weight, and power (SWaP) consumed and heat generated by the processing system. These solutions could comprise large networks leading to data latencies between processing components. However, multi-core processors place multiple processing cores on a single chip to increase processing power without noticeably increasing the system's SWaP and heat dissipation. Also, with multiple cores on a single chip the data latencies of distributed programming are mostly negated. With multi-core processing, the computer industry continues pushing the performance/power envelope through parallel processing rather than increasing the processor clock speed. For the most part, serial computing has been the standard software development model, with multiple cores on a processor, now parallel computing is emerging as the new standard and very few programmers are well versed in parallel computing. A multi-core processor, in general, appears similar to the dual core and quad core processors displayed in Figure 2. In both cases, each core has an associated L1 cache while the L2 cache is shared between all the cores. For systems with L1, L2, and L3 cache, normally the L3 cache is shared between all cores, each core has its own segregated L1 cache, and the L2 cache may be shared between cores or segregated L2 caches will be devoted to each core.

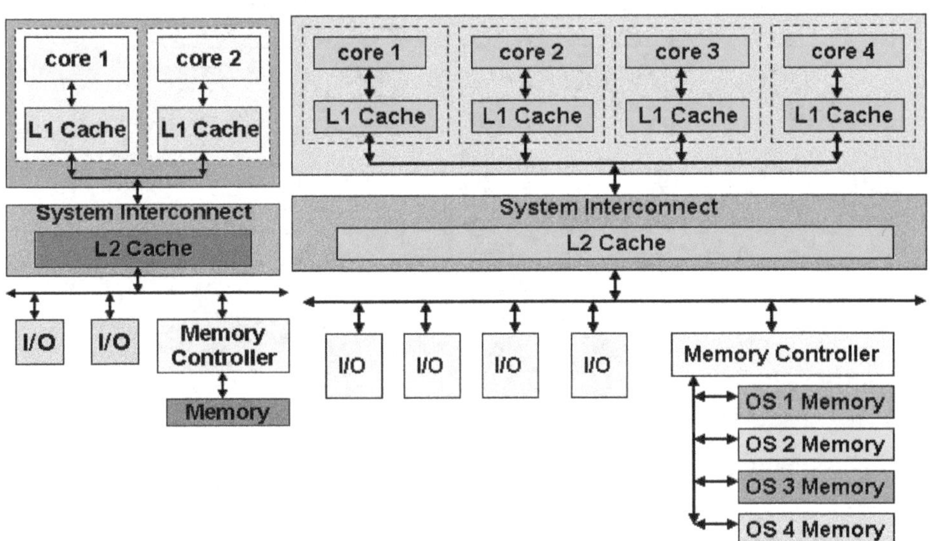

Fig. 2. Example Dual Core (left) and Quad Core (right) Multi-core Processors.

3. Multiprocessing models and frameworks

Traditionally, there were two multiprocessing models: Asymmetric Multi-Processing (AMP) and Symmetric Multiprocessing (SMP). For highly integrated processing, AMP designs incorporate several cores on a chip with each processor using its own L1 cache, and all processors share a common global memory. The AMP model can incorporate either heterogeneous cores executing different operating systems (OS) or homogeneous cores executing the same OS. With heterogeneous cores, the AMP architecture looks like a Digital Signal Processing (DSP) architecture. In AMP designs, application tasks are sent to the system's separate processors. These processors are collocated on the same board, but each is a separate computing system with its own OS and memory partition within the common global memory. See Figure 3.

The advantages of the AMP multiprocessing model include:

- The operating systems, tasks, and peripheral usage can be dedicated to a single core. Hence, it offers the easiest and quickest path for porting legacy code from single core designs to multi-core designs. Therefore, it is the easier multiprocessing model for serial computing software engineers to start with.

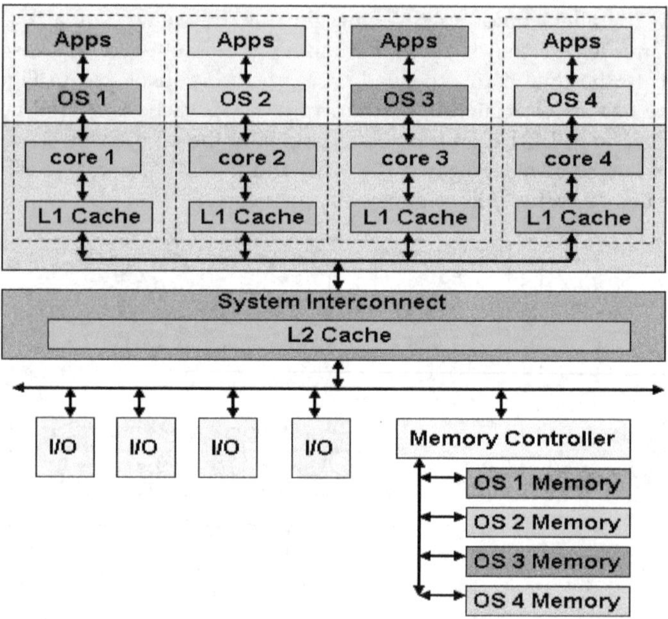

Fig. 3. Traditional AMP Model.

- Migrating existing (non-SMP) OSs to the model is relatively simple and usually offers superior node-to-node communication compared to a distributed architecture.
- AMP also allows software developers to directly control each core and how the cores work with standard debugging tools and methodologies. AMP supports the sharing of large global memories asymmetrically between cores.
- AMP provides software developers with greater control over efficiency and determinism.
- AMP allows engineers to embed loosely coupled applications from multiple processors to a single processor with multiple cores.

The disadvantages of the AMP multiprocessing model include:

- For tightly coupled applications, AMP approaches work best when the developers need no more than two cores while developing a solution. As more cores are added, the AMP multiprocessing model becomes exponentially more difficult especially for tightly coupled applications executing on all cores.

- AMP can result in underutilized processor cores. For example, if one core becomes busy, applications running on that core cannot easily migrate, to an underutilized core. Although dynamic migration is possible, it involves complex check pointing of the application's state which can result in service interruption while the application is stopped on one core and restarted on a different core. This migration may be impossible if the cores use different OSs.
- None of the OSs owns the entire application system. The application designer must manage the complex tasks of handling shared hardware resources. The complexity of these tasks increases significantly as more cores are added. As a result, AMP is ill-suited for tightly coupled applications integrating more than two cores.
- Memory latency and bandwidth can be affected by other nodes.
- The AMP multiprocessing model does not permit system tracing tools to gather operating statistics for the multi-core chip as a whole since the OSs are distributed on each core. Instead, application developers gather this information separately from each core and then combine the results for analysis purposes. This is only a concern for systems where the applications on the individual cores are tightly coupled.
- Cache "thrashing" may occur in some applications.

In SMP architectures, each node may have two or more processors using homogeneous cores, but not heterogeneous cores, while the multiple processors share the global memory. In addition, the processors may also have both local and shared cache, and the cache is coherent between all processors and memory. See Figure 4. SMP executes only one copy of an OS on all of the chip's cores or a subset of the chip's cores. Since the OS has insight into all system elements, it can transparently and automatically allocate shared resources on all cores. It can also execute any application on any core. Hence, "SMP was designed so you can mimic single-processor designs in a distributed computing environment," said Enea's Michael Christofferson[5]. The OS provides dynamic memory allocation, allowing all cores to draw on the full pool of available memory, without a performance penalty. The OS may use simple POSIX primitives for applications running on different cores to communicate with each other. POSIX primitives offer higher performance and simpler synchronization than the AMP system networking protocols.

Other SMP multiprocessing model advantages include:

- A large global memory and better performance per watt is due to using fewer memory controllers. Instead of splitting memory between multiple central processing units (CPU), SMP's large global memory is accessible to all processor cores. Data intensive applications, such as image processing and data acquisition systems, often prefer large global memories that can be accessed at data rates up to 100s of Megabytes/second (Mbytes/sec).
- SMP also provides simpler node-to-node communication, and SMP applications can be programmed to be independent of node count. SMP especially lends itself to newer multi-core processor designs.
- Systems based on SMP, have the OS perform load-balancing for the tasks between all cores.

[5] Morgan, Lisa L., (December 15, 2006), Making the Move to Multicore, *SD Times*.

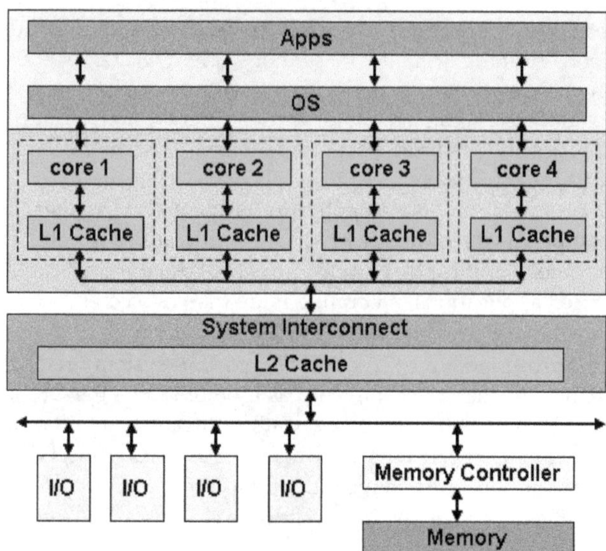

Fig. 4. Traditional SMP Multiprocessing Model Example.

- One copy of an OS can control all tasks performed on all cores, dynamically allocating tasks or threads to the underutilized core to achieve maximum system utilization.
- The SMP multiprocessing model permits system tracing tools to gather operating statistics for the multi-core chip as a whole, providing developers insights into optimizing and debugging applications. The tracing tools can track thread migration between cores, scheduling events, and other information useful for maximizing core utilization.
- An SMP approach is best for a larger number of cores and for developers who have time to adequately develop a long term solution that may eventually add more cores.
- SMP, versus AMP, is usually the preferred choice for applications implementing dynamic scheduling.

The disadvantages of the SMP multiprocessing model include:

- The memory latency and bandwidth of a given node can be affected by other nodes, and cache "thrashing" may occur in some applications.
- Legacy applications ported to an SMP environment generally require a redesign of the software. Legacy applications with poor synchronization among threads may work incorrectly in the SMP concurrent environment. Therefore, an SMP approach is better for software developers with parallel computing experience.
- Enea's Christofferson said that in many designs there are components within an operating system that may have hidden requirements that may not be running at the same time as another thread. To avoid the problem, Christofferson recommended that designers consider all OS and application threads to make sure there are no concurrency problems.[6]

[6] Morgan, Lisa L., (December 15, 2006), Making the Move to Multicore, *SD Times*.

- When moving legacy architectures from single core processing to multi-core processing, the major issue is concurrency. In a single operating environment, running multiple threads is a priority, so two threads with different priority levels can execute in parallel when they are distributed to different cores.
- SMP systems exhibit non-determinism. Hence any computing solutions that require determinism may need to stay away from an SMP model.

After listing the advantages and disadvantages of both AMP and SMP, a comparison between both multiprocessing models on several important programming concepts would be beneficial. See Table 1. With most programming concepts, the support that AMP provides is diametrically different from the support provided by SMP. However, as a software architect or developer of a system being ported to a multi-core processor, you want AMP support for some programming concepts and SMP support for other programming concepts. It was for this very reason that RTOS suppliers began to provide CPU affinity with their SMP support. What has become more prevalent in the past several years is developing hybrid models that combine some AMP support with some SMP support based on the system needs of the computing solution being developed. Two of the more popular hybrid models include:

- Combined AMP/SMP Model which executes both processing models on one processor. For example, for a quad-core processor, two cores will be executing an AMP model while the remaining two cores will be executing a SMP model. See Figure 5. In this hybrid model, there is no cross pollination between the models running on any of the cores. One benefit of this model is that architects can implement tasks that achieve better performance on AMP such as task parallelism on the AMP cores and tasks that achieve better performance on SMP such as data parallelism on the SMP cores, resulting in an overall system performance than an AMP or SMP only system.
- Supervised AMP Model which includes a layer of software executing between the OSs and the cores. The supervisor's primarily benefit is additional communication software that allows for improved system communication between the OSs running on the different cores. The benefits of this include:
  - Improving scalability for additional cores.
  - Providing better system debugging between processes on different cores.
  - Enabling reboot of individual cores on your system.[7]

Hence, Supervised AMP model has improved system debugging capabilities over a system implementing a traditional AMP model. See Figure 6.

Several embedded software frameworks have been developed for multi-core processors, but more are needed for improved software development and performance. The frameworks discussed in the rest of this chapter are a sampling of available frameworks. The mention of each framework is not intended as a recommendation. The Georgia Institute of Technology, through the Software and Algorithms for Running on Multi-core (SWARM) program, developed a framework consisting of portable open source parallel library of basic primitives that exploit multi-core processors. This framework allows developers to implement efficient parallel algorithms for operations like combinatorial sorting and

[7] Wlad, Joe. (2011), Freescale Multi-Core Forum, Freescale Multi-core Forum, St. Louis, September, 2011.

Programming Concept	AMP	SMP
Seamless resource sharing	No	Yes
Scalable beyond dual core	No/Complicated for tightly coupled apps	Yes
Mixed OS environment (ex: VxWorks & Linux)	Yes	No
Dedicated processor by function (CPU affinity)	Yes	Yes/No. CPU affinity is not supported in traditional SMP models, but most RTOS suppliers provide CPU affinity for their SMP models.
Inter-core messaging	Slower (application)	Fast (OS primitives)
Thread synchronization between cores	No/Complicated	Yes
Dynamic load balancing	No	Yes
System-wide debug and optimization	No/Complicated for tightly coupled apps	Yes
Migrating Legacy Apps/New App Development	Best at Migrating Legacy Apps. Good choice for New App Development.	Best for New App Development
Data/Task Parallelism	Task preferred	Data preferred
Engineer experienced in Serial Computing Only	Better choice than SMP	More difficult for a novice parallel computing developer

Table 1. AMP and SMP Model Comparisons.

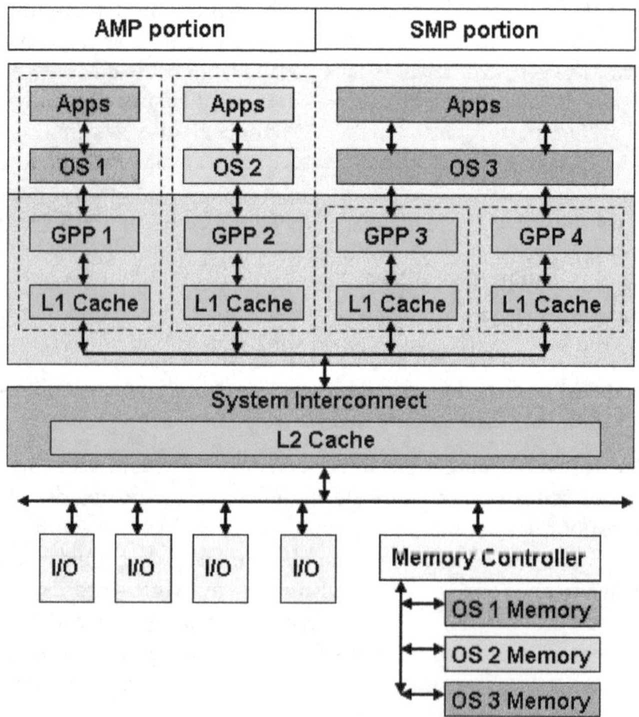

Fig. 5. Combined AMP/SMP Model.

selection algorithms. The University of California-Berkeley (UCB) and University of Illinois at Urbana-Champaign (U of I) are concentrating on software frameworks for multi-core processors. Both universities were partially funded by a $10 million grant from Intel and Microsoft. In particular, UCB is concentrating on developing frameworks and a composing language to assist programmers in creating and coordinating parallel programming models. Meanwhile, U of I is exploring new frameworks for extracting parallelism from serial code and developing software component building blocks required for parallel programming frameworks. Several software and hardware companies including AMD, IBM, Hewlett-Packard, Intel, and NVidia are funding Stanford University's Pervasive Parallelism Lab to investigate new parallel programming models including improved synchronization techniques between the cores on a multi-core processor.

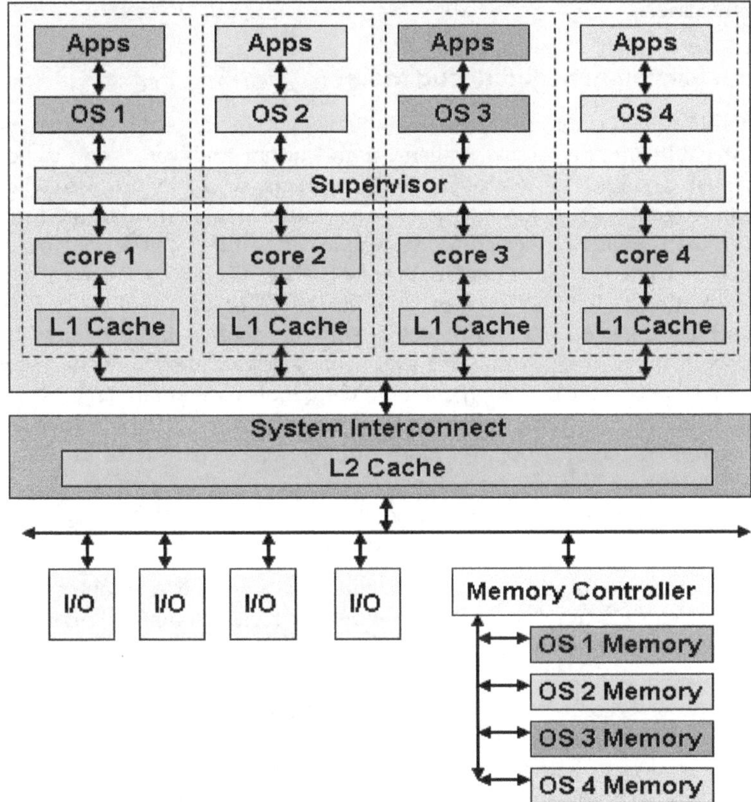

Fig. 6. Supervised AMP Model.

Of software suppliers, Microsoft has included multi-core support for its .NET framework. The .NET framework contains the Task Parallel Library (TPL) with software to support task parallelism and the Parallel Language Integrated Query (PLINQ) to support data parallelism. PLINQ provides the ability to parallelize data queries. Meanwhile, TPL provides parallelized versions of the C# for and foreach loops and partitions work for parallel processing and spawning, executing, and terminating threads that execute in parallel. Intel markets its Threaded Building Blocks (TBB) which are used for parallelizing serial software. TBB is a C++ template library which treats a program's operations as tasks. The tasks are assigned to individual cores by TBB's run-time executables. The operations or tasks then execute in a sequence where synchronization bugs between the threads or tasks have been minimized or removed.

OpenMP provides a framework for parallelizing serial software written in C, C++, or Fortran using roughly fifty pre-processor declarations. In this model, one core acts as the master assigning tasks/work to the other cores. Using this framework, the developer writes a control software for the master core and complementary software for the tasks that the other cores perform. The MCF library of functions manages concurrent processes and distributes data among the cores. The biggest problem with MCF is that it only supports IBM's Cell processor.

4. Software development and debug tools

Software tools have and continue to be one of the biggest challenges for software developers working with multi-core processors. In general, the author finds most tools to be narrowly focused on just a single hardware vendor's products, a single processor, or a single programming language. These tools often provide results of limited value, or require greater manual labor than what is expected. For example, often times the output from one tool cannot simply be routed as input into another tool. These tasks may require a good deal of manual reformatting or manipulation prior to inputting the data into the next tool. Some tool vendors repackaged their multi-processor software tools with a few modifications to handle inter-core processing as tools for multi-core software development. However, the good news is a few software development and debug tools have entered the market that are mature, are focused on products from multiple vendors, and provide a good deal of automation to free up the developer for more pertinent, non-repetitive tasks. The rest of this section will discuss a few software development tools for multi-core processing. Most of the information below comes from the tool vendors themselves, tool investigations that the author has performed, or demonstrations that the author has witnessed.

Clean C overcomes some single core to multi-core conversion problems. IMEC has developed the Clean C utility as an Eclipse plug-in which automatically converts C code from a single core processor to a multi-core processor. However, Clean C has 29 programming rules that must be manually applied to the code base prior to using the utility. Once the C code base conforms to all 29 programming rules, the Clean C utility can be executed on the software with few updates for an optimized multi-core application. If the Clean C utility is applied without implementing the 29 programming rules to the C code base, the result will likely be non-operational. The Clean C utility can only be applied to C language software code bases. Clean C does not properly convert C++ based applications. The author has not tested this product.[8]

Intel's Parallel Studio is a C/C++ multi-core tool suite that integrates with Microsoft's Visual Studio 2005, 2008, and 2010 Integrated Development Environments (IDE). Parallel Studio is comprised of:

---

[8] http://www.imec.be/CleanC

- Intel Parallel Advisor which models an application and analyzes the best locations to implement parallelism within your application.
- Intel Parallel Composer which contains a C++ compiler, performance libraries, software thread building blocks, and parallel debugging extensions for improved performance on multi-core processors.
- Intel Parallel Inspector which automatically identifies memory and threading errors for the software developer.
- Intel Parallel Amplifier which analyzes processing hot spots, concurrency, and lock and waits with the goal of improving performance and scalability.[9]

Cilk++, Cilk, and jCilk, developed by Supertech Research Group who sold their product to Intel, assists developers with converting from single core to multi-core software systems. First, it implements its own three command standard for multi-core development. This standard allows developers to insert these commands in their existing code for spawning and synchronizing tasks, rather than restructuring their code base. Second, these products contain a number of debugging and run-time analysis tools to assist developers with optimizing their applications in a multi-core environment. Cilk++, Cilk, and jCilk apply to applications written in C++, C, and Java, respectively. Some of the Cilk components have been embedded in Intel's Parallel Studio tool. The author has witnessed a demonstration of Cilk++.[10]

The objective of Critical Blue's Prism tool is to provide analysis and an exploration and verification environment for embedded software development using multi-core architectures. A software developer could use this tool to assist in converting an application from a single core microprocessor to a multi-core microprocessor. It implements a Graphical User Interface (GUI) to assist with a developer's multi-threaded software development. The GUI provides multiple views for a look 'under the covers'. It provides detailed analysis of your application. The tool works for many processor chips including x86, PowerPC (PPC), Microprocessor without Interlocked Pipeline Stages (MIPS), and Advanced Reduced Instruction Set Computer (RISC) Machine (ARM). The author has tested this product and found it to be one of the better tools for moving an application from a single core to multi-core processor.[11]

Poly Core Software provides a multi-core software communications framework. The Poly Core software tool suite consists of:

- Poly-Mapper which is a Graphics User Interface (GUI) tool that allows developers to map software communications across multiple cores using XML commands.
- Poly-Generator converts the Poly-Mapper XML commands to C source code files.
- Poly-Messenger contains a software communications library for distributing processing on multiple cores.
- Poly-Inspector allows developers to inspect and analyze applications for communication 'hot spots'. A 'hot spot' occurs where a single or more cores have an increased amount of processing activity and while other processing cores are idle.

---

[9] http://en.wikipedia.org/wiki/Intel_Parallel_Studio
[10] http://supertech.csail.mit.edu/cilk
[11] http://www.criticalblue.com

The Poly Core Software suite of tools is used for generating only C code files that can be ported to multiple OSs. The code files execute on most processor chips such as x86, PPC, ARM, and MIPS.[12]

Transparent Inter Process Communication (TIPC) is an Open Source implementation that allows software designers to create applications that can communicate quickly and reliably with other applications within the computing core cluster. The TIPC protocol originated with Ericsson and has been deployed in their products for several years. TIPC is available for Linux, Solaris, and VxWorks OSs. Most applications using TIPC are written in C/C++ languages and support is available for Perl and Python.[13]

VLX by Red Bend Software is a real-time hypervisor that assists developers with migrating embedded systems from single core to multi-core processors. Their tool allows developers to run applications using a mixture of traditional Real-time Operating Systems (RTOS) along with Linux and Windows OSs concurrently on a shared hardware platform. Virtual Logix claims VLX maintains determinism and the same high performance that a RTOS provides. VLX has been certified to Common Criteria (CC) Evaluation Assurance Level (EAL) 5. VLX executes on ARM, Texas Instruments (TI), PPC, and x86 microprocessors. The author has witnessed a demonstration of VLX.[14]

Simics is primarily a virtualization emulation tool used by software developers to develop, test, and debug embedded software that will eventually execute on multi-core processors or in a simulated environment. Simics is produced by Intel's Wind River subsidiary. Simics can emulate many multi-core chip manufacturer's processors. However, Simics specializes in its support for Freescale Semiconductor processors. Simics claims to provide additional visibility into your system to improve overall debugging performance. Simics models hardware systems using software running on ordinary workstation computers for an improved development and debugging experience for software engineers. Simics allows developers greater control by varying the number and speed of the cores and injecting actual faults into the system. The author has witnessed a demonstration of Simics.[15]

QEMU is an open source virtualization emulation tool used by software developers to develop, test, and debug embedded software that will eventually execute on multi-core processors or in a simulated environment. It provides solutions for x86, ARM, MIPS, PPC, Scalable Processor Architecture (SPARC), and several other microprocessor families. A developer can simulate multiple communication channels by creating multiple QEMU instances. The author is currently working on a team using QEMU for its virtualization efforts.[16]

TRANGO Virtual Processors, a subsidiary of VMware, uses an Eclipse based IDE to provide secure virtual processes for software engineers to migrate legacy single core processors to multi-core platforms. TRANGO virtual processors assist with migration to multi-core by first instantiating multiple virtual processor units on a single core. Next, the developer populates each virtual processor unit with its own OS and application(s). Then, the

[12] http://www.polycoresoftware.com
[13] http://tipc.sourceforge.net
[14] http://www.redbend.com
[15] http://www.windriver.com/products/simics
[16] http://wiki.qeu.org/Main_Page

developers move the OSs and applications onto a physical multi-core hardware system. TRANGO recommends mapping one TRANGO hypervisor to each core. TRANGO hypervisors also support the SMP multiprocessing model and RTOSs. The author has not tested this product.[17]

Sysgo markets their PikeOS which is a paravirtualization RTOS based on a separation microkernel. It uses an Eclipse based IDE. This RTOS has been certified to DO-178B Level B. Sysgo claims that the PikeOS implements a Multiple Independent Levels of Security (MILS) architecture and that it is completing formal code verification for a CC EAL 7 certification during the Summer 2011. In 2009, Sysgo began marketing the PikeOS in North America. The author has not tested this product.[18]

Most of the major embedded RTOS suppliers including QNX, Wind River, Lynux Works, Green Hills, and DDC-I also support software development for multi-core processors. However, they do not offer identical support. Most of the suppliers also provide their own hypervisor that works with their own line of products. The author has tested Wind River's VxWorks OS with multi-core support and has witnessed demonstrations of QNX and Lynux Works RTOSs with multi-core support. When analyzing the RTOS's multi-core support, pay attention to the product's performance profiling tools which allow the developer to examine more closely what is happening 'under the hood'. Understand which software languages each RTOS supports and whether real-time support is provided for each language. Wind River, Green Hills, and Lynux Works also market their own real-time hypervisors.

This section has discussed several tools for developing software aimed at a multi-core processor. Very few tools are direct competitors with another tool. Currently most tools are attempting to solve one small piece of the software developer's task in writing software for a multi-core environment. When choosing software development tools for multi-core processors, keep in mind that most tools are still immature, are usually programming language specific, processor specific, and/or vendor specific. Make sure you have a thorough understanding of the application you are developing or migrating and the development needs are for the application. Ask very detailed, pointed questions of the tool vendors to make sure you understand what their tool can and cannot perform at the time of purchase or use.

5. Virtualization

Virtualization technology can be used to create several virtual machines to run on a single virtual machine. Virtualization technology allows multiple OSs to run on a single processor. Processors with multiple cores could easily simulate one virtual machine on each core of the physical processor or machine. Virtualization technology was first introduced in the 1960s with IBM mainframe computers with many benefits. First, virtualization allowed many users to concurrently use the same mainframe platform where each user had their own virtual machine and where each virtual machine can execute a different OS resulting in increased productivity from the expensive IBM mainframes. Second, the technology allowed legacy applications to run on future mainframe hardware designs. Third, the virtualization

[17] http://en.wikipedia.org/wiki/Trango_Virtual_Processors

[18] http://www.sysgo.com/products/pikeos-rtos-technology

technology all resided in a thin layer of software that executed on top of the hardware or an underlying OS.

With the introduction of the Personal Computer (PC), interest in virtualization technology died. However, with PCs and processors becoming more and more powerful in the last ten years, there is a resurgence in the technology for this computing equipment. The benefits of virtualization achieved with mainframe computers are the same for single core and multi-core processors. Virtualization products can be found for both real-time and non-real time embedded systems.

There are three main types of virtualization as shown in Figure 7. They are:

- Full Virtualization, which is the most flexible approach, can usually support any OS type. Most processor manufacturers have been adding full virtualization support for their processors. This approach allows any legacy or new OS designed for the processor to run virtualized. This approach can be implemented with a host OS executing between the hypervisor and the hardware, but it is not necessary. This approach can also be implemented with special virtualization technology built into the processor. Since this approach does not require any modifications to the OS, it is expected to eventually be the preferred virtualization type.
- Para Virtualization which can only support OSs that have been modified to run in their virtual machine. In this approach the OS is modified so that it would use the virtualized layer of software's interface to communicate between the guest OSs and the virtualized layer of software. Para virtualization is usually built into the host OS and then allows multiple guest OSs to execute in virtual machines. This approach executes faster at run-time than the full virtualization approach.
- Container Virtualization can only support OSs that have been modified to run in their virtual machine like a Para Virtualization approach, but here there is no attempt to virtualize the entire processor. Instead most of the OS components are reused between the container based OSs. Container virtualization implements a host OS and guest OSs for sharing the host code with one restriction. The guest OSs must be the same as the host OS.

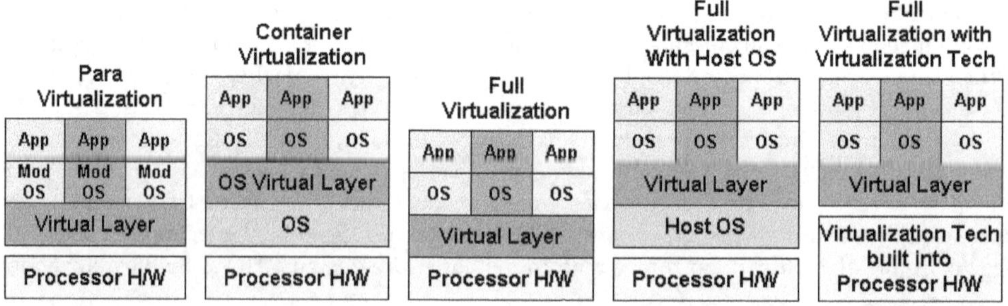

Fig. 7. Virtualization Technology Types.

Virtualization technology led to the development of Multiple Levels of Security (MLS). An MLS embedded system is a trusted system at a high robustness level that securely handles processing data at more than one classification level. An MLS system is similar to virtualization technology whereby a processor is divided into several virtual machines or partitions. The difference is that in a MLS system the partitions are based on security levels. For example, one partition may be unclassified, a second partition may be Secret, while a third partition may be classified Top Secret.

6. Software programming languages

Software language support for multi-core processors generally falls into two categories. New languages designed with parallelism from the beginning or extensions to current popular software languages. Most language extensions are focused on single Fortran and C/C++ standards. Some language extensions include:

- OpenMP Fortran which is an extension to Fortran 95. Basically, it implements OpenMP compiler directives, library functions, and environment variables for the Fortran language.[19]
- Co-array Fortran which is an extension to Fortran 95 and the 2008 Fortran standards. Co-array Fortran syntax is architecture independent and can be used in shared memory and distributed memory machines and on clustered machines. Co-array Fortran can be applied to a greater range of machine architectures than OpenMP Fortran, hence a Subset Co-Array Fortran has been generated which can be translated into OpenMP as part of the compilation process.[20]
- High Performance Fortran (HPF) is an extension to Fortran 90. HPF uses a data parallel model of computation to spread the work of a single array computation over multiple processors. Many users and vendors who initially used HPF have migrated to OpenMP Fortran or Co-array Fortran.[21]
- OpenMP C/C++ contains compiler directives, library functions, and environment variables that assist developers with managing parallel programs coded in the C/C++ languages. The directives extend the sequential C/C++ programming languages with parallel constructs.[22]
- Parallel Unified C, also known as Unified Parallel C, is an extension of the C programming language designed for computing on large-scale parallel machines. Parallel Unified C extends ISO C 99 with the following constructs:
    - An explicitly parallel execution model
    - A shared address space
    - Synchronization primitives and a memory consistency model
    - Memory management primitives[23]
- pC++ is a language extension to C++ that contains parallel constructs for C++ applications on high performance computers. pC++ allows programmers to develop distributed data structures with parallel execution semantics.[24]

---

[19] http://en.wikipedia.org/wiki/OpenMP
[20] http://www.co-array.org
[21] http://hpff.rice.edu
[22] http://en.wikipedia.org/wiki/OpenMP
[23] http://upc.lbl.gov

Some new languages designed with parallelism from the start include:

- Erlang is a concurrent/functional programming language with dynamic typing and strict evaluation. It supports hot swapping so code can be modified without stopping a system. It is used primarily in the telecom industry.[25]
- Fortress is an open source language that is being targeted for the multi-core and supercomputing software communities. The current Fortress prototype runs on top of a standard Java Virtual Machine (JVM). Fortress supports both task and data parallelism. The runtime implicitly farms out computations to the available processor cores using a fine-grained threading model. Basically, the designers implemented parallelism into the language at every possible location. Sun's Fortress language was originally funded by the Defense Advanced Research Projects Agency (DARPA) High Productivity Computing System (HPCS) program.[26]
- Z-level Programming Language (ZPL) is a portable, high-performance parallel programming language for science and engineering computations. It is an array programming language that uses implicit parallelism and can execute on both sequential and parallel computers.[27]
- Chapel is an open source language that is expected to support a multi-threaded parallel programming model. It is expected to support data parallelism, task parallelism, and nested parallelism. Chapel is expected to support object-oriented concepts, generic programming features, and code reuse. This language is being developed by Cray, Inc. Some Chapel concepts come from HPF and ZPL. Cray's Chapel language was originally funded by DARPA's HPCS program.[28]
- Haskell is a purely functional programming language that engineers from Galois are embracing that is richly statically typed. Functional programming languages lack side effects. These languages handle structures as values. Functional languages reduce code count. Functional programming languages like Haskell require a paradigm shift from both object oriented and modular programming languages. Parallel evaluation strategies and nested data parallelism are built into the language.[29]

Most of the above languages have been developed within the past six years. Erlang is the exception to this.

7. Multi-core processing standards

One of the goals of the Multi-Core Association has been developing standards for multi-core processors. The Multi-core Association is an industry consortium whose members include embedded software and hardware companies such as Intel, Freescale Semiconductor, Nokia Siemens Networks, QNX, Texas Instruments, and Wind River Systems. The Multi-core Association's goal is to support the multi-core ecosystem which includes vendors of development tools, debuggers, processors, operating systems, compilers, and simulators

[24] http://www.extreme.indiana.edu/sage
[25] http://www.erlang.org
[26] http://en.wikipedia.org/wiki/Fortress_(programming_language)
[27] http://en.wikipedia.org/wiki/ZPL_(programming_language)
[28] http://chapel.cray.com
[29] http://www.haskell.org/haskellwiki/Haskell

along with application and system developers. The Multi-core Association has either completed, started work, or has plans to develop the following standards:

- The Multi-core Communications Application Programmer Interface (MCAPI) is a high-performance, low latency communications and synchronization Application Programmer Interface (API) for closely distributed cores and processors in embedded systems. MCAPI is expected to support streaming communications that are fast and efficient and are similar to the sockets used for networking applications. The MCAPI is expected to support "socket like" stream-based API which would benefit multi-core devices. The MCAPI has the goal to support just the specific needs of embedded systems such as tighter memory constraints, high system throughput, and tighter task execution time constraints.
- Multi-core Resource Management API (MRAPI) provides a standardized API for the management, synchronization, and scheduling of processing resources. The MRAPI will support features for state management, context management, scheduling, and basic resource synchronization. The RAPI has the goal to support existing operating systems and the CAPI, Multicore Task Management API (MTAPI), and Debug API.
- Multi-core Programming Practices (MPP) provides a "best practices" guide for C/C++ developers to write "multi-core ready" software. The goals for this standard is to assist software developers in developing portable multi-core code which can be targeted at multiple platforms, reducing bugs due to multi-core related issues, and reduce the learning curve for multi-core software development.
- Multi-core Virtualization will provide users of embedded virtualization solutions with improved interoperability of applications and middleware between different virtualization vendors through the properties in its standard.
- MTAPI will provide a standardized API for dynamic scheduling and managing software tasks, including task creation and deletion for a large variety of architectures. The MTAPI goal is to support existing operating systems and the MCAPI, MRAPI, and Debug API.
- Debug API will enhance multi-core development systems with development tools to address problems in communication and interpretation of debug tools and on-chip debug components. This work includes:
    - Identifying and mapping multi-core debugging high level requirements to specific requirements for underlying infrastructures
    - Extending and standardizing current debug interfaces for multi-core debugging needs
    - Standardizing debugging and Joint Test Action Group (JTAG) interface connections.

The purpose of these APIs is to make the source code portable and reusable so that software multi-core architectures can be processor independent. The expectation is that the standards should complement one another. See Figure 8.

So far, the MCAPI and MRAPI standard APIs have been released. The MPP standard is expected to be released in later 2011 or early 2012. The scheduled release dates for the Multi-core Virtualization, and Debug standards have all passed without the standards being released. These standards are developed by the Multi-core Association's member organizations. Most of these organizations are companies with their own deadlines for shipping software and hardware tools and products to market. Hence, their main priorities are satisfying their customers with their products and services. So the Multi-core Association's processing standards development is progressing at a slower rate than originally anticipated.

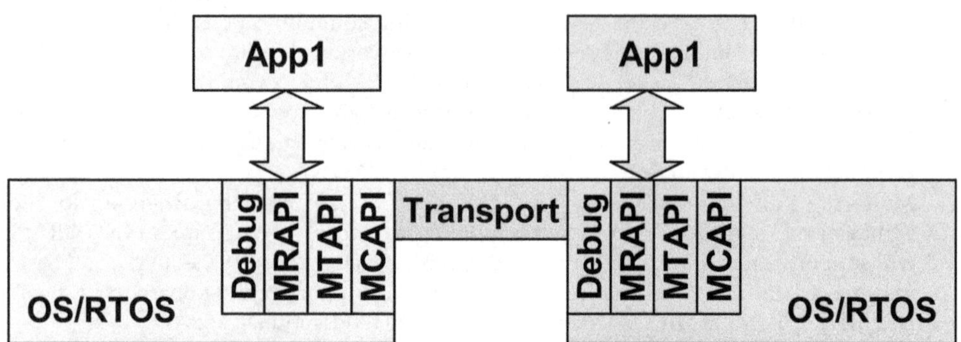

Fig. 8. MCAPI, MRAPI, MTAPI, and Debug Implementation View for Multi-core Devices.

OpenMP is a specification for a set of compiler directives, Runtime Library Routines, and environment variables that can be used to specify multithreaded, shared memory parallelism in Fortran and C/C++ programs. The OpenMP specification is being developed by the OpenMP Architecture Review Board (ARB). The OpenMP Version 3.0 Specification has been released to the public and addresses many multi-core processor needs. OpenMP is a portable, scalable model that provides shared memory parallel programmers a flexible API for developing parallel applications for multiple platforms. OpenMP contains a set of compiler directives and library routines for parallel application programmers. Typically OpenMP is used to parallelize looping constructs among multiple threads. OpenMP has the following advantages[30]:

- Provides both coarse-grained and fine-grained parallelism.
- When updating a serial application to run in a multi-core parallel environment, the original code set will most likely not require to be modified when parallelized with OpenMP pragma compiler directives.
- When executing a parallelized application in a serial environment, the OpenMP directives can be treated as comments.
- Data decomposition and layout are handled automatically by pragma directives.

OpenMP has the following disadvantages:

- Cannot be used on Graphics Processing Units (GPU).
- Scalability is limited. Easier to work with on small software applications of less than 1000 lines than large applications with several hundreds of thousands of lines of code.
- Can introduce synchronization bugs and race conditions without providing any assistance in removing these bugs.

---

[30] http://en.wikipedia.org/wiki/OpenMP

- Requires a compiler that supports OpenMP.
- Possible to accidently write false sharing code. False sharing occurs when multiple threads on different cores write to a shared cache line but not at the same location. Since the memory is changing, each core must update its copy of its cache resulting in much greater memory transfers than in a serial application with a single thread.

Other standards that are focused on issues pertaining to multi-core processors include:

- Mobile Industry Processor Interface (MIPI) is addressing a range of debug interface efforts for multi-core devices. However, its specifications are focused on mobile devices and not multi-core processors in general.[31]
- Message Passing Interface (MPI) is an API specification that allows multiple computers to communicate with each other. It is often used for parallel programs running on computer clusters and supercomputers, where accessing non-local memory can be expensive.[32]
- System C is a standard that allows engineers to design a system that spans both hardware and software. It contains a set of C++ classes and macros. It is often used for system simulations, modeling, and functional verification involving parallel processes. Multiple software suppliers support the System C standard.[33]

8. Software community parallel programming experience

The vast majority of software developers are experienced in serial software development. Few software engineers are experienced in parallel software development. First, training for software engineers has traditionally been focused on serial development efforts. Very few universities and colleges offer undergraduate courses aimed at parallel software development. The author has sponsored a short parallel and multi-core programming course at Boeing. One Boeing engineer with a PhD in Computer Science from a major university remarked that he planned to take the course since they had one course in parallel software development at his university and that he just did not understand the concepts. If PhDs from major universities are having problems with parallel software development, clearly software engineers with Bachelor degrees will also have problems. Second, the author and several Boeing teammates have investigated universities and colleges throughout the United States for course offerings in parallel software development. Unfortunately, we did not find many universities nor colleges offering any courses. Some of the better educational opportunities that were investigated include the University of Illinois at Urbana-Champaign, University California-Berkeley, Stanford University, MIT, and Washington University at St. Louis. Both the University of Illinois at Urbana-Champaign and University California-Berkeley offer Summer school courses in parallel software development. The author has found many recommendations for both universities' courses. Stanford University is offering training through its Pervasive Parallelism Lab. Also, the MIT professors at Supertech Research Group who developed the Cilk applications have been offering classes on parallelism topics that use the Cilk tool. There are some professional

[31] http://www.mipi.org

[32] http://www.mcs.anl.gov/research/projects/mpi

[33] http://www.systemc.org/home

training organizations such as ProTech which will provide training in parallel and multi-core software development. In conclusion, the availability for training in parallel software development has been and continues to be very slim.

One of the major challenges in migrating serial software to a parallel environment is ensuring that your system's functionality is still correct after spreading the functionality across several cores all executing simultaneously. In parallelizing your application there are several concurrency issues that a software developer needs to watch for:

- Dead lock: Occurs when two or more threads or processes are both waiting for the other to release a resource.
- Live lock: Similar to dead lock where tasks require a resource held by another thread or process, but the state of the waiting threads or processes are changing in regards to other tasks. A live lock example are when the Three Stooges are each trying to get through a doorway and they get stuck.
- False Sharing: Occurs when two or more cores access different data in a shared cache line. If one core writes to the cache line, the caching protocol may force the second core to reload the cache line even though the data has not changed.

A second major challenge for software developers is to analyze their software for data dependencies based on the execution of threads for the entire system. A data dependency occurs when two data references read from or write to the same variable, whether it is stored in memory or in a register. If a data dependency is detected, the software developer shall either reorder the statements or modify the thread execution on different cores. Look at the statements below which are executed in order from instruction 1 to instruction 5 and determine where the dependencies exist:

1. variable1 = 3;
2. variable2 = 5;
3. variable3 = variable2;
4. variable4 = variable1 + variable2;
5. variable1 = -8;

There are data dependencies between instructions 2 and 3 and between instructions 4 and 5. This means that if you switch instructions 2 and 3 and instructions 4 and 5, respectively, the application results will be different. If a software developer switches instructions 1 and 2, the application results will be the same. Hence, a data dependency does not exist between instructions 1 and 2. There are several data dependency types. First are true dependencies which exist when an instruction is dependent on the previous instruction, such as:

1. variable1 = 2;
2. variable2 = variable1;

True dependencies occur where a variable is defined in one statement and then used in the following statement. This is also known as "Write after Read" and these statements are not safe to be reordered. Second are anti-dependencies which exist when an instruction requires a value that is later updated, such as:

1. variable1 = variable2;
2. variable2 = 5.0;

Anti-dependencies occur where a variable is read prior to the variable later being reset to a different value. This is also known as "Read after Write" and these statements are not safe to be reordered. Third are input dependencies which exist where a variable is read prior to being read a second time, such as:

1. variable1 = variable2;
2. variable3 = variable2;

Input dependencies occur where a variable is read twice in a row. This is also known as "Read after Read" and these statements are safe to be reordered. Fourth are output dependencies also known as false dependencies. These dependencies exist where a variable is written to prior to being written to a second time, such as:

1. variable1 = 0.0;
2. variable1 = 3.0;

Output dependencies occur where a variable is written twice in a row. This is also known as "Write after Write" and these statements are not safe to be reordered. Fifth are control dependencies which exist when the output of an instruction was referenced in a previous decision block. An example of this is displayed below where variable2 is set in statement 3, but was referenced in a decision block in statement 1:

1. if (variable1 == variable2)
2. variable1 = variable1 + variable2;
3. variable2 = variable2 + variable1;

A control dependency does not exist between instructions 1 and 3. However, a control dependency may exist between instructions 1 and 2 if instruction 1 can be executed prior to instruction 2 or if the output of instruction 1 determines if instruction 2 will be executed. The control dependency displayed may exhibit "Write after Read" and instructions 1 and 2 may not be safe to reorder.[34]

With the challenges listed above, there are several solutions that software developers can use.

- First, there are software locks that can be placed around code that may lead to deadlock, live lock, or data dependency conditions. A software developer would place the lock start prior to a block of problematic code and the lock end after the block of problematic code. See Figure 9 where the synchronized command is used to place locks around the moveBox and updateBox functions. In using software locks, software developers can use them during writes to memory or a register or during reads from memory or registers that may have been updated. Software locks should not be used when invoking methods on other objects. The advantage of software locks is that it increases safety by guaranteeing that only the block of problematic code is functioning with other threads or processes are halted. The disadvantage of software locks is that all other threads and processes are halted during this execution, thus slowing the system execution to a serial environment.
- A second solution is to make your code immutable. A software developer accomplishes this by replacing public class variables and global variables with private class variables

[34] http://en.wikipedia.org/wiki/Data_dependency

and local variables and passing class variables into functions via the function call. The advantage of designing immutable software is that it eliminates data dependencies while increasing their parallel execution of your software. The disadvantage is that it may require significant modifications to your software.

- A third option is software confinement. Here the software developer confines all processing to execute on a single thread or single core. When this practice is followed, your resulting software is more loosely coupled and is a good software architecture strategy. The advantage of software confinement is that it eliminates data dependencies while increasing their parallel execution of your software. The disadvantage is that it may require significant modifications if your software was originally designed without confinement as a goal. This may also include ordering your system's code blocks so that any code with potential data dependency problems execute at different times on different threads or cores.

```
Thread on core 1:
Void synchronized moveBox(){
   x += getUpdatedX();
   ....
   y += getUpdateY();
   ....
}
```

```
Thread on core 2:
Void synchronized updateBox(int x, int y){
   y_ = y;
   x_ = x;
}
```

Fig. 9. Lock Example.

- A fourth option is decomposing large blocks of code where data dependencies and dead locks take place into smaller blocks and place the locks around the smaller blocks of software. The advantage of this approach is that the software will be safer without spending significant time re-architecting your system. The disadvantage of this approach still involves halting all other threads and processes while the problematic code is still functioning.

As we saw in this section there are a number of issues such as dead locks, live locks, and data dependency situations that may cause applications to ineffectively run when they are parallelized. The good news is that there are several options for software developers to implement to correct these problems. While some options can be quickly implemented like software locks, they degrade overall system performance, while other options like software confinement and immutable software improve software performance, they can take many developer hours to correctly implement.

9. Differentiated multi-core processors

On the positive side, the differentiated multi-core processors have provided greater options for software developers. In the past, a large system would consist of several processors with different single core processing units. Some of the processors would have GPUs for display processing while other processors would have CPUs to perform the actual non-display processing. Now, multi-core processors are coming into vogue with multiple CPU cores and multiple GPU cores for both non-display and display processing, respectively. Hence, with these multiple heterogeneous and homogeneous hardware multi-core processors, developers have greater and better choices for developing new large scale software systems.

The increase in differentiated multi-core processors has its share of problems on the software side. As we have seen with several frameworks and tools mentioned earlier, often times there is only support for certain processors or processor families. Of course, the microprocessor vendor is attempting to tie the software development to their own multi-core processor which can cause several problems. First, while most multi-core microprocessor vendors have developed some software tools, no vendor has developed a complete suite of tools to assist the software developer with requirements, architecture, code, and test. Second, with the hardware vendors entering this market, the software tool vendors' market share is reduced. They may decide against providing a new tool or supporting a particular multi-core microprocessor's chipset if the vendor themselves is already providing the support. Third, with so many software developers not trained nor experienced with developing parallel software, the addition of many differentiated multi-core processors increases the learning curve for developers. The software developer may be working on different multi-core processors at the same time. Hence, in this case the role of differentiated multi-core processors has probably slowed, rather than enhanced, their adoption by the computing industry.

10. Conclusion

By reviewing some of the key software development issues for multi-core processors, including:

- Immaturity of software tools
- Lack of standards
- Inexperience of current software developers
- Lack of software models and frameworks
- Lack of System software like libraries
- Differentiated processors with minimal support

Current software development for multi-core processors is at an immature level when compared to both software development for single core processors and hardware development for multi-core processors. Therefore, this chapter has provided details to support Chuck Moore's statement that "To make effective use of Multi-core hardware today, you need a PhD in computer science."[35] Even though the statement is a few years old, it still applies as of the writing of this chapter. There is still much research to be performed for improved parallel processing models and frameworks. Both Microsoft and Intel have spent millions in this research along with several small startup companies. The biggest question continues to be how to identify promising solutions along with attracting the research dollars to fund the work to develop the solutions. More attention needs to be paid towards standards development which should naturally improve over time. The biggest concern is the education and training of software professionals. Currently, some 'best practices' documents are being developed for beginner multi-core software developers. The biggest challenge is for the universities, colleges, and other training organizations to educate new and experienced software developers. While analyzing the improvements over the past several years, many more breakthroughs are still needed before the software industry can receive the full benefit from upgrading to multi-core processors.

---

[35] Moore, Chuck, (May 12, 2008) "Solving the Multi-core Programming Problem", *Dr. Dobbs Journal*.

11. Acknowledgments

Kenn Luecke would like to thank Andrea Egan, Shawn Rahmani, and Wayne Mitchell for assisting him with his initial research into software development for multi-core processors for the Boeing Company. He would also like to thank fellow Boeing engineers David Cacchia, Tom Dickens, Jon Hotra , David Sharp, Don Turner, Homa Ziai-Cook, and Heidi Ziegler for their assistance with multi-core related issues.

12. References

[1] http://en.wikipedia.org/wiki/Moore's_law
[2] Sutter, H., (March, 2005). "The free lunch is over. A fundamental turn toward concurrency in software," *Dr. Dobb's Journal, Volume 30, Number 3.*
[3] Fittes, Dale, (October 30, 2009) Using Multicore Processors in Embedded Systems - Part 1, *EE Times.*
[4] Moore, Chuck, (May 12, 2008) "Solving the Multi-core Programming Problem", *Dr. Dobbs Journal.*
[5] Morgan, Lisa L., (December 15, 2006), Making the Move to Multicore, *SD Times.*
[6] Morgan, Lisa L., (December 15, 2006), Making the Move to Multicore, *SD Times.*
[7] Wlad, Joe. (2011), Freescale Multi-Core Forum, Freescale Multi-core Forum, St. Louis, September, 2011.
[8] http://www.imec.be/CleanC
[9] http://en.wikipedia.org/wiki/Intel_Parallel_Studio
[10] http://supertech.csail.mit.edu/cilk
[11] http://www.criticalblue.com
[12] http://www.polycoresoftware.com
[13] http://tipc.sourceforge.net
[14] http://www.redbend.com
[15] http://www.windriver.com/products/simics
[16] http://wiki.qeu.org/Main_Page
[17] http://en.wikipedia.org/wiki/Trano_Virtual_Processors
[18] http://www.sysgo.com/products/pikeos-rtos-technology
[19] http://en.wikipedia.org/wiki/OpenMP
[20] http://www.co-array.org
[21] http://hpff.rice.edu
[22] http://en.wikipedia.org/wiki/OpenMP
[23] http://upc.lbl.gov
[24] http://www.extreme.indiana.edu/sage
[25] http://www.erlang.org
[26] http://en.wikipedia.org/wiki/Fortress_(programming_language)
[27] http://en.wikipedia.org/wiki/ZPL_(programming_language)
[28] http://chapel.cray.com
[29] http://www.haskell.org/haskellwiki/Haskell
[30] http://en.wikipedia.org/wiki/OpenMP
[31] http://www.mipi.org
[32] http://www.mcs.anl.gov/research/projects/mpi
[33] http://www.systemc.org/home
[34] http://en.wikipedia.org/wiki/Data_dependency
[35] Moore, Chuck, (May 12, 2008) "Solving the Multi-core Programming Problem", *Dr. Dobbs Journal.*

3

Determining a Non-Collision Data Transfer Paths in Hypercube Processors Network

Jan Chudzikiewicz and Zbigniew Zieliński
Military University of Technology
Poland

1. Introduction

Fault tolerant systems are called systems capable of performing certain tasks despite of some unfitness (Kulesza et al., 1999; Kulesza, 2000; Chudzikiewicz, 2002; Chudzikiewicz & Zielinski, 2010). One of the conditions to be met by the structure used in fault tolerant systems is redundancy of the system components, namely use of redundant structures (see definition 2). Example of a structure, which ensures adequate number of communication lines is a binary n-dimensional hypercube H^n structure (see definition 1). Structures of this type have large reliability (Kulesza, 2000, 2003) and large diagnostic deepness in the sense of network coherence (Kulesza, 2000; Chudzikiewicz, 2002). The hypercube structures find wide application in data processing systems, especially for building fault tolerant systems, because such structures have natural features of redundancy.

Interconnection networks with the hypercube logical structure possess already numerous applications in critical systems and still they are the field of interest of many theoretical studies. In this kind of network the faulty processor may be replaced with a spare fault free processor (e.g. after network reconfiguration) or may be eliminated from the network and the new (degraded) network continues to operate, provided that it meets certain requirements. The last kind of such network is called a soft degradation network. A system's dependability is maintained by ensuring that it can discriminate between faulty and fault-free processors. The process of identifying faulty processors is called diagnosis of the processors' network.

We assume, that processors that are determined as faulty could not be repaired or replaced with spare equipment. The elimination of the faulty processor from the network induces (in the general case) the structure of several components of consistency. If the obtained (reduced) logical structure of the network is not the working structure, then the network loses its ability to operate (this network state will be determined as the network failure).

Correct diagnosis is another condition to tolerate failures in such systems. The quality of this diagnosis is critical to restore the suitability of the system by replacing the failure units, or isolation of such elements (soft system degradation) and perform reconfiguration tasks (Wang, 1999; Kulesza, 2000; Chudzikiewicz & Murawski, 2006; Zielinski et al., 2010). This requires the use of most effective diagnosis methods (Chudzikiewicz & Zielinski, 2003; Zielinski, 2006). In the case of distributed processing systems, a methods which uses the results of mutual testing of the system elements may be used (Kulesza & Zieliński 2010; Zielinski et al., 2011).

Both, from the viewpoint of functional tasks for which the system was built as well as the implementation of a system diagnosis it is important to ensure an effective mechanism for communication between system components (Chudzikiewicz & Zielinski, 2010; Kulesza et al., 1999).

In multiprocessor systems, effective communication between processors is one of the critical elements of data processing. Processors in multiprocessor systems communicate with each other by sending messages. The problem of data transfer in hypercube systems has been widely analyzed in the literature. Among other things, Gordon and Stout present the method called by them "sidetracking" (Gordon & Stout, 1988). This method assumes that each node stores information about the reliability state of their neighbors. Information from a given node is sent by a random path which is adjacent to a faulty free node. In the case of no path adjacent to the faulty free nodes, information is blocked and sent back to the node from which it was originally sent. A disadvantage of this method is little probability to submit information for a specified number of unfit nodes and large time delay. Another method proposed by Chen is called "backtracking" (Chen & Shin, 1990). This method assumes that the information on subsequent nodes, which mediated in data transmission is stored in the transmitted data. In the case that the data reaches the node that is adjacent to the unfit nodes, the information is used to send data back to the earlier node. Disadvantage of this solution is that the redundant information is moved in transmitted data and large time delays. Both methods - "sidetracking" and "backtracking" may lead to situation where the same intermediate nodes will be used to send data from different system components that communicate with each other (pairs of nodes). This may cause significant overload of individual links, while others will have unused resources. Moreover, individual data packets can be sent over different paths and reach out customers in a different (not always consistent with the assumed) sequence. This is especially inadvisable in the case of the need to ensure the efficiency of communication e.g. video conference realization.

This chapter presents the method of the data transmission paths reconfiguration in a hypercube-type processor network. The method is based on the determining strongly and mutually independent simple chains (see definition 4) between communicating pairs of nodes, which are called - I/O ports[1]. The method assumes that each node stored information about the reliability state of the system. The implementation problem of the presented method in embedded systems has also been raised. Mechanisms based on operating systems of Windows CE class are also presented, which will facilitate the implementation of the developed method.

2. Basic definitions

Let Z^n indicate the set of n-dimensional binary vectors.

Let us determine:

$$(s_1,...,s_2) = \{z \in Z^n : ((s_i \neq x) \Rightarrow (z_i = s_i)) \wedge ((s_i = x) \Rightarrow (z_i = \{0,1\}))\} \; (s_i \in \{0,1,x\}, 1 \leq i \leq n),$$

[1] I/O port is a node representing an element in a real system which can communicate with external networks.

where:

x indicates the indefinite value (0 or 1),

$Z(s)$ – is a set of 0-dimensional cubes (vector set $z=(z_1,...,z_n)$ $(z_i \in \{0,1\},\ 1 \le i \le n)$ of cube s $(s \in S^n)$).

Definition 1

An n-dimensional binary hypercube is the ordinary graph G $(G=<E,G>$, $|E|=2^n, |U|=n \cdot 2^{n-1})$ with 2^n nodes, each of which is described with an adequate binary vector z $(z=(z_1,...,z_n),\ z_i \in \{0,1\},\ 1 \le i \le n,\ z \in Z^n,\ |Z^n|=2^n)$ and $n \cdot 2^{n-1}$ edges connecting these nodes, which vectors that describe them are distant by 1 according to the Hamming measure.

Hereinafter the a nodes graph H^n will represent real processors, and its edges the data transmission paths between processors, which are adjacent to a specific edge.

The Hamming distance between two binary vectors $b'(\tau_i)$ and $b''(\tau_i)$, which are the poles of the chain τ_i, complies with the dependency:

$$\delta(b'(\tau_i), b''(\tau_i)) = \sum_{k \in \{1,...,n\}} (b'(\tau_i)_k \oplus b''(\tau_i)_k)$$

where:

$b'(\tau_i)_k$ – the k-th element of the binary vector $b'(\tau_i)$,

$\oplus$ –modulo 2 sum.

Definition 2

Redundant network logical structure is a structure whose graph G $(G=<E,U>)$ meets the condition: $|U| \ge |E|$.

Definition 3

A chain τ with a length k $(0 \le k \le 2^n)$ in H^n is called a coherent subgraph of the H^n graph if it includes $k+1$ nodes from which only two are of the first degree.

The node of the first degree chain is called the pole of this chain.

Let $Z(\tau)$ and $B(\tau)$ $(B(\tau) \subseteq Z(\tau))$ indicate the set of nodes and the poles of the τ chain respectively.

The chain τ will be presented both in the form of a subgraph $<Z(\tau)> H^n$ as well as in the form of a set $S(\tau)$ of s $(s \in S_1^n)$ 1-dimensional subcubes such that: $[s \in S(\tau)] \Leftrightarrow [\exists\, z', z'' \in Z(\tau): z'+z''=s]$.

Definition 4

It is said that chains τ' and τ'' in H^n are strongly and mutually independent, if $Z(\tau') \cap Z(\tau'') = \varnothing$.

An example of hypercube structure H^4 is shown in Figure 1. This structure is characterized by $|E| = 2^4 = 16, |U| = 4 \cdot 2^{4-1} = 32$. In parentheses in Figure 1 the binary label values assigned to individual nodes are given. The set Z^n of nodes is of the form as below:

$$Z^n = \{0000, 0001, 0010, 0011, 0100, 0101, 0110, 0111, 1000, 1001, 1010, 1011, 1100, 1101, 1110, 1111\}$$

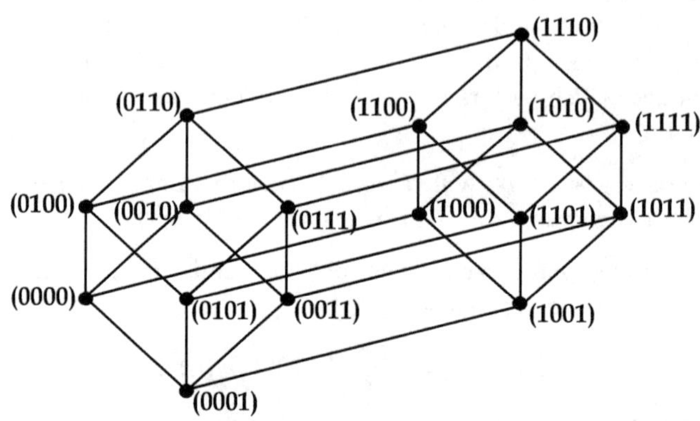

Fig. 1. An example of the H^4 structure.

Damage to the processor in the system described by the H^n graph and a lack of interchangeability causes the creation of a working structure, which is a partial subgraph of the graph H^n. An example of this type of structure is the structure shown in Figure 2, which is a partial subgraph of the graph H^4 shown in Figure 1. The processors labeled 0111 and 1000 are damaged.

3. The method of determining non-collision paths in a cube-type structure

The method of determining non-collision paths in hypercube structures is based on determination of simple chains between the nodes representing processors, which want to communicate with each other. An example of such a structure is shown in Figure 3.

Suppose that in the present structure the nodes from the E' set (nodes: 0000, 0010, 0100) and E'' set (nodes: 0011, 1011, 1110) $((E', E'' \subset E) \wedge (E' \cap E'' = \varnothing))$ represent processors, which are connected to I/O ports. Sending data from the processor represented by a node from the E' set to the processor represented by a node from the E'' set, requires a mediation of processors represented by nodes from the E''' set $(E''' = E \setminus (E' \cup E''))$.

Let us accept the following assumptions:

- minimum cost to send data - interpreted as the minimum number of elements in the transmission of intermediary data;
- possibility of implementing parallel data transfer between several pairs of processors – each pair communicates through independent pathways.

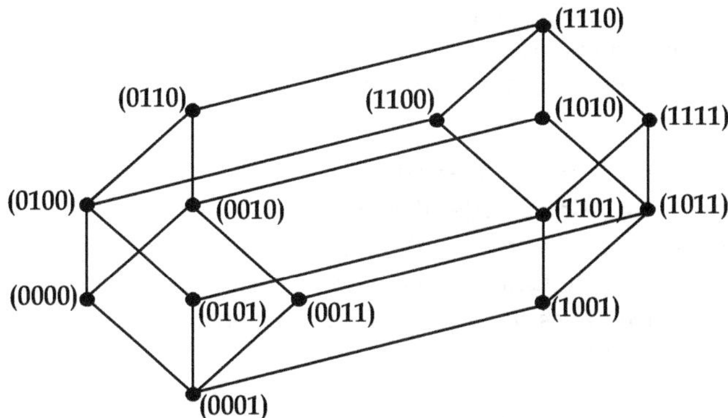

Fig. 2. An example of a partial subgraph of the structure shown in Figure 1.

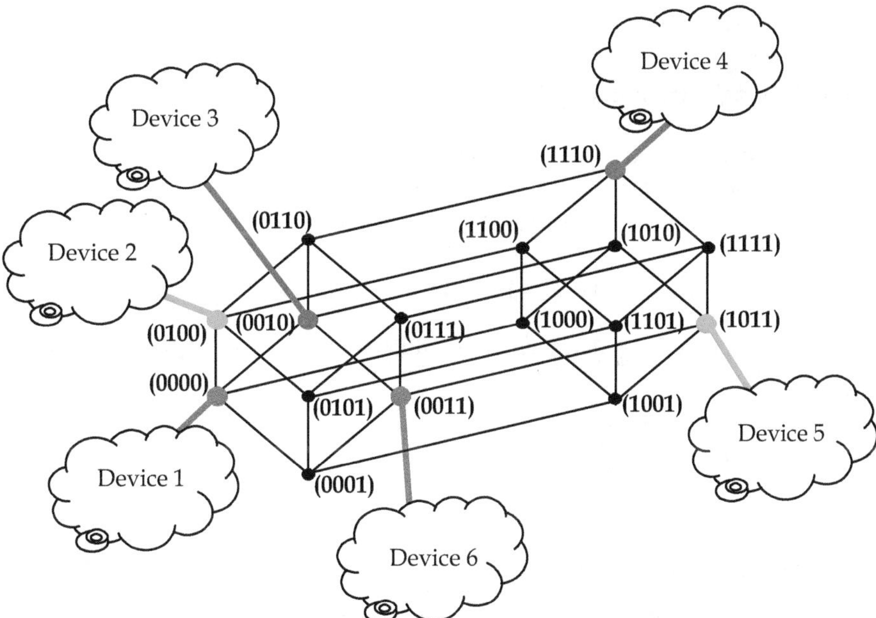

Fig. 3. An example of the H^4 structure with indicated I/O ports.

Determining connections between the nodes $e'(e' \in E')$ and $e''(e'' \in E'')$ means determination of the shortest chain (see definition 3) between these nodes. Implementation of parallel transmission between nodes from the set E' and the nodes from the set E'' requires calculation of strongly and mutually independent chains between specific nodes.

The final result of the method is to determine all paths between elements, which at the given moment intend to exchange data in such a way so that they do not interfere with other transmissions.

The proposed method is implemented in two phases. In the first phase, all possible simple chains between nodes that want to implement data exchange are determined. Determined for a specific pair of nodes, simple chains can't contain other nodes that are I/O ports.

In the second phase, from the set of simple chains, strongly and mutually independent chains are determined for pairs of nodes that communicate with each other. The method to determine the simple chain uses the algorithm based on the adjacency binary matrix. The algorithm determining data transmission paths between node pairs is given below and the adjacency binary matrix for the structure from Figure 3 is shown in Figure 4.

Let us denote:

$Ł(z', z'')$ - a set of chains connecting nodes z' and z'',

$Z(\tau_j)$ - a set of nodes that create chain τ_j,

$B(\tau_j)$ - a set of poles of chain τ_j,

W - a set of pairs of poles among, which simple chains $W = \{(z(e'), z(e'')) : (e', e'' \in E) \wedge (z(e'), z(e'') \in B(\tau))\}$ will be determined;

P - a set of strongly and mutually independent chains connecting communicating pairs of nodes.

Step 1. Select an unselected node as initial pole z' from the set W with the smallest label. As the end pole, select the node z'', so that: $(z', z'') \in W$.

Step 2. Determine the set $Ł(z', z'')$ of chains connecting nodes z' and z'', so that:

$$Ł(z', z'') = \{\tau : (Z(\tau) \setminus B(\tau)) \cap W = \varnothing\}.$$

If the set of chains is determined for all pairs of the set W go to step 3, otherwise go to step 1.

Step 3. Take the chain τ from the chain set $Ł(z', z'')$ for $(z', z'') \in W$. $Ł(z', z'') = Ł(z', z'') \setminus \tau$.

Step 4. Step 4Add the selected chain to set P, if:

$$((B(\tau) \neq B(\tau_i)) \wedge (Z(\tau) \neq Z(\tau_i)) \quad \forall \tau_i \in P, i = \{1, ..., |P|\}).$$

If the condition is met go to step 5.

If the condition is not met and $Ł(z', z'') \neq \varnothing$ go to step 3.

If the condition is not met and $Ł(z', z'') = \varnothing$ go to step 5.

Step 5. If $|P| = |W|$ the set of chains for all pairs $(z', z'') \in W$ is determined. Go to step 6.

If $|P| \neq |W|$ determine the next pair $(z', z'') \in W$. Go to step 3.

Step 6. The end of the algorithm.

On the adjacency matrix from Figure 4 colors mark rows and columns corresponding to the I/O ports.

		0000 0	0001 1	0010 2	0011 3	0100 4	0101 5	0110 6	0111 7	1000 8	1001 9	1010 10	1011 11	1100 12	1101 13	1110 14	1111 15
0000	**0**		1	1		1				1							
0001	1	1			1		1				1						
0010	**2**	1			1			1				1					
0011	3		1	1					1				1				
0100	**4**	1					1	1						1			
0101	5		1			1			1						1		
0110	6			1		1			1							1	
0111	7				1		1	1									1
1000	8	1									1	1		1			
1001	9		1							1			1		1		
1010	10			1						1			1			1	
1011	**11**				1						1	1					1
1100	12					1				1					1	1	
1101	13						1				1			1			1
1110	**14**							1				1		1			1
1111	15								1				1		1	1	

Fig. 4. Adjacency matrix for the structure shown in Figure 3.

For illustration of the algorithm let us trace designation of a simple chain between nodes: 0100 and 1011. In the first step the algorithm has appointed the node 0101 moving along the 4-th column to 5 row of this matrix. This is shown in Figure 5.

		0000 0	0001 1	0010 2	0011 3	0100 4	0101 5	0110 6	0111 7	1000 8	1001 9	1010 10	1011 11	1100 12	1101 13	1110 14	1111 15
0000	0																
0001	1						1				1						
0010	2																
0011	3																
0100	4						1	1						1			
0101	5		1			1			1						1		
0110	6					X			1								
0111	7						1	1									1
1000	8										1	1		1			
1001	9		1							1			1		1		
1010	10									1			1				
1011	11										1	1					1
1100	12					X				1					1		
1101	13						1				1			1			1
1110	14																
1111	15								1				1		1		

Fig. 5. Illustration of the first step of the algorithm. The matrix does not contain others I/O ports.

In the second step the algorithm has appointed 0001 node moving along the 5th row of the matrix. This is shown in Figure 6.

The algorithm in the next steps, alternating moving along columns and rows has appointed simple chain linking nodes: 0100 and 1011. This is shown in Figure 7.

The algorithm in six steps, has appointed the single simple chain linking nodes: : 0100 and 1011 the following form: {0100, 0101, 0001, 1001, 1000, 1010, 1011}.

For the structure from Figure 3 the algorithm determined sets of simple chains $Ł(z', z'')$ as shown in Table 1.

In the second phase of the method from the set of a simple chains, as shown in Table 1, for each pair of I/O ports, will be chosen the shortest simple chains allowing for the implementation of collision-free data transfer, as shown in Figure 8.

Let us consider the case when nodes: 0111 and 1000 are damaged. According to the presented method the new configuration will be determined by choosing from the set shown in Table 1 simple chains, which do not contain damaged nodes. The algorithm assigned new sets of simple chains $Ł(z', z'')$ shown in Table 2. Figure 9 shows the network configuration rejecting the unfit nodes: 0111 and 1000 and allows implementation of the collision-free data transfer.

	0000 0	0001 1	0010 2	0011 3	0100 4	0101 5	0110 6	0111 7	1000 8	1001 9	1010 10	1011 11	1100 12	1101 13	1110 14	1111 15
0000 0																
0001 1						1				1						
0010 2																
0011 3																
0100 4						1	1						1			
0101 5		1			1			X						X		
0110 6					X			1								
0111 7						1	1									1
1000 8										1	1		1			
1001 9		1							1			1		1		
1010 10									1			1				
1011 11										1	1					1
1100 12					X				1					1		
1101 13						1				1			1			1
1110 14																
1111 15								1				1		1		

Fig. 6. Illustration of the second step of the algorithm.

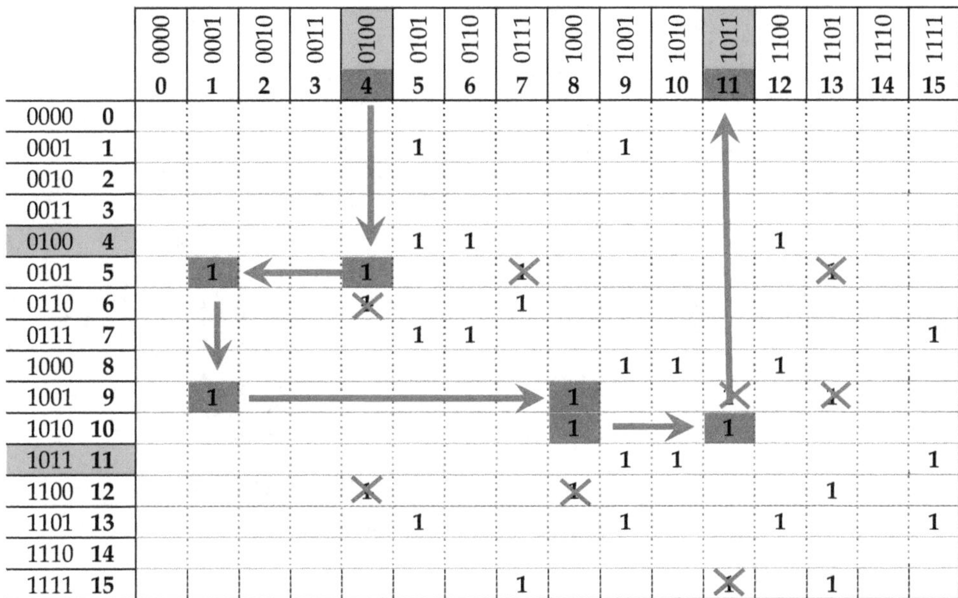

	0000 0	0001 1	0010 2	0011 3	0100 4	0101 5	0110 6	0111 7	1000 8	1001 9	1010 10	1011 11	1100 12	1101 13	1110 14	1111 15
0000 0																
0001 1						1				1						
0010 2																
0011 3																
0100 4						1	1						1			
0101 5		1			1			~~1~~						~~1~~		
0110 6					~~1~~			1								
0111 7						1	1									1
1000 8										1	1		1			
1001 9		1							1			~~1~~		~~1~~		
1010 10									1			1				
1011 11										1	1					1
1100 12					~~1~~				~~1~~					1		
1101 13						1				1			1			1
1110 14																
1111 15								1				~~1~~		1		

Fig. 7. Illustrate appointed by the algorithm the single simple chain between nodes: 0100 and 1011.

Ł(0000, 0011)	Ł(0010, 1110)	Ł(0100, 1011)
0 ; 1 ; 3	2 ; 6 ; 7 ; 5 ; 1 ; 9 ; 8 ; 10 ; 14	4 ; 5 ; 1 ; 9 ; 8 ; 10 ; 11
0 ; 1 ; 5 ; 7 ; 3	2 ; 6 ; 7 ; 5 ; 1 ; 9 ; 8 ; 12 ; 13 ; 15 ; 14	4 ; 5 ; 1 ; 9 ; 8 ; 12 ; 13 ; 15 ; 11
0 ; 1 ; 5 ; 13 ; 15 ; 7 ; 3	2 ; 6 ; 7 ; 5 ; 1 ; 9 ; 8 ; 12 ; 14	4 ; 5 ; 1 ; 9 ; 11
0 ; 1 ; 9 ; 8 ; 12 ; 13 ; 5 ; 7 ; 3	2 ; 6 ; 7 ; 5 ; 1 ; 9 ; 13 ; 12 ; 8 ; 10 ; 14	4 ; 5 ; 1 ; 9 ; 13 ; 12 ; 8 ; 10 ; 11
0 ; 1 ; 9 ; 8 ; 12 ; 13 ; 15 ; 7 ; 3	2 ; 6 ; 7 ; 5 ; 1 ; 9 ; 13 ; 12 ; 14	4 ; 5 ; 1 ; 9 ; 13 ; 15 ; 11
0 ; 1 ; 9 ; 13 ; 5 ; 7 ; 3	2 ; 6 ; 7 ; 5 ; 1 ; 9 ; 13 ; 15 ; 14	4 ; 5 ; 7 ; 15 ; 11
0 ; 1 ; 9 ; 13 ; 15 ; 7 ; 3	2 ; 6 ; 7 ; 5 ; 13 ; 9 ; 8 ; 10 ; 14	4 ; 5 ; 7 ; 15 ; 13 ; 9 ; 8 ; 10 ; 11
0 ; 8 ; 9 ; 1 ; 3	2 ; 6 ; 7 ; 5 ; 13 ; 9 ; 8 ; 12 ; 14	4 ; 5 ; 7 ; 15 ; 13 ; 9 ; 11
0 ; 8 ; 9 ; 1 ; 5 ; 7 ; 3	2 ; 6 ; 7 ; 5 ; 13 ; 12 ; 8 ; 10 ; 14	4 ; 5 ; 7 ; 15 ; 13 ; 12 ; 8 ; 9 ; 11
0 ; 8 ; 9 ; 1 ; 5 ; 13 ; 15 ; 7 ; 3	2 ; 6 ; 7 ; 5 ; 13 ; 12 ; 14	4 ; 5 ; 7 ; 15 ; 13 ; 12 ; 8 ; 10 ; 11
0 ; 8 ; 9 ; 13 ; 5 ; 1 ; 3	2 ; 6 ; 7 ; 5 ; 13 ; 15 ; 14	4 ; 5 ; 13 ; 9 ; 8 ; 10 ; 11
0 ; 8 ; 9 ; 13 ; 5 ; 7 ; 3	2 ; 6 ; 7 ; 15 ; 13 ; 5 ; 1 ; 9 ; 8 ; 10 ; 14	4 ; 5 ; 13 ; 9 ; 11
0 ; 8 ; 9 ; 13 ; 15 ; 7 ; 3	2 ; 6 ; 7 ; 15 ; 13 ; 5 ; 1 ; 9 ; 8 ; 12 ; 14	4 ; 5 ; 13 ; 12 ; 8 ; 9 ; 11
0 ; 8 ; 9 ; 13 ; 15 ; 7 ; 5 ; 1 ; 3	2 ; 6 ; 7 ; 15 ; 13 ; 9 ; 8 ; 10 ; 14	4 ; 5 ; 13 ; 12 ; 8 ; 10 ; 11
0 ; 8 ; 12 ; 13 ; 5 ; 1 ; 3	2 ; 6 ; 7 ; 15 ; 13 ; 9 ; 8 ; 12 ; 14	4 ; 5 ; 13 ; 15 ; 11
0 ; 8 ; 12 ; 13 ; 5 ; 7 ; 3	2 ; 6 ; 7 ; 15 ; 13 ; 12 ; 8 ; 10 ; 14	4 ; 6 ; 7 ; 5 ; 1 ; 9 ; 8 ; 10 ; 11
0 ; 8 ; 12 ; 13 ; 9 ; 1 ; 3	2 ; 6 ; 7 ; 15 ; 13 ; 12 ; 14	4 ; 6 ; 7 ; 5 ; 1 ; 9 ; 8 ; 12 ; 13 ; 15 ; 11
0 ; 8 ; 12 ; 13 ; 9 ; 1 ; 5 ; 7 ; 3	2 ; 6 ; 7 ; 15 ; 14	4 ; 6 ; 7 ; 5 ; 1 ; 9 ; 11
0 ; 8 ; 12 ; 13 ; 15 ; 7 ; 3	2 ; 6 ; 14	4 ; 6 ; 7 ; 5 ; 1 ; 9 ; 13 ; 12 ; 8 ; 10 ; 11
0 ; 8 ; 12 ; 13 ; 15 ; 7 ; 5 ; 1 ; 3	2 ; 10 ; 8 ; 9 ; 1 ; 5 ; 7 ; 6 ; 14	4 ; 6 ; 7 ; 5 ; 1 ; 9 ; 13 ; 15 ; 11
	2 ; 10 ; 8 ; 9 ; 1 ; 5 ; 7 ; 15 ; 13 ; 12 ; 14	4 ; 6 ; 7 ; 5 ; 13 ; 9 ; 8 ; 10 ; 11
	2 ; 10 ; 8 ; 9 ; 1 ; 5 ; 7 ; 15 ; 14	4 ; 6 ; 7 ; 5 ; 13 ; 9 ; 11
	2 ; 10 ; 8 ; 9 ; 1 ; 5 ; 13 ; 12 ; 14	4 ; 6 ; 7 ; 5 ; 13 ; 12 ; 8 ; 9 ; 11
	2 ; 10 ; 8 ; 9 ; 1 ; 5 ; 13 ; 15 ; 7 ; 6 ; 14	4 ; 6 ; 7 ; 5 ; 13 ; 12 ; 8 ; 10 ; 11
	2 ; 10 ; 8 ; 9 ; 1 ; 5 ; 13 ; 15 ; 14	4 ; 6 ; 7 ; 5 ; 13 ; 15 ; 11
	2 ; 10 ; 8 ; 9 ; 13 ; 5 ; 7 ; 6 ; 14	4 ; 6 ; 7 ; 15 ; 11
	2 ; 10 ; 8 ; 9 ; 13 ; 5 ; 7 ; 15 ; 14	4 ; 6 ; 7 ; 15 ; 13 ; 5 ; 1 ; 9 ; 8 ; 10 ; 11

	2 ; 10 ; 8 ; 9 ; 13 ; 12 ; 14	4 ; 6 ; 7 ; 15 ; 13 ; 5 ; 1 ; 9 ; 11
	2 ; 10 ; 8 ; 9 ; 13 ; 15 ; 7 ; 6 ; 14	4 ; 6 ; 7 ; 15 ; 13 ; 9 ; 8 ; 10 ; 11
	2 ; 10 ; 8 ; 9 ; 13 ; 15 ; 14	4 ; 6 ; 7 ; 15 ; 13 ; 9 ; 11
	2 ; 10 ; 8 ; 12 ; 13 ; 5 ; 7 ; 6 ; 14	4 ; 6 ; 7 ; 15 ; 13 ; 12 ; 8 ; 9 ; 11
	2 ; 10 ; 8 ; 12 ; 13 ; 5 ; 7 ; 15 ; 14	4 ; 6 ; 7 ; 15 ; 13 ; 12 ; 8 ; 10 ; 11
	2 ; 10 ; 8 ; 12 ; 13 ; 9 ; 1 ; 5 ; 7 ; 6 ; 14	4 ; 12 ; 8 ; 9 ; 1 ; 5 ; 7 ; 15 ; 11
	2 ; 10 ; 8 ; 12 ; 13 ; 9 ; 1 ; 5 ; 7 ; 15 ; 14	4 ; 12 ; 8 ; 9 ; 1 ; 5 ; 13 ; 15 ; 11
	2 ; 10 ; 8 ; 12 ; 13 ; 15 ; 7 ; 6 ; 14	4 ; 12 ; 8 ; 9 ; 11
	2 ; 10 ; 8 ; 12 ; 13 ; 15 ; 14	4 ; 12 ; 8 ; 9 ; 13 ; 5 ; 7 ; 15 ; 11
	2 ; 10 ; 8 ; 12 ; 14	4 ; 12 ; 8 ; 9 ; 13 ; 15 ; 11
	2 ; 10 ; 14	4 ; 12 ; 8 ; 10 ; 11
		4 ; 12 ; 13 ; 5 ; 1 ; 9 ; 8 ; 10 ; 11
		4 ; 12 ; 13 ; 5 ; 1 ; 9 ; 11
		4 ; 12 ; 13 ; 5 ; 7 ; 15 ; 11
		4 ; 12 ; 13 ; 9 ; 1 ; 5 ; 7 ; 15 ; 11
		4 ; 12 ; 13 ; 9 ; 8 ; 10 ; 11
		4 ; 12 ; 13 ; 9 ; 11
		4 ; 12 ; 13 ; 15 ; 7 ; 5 ; 1 ; 9 ; 8 ; 10 ; 11
		4 ; 12 ; 13 ; 15 ; 7 ; 5 ; 1 ; 9 ; 11
		4 ; 12 ; 13 ; 15 ; 11

Table 1. Sets of simple chains determined by algorithm for the structure from Figure 3.

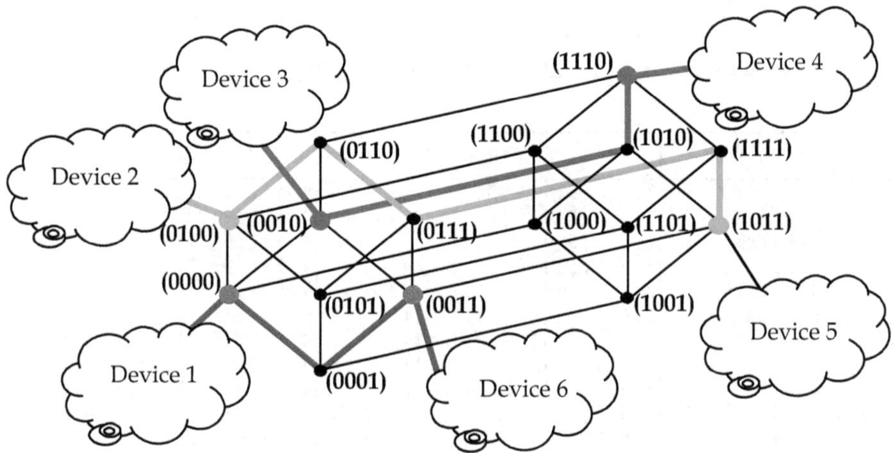

Fig. 8. An example of network configuration that allows collision-free communication between I/O ports.

Ł(0000, 0011)	Ł(0010, 1110)	Ł(0100, 1011)
0 ; 1 ; 3	2 ; 6 ; 14	4 ; 5 ; 1 ; 9 , 11
	2 ; 10 ; 14	4 ; 5 ; 1 ; 9 ; 13 ; 15 ; 11
		4 ; 5 ; 13 ; 9 ; 11
		4 ; 5 ; 13 ; 15 ; 11
		4 ; 12 ; 13 ; 5 ; 1 ; 9 ; 11
		4 ; 12 ; 13 ; 9 ; 114 ; 12 ; 13 ; 15 ; 11

Table 2. The sets of simple chains without damaged nodes (0111, 1000).

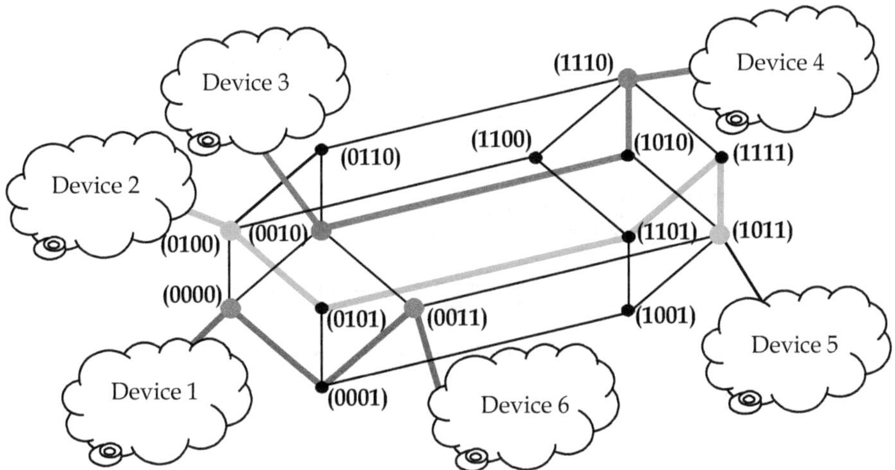

Fig. 9. The sets of simple chains without damaged nodes (0111, 1000).

4. Implementation of the method of determining non-collision paths in Windows CE

The processor network is based on S3C2440 processor on S3C2440SBC board. This is a 32-bit RISC processor. It is compatible with the Harvard Architecture model, characterized by a separate cache for commands (16KB) and data (16KB). It is equipped in: Memory Management Unit and Internal Advanced Microcontroller Bus Architecture. The family ARM920T processor is chosen (S3C2440 processor belongs to it), because of the possibility of installing Windows Embedded CE operating system on S3C2440SBC board. S3C2440SBC board provides a rich set of communication interfaces: three RS-232 interfaces, four USB 2.0 and one RJ-45 Ethernet. In the developed model of processor network the RS 232 interface is used to implement communication between the processor modules while the Ethernet interface is used for communication with external elements in relation to the network of processors.

To implement communication through the Ethernet interface the mechanism uses NDIS network drivers. Network driver interface specification is implemented in Windows® as a library, which defines interfaces between different layers of drivers and separates hardware drivers (low level) from upper layer drivers such as transport layer (Phung, 2009). NDIS also stores information on the status and parameters of the network drivers including indicators for functions, handlers and other values.

NDIS distinguishes the following types of drivers (see Figure 10):

- Miniport driver;
- Intermediate driver;
- Protocol driver.

The protocol driver is the highest in the stack of the NDIS driver and at the same time it is the lowest located component in an implemented network protocol. The protocol driver

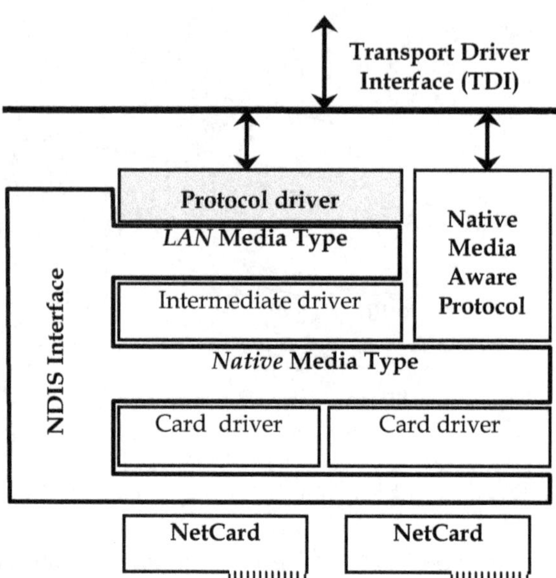

Fig. 10. Types of NDIS drivers.

allocates suitable memory area for the packet, copies data from the application to the prepared packet and - by calling the NDIS function - sends it to the network adapter. It also creates an interface for incoming data from the network adapter and sends them to the application.

Cooperation with other elements of the system is implemented using *ProcolXxx* functions, which constitute the interface for drivers situated lower in the stack. The protocol driver works with situated lower miniport or intermediate drivers in the stack that export a set of *MiniportXxx* functions. Transfer of packets by this driver is realized through the NDIS library by calling the appropriate functions. For example, functions *NdisSend* and *NdisSendPackets* can be used for sending packets.

The network software architecture with division on software layers is shown in Figure 11 (Zieliński et al., 2011).

In the operating system layer it is included a software layer which enables direct access to communication interfaces. In the communication software layer the dynamic library (*.dll) was realized to make available SEND() and RECIVE() functions. These functions enable sending and receiving messages in homogeneous manner - independently of physical interface.

The SEND() function makes it also possible to send broadcast messages that are used for broadcasting a new configuration of a degraded network structure. In the "Network Reconfiguration software" module the method of simple chains determining is implemented which is presented in Section 3. The structure of communication software layer is shown in Figure 12.

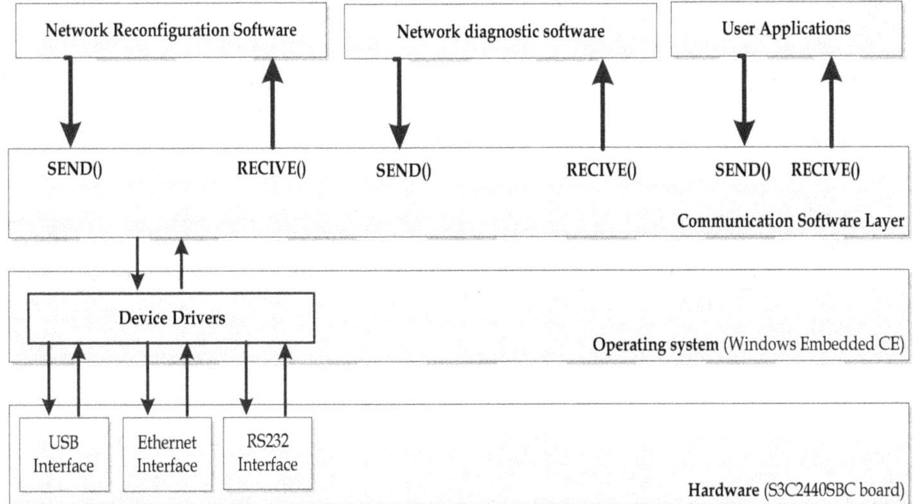

Fig. 11. The Network Software System Architecture.

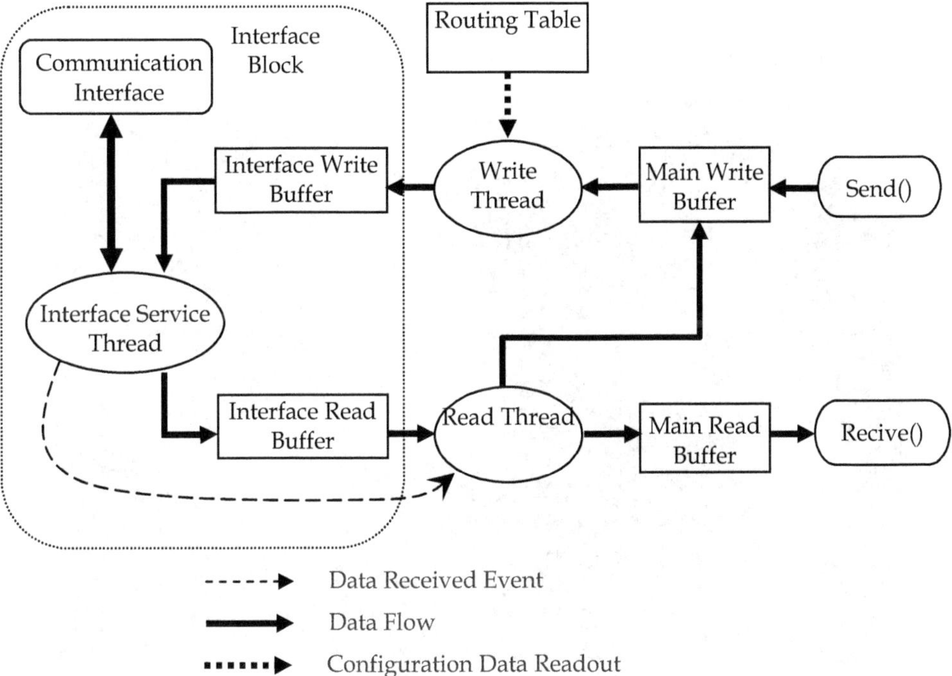

Fig. 12. Block diagram of the software communication layer.

Interface block includes hardware and software components that support a single interface. The notion of interface determines both a network card, as well as RS232 or USB 2.0. The number of blocks depends on the number of active interfaces. Identification of the active interface is realized at the stage of initial system configuration.

Write thread performs operations of: data download from main write buffer, adding additional information to a data packet and forwarding the package to the interface write buffer. Choosing an interface to be used to send a package is realized based on destination host ID and Routing Table.

Read thread performs operations of: data download from the interface read buffer and forwarding the data to the Main Read Buffer. Data read is performed after receiving an event – "data ready" generated by the handler of thread interface. In the case of a broadcast message, this data is copied back to the Main Write Buffer. This allows sending data to other network elements.

5. Conclusions

Designed method of data paths reconfiguring allows determining parallel data paths in degradable hypercube processor network. In view of the searching independent parallel data paths transmission in a distributed manner and small computational overhead the method may be used in the systems with high performance requirements and due to possibility of adapting solutions to the current reliability state also in fault tolerant systems.

The method was implemented in the experimental 4-dimensional hypercube processor network. The photo of this network with running modules is shown in Figure 12.

Fig. 13. The experimental network operating.

The appearance of the user interface shown in Figure 14. The procedure of diagnosing comparison method is periodically run in that network. After identifying damaged processors the reconfiguration algorithm is run on the set of fault-free processors. Currently, are realized adaptive tests of the experimental network model. Preliminary results of these tests show that the diagnostic messages are no more than 10% of all traffic in the network and time of the structure reconfiguration does not exceed 100 ms. Further work are directed to determine a degradation characteristics of the 4-dimensional hypercube processor network. Analytical methods were determined. Sets and images of all non-labeled coherent structures of order p where $p \in \{6,...,16\}$ and the powers of sets of labeled structures was determined by analytical methods. On this basis, it will be possible to build software tool to determine the cycle of life of such a network. The life cycle of the network can be expressed as a probability that the network keeps communication skills between defined sets of I/O ports and certain diagnostic properties after damaging the k processors $(k \in \{1,...,10\})$. Knowing degradation characteristics will allow selection of the best exploitation strategies of the network. The strategy consists of selecting the optimal (in the sense of communications capabilities, i.e. number of parallel data transmission paths) new working network structure and selection of a rational diagnosis method and tests.

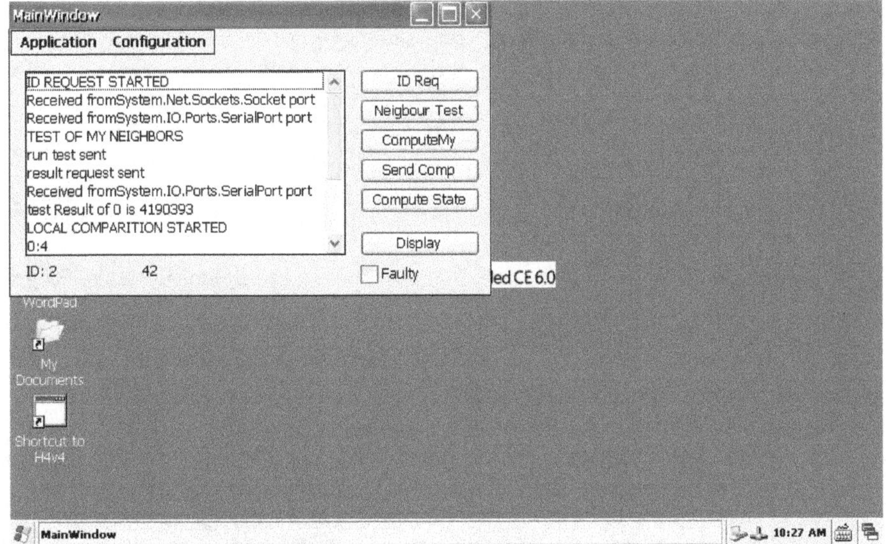

Fig. 14. Application User Interface.

6. References

Chen M.-S., Shin K.G. (1990). Depth-first search approach for faulttolerant routing in hypercube multicomputers, *IEEE Transactions Parallel and Distributed Systems*, vol. 1, no. 2, (April 1990), str. 152-159, ISSN: 1045-9219

Chudzikiewicz J. (2002), *Sieci komputerowe o strukturze logicznej typu hiperszeœcianu*; Institute of Automatics and Robotics, Faculty of Cybernetics, Military University of Technology, ISBN 83-916753-0-0, Warsaw, Poland

Chudzikiewicz J., Zieliński Z. (2003). Wyznaczanie *m*-diagnozowalnych struktur typu PMC w systemach o zwiększonej odporności na uszkodzenia, *Materiały X Konferencji SCR' 2003*, Ustroń, September 2003

Chudzikiewicz J., Murawski K. (2006). Determining A Non Collision Data Transfer Path In Hypercube Telecomunication Network, *Diagnostyka*, No. 3 (39), (2006), pp. 131-136, ISSN 641-6414

Chudzikiewicz J, Zieliński Z. (2010). Reconfiguration of a processor cube-type Network, *PRZEGLĄD ELEKTROTECHNICZNY (Electrical Review)*, NR 9, pp. 139-145, ISSN 0033-2097

Gordon J.M., Stout Q.F. (1988). Hypercube message routing in the presence of faults, *Proc. Third Conf. on Hypercube Concurrent Computers and Applications*, vol. 1, (Jan. 1988), str. 318-327

Kulesza R., Zieliński Z., Chudzikiewicz J. (1999). Reconfiguration of a ring structure in a hypercube computer network with faulty links; *International Conference on Technical Diagnostics 9th IMECO TC-10*, pp. 159-164, Wroclaw 1999.

Kulesza R. (2000). *Podstawy diagnostyki sieci logicznych i komputerowych (Secend edition)*, Institute of Automatics and Robotics, Faculty of Cybernetics, Military University of Technology, ISBN 83-9127747-6-4, Warsaw, Poland

Kulesza R. (2003). Struktury samodiagnozowalne w systemach cyfrowych, In: *Bulletin of Institute of Automatic and Robotics*, No 18, (2003), pp. 19-31, ISSN 1427-3578

Kulesza R., Zieliński Z. (2010). The life period of the hypercube processors' network diagnosed with the use of the comparison method, Monographs On System Dependability, In: *Monographs of System Dependability. Technical Approach to Dependability*, Sugier J., Mazurkiewicz J., Walkowiak T., Zamojski W., pp. 65-78, Oficyna Wydawnicza Politechniki Wrocławskiej, ISBN 978-83-7493-528-9, Wrocław

Phung S. (2009). *Professional Windows® Embedded CE 6.0*, Wiley Publishing, Inc., ISBN: 978-0-470-37733-8, USA, Canada

Sengupta A., Dahbura A.T. (1992). On Self-Diagnosable Multiprocessor Systems: Diagnosis by the Comparison Approach, *IEEE Transactions on Computers*, vol. 41, no. 11, (November 1992), pp. 1386–1396

Wang D. (1999). Diagnosability of Hypercubes and Enhanced Hypercubes under the Comparison Diagnosis Model, *IEEE Transactions on Computers*, vol. 48, no. 12, (December 1999), pp. 1369–1374

Zielinski Z. (2006). The Simulation Model Of Distributed Network System Diagnostic Procedures, *Diagnostyka*, No. 3 (39), (2006), pp. 209-214, ISSN 641-6414

Zielinski Z., Chudzikiewicz J., Arciuch A., Kulesza R. (2011). Sieć procesorów o łagodnej degradacji i strukturze logicznej typu sześcianu 4-wymiarowego, In: *Projektowanie i implementacja systemów czasu rzeczywistego*, Trybus L., Samolej S., pp. 219-232, Wydawnictwo komunikacji i Łączności, ISBN 978-83-206-1822-8, Warszawa

Zieliński Z., Kulesza R., Strzelecki Ł. (2011). Diagnosability characterization of the 4-dimensional cube type soft degradable processors' network, In: *Monographs On System Dependability – Problems of Dependability and Modeling*, Mazurkiewicz J., Sugier J., Walkowiak T., Michalska K., pp. 283–296, Oficyna Wydawnicza Politechniki Wrocławskiej, ISSN 978-83-7493-612-5, Wrocław

4

Concepts of Communication and Synchronization in FPGA-Based Embedded Multiprocessor Systems

David Antonio-Torres
Tecnologico de Monterrey Campus Puebla
Mexico

1. Introduction

The advent of deep submicron (DSM) technologies has driven the evolution of very large scale of integration (VLSI) chip design to new frontiers. In the early days, digital system design was tackled as an integration of discrete systems in a printed circuit board (PCB), the so-called jelly-bean design (Maxfield, 2004). If the complexity of the task was large, the resulting PCB was expected to be full packed with discrete components, thus pressing the designers with concerns such as area, power consumption, speed, etc. The further shrinking dimensions of the transistors allowed the designers to pack some similar discrete components together into a single one, thus alleviating design concerns about signal integrity, connectivity, etc. However, it was later found that some other aspects of design could also be alleviated if a larger number of the discrete components of the PCB were integrated into a single chip; this design strategy introduced the concept of System on Chip (SoC); an SoC is then defined as an integrated circuit that incorporates on-chip memory, hardware and software components, where the software components are to be run by one or more microprocessors or digital signal processors (DSP) (Chang et al., 1999).

It can be argued that SoC design has caused a great impact on consumer markets such as mobile communications. However, the market, in return, has pushed for convergence of multimedia, communication and signal processing into a single consumer electronic device, the so-called multimedia embedded systems, leading the designers to rethink the design strategy. Due to the massive data processing, the number of hard deadlines that such systems impose and the parallelism that the previous two entail, the presence of more microprocessors was mandatory. As a result, the latest incarnations of SoC are now termed Multiprocessor System on Chip (MPSoC). An MPSoc truly implements parallelism in the form of hardware threads, that is, each microprocessor present in an MPSoC executes a thread of execution in its own right. While the inclusion of more microprocessors provides more computing power to deal with stringent processing conditions, several other design concerns have been brougth about. Indeed, low-power operation, architecture design, performace predictability, on-chip communication, among others, are still open to design and exploration in the MPSoC field (Jerraya & Wolf, 2005).

Design of MPSoCs is a complex task that requires the contribution of several disciplines: computer architecture, embedded microprocessors, low-power design, physical and layout implications of DSM technologies, parallel computing, operating systems, network protocols, etc. In addition, the type of applications that an MPSoC is expected to run is not trivial and a correct tuning between the selected MPSoC architecture and the application is a lengthy process (Jerraya & Wolf, 2005). As a consequence, a few papers report performance comparisons between several architectures for a given application. Furthermore, due to the number of complexities around an MPSoC design, low-level details about synchronization and communication, which play a differentiation factor between architectures, are not fully clarified (Li & Hammami, 2009), (Yu & Schaumont, 2006). This chapter intends to shed some light to internal mechanisms of synchronization and communication in three dominant architectures in MPSoC: shared memory, message passing and Network on Chip (NoC). With the purpose of further clarifying those mechanisms, this chapter also proposes the use of an easy-to-program embedded microprocessor: PicoBlaze (Xilinx, 2011a). PicoBlaze is an 8-bit embedded microprocessor, in the form of soft core, developed by Xilinx and targeted for some families of FPGAs. These important characteristics of PicoBlaze are further reinforced with its programming in assembly language. Likewise, a generic dual core architecture proposed by Xilinx (Asokan, 2007) influences the development of the MPSoc architectures reported in this chapter. Consequently, PicoBlaze lends itself to implement a design flow for embedded systems whose architecture can be very easily simulated and prototyped. It is expected that with the use PicoBlaze and a design environment built around it, intricacies of communication and synchronizarion of those three MPSoC architectures can be unveiled and compared.

This chapter is organized as follows. Section 2 describes the tools of the design environment for the design and verification of the three proposed MPSoC architectures and provides details of the programming and simulation of PicoBlaze. Architectural features and the hardware blocks that provide the mechanisms of synchronization and communication for the multiprocessor architectures are identified and explained in section 3. Section 4 provides the details of implementation of the multiprocessor architectures using PicoBlaze. As the main focus of this chapter is on low-level details, the information provided in section 4 comes in the form of VHDL and assembly-language code. Also, section 4 evaluates the performance of the MPSoC architectures in terms of latency and area. Section 5 draws some conclusions and outlines the future work. Finally, acknowledgements and references are provided in sections 6 and 7 respectively.

2. FPGA-based design platform

One of the proposals of this chapter is the use of FPGAs as a platform for the evaluation of multiprocessor architecture. Due to its reconfigurable fabric and short design times, FPGAs lend themselves quite readily for the exploration of new architectures. Along with the selection of FPGAs for the exploration of new architectures, the proposed design platform includes a set of tools that speeds up the design flow and facilitates the evaluation of the designed architectures. This section explores the three components that make up the proposed platform design: FPGAs, PicoBlaze and Xilinx ISE.

2.1 FPGAs

The use of FPGA platforms in the exploration of new computer architectures and embedded systems has proven successful (Li & Hammami, 2009), (Yu & Schaumont, 2006). Along with the introduction of FPGAs in this field, languages for hardware description (HDL) such as VHDL and Verilog also help promote the use of reconfigurable logic devices in the exploration of new digital systems (Skahill, 1996), (Brown & Vranesic, 2000). An example of a design environment for the design of hardware and software components of embedded systems is EDK of Xilinx (Xilinx, 2011b). EDK relies on a library of reusable software components, a library of reusable hardware blocks and a set of tools that enable the programming and evaluation of embedded systems in an FPGA. Relying on the use of EDK for the design of embedded systems, Xilinx has also proposed a multiprocessor architecture based on two 32-bit microprocessors. Features of this proposed architecture are given later in this chapter.

2.2 PicoBlaze

PicoBlaze is an 8-bit embedded microprocessor developed by Xilinx and targeted for some families of FPGAs. The rationale for the selection of PicoBlaze for the development of MPSoC architectures are listed below.

- PicoBlaze has a simple and very flexible architecture in terms of the configurability and inclusion of peripherals
- Reduced instruction set and easy programming and simulation
- Because of the port-mapped peripherals approach that it implements, communication with peripherals is simplified and coding effort is reduced
- Its simple architecture and easy programming is in line with one of the objectives of this chapter, which is to highlight the characteristics of the syncronization and communication aspects of three multiprocessor architectures.

  While complex applications call for the use of more robust embedded microprocessors, it is the belief of the author that by reducing the complexity of the programming of the microprocessors and its necessities for communication the low-level exploration can be more focused on the characteristics of synchronization and communication required by the multiprocessing architecture.

2.3 Xilinx ISE

ISE is the flagship tool of Xilinx in the market of digital design (Xilinx, 2011c). ISE plays a key role in the proposed design environment, as it provides a set of entry tools for the capture of functionality of the design, a gate synthesizer and an FPGA programmer. In particular, this chapter makes use of a well proven approach: synthesizable VHDL descriptions for the hardware components of the MPSoC architectures and development of assembly-language code for the applications that the PicoBlaze instances are to run (Antonio-Torres et al., 2009). As ISE is focused on the development of hardware blocks, its use is complemented with the use of a couple of tools for assembly-language programming: the assembler KCPSM3 (Xilinx, 2011a) and the instruction-set simulator for PicoBlaze pBlazeIDE (Mediatronix, 2001). The three tools give shape to the design flow outlined below.

- The assembly language applications are developed for all the PicoBlaze instances of the architecture
- The applications are then assembled with KCPSM3 and translated into VHDL descriptions of read-only memories that hold the applications. The assembly-language applications translated into VHDL code allow the integration of the software development stages with the hardware design phases
- The design of the MPSoC architecture is further developed within ISE under a hardware design approach. If needed, the simulation of the software applications interacting with the hardware components can be conducted in the form of waveform analysis. As a matter of fact, this is the approach that is used to validate the proposed MPSoC architectures
- Upon completion of hardware design and simulation, the MPSoC architectures can be synthesized in an FPGA and concerns, such as area, can be evaluated

Once the proposed design flow and its supporting tools have been presented, the next section introduces the three multiprocessor architectures proposed for exploration.

3. Multiprocessor architectures

Due to its complexity and the huge design space that multiprocessor architectures call for, it can be argued that FPGA is a good candidate as a platform for evaluation and prototyping. In line with this idea, Xilinx has proposed a Generic Dual Processor Architecture (Asokan, 2007), (Kowalczyk, 2003), which is shown in Figure 1. This architecture is to be developed with two Xilinx tools: the Embedded Design Kit (EDK) and Software Design Kit (SDK), both of which are components of the tool Xilinx Platform Studio.

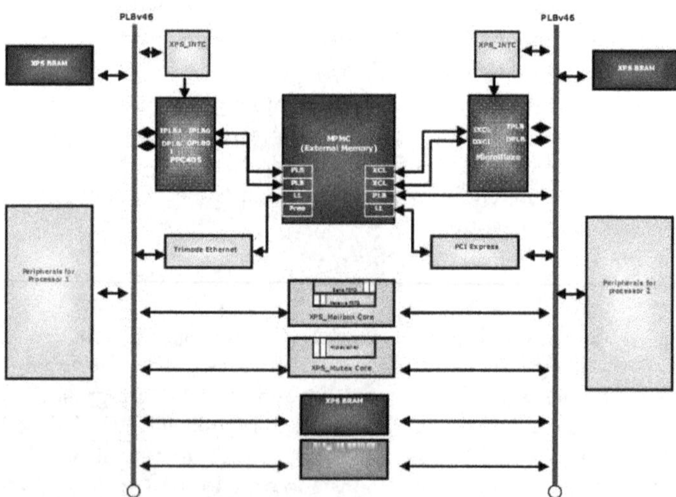

Fig. 1. Generic dual processor architecture proposed by Xilinx

The Generic Dual Processor Architecture is composed of two microprocessors. Depending upon the selected family of FPGAs, the microprocessor instances can be MicroBlaze or PPC405; MicroBlaze is a 32-bit soft core, while PPC405 is a 32-bit hard core available in some families. Additionally, each microprocessor can be deployed with a set of local peripherals, optionally supported by an interrupt controller. Playing the role of shared resources, an external memory with a multiport memory controller (MPMC) and an XPS BRAM are considered in the architecture; a bus bridge is also included, allowing the access of the two microprocessors to the two sets of, no longer, private peripherals. Implementing the mechanisms for communication and synchronization of the microprocessors are a mutex, XPS_Mutex (Xilinx, 2009b), and a mailbox, XPS_Mailbox, (Xilinx, 2009a); note that both are supplied by EDK in the form of VHDL descriptions and complemented with low-level software drivers. The mutex is in charge of arbitrating the accesses of the microprocessors to the shared resources, thus avoiding contention in case of simultaneous accesses. On the other hand, the mailbox embodies a channel of bidirectional communication between the microprocessors. As the mutex and the mailbox supplied by EDK are targeted to MicroBlaze and PPC405, the following sections provide details of how they can be tailored to the communication needs of PicoBlaze.

3.1 Shared memory

Figure 2 shows the concept of the shared memory architecture, where two microprocessors are attached to a bus along with a set of memory blocks and controllers of input/output devices. Before a microprocessor accesses one of the shared resources, it must request control to the mutex; in high-level language, this request comes in the form of a LOCK command (Culler et al., 1998). Once the control over the resource is granted by the mutex, the microprocessor is free to access the shared resource. When the task is completed, the microprocessor must release the control over the resource; in high-level language, the release operation comes in the form of an UNLOCK command (Culler et al., 1998).

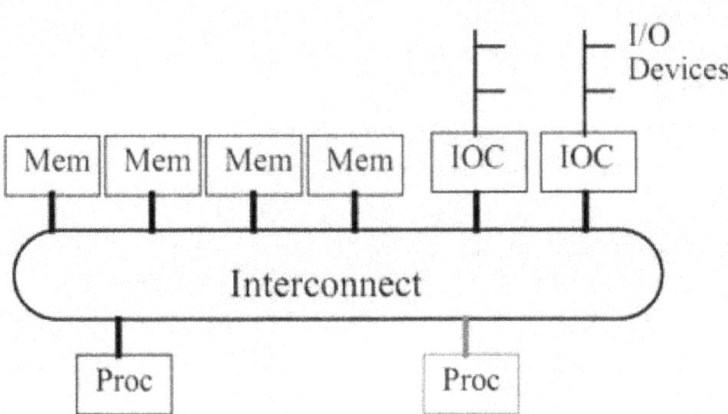

Fig. 2. Traditional organization of a shared memory architecture

At the core of a mutex, there is a finite-state machine (FSM) playing the role of an arbiter (Brown & Vranesic, 2000). Figure 3 shows an arbiter for three microprocessors that can lock/unlock one shared resource. The FSM must have as many *Gnt* states as microprocessors present in the system. Furthermore, the mutex, as a component, must provide an access port to each microprocessor in the architecture.

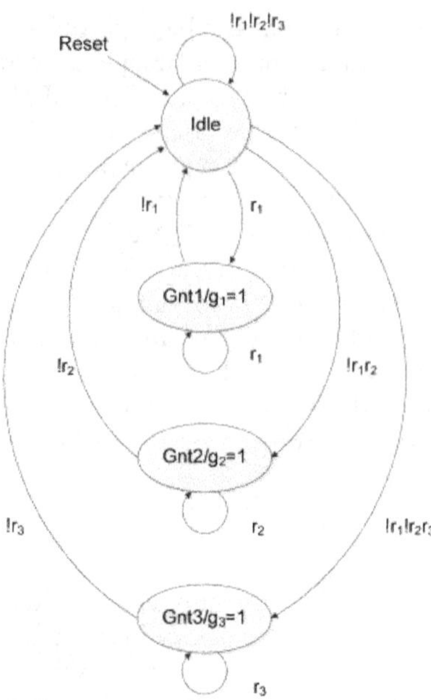

Fig. 3. A finite-state machines as a mutex for the arbitration in a shared memory architecture

As can be seen in Figure 3, the arbiter resolves contention by assigning priorities to all the microprocessors present in the system. The interaction between a requesting microprocessor and the arbiter is described as follows

- The microprocessor issues the command LOCK to the arbiter along with its identifier (this identifier is usually termed CPUID)
- If more than one microprocessor simultaneously try to LOCK the arbiter, the contention is resolved according to priorities
- The microprocessor reads back an internal register of the arbiter to retrieve the CPUID of the microprocessor that currently holds control over the shared resource
- If the CPUID read back from the arbiter coincides with that of the requesting microprocessor, the microprocessor can then take control over the shared resource; else the microprocessor issues again the LOCK command until it gains control over the resource
- Once a microprocessor has gained control over the shared resource, it proceeds with the required task and, upon completion, it must relinquish the control by issuing the command UNLOCK along with its CPUID

3.2 Message passing

Instead of relying on shared resources and requesting their access to a mutex, the message passing architecture identifies a mailbox as a bidirectional channel of communication between microprocessors. A mailbox allows two microprocessors to synchronize, share data and exchange status information. Figure 4 shows a typical message passing architecture that relies on mailboxes for interprocessor communication.

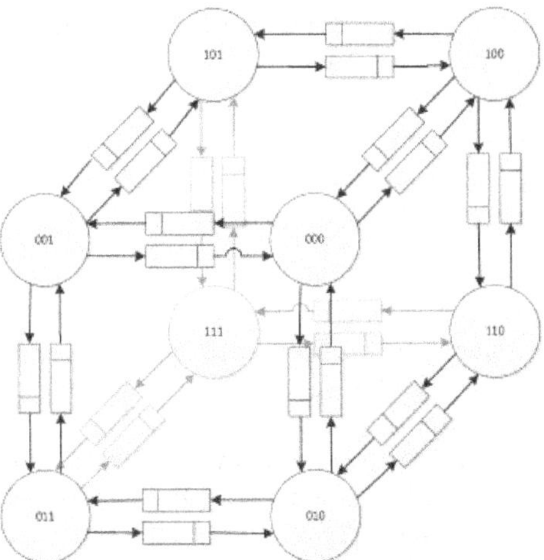

Fig. 4. Message passing architecture relying on mailboxes for interprocessor communication

As will be discussed later, a mailbox is composed of two first-in first-out (FIFO) memory buffers. A FIFO features two access ports, a read port and write port, see Figure 5. The important characteristic of a FIFO is that it keeps the data stored according to the order they were pushed into. A FIFO also features two status flags: an EMPTY flag that, when asserted, indicates that no data is available to be read and a FULL flag that, when asserted, indicates that there is no room for a new data to be written.

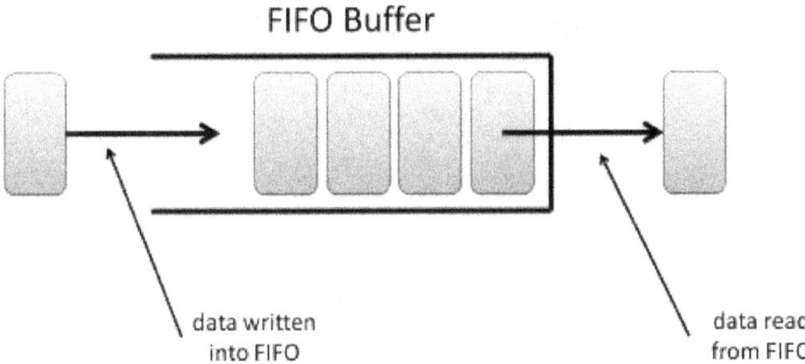

Fig. 5. Concept of a FIFO memory buffer with two access ports

The implementation of a mailbox with two FIFO buffers allows the communication between two microprocessors to be bidirectional, that is, one microprocessor is assigned the read port of FIFO 0 and the write port of FIFO 1, while the other microprocessor is assigned the read port of FIFO 1 and the write port of FIFO 0. The communication between the microprocessors initiates when microprocessor 0 writes a data to a write port, in which case it is said that the microprocessor 0 has issued a SEND command, and completes when microprocessor 1 reads that same data at the corresponding read port, in which case it is said that microprocessor 1 has issued a RECEIVE command (Culler et al., 1998). The interaction of the two microprocessors with the mailbox follows the procedure described below.

- Microprocessor 0 inspects the FULL flag of its corresponding write port and if the flag is zero it issues a SEND command
- Microprocessor 1 inspects the EMPTY flag of its corresponding read port and if the flag is zero it issues a RECEIVE command
- To implemente the communication in the opposite direction, microprocessor 0 and microprocessor 1 shift places with respect to the conditions given above

3.3 Network on chip

In addition to the well-known architectures described above, a recent exploration in the design of MPSoCs is Network on Chip (NoC). An NoC builds up interprocessor communication by borrowing some concepts from macronetworks theory (De Micheli & Benini, 2006), (Bjerregaard & Mahadevan, 2006). Instead of allowing microprocessors, or, in general, any processing element (PE), to be attached to a bus, an NoC provides each PE with a multipoint access to the rest of PEs in the system. Figure 6 shows the concept of an NoC. Note that the small circles represent routers that define the path of the data.

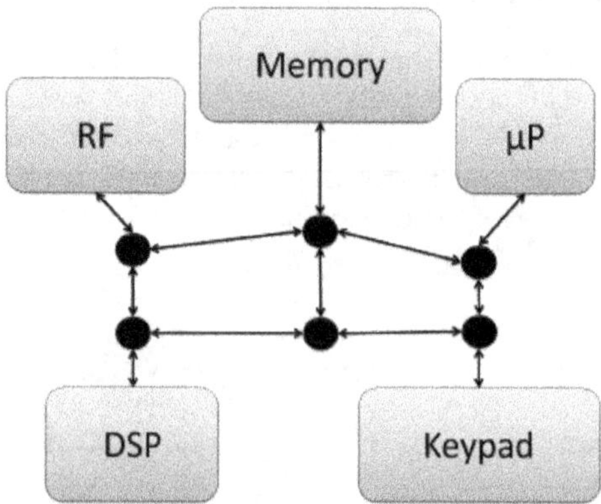

Fig. 6. Concept of a network on chip

From the perspective of an NoC, each PE implements a piece of functionality in the architecture and their interaction gives shape to the functionality of the whole system. In order to provide each PE with a channel of communication with the rest of the system, the concept of a network is introduced. Among the main tasks of the network are to identify the receiver of the message and establish a link between the source and the destination point; at each end of the link is a PE. Figure 7 shows a simple 4-by-4 grid NoC with global on-chip communication for the existing PEs.

Figure 7 is also helpful for the identification of the fundamental components of the network, which are described next.

- A network adapter interfaces between the core and the NoC, thus separating aspects of computation and communication in the system
- The routing nodes establish the path of the data according to the protocol of the network
- The links provide the channels of communication for the routing nodes

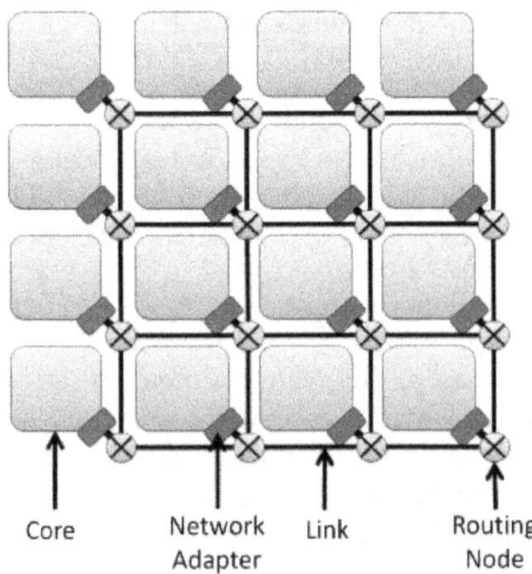

Fig. 7. 4-by-4 grid NoC with the main components of a network

The next section provides the hardware and software details of the implementation of the three multiprocessor architectures just presented. The hardware details are given in the form of VHDL descriptions, while software details come in the form of assembly-language routines. Additionally, aspects of evaluation are also discussed in order to put into perspective two important aspects of an MPSoC: latency and scalability.

4. Programming and evaluation

This section provides the low-level details of the comunication between a number of PicoBlaze instances and the components of the on-chip communication for the three types of multiprocessor architectures described in the previous section. In addition, the performance of the architectures will be evaluated in terms of latency and scalability. The latency of each architecture will be reported in terms of clock cycles or instruction cycles; as PicoBlaze features a fixed instruction cycle for the whole instruction set, the relation between clock and instruction cycles is quite straightforward. The scalability will be reported in terms of further modifications of the hardware components currently present in each architecture.

The three architectures are going to run a simple application that consists in adding eight 8-bit numbers that are stored locally. All the microprocessors run an exact copy of the application. Each microprocessor is going to be identified with a unique CPUID. As part of the evaluation and to facilitate debugging, microprocessor 1 is assigned CPUID 0x01 and adds numbers from 0x10 to 0x17; microprocessor 2 is assigned CPUID 0x02 and adds numbers from 0x20 to 0x27 and so on. The benefits of defining CPUID and a simple summation are that the effort during the visual inspection of waveforms is reduced and the exchange of data, for the sake of communication and synchronization, can be very easily identified. The final result of the application is the addition of all the individual additions conducted locally by each microprocessor. From a high-level language programming environment, this application can be seen as a long summation that is partitioned into a number of equal parts and that the number of partitions are allocated to an equal number of microprocessors. The mechanisms of synchronization or communication will allow the obtention of the total result of the summation (Culler et al., 1998).

Depending on the type of the architecture, a specific interprocessor communication mechanism is to allow the microprocessors to share their local results and a global variable is to account for the addition of the local results. The global variable may come in the form of a shared resource or an internal register of one of the microprocessors.

4.1 Mutex

As has been previously discussed, in a shared-memory architecture the mutex must provide a port of communication with each microprocessor present in the system. For the demonstration of this architecture, a system with eight PicoBlaze instances is evaluated. Figure 8 shows the organization between the eight PicoBlaze microprocessors, the shared resource and the mutex. Note that, due to the type application to be deployed in the architecture, the communication between the shared resource and the microprocessors is bidirectional. The shared resource is a multiport register that will hold the final result of the additions.

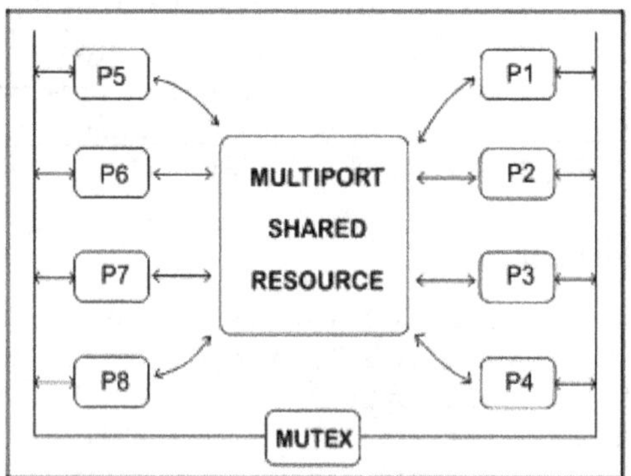

Fig. 8. MPSoC with a mutex and eight PicoBlazes

The VHDL entity of a mutex with ports for the eight PicoBlazes is shown below. Note that the ports and flags of PicoBlaze are encapsulated into a bus with the purpose of reducing the effort of the structural design of the whole system.

```
entity mutex_8 is
    Port ( CLK : in  STD_LOGIC;
           RST : in  STD_LOGIC;
           P1_BUS : in  STD_LOGIC_VECTOR (17 downto 0);
           P2_BUS : in  STD_LOGIC_VECTOR (17 downto 0);
           P3_BUS : in  STD_LOGIC_VECTOR (17 downto 0);
           P4_BUS : in  STD_LOGIC_VECTOR (17 downto 0);
           P5_BUS : in  STD_LOGIC_VECTOR (17 downto 0);
           P6_BUS : in  STD_LOGIC_VECTOR (17 downto 0);
           P7_BUS : in  STD_LOGIC_VECTOR (17 downto 0);
```

```
            P8_BUS : in  STD_LOGIC_VECTOR (17 downto 0);
            CPUID : out  STD_LOGIC_VECTOR (7 downto 0));
end mutex_8;
```

Each Px_BUS, where x stands for 1, 2, etc., is decomposed into the following signals

- Px_BUS(17) carries the request of the microprocessor: the LOCK or the UNLOCK command
- Px_BUS(16:10) carry the CPU ID of the requesting microprocessor
- Px_BUS(9:2) carry the address of the mutex in the bus system
- Px_BUS(1) and Px_BUS(0) carry the strobes that enable the communication

As can be seen in its entity, the mutex also provides an output port for all the microprocessors to read back the CPUID of the microprocessor that currently owns the shared resource; this reading back usually takes place after a microprocessor has tried to lock the mutex. The assembly-language code shown below is the routine that every microprocessor must execute to lock the mutex; the execution of the application will not continue until the microprocessor succeeds in locking the mutex. Note that PicoBlaze uses the instruction `OUTPUT` to write a data to an output port and the instruction `INPUT` to read a data from an input port. On the other hand, the combination of instructions `COMPARE` and `JUMP NZ` allows PicoBlaze to test a data (Xilinx, 2011a).

```
;requests access to the shared resource
LOAD    OutReg, CPUID
OR      OutReg, Lock ;CPU tries to lock the mutex
locked:
OUTPUT  OutReg, MutexAddress
INPUT   InReg, MutexAddress
COMPARE InReg, CPUID
JUMP    NZ, locked ;if not locked, tries it again
```

Upon succeeding locking the mutex, the microprocessor reads the multiport register, which for this example implements the global variable, executes another addition between the local and the global variable and saves the result into the global variable by writing back to the register. The VHDL entity of the multiport register is shown below.

```
entity mp_register_16 is
    Port ( CLK : in  STD_LOGIC;
           RST : in  STD_LOGIC;
           P1_BUS : in  STD_LOGIC_VECTOR (17 downto 0);
           P2_BUS : in  STD_LOGIC_VECTOR (17 downto 0);
           P3_BUS : in  STD_LOGIC_VECTOR (17 downto 0);
           P4_BUS : in  STD_LOGIC_VECTOR (17 downto 0);
           P5_BUS : in  STD_LOGIC_VECTOR (17 downto 0);
           P6_BUS : in  STD_LOGIC_VECTOR (17 downto 0);
           P7_BUS : in  STD_LOGIC_VECTOR (17 downto 0);
```

```
        P8_BUS : in  STD_LOGIC_VECTOR (17 downto 0);
        REG_OUT : out  STD_LOGIC_VECTOR (7 downto 0));
end mp_register_16;
```

The assembly-language routine for accessing the multiport register is shown below. Note that the local variables are `LowByte` and `HighByte`, while `ReadRegLow` and `ReadRegHi` are the addresses for a reading access to the register and `WriteRegLow` and `WriteRegHi` are the addresses for a writing access to the register.

```
INPUT   Acc, ReadRegLow          ;reads the global low byte and
ADD     LowByte, Acc             ;adds it to the local low byte
INPUT   Acc, ReadRegHi           ;reads the global high byte and
ADDCY   HighByte, Acc            ;adds it to the local high byte
OUTPUT  LowByte, WriteRegLow     ;the shared resource is updated
OUTPUT  HighByte, WriteRegHi     ;accordingly
LOAD    OutReg, CPUID
OR      OutReg, Unlock
OUTPUT  OutReg, MutexAddress     ;CPU unlocks the shared resource
```

Figure 9 shows a typical situation when all the microprocessors contend for the shared resource. Note that each microprocessor is represented by their lock command and CPUID. As the microprocessor with CPUID 0x01, which is that with the highest priority, is contending, the mutex resolves the contention by granting the access to this microprocessor. The signal *mutex_debug*, which is provided for debugging purposes, accounts for this situation. It can be verified that the contention is resolved by the mutex in four clock cycles.

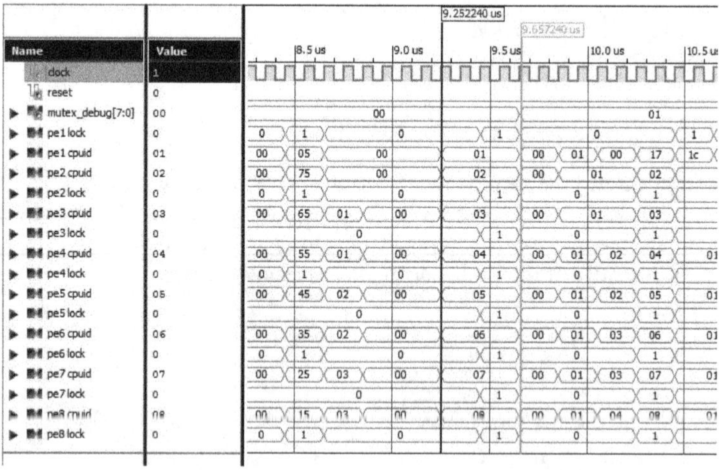

Fig. 9. The eight microprocessors contend for the shared resource and the mutex resolves the contention and grants access to microprocessor with CPUID 0x01

Figure 10 shows that the interval of time that the microprocessor with CPUID 01 owns the mutex is 24 clock cycles. The signal *mutex_debug* provides this information. Knowing that each instruction of PicoBlaze takes two clock cycles, each microprocessor own the mutex for 12 intruction cycles. This number of instruction cycles was expected, as can be verified in the code excerpt that was shown previously. As the application that every microprocessor is running is exactly the same, all the microprocessors own the mutex for the same period of time.

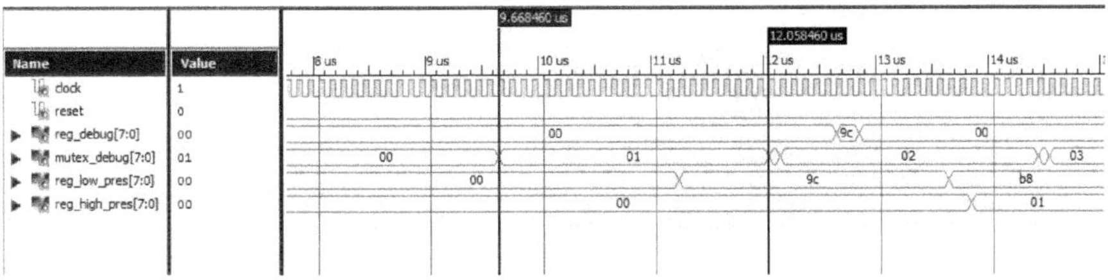

Fig. 10. Microprocessor with CPUID 0x01 owns the shared resource for 24 clock cycles

Figure 11 shows the moment when the PicoBlaze instance with the lowest priority, CPUID 0x08, accesses the multiport register, signals *reg_low_pres* and *reg_high_pres*, and updates its current contents. Note also that the completion of the work is indicated once this microprocessor unlocks the mutex, which happens at the time 28850 ns, approximately. Given a simulated clock period of 100 ns, it can be concluded that the task of the system is completed in an equivalent time to 289 instruction cycles.

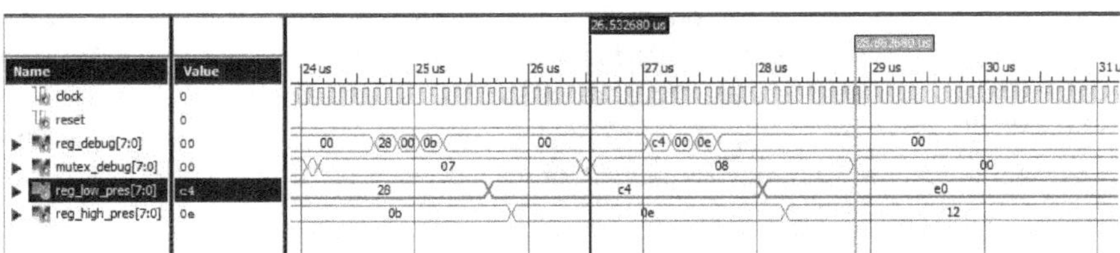

Fig. 11. The application is completed once the microprocessor with CPUID 0x08 unlocks the mutex

The main disadvantage of the use of a mutex in an MPSoC architecture is that the microprocessor with the lowest priority will have a latency to access the shared resource directly proportional to the number of microprocessors present in the architecture. The main advantage of this architecture is that the final result of the application is kept in just one memory location.

In terms of scalability, the number of states of the arbiter is dependant of the number of microprocessors of the architecture. If more microprocessors are to be added, more states are to be added to the arbiter. Additionally, the structure of the arbiter must be replicated as many times as shared resources present in the MPSoC. It can be concluded that the area of the communication components is linearly proportional to the number of microprocessors and the number of shared resources.

4.2 Mailbox

The structure of a mailbox composed by two FIFOs is shown in Figure 12. The mailbox features two ports: Port 0 and Port 1. The microprocessor attached to Port 0 must make use of the addresses 0xB0 through 0xB4 for the communication with the mailbox, for a writing access the data must be written to FIFO 0 and for a reading access the data must be read from FIFO 1. The microprocessor attached to Port 1 must make use of the addresses 0xC0 through 0xC4 for the communication with the mailbox; for a writing access the data must be written to FIFO 1 and for a reading access the data must be read from FIFO 0.

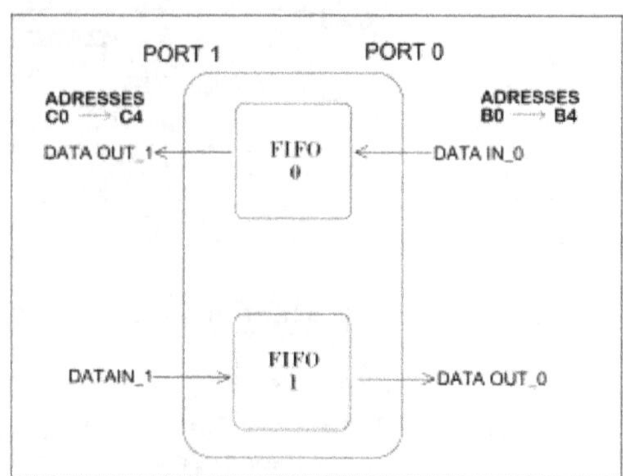

Fig. 12. Structure of a mailbox composed by two FIFOs

The labels given to the two ports of each FIFO are provided for easy identification when two PicoBlazes are attached. The definition of the entity of the mailbox is shown below. Note that the design of the mailbox is generic in terms of the depth of the two FIFOs and the number of bits of the memory locations. In addition, the port that was previously defined as Port 0 now is identified as the right port, while the port that was previously defined as Port 1 is now identified as the left port. Finally, the definition of the elements of each port are defined in accordance to the ports of PicoBlaze.

```
entity mailbox is
   generic(
        NBIT : integer := 8; --number of bits
        WIDTH : integer := 3 --addressing lines
        );
   Port( CLK, RST : in  STD_LOGIC;
        --right port
        DATAIN_0 : in  STD_LOGIC_VECTOR(7 downto 0);
        PORTID_0 : in  STD_LOGIC_VECTOR(7 downto 0);
        RD_0, WR_0 : in  STD_LOGIC;
        DATAOUT_0 : out  STD_LOGIC_VECTOR(7 downto 0);
        --left port
        DATAIN_1 : in  STD_LOGIC_VECTOR(7 downto 0);
        PORTID_1 : in  STD_LOGIC_VECTOR(7 downto 0);
        RD_1, WR_1 : in  STD_LOGIC;
        DATAOUT_1 : out  STD_LOGIC_VECTOR(7 downto 0));
end mailbox;
```

Figure 13 shows a multiprocessor system with nine PicoBlaze instances. The PicoBlaze instances are numbered from P1 to P9 in a typical tree organization (Bjerregaard & Mahadevan, 2006). The arrowheads between the microprocessors represent the mailboxes establishing the interprocessor communication channel. The mailboxes are numbered from 1 to 8.

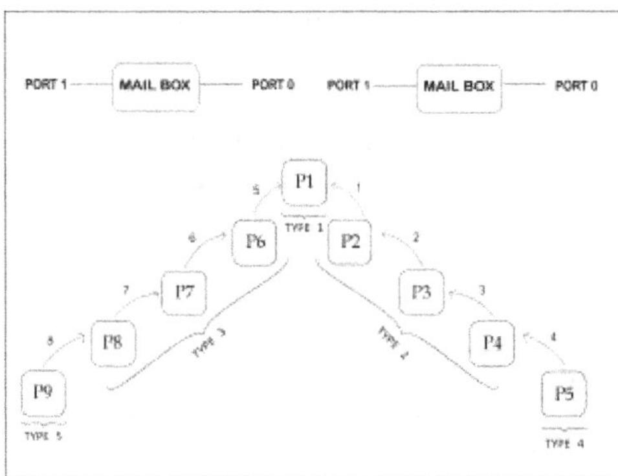

Fig. 13. Message passing architecture with nine PicoBlazes and eigth mailboxes in a tree structure

While the application is exactly the same for all the microprocessors, they do not implement the same functionality in the three organizations; this is the reason why a TYPE feature is also defined for each microprocessor. As a consequence, while all the PicoBlaze instances run the same application, they differ in the CPUID and TYPE that they are assigned. The execution of the application according to the definition of TYPE is explained next. Note that the TYPE-1 microprocessor has the longest execution.

- TYPE-1 microprocessor is in charge of holding the total result of all the individual additions. Once it concludes its local addition it starts to read the mailboxes and then update their local addition accordingly. The application is complete once both mailboxes indicate that are empty.
- TYPE-2 microprocessors write the result of their local addition to the mailbox to the left (Port 0 of mailbox) and then start to read data from the mailbox to the right (Port 1 of mailbox) and writing it to the mailbox to the left (Port 1 of mailbox) until the mailbox to the right indicates that it is empty, thus reaching an end to their execution.
- TYPE-3 microprocessors follow the same execution as TYPE-2 microprocessor, except that in the opposite direction. TYPE-3 microprocessors complete their local addition and write their result to the mailbox to the right (Port 1 of mailbox) and then start to read data from the mailbox to the left (Port 0 of mailbox) and writing it to the mailbox to the right (Port 1 of mailbox) until the mailbox to the left indicates that it is empty, thus reaching an end to their execution.
- TYPE-4 microprocessor completes its local addition and then it writes it to the mailbox to the left (Port 0 of mailbox), thus completing its job
- TYPE-5 microprocessor completes its local addition and then it writes it to the mailbox to the right (Port 1 of mailbox), thus completing its job

The assembly-language directives for PicoBlaze shown below provide the necessary functionality for the definition of the CPUID and the TYPE. Note that the CPUID definition is no longer necessary for the organization of the architecture.

```
;constants and registers
CONSTANT CPUID, 01        ;unique identifier of the CPU
CONSTANT TYPE, 01         ;classification in the architecture
```

As part of the assembly-language application of the system, a decoding subroutine is provided for each microprocessor to branch to their corresponding thread of execution according to the TYPE they were assigned. The code excerpt below shows this subroutine. Again, the combination of the instructions `COMPARE` and `JUMP Z` facilitates the required branching.

```
;the type of communication is determined according
;to the TYPE assigned to each CPU
;type 1 is the last to initiate in order to allow
;the fifos to be loaded at its both sides
LOAD      InReg, TYPE
COMPARE   InReg, 04
JUMP      Z, commType4
COMPARE   InReg, 05
JUMP      Z, commType5
COMPARE   InReg, 02
JUMP      Z, commType2
COMPARE   InReg, 03
JUMP      Z, commType3
JUMP      commType1
```

Subroutines for the TYPE-2 and TYPE-4 microprocessors are shown below. Both subroutines make use of a set of routines that implement even lower-level communication between PicoBlaze and the mailboxes. Note that in both subroutines a `JUMP` to the address `loop` represents the completion of the job.

```
commType2:
    ;this type writes to port 0 and reads from port 1
    LOAD    FirstData, LowByte
    LOAD    SecondData, HighByte
    CALL    writeAccessPort0        ;shares local variables
askIfEmptyType2:
    INPUT   InReg, ReadEmptyPort1  ;asks if fifo is empty
    COMPARE InReg, isFifoEmpty
    JUMP    Z, loop                ;if fifo is empty job is done
    CALL    readAccessPort1        ;if fifo is not empty it passes
    CALL    writeAccessPort0       ;a new pair of data
    JUMP    askIfEmptyType2
```

```
commType4:
    LOAD     FirstData, LowByte
    LOAD     SecondData, HighByte
    CALL     writeAccessPort0       ;shares local variables
    JUMP     loop
```

Figure 14 shows how the TYPE-4 microprocessor writes its local variables, two 8-bit variables that hold the result of its local addition, to a mailbox. Note the use of the address 0xB0 by the port portid_pe5 and the two short pulses of the port writest_pe5 to indicate a writing access to the Port 0 of the mailbox.

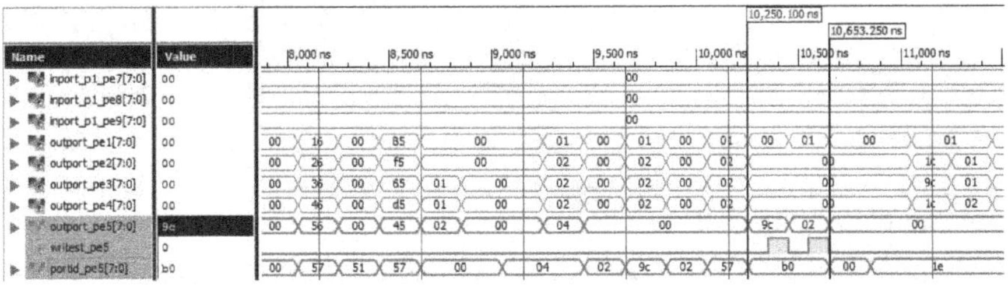

Fig. 14. Communication of the TYPE-4 microprocessor with a mailbox

Figure 15 shows the communication of the microprocessor P2, which is a TYPE-2, with its both mailboxes. The cursor indicates the beginning of such communication. This microprocessor starts by writing its local addition variables to the mailbox to the left, note the use of the address 0xB0 and the two pulses in writest_pe2. Next, the microprocessor reads the empty flag of the mailbox to the right, note the single pulse of readst_pe2; the flag is reflected in inport_p1_pe2 (Port 1 of the mailbox to the right). As the mailbox indicates that it is not empty, the microprocessor proceeds to read the mailbox in four read accesses (note that the addresses for these accesses are 0xC1, 0xC4, 0xC1 and 0xC4); the data read is verified in inport_p1_pe2, which is then written to Port 0 of the mailbox to the left, the port output_pe2 transports the data.

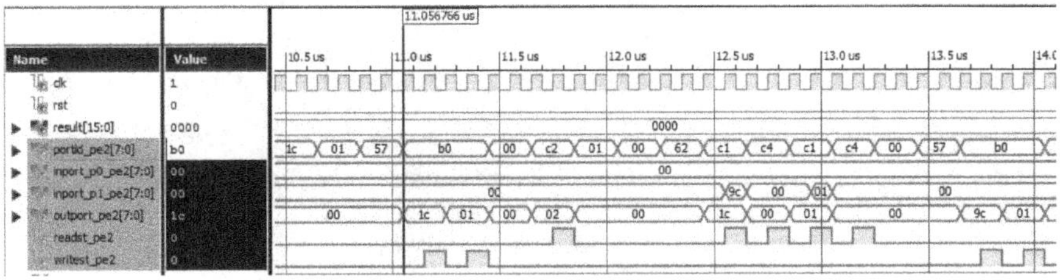

Fig. 15. Communication of a TYPE-2 microprocessor with its mailboxes

Figure 16 shows the operation of the microprocessor P1, the only TYPE 1 in the architecture, before completing its job. The cursor coincides with moment the microprocessor reads the empty flag of the mailbox attached to the right. As can be seen, the port inport_p1_pe1 carries the value 0x01 indicating that the mailbox is empty. This also indicates that the microprocessor has completed the processing of all the data generated by the microprocessors to the right (P2, P3, P4 and P5). Next, microprocessor P1 reads a new data from the mailbox attached to left through the port inport_p0_pe1 (the data is 0x040C) issuing the address sequence: 0xB1, 0xB4, 0xB1 and 0xB4. Around the time 32 microseconds, microprocessor P1 reads the empty flag of the mailbox to the left; as the value in port inport_p0_pe1 is 0x01, microprocessor P1 is indicated that the mailbox to the left is empty. This leads microprocessor P1 to write the final result of all the additions to an external register for debugging purposes; this takes place around the time 32.5 microseconds and the data written is 0x177C. Note that the register is mapped to the addresses 0xE1 and 0xE2.

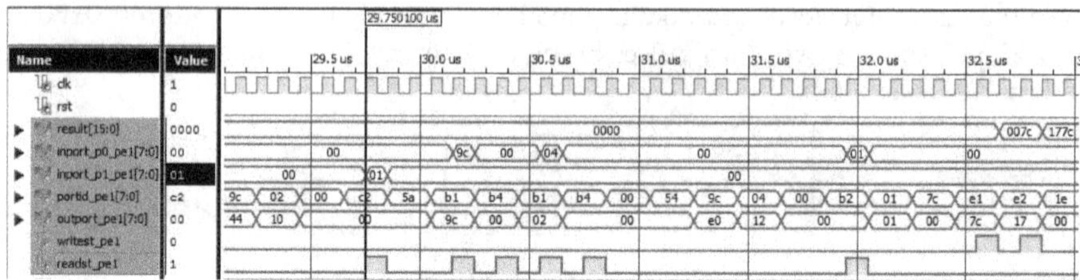

Fig. 16. Communication of the TYPE-1 microprocessor with its mailboxes and the completion of the application

Due to the tree structure of the MPSoC and the point-to-point communication implemented by the mailboxes, the messages take a long path, and, as a result, a long latency, to reach the microprocessor at the top of the tree for them to be processed. It can be demonstrated that the time it takes for a message to be transferred from one mailbox to the other equals eigth instruction cycles. This number can be used for the calculation of the total latency of the system given the number of mailboxes present. The time a message takes from its source to its destination can be computed as the number of mailboxes in the path times eight instruction cycles. In order to avoid that the latency of the messages adds up, the messages can be parallelized through the branches of the tree.

In terms of scalability, the message-passing architecture is simple. For each point-to-point communication between two microprocessors, one mailbox is needed. In addition, for one more microprocessor that is added to the architecture, at least one more mailbox needs to be introduced. While the communication mechanism in a message-passing architecture is not complex, its main disadvantage is the area required by each mailbox. As each mailbox is made up of two FIFOs and a FIFO is made up of registers, the requirement of memory for a large number of mailboxes in an architecture can be high.

The latency and area penalties in a message-passing architectures can be reduced if a more flexible communication approach is devised. The next section explores the use of a router for the implementation of a multipoint communication network.

4.3 NoC

Several NoC architectures have been explored and successfully implemented (De Micheli & Benini, 2006), (Bjerregaard & Mahadevan, 2006); however, in line with the proposal of this chapter, the design of a specific router has been chosen. This router is adequate for the FPGA fabric and its functionality has already been reported in VHDL (Bakr, 2008), see Figure 17. It is worth noting that the VHDL description has been modified to support the communication needs of PicoBlaze.

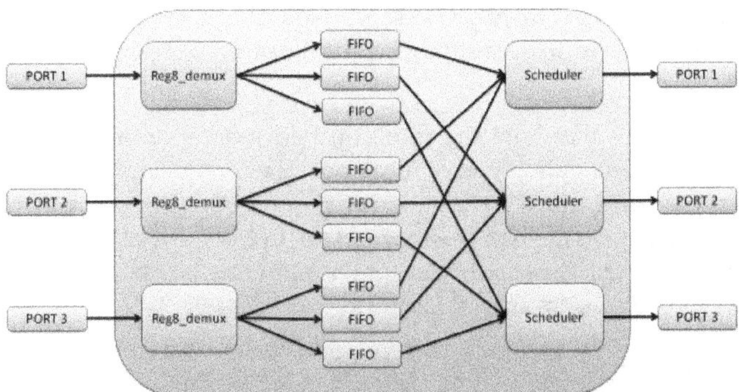

Fig. 17. Structure of an NoC router adequate for FPGA implementation

The router shown in Figure 17 allows the communication of up to three PEs. The router requires that each PE features separate input and output ports. The operation of the router is as follows. The incoming messages, at the left-hand side ports, are inspected and their header extracted in order to determine their destination. This inspection is conducted by the joint operation, at each port, of a register and a demultiplexor. Once the destination is identified, the messages are stored in the corresponding FIFO; the number of the internal FIFOs is determined by the number of ports of the router. From the FIFOs, the messages are finally routed to their destination based on the operation of a round-robin scheduler.

In order to take advantage of the 8-bit communication data of PicoBlaze, each packet of communication between two microprocessors is composed of two 8-bit data. The first 8-bit data, the address, identifies the destination of the message; this address data is coded as one-hot code, thus allowing up to eight microprocessors to be addressed in the architecture. The second 8-bit data is the message itself. For purposes of evaluation, eigth PicoBlaze instances are connected to the router; as a result, the router is composed of 8 register-demultiplexer modules, 64 4-level FIFOs and 8 schedulers. Similar to the implementation of the other two multiprocessor architectures evaluated in the chapter, each microprocessor is to implement the addition of eight 8-bit data and the goal is to exploit parallelism to produce the addition of all the individual results. Figure 18 shows the

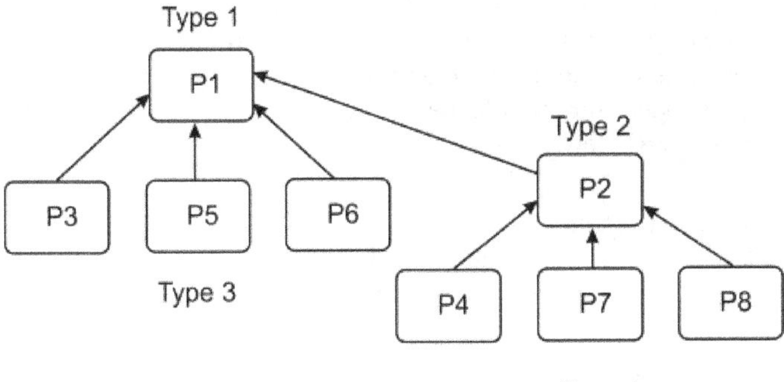

Fig. 18. Communication of eight microprocessors making use of an NoC

communication between eight microprocessors. Note that the eight microprocessors have been classified into four types in order to define the data flow that will allow the computation of the final result.

Along with the two bytes that hold the result of their local additions, the microprocessors issue the address of the destination microprocessors. The router extracts the address from the communication packet and stores the data in internal FIFOs. The arrival of new data to the FIFOs is indicated to the destination microprocessor in the form of an interrupt. The code excerpt below shows the entity of the router for the eight microprocessors. Note that only the ports of two microprocessors are shown for the sake of brevity.

```
entity noc_router is
    Port ( CLK : in  STD_LOGIC;
           RST : in  STD_LOGIC;
           INPORT1     : in  STD_LOGIC_VECTOR (7 downto 0);
           PORTID1     : in  STD_LOGIC_VECTOR (7 downto 0);
           WRITE1      : in  STD_LOGIC;
           INPORT2     : in  STD_LOGIC_VECTOR (7 downto 0);
           PORTID2     : in  STD_LOGIC_VECTOR (7 downto 0);
           WRITE2      : in  STD_LOGIC;
     ...
           OUTPORT1    : out  STD_LOGIC_VECTOR (7 downto 0);
           INTERRUPT1  : out  STD_LOGIC;
           OUTPORT2    : out  STD_LOGIC_VECTOR (7 downto 0);
           INTERRUPT2  : out  STD_LOGIC;
     ...
     );
end noc_router;
```

The differences between the four types of microprocessors in the NoC architecture are explained next. Once they complete their local additions, type-3 and type-4 microprocessors share their results with their destination microprocessor. As a consequence, these two types of microprocessors do not support interrupts. Upon the occurrence of an interrupt, type-1 microprocessor updates its local result with the new data. Type-2 microprocessor updates its local result upon the arrival of new data and waits for the occurrence of all the interrupts to share its updated local result with type-1 microprocessor. The assembly-language application that the microprocessors execute include the CPUID and the type of each; this is demonstrated in the code excerpt shown below.

```
;constants and registers
CONSTANT CPUID, 01        ;unique identifier of the CPU
CONSTANT TYPE, 01         ;classification in the architecture
```

The assembly-language routine that allows the microprocessors to share their local result is shown below.

```
;type_2 retransmits local values to cpu1,
;data first, address second
;until interrupt counter counts six interrupts
;(low and high byte from three cpus)
type_2:
    COMPARE  InterruptCounter, 06
    JUMP     NZ, type_2
    LOAD     DataReg, LowByte
    OUTPUT   DataReg, RouterWriteData
    LOAD     AddressReg, CPU1
    OUTPUT   AddressReg, RouterWriteAddress
    LOAD     DataReg, HighByte
    OUTPUT   DataReg, RouterWriteData
    OUTPUT   AddressReg, RouterWriteAddress
    JUMP     loop
    ;
    ;type_3 retransmits local values to cpu1,
    ;data first, address second
type_3:
    LOAD     DataReg, LowByte
    OUTPUT   DataReg, RouterWriteData
    LOAD     AddressReg, CPU1
    OUTPUT   AddressReg, RouterWriteAddress
    LOAD     DataReg, HighByte
    OUTPUT   DataReg, RouterWriteData
    OUTPUT   AddressReg, RouterWriteAddress
    JUMP     loop
```

As has been discussed before, interrupts play a key role for the communication of messages in the architecture. A simple routine that handles interrupts and allows the microprocessors to update their local results is shown below.

```
;depending on the CPU the data are retransmitted or not
;the interrupt flag of router is cleared after data is read
isr:
    ;data in router is read
    INPUT   Temporal, RouterReadData
    ;verifies the flag to proceed with the addition
    COMPARE OrderByteFlag, 01
    JUMP    Z, add_high_byte
    ADD     LowByte, Temporal
    ;next interrupt addition of high byte will take place
    LOAD    OrderByteFlag, 01
isr_continuation:
    ;this counter only applies to cpu type 2
    ADD     InterruptCounter, 01
```

```
    LOAD     Temporal, 00
    ;interrupt flag of router is cleared
    OUTPUT   Temporal, RouterClearFlag
    RETURNI ENABLE
    ;
add_high_byte:
    ADDCY    HighByte, Temporal
    ;next interrupt addition of low byte will take place
    LOAD     OrderByteFlag, 00
    JUMP     isr_continuation
;
```

Figure 19 shows low-level details of the communication between type-3 and type-1 microprocessors. The signals *out_port*, *port_id* and *writest_strobe* of the PicoBlaze instances P3, P5 and P6 allow sending the two bytes of their local additions to PicoBlaze P1; note that the three messages are composed of four write accesses: the number 0xB0 in port_id identifies the data, while the number 0xB1 identifies the CPUID of the receiver. It can be seen that the three writes accesses complete around 12.05 microseconds of simulation time. The bottom half of Figure 19 shows the arrival of the data shared by P3 and P5 (first the low byte first and then the high byte); the completion of the two messages occur at 14.86 and 20.06 microseconds.

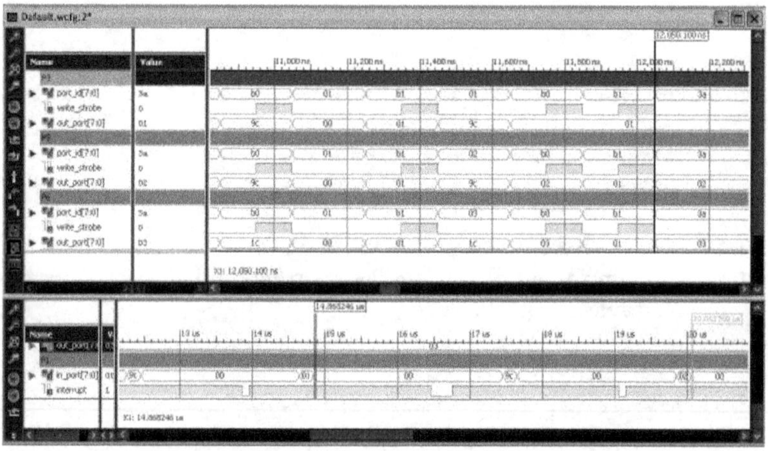

Fig. 19. Communication between type-3 and type-1 microprocessors

Details about the communication between a type-4 and a type-2 microprocessor are shown in Figure 20. For this communication scenario, P4, P7 and P8 are the senders and P2 is the receiver. The three messages are completed around 11.65 microseconds, while the messages from P7 and P8 are received at 14.44 and 19.45 microseconds.

Communication between P2, the sender, and P1, the receiver, is shown in Figure 21. The number sent by P2 is 0x0AF0, which accounts for the local additions of P2, P4, P7 and P8. As indicated previously, P1 is to hold the result of the eight local additions. Note that the latency in this communication is of around 3.39 microseconds.

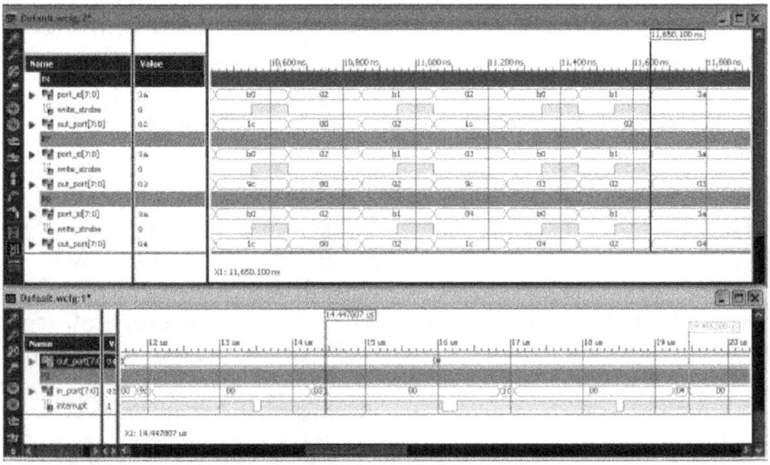

Fig. 20. Communication between type-4 and type-2 microprocessors

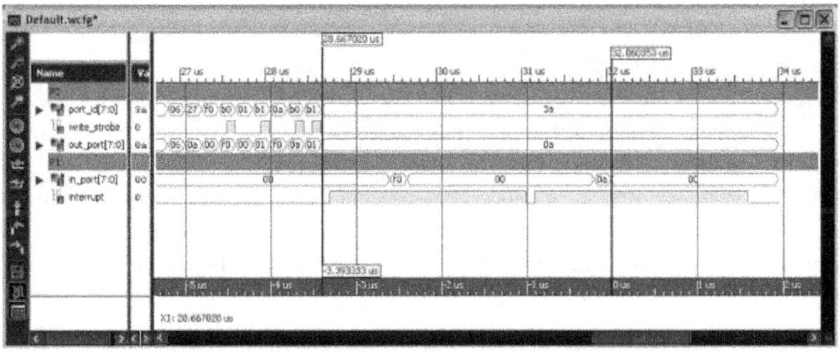

Fig. 21. Communication between type-2 and type-1 microprocessors

It can be demonstrated that the latency in the communication between a sender and a receiver in the NoC has two sources: the inherent operation of the router and the ISR latency of PicoBlaze. Inside the router, the joint operation of the register and demultiplexer incurs in a delay that is mostly combinational; however, the scheduler consists in a 32-state FSM (4 states for each microprocessor operation), whose operation is influenced by the time PicoBlaze takes to service an interrupt. In a worst-case scenario, the ISR takes 20 instruction cycles (10 for each byte of the local addition that is sent), which equal 40 clock cycles; adding 4 clock cycles for the operation of the FSM for each microprocessor and multiplying by the 8 microprocessors in the system, it results in a 352-clock-cycles delay. The simulation that is being reported is based on a period of 100 nanoseconds.

In terms of the hardware provisions of the NoC, the depth of the FIFOs should reflect the needs of the application, as the number of FIFOs present in the router is exponentially dependant of the number of microprocessors in the architecture. Despite the high demands for FIFOs, an NoC offers the most flexible approach for the communication and synchronization of multiple microprocessors. Indeed, the sender has control over the selection of the microprocessor that is to receive the message and, depending on the existing traffic conditions of the system, the sender may intelligently define new routes of communication to comply with hard deadlines of communication.

5. Conclusions and future work

Multiprocessor system-on-chip (MPSoC) is the last incarnation of complex system-on-chip. The market push for digital convergence and multimedia systems has put a lot pressure on the capabilities of integrated circuits and the only possible way designers can take up the challenge is to deploy a number of microprocessors in a single chip. This new era in the VLSI design is possible thanks to the latest deep submicron (DSM) technology, as DSM technologies allow a larger number of transistors and more processing available per area. As the design and programming of microprocessors have currently reached a level of maturity, the design focus of current SoCs is on the on-chip communication. On-chip communication defines the structure of communication and synchronization between all the microprocessors present in the architecture.

This chapter has intended to shed some light into the low-level details of communication and synchronization between a number of microprocessors in the architecture. For that purpose, a design platform has been proposed; this platform is composed of the tool ISE and the microprocessor PicoBlaze, both from Xilinx, and FPGAs for prototyping and evaluation. Likewise, three multiprocessor architectures have been proposed for evaluation: memory shared, message passing and Network-on-Chip (NoC). The communication and synchronization components necessary in each architecture have been described in VHDL and the software applications have been developed in assembly language. Programming of the applications at low level has allowed a deep inspection into the mechanisms surronding on-chip communication. Additionally, the low-level approach has served to identify aspects of latency and scalibility in the three architectures.

From the exploration and evaluation of the three architectures, it can now be concluded that NoC has the most promising results. This is not surprising, as NoC design has received a great deal of attention from several research groups around the globe. Among the most important characteristics of NoC design are: parallel architectures are naturally implemented; multipoint communication between microprocessors increases the design space, leading to well-explored architectures and high-performance applications and the on-chip communication structure is now separated from the computation structure implemented by the microprocessor instances.

NoC design is an open research area that still requires a great deal of exploration and evaluation. With the aid of FPGAs, NoC designs can be prototyped and evaluated early in the design flow. However, in order to get the most out of NoCs, more aspects need to be considered in this design area. A variety of microprocessors, parallel programming, networking standards, operating systems, high-level programming languages, exploration of data-intensive applications, among others, need to be considered as part of the design space that NoC brings about. In particular, automatic deployment of an application on a given number of microprocessor instances and that the process of deployment be aware of the network of communication in the architecture are still under research. It is the author's belief that the use of high-level design languages, such as SystemC, can be of great help to NoC design when it comes to predicting performance, modelling behaviour and functionality, predicting network trafic and, finally, mapping the application efficiently on the architecture.

Additionally, by making use of the support of SystemC for higher levels of abstraction, the design time and the exploration of the design space of NoCs can be drastically reduced.

6. Acknowledgements

The author would like to thank the following institutions and people: Xilinx Inc. for the donation of their tools for the preparation of this work, IMEC and the Microelectronics Training Center for sharing the design of the NoC router and the students Mr. D. Sosa-Ceron, Mr. R. Ramirez-Mata, Mr. P. Galicia-Rojas, Mr. R. Garcia-Baez and Mr. L. Cortez-Eliosa at the Tecnologico de Monterrey Campus Puebla for the elaboration of the images of this chapter.

7. References

Antonio-Torres, D.; Villanueva-Perez, D.; Sanchez-Canepa, E.; Segura-Meraz, N.; Garcia-Garcia, D.; Conchouso-Gonzalez, D.; Miranda-Vergara, J.; Gonzalez-Herrera, J.; Riquer-Martinez de Ita, A.; Hernandez-Rodriguez, B.; Castaneda-Espinosa de los Monteros, R.; Garcia-Chavez, F.; Tellez-Rojas, V. & Bautista-Hernandez, A. (2009). A PicoBlaze-Based Embedded System for Monitoring Applications, *CONIELECOMP '09 Proceedings of the 2009 International Conference on Electrical, Communications, and Computers*, 978-0-7695-3587-6, Cholula, Puebla, Mexico, 2009

Asokan, V. (2007). Designing Multiprocessor Systems in Platform Studio, White Paper 262 (WP262), Xilinx Inc., USA, 2007

Bakr, S. (2008). Network-on-Chip Router, *Lab Exercise no. 29*, IMEC, Microelectronics Training Center, Belgium, 2008

Bjerregaard, T. & Mahadevan, S. (2006). A Survey of Research and Practices on Network-on-Chip. *ACM Computing Surveys*, Vol. 38, March 2006, ACM

Brown, S. & Vranesic, Z. (2000). *Fundamentals of Digital Logic with VHDL Design*, McGraw-Hill, 0070125910, USA

Chang, H.; Cooke, L.; Hunt, M.; Martin, G.; McNelly, A. & Todd, L. (1999). *Surviving the SoC Revolution: A Guide to Platform-Based Design*, Kluwer Academic Publisher, The Netherlands

Culler, D.; Singh, J. & Gupta, A. (1998). *Parallel Computer Architecture: A Hardware/Software Approach*, Morgan Kaufmann Publisher, 1558603433, USA

De Micheli, G. & Benini, L. (2006). *Networks on Chips*, Morgan Kaufmann Publisher, 0123705211, USA

Jerraya, A. & Wolf, W. (2005).*Multiprocessor Systems-On-Chips*, Ahmed Amin Jerraya & Wayne Wolf, (Ed.), Morgan Kaufmann Publisher, 012385251X, USA

Kowalczyk, J. Multiprocessor Systems. White Paper 162 (WP162), Xilinx Inc., USA

Li, X. & Hammami, O. (2009). An Automatic Design Flow for Data Parallel and Pipelined Signal Processing Applications on EmbeddedMultiprocessor with NoC: Application to Cryptography. *International Journal of Reconfigurable Computing*, Vol. 2009, Article ID 631490, September 2009

Maxfield, C. (2004). *The Design Warrior's Guide to FPGAs*, Newnes, 0-7506-7604-3, USA

pBlazeIDE Instruction Set Simulator, available at: http://www.mediatronix.com/pBlazeIDE.htm

Skahill, K. (1996). *VHDL for Programmable Logic*, Addison-Wesley Publishinh Company, Inc., 0201895862, USA

XPS Mailbox (v2.00a) Datasheet, Xilinx Inc., USA, 2009

XPS Mutex (v1.00c) Datasheet, Xilinx Inc., USA, 2009

PicoBlaze User Resources, available at: http://www.xilinx.com/ipcenter/processor_central/picoblaze/

Platform Studio and the Embedded Development Kit (EDK), available at: http://www. xilinx.com/tools/platform.htm

Xilinx ISE Design Suite, available at: http://www.xilinx.com/products/design-tools/ise-design-suite/

Yu, P. & Schaumont, P. (2006). Executing Hardware as Parallel Software for Picoblaze Networks, *International Conference on Field Programmable Logic and Applications, 2006. FPL '06*, 1-4244-0312-X, Madrid, August, 2006

Part 2

Application and Implementation

5

Networked Embedded Systems – Example Applications in the Educational Environment

Fernando Lopes[1,2] and Inácio Fonseca[1]
[1]*Instituto Superior de Engenharia de Coimbra*
[2]*Telecommunication Institute*
Portugal

1. Introduction

In this chapter we present a network architecture and two field application examples involving the deployment of embedded systems for distributed applications in the educational environment. The main contribution intended for this chapter is the proposed network architecture, with emphasis in the specific distributed implementation of networked embedded systems. The contribution also includes the detailed description of the technology options, the choices for the hardware and the development tools, as well as the implementation steps required to achieve a successful fully working system.

A very wide group of automation applications can benefit from embedded networked technology for more flexible and efficient implementations [1]. This technology allows for better integrated communications, integrated local and global control, supervision and maintenance. The educational environment has a set of management requirements that can be fulfilled using networked embedded systems and a well defined communication concept [1,2,3,4].

In this chapter we will present an applied research work using embedded systems. The work targets applications in the educational environment, specifically in the automated access control, access management and course management areas. Two field applications are presented, that allow demonstrating the suitability of the proposed networked embedded system concept for applications in these areas. These applications are fully deployed and in service in a higher education institution. The developed system concept can find applications in other fields such the residential, infrastructure and industrial areas.

A first example application, to be presented in this chapter, is in the automated access control and access management area, where distributed and networked intelligent systems interface with remote sensors to validate user credentials, granting or denying individual access to premises. The presented system uses a microcontroller with a standard Ethernet interface, to validate users presenting a compatible *Ibutton* or *RFID* Card. The user credentials are validated locally or in a central database. Authorized users are given access to reserved areas. By using a powerful database, very flexible and complex high level administration and management functions can be implemented. By sharing the local IP network infrastructure, maximum commonality and flexibility are achieved. Both microcontroller and database server software are fully implemented using Open Source developing tools.

A second example application to be described in this chapter deals with a Linux-based Embedded Identification Module (EIM), which is integrated in an Information System specifically tailored for course management. The Embedded Identification System allows for networked fingerprint and RFID reading and identification. The Information System permits ubiquitous network access to teachers and course directors, while tasks such as calendar and timetable setting and correction, student class attendance and class progress information are integrated and efficiently managed. Student and teacher identification is achieved through the networked Embedded Identification Systems with fingerprint and RFID sensors.

This chapter is organized in five sections. The first section consists of this introduction, presenting the global objectives and shortly describing the two example applications to be detailed. The second section will present an application and technology review in the embedded systems area with especial emphasis on development tools and operating systems. The third section will detail the first application example, featuring the architecture and a field implementation for a flexible and scalable distributed access control and access management system. The fourth section of the chapter will present the second application example, describing the hardware and software developed to create an information system specifically tailored to be used as a distributed course management application. The last section concludes the chapter and includes a short discussion on the creation of specific firmware and the future use of real-time operating systems.

2. Applications and technology review

Embedded systems can find applications in a very wide group of automation environments. These include, in addition to the ones in the educational management area presented in Section 1, a whole set in the industrial, residential, medical, economic, consumer and sensor networks areas.

In the industrial field, embedded systems can be widely used for fault monitoring and diagnosis, with automated reports, scheduling, triggering and registering specialized maintenance actions [5].

In the residential area, many future applications are envisaged such as intelligent appliances with automated management capabilities as for example the signalling of missing or out-of-date items while creating and automatically emailing or SMS-forwarding shopping lists and other required tasks. A very active research topic in the joint medical and residential areas is the concept of Ambient Assisted Living [6]. This research topic targets the home assistance to the elderly or autonomy impaired patients. The remote monitoring and interaction possibilities, allow for specialized individual care. The goal is to dramatically improve the autonomy and quality of life of these patients, by not requiring long and frequent hospital attendance.

The international tracking and quality control of goods can also be efficiently managed by using RFID Tags supported by a communication and information infrastructure. Border control and product taxing are examples of tasks that can highly benefit from the implementation of such technologies. Another area of special interest is animal farming, where sub-dermal transponders are used for identification, health monitoring and management, registering and transport control.

Embedded systems and embedded operating systems are now pervasive in consumer and network equipment such as mobile phones, PDAs, tablets, Webpads, VoIP phones, robots, audio and video appliances such as set-top-boxes, media players and televisions, thin client devices, switches and routers, among many other consumer examples.

Another specific application area, which has received special interest recently, is the ubiquitous deploying of networked embedded systems for the global monitoring of large civil strategic buildings and infrastructures. These include forests, sensitive ecosystems, power plants and power grids, government buildings and communication infrastructures such as bridges, motorways, sea ports, railways and airports.

Integrated with Identification, Wireless, Localization (GPS), and Internet technologies, networked embedded systems can be used to create true global monitoring, control and management solutions. A related and very prominent area of research in this field is the advanced concept of Sensor Networks [7].

According to [8] "Many embedded systems have substantially different design constraints than desktop computing applications. No single characterization applies to the diverse spectrum of embedded systems. However, some combination of cost pressure, long life-cycle, real-time requirements, reliability requirements, and design culture dysfunction can make it difficult to be successful applying traditional computer design methodologies and tools to embedded applications. Embedded systems in many cases must be optimized for life-cycle and business-driven factors rather than for maximum computing throughput".

Other important issues to be faced by the embedded developer are: real-time components, adaptive real-time requirements, compilers and timing analysis, development and execution platforms, control for embedded systems, testing and verification tools and strategies [9]. In what concerns the real-time components, which are one of the greatest implementation challenges, there are design tools in which systems are designed by putting together pieces that might be termed components. Examples are *MetaH*, *Ptolemy* and *Metropolis* tools [9].

In [10] and [11] the authors present the state of the art in Real-Time Operating Systems (RTOS) for embedded platforms. Definition of Hard *versus* Soft Real-Time Systems is presented, together with the scheduling policies - preemptive, non preemptive - and the typical design workflow of a real-time system. Some examples of RTOS are described such as QNX (POSIX compatibility), VxWorks, Kurt-Linux, Red-Linux and Windows. In these types of Operating Systems (OS), virtualization can also be used to allow different OS running in the same hardware: typically one RTOS and Windows. The characteristics regarding the handling of highly demanding deadlines can classify the types of RTOS to be used in: hard real-time system, critical real-time system and safety-critical real-time system.

The steps required to build a Linux Embedded System from scratch are presented in [12]. The document shows how to build *toolchains*, how to use embedded *bootloaders*, how to perform setup and configuration among other required tasks. An important issue discussed in this reference is the recent advances in free and Open Source software for embedded systems. The author presents a comparison between the number of installed systems with

Windows Embedded and Linux Embedded for different device categories such as PDAs, mobile phones, VoIP phones, robots, audio and video devices, thin client devices, gateways, tablets and Webpads. A slightly higher score is achieved by Linux, with about 51% against 49% for the number of devices at the time of analysis. This comparison is based on reports published by online sites *linuxdevices.com* and *windowsfordevices.com*.

In [13] and [14] the authors present the steps towards the installation and use of a *toolchain* compiler for ARM LPC based processors. The ARM/MIPS architecture has been steadily growing in the community for microcontroller firmware development and is now widely used. Other architectures for microcontrollers used in embedded systems are mostly based on RISC or CISC concepts. Example manufactures are ST, Infineon, Intel, Zilog, Texas, NXP and Microchip among others.

In another segment of tools are those related to HDL and VHDL circuit synthesizing. In these cases the real-time project is typically programmed in C and the tool will synthesize the HDL code to be uploaded to a FPGA circuit. This kind of systems uses RTOS that are highly hardware based and that make intensive use of hardware resources [15].

An important class within embedded systems groups includes those categorized as "little embedded systems" which exhibit small amount of memory usage. In this group are 8bit, 16 bit and 32 bit microcontrollers with memory sizes ranging from less than 25 kBytes up to 32 kBytes and low clock frequencies, with a typical value of 100 MHz. In this category small and light RTOS are necessary such as FreeRTOS, Contiki and SalvoRTOS. Other examples outside this segment are FreeOSEK, Toppers and Trampoline [15].

The development of complete embedded hardware and firmware solutions for specific applications is a very demanding task with many aspects to be considered. Generally speaking an embedded system should respect [15]:

- *Functional specifications*: observing the physical values and collecting them in real-time. Since the state of the controlled object is a function of real-time, the observed values are only temporarily present within a time-limited window. The update can be triggered in two possible ways: periodically - time-triggered observation; events - change of state observation or event-triggered;
- *Temporal specifications*: guaranteeing that all tasks are performed within their defined relative time sequence and individual time constraints;
- *Reliability specifications*: the most important attributes for the measurement of reliability are: fault tolerance, maintenance, availability and security.

When developing the hardware, firmware and software for the networked systems to be presented in Section 3 and Section 4, these global and other more specific aspects were thoroughly considered in the choices that were made.

3. Embedded access control and access management

Different technologies can be used when designing an automated access control and management system. See [16,17,18] and for commercial systems [19]. A starting point is the decision on how individual users are identified. This identification can be based on the presentation of unique credentials such as manual codes or *RFID* Tags. The credentials can also be based on biometric patterns. The most common are fingerprints and iris prints.

Other forms of biometric data can be used for identification, such as gait, voice and face recognition. These latter forms, however, are much more processing intensive.

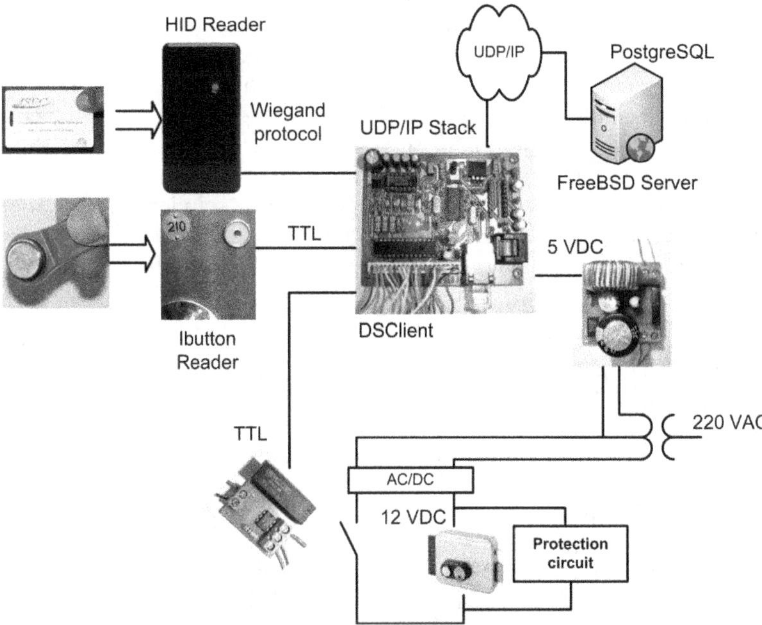

Fig. 1. Architecture of the developed access control system.

The second step is the decision on how individual identification credentials are validated. This action aims to answer the question: "Does this user have the permission to access this location?" The developed system infers identity through the presentation of an *RFID* Card or an *Ibutton*. Both technologies have in chip, hard stored, unique serial numbers, which can be used as identification credentials. Validation is performed using IP connectivity for the tentative matching of presented credentials with those stored in a local table or in a central *PostgreSQL* database server [20]. The complete architecture is shown in Figure 1. Noteworthy is the fact that the access system shares the local IP network infrastructure with existing services. This allows high hardware and software commonality, high flexibility, minimum deployment complexity and minimum cost.

In addition to the specific design of the *DSClient* hardware module, to be detailed in Section 3.1, the most significant decisions on the design of the presented distributed system are related to the communications infrastructure. Figure 1 includes a representation of the information flow between the various system components. The considered options for the IP communication architecture were the following:

- TCP/IP networking with HTTP 1.0 support. In this option the embedded system represented by the *DSClient* would remotely execute a PHP [21] script on the FreeBSD server [22]. This script would validate the user presented credentials. This simple setup has some advantages. In terms of the information flow only a TCP connection must be established. A disadvantage is the need to implement the TCP protocol. The HTTP protocol is not a difficulty in this approach, since it consists in the simple action of sending a read command, similar to a browser HTTP read;

- Use of TCP/IP networking with an active service running in the *FreeBSD* server. The running service would receive the user data from the *DSClient*, query the database for a matching and would answer the request. A clear advantage would be the simple protocol implementation, only requiring a socket definition and simple read and write operations. Disadvantages are the need to implement the TCP protocol and the additional need to establish a running service on the server;
- Use of UDP networking to send a validation request and wait for a probable answer in a defined timeframe. The main advantage of this solution is the simple UDP implementation and the fact that there is no need for the TCP implementation in firmware. A disadvantage is the absence of flow control. A service must also be setup on the server.

Given the above described options, a decision was made on the implementation of the simpler and faster UDP packet transmission when compared to TCP. Data encryption was also implemented with this approach. In addition, a simpler and faster *DSClient* can be built, without the need for the TCP firmware.

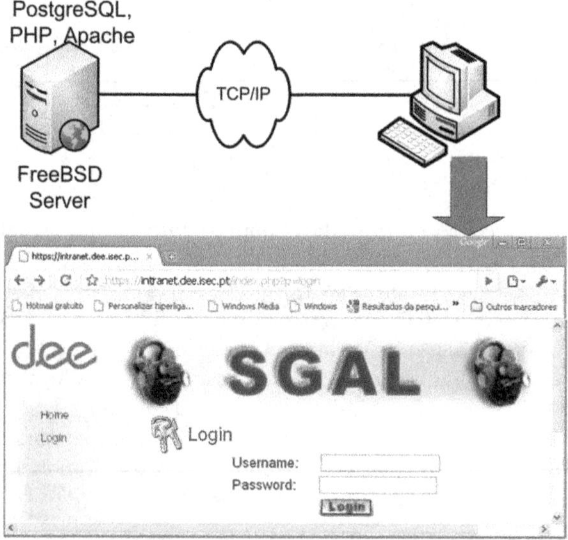

Fig. 2. Browser interface for the administration system.

In order to increase the security of the access control system, an additional packet identification technique was implemented, based on the positive matching between *DSClient* requests and server generated answers at the Layer 3 packet level. The request packet includes a security field computed using an elapsed time value and a generator polynomial. This field allows the positive identification of the server answer, guarantying the correspondence between the received packet and the sent UDP *DSClient* request. This technique avoids the non-authorized future use of the same answer packet, which may represent a positive validation, intended only for the ongoing query.

The high level administration of the system is accomplished using a Browser interface (Figure 2) (https://intranet.dee.isec.pt/SGAL_WEB_DEE). The interface consists of a set of WEB pages accessed through a secure connection. The pages are implemented using PHP language and an Apache server. The interface allows for the configuration and updating of the access database. With global administrator permissions the interface has the following main features:

- Add, Edit and Delete room administrators and associated fields;
- Add, Edit and Delete general users and associated fields;
- Add, Edit and Delete user permissions for individual rooms;
- Browsing and Exporting of registered accesses if enabled.

The main administration interface page is shown in Figure 2. It allows room administrator creation and editing; general user creation and editing; permission editing and general access management. SGAL relates to the initial name for the Web administration application which is, in Portuguese: "*Sistema de Gestão de Acesso a Laboratórios*".

It should be noted the intentional choice of Open Source software in this application, demonstrating the high potential of the available tools also in this field. The aforementioned embedded systems and many other small intelligent systems are also increasingly Linux based, with several examples previously given in Section 2.

3.1 Hardware and software implementation

The detailed implementation of the hardware considered a balance between the cost and dependability of the system. In a first prototype the Microchip *18F2685* microcontroller [23] was chosen, and was associated with the *ENC28J60* Ethernet Controller chip, also from Microchip. The *ENC28J60* implements the Ethernet physical layer at 10 Mbps in half or full-duplex modes. It has however some limitations negotiating with active network nodes such as some types of switches. The limitations reside on the speed and half/full duplex negotiation. It has a SPI control interface, available in most current microcontrollers, allowing very simple and cost effective solutions, which do not require high performance communications. The choice of the *18F2685* microcontroller was based on the availability of an on-chip CAN controller, which adds the flexibility to further associate hardware using the CAN interface. The simple hardware architecture for the *DSClient* module, presented in Figure 1, is shown in Figure 3.

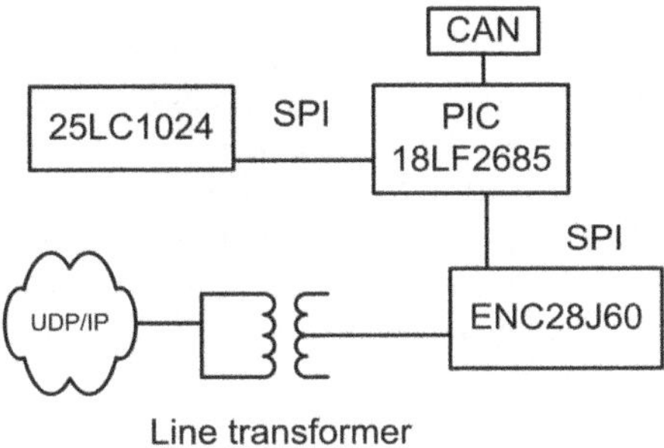

Fig. 3. Hardware architecture for the *DSClient* module.

A second prototype implemented the *DSClient* module using the PIC18F67J60 microcontroller, which includes an internal 10Mbps Ethernet controller compatible with the external ENC28J60 controller. Both prototypes include an external memory, using the 25LC1024 chip. This memory can be used to store encrypted credentials for the local room, providing redundancy for a temporary non-operational network. A third prototype uses an ARM Cortex-M3 [24] *Stellaris* microcontroller with integrated 100Mbps Ethernet, fully compatible in terms of behaviour with the two previous versions (Figure 4).

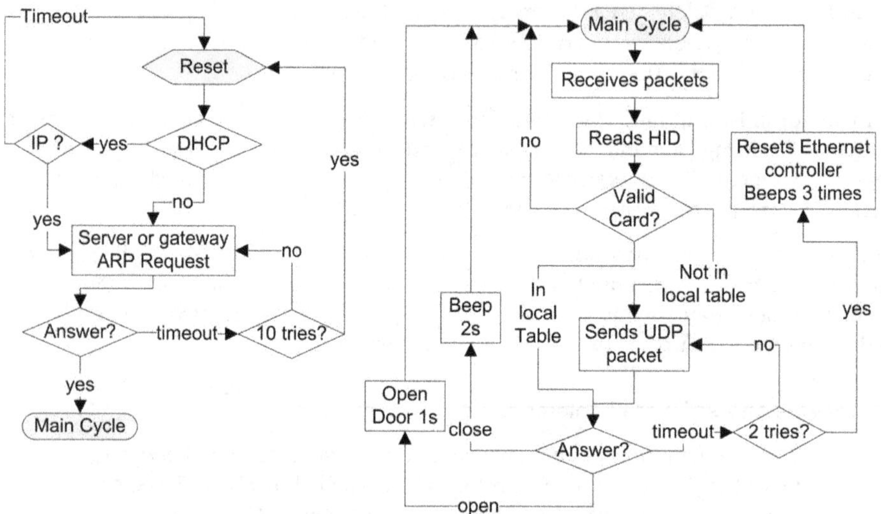

Fig. 4. Simplified flowchart illustrating the *DSClient* software. Left: initialization phase showing an ARP request that can be answered by the server or gateway, depending on the *DSClient* being on the same or on a different network. Right: main operation cycle for access control.

A flowchart representation, describing the main software decision flow implemented in the *DSClient* programmed firmware, is presented in Figure 4. It illustrates the *DSClient* software, with the initialization phase showing an ARP request that can be answered by the server or gateway, depending on the *DSClient* being on the same or on a different network. It also shows the main operation cycle for access control.

A detail that should be highlighted in the flowcharts of Figure 4 is the intentional reset of the Ethernet chip. This action is required since the Ethernet interface can stop answering network packets. This situation can arise if there is a faulty non answering *FreeBSD* server, but can also result from excessive IP traffic - for instance, due to an intentional denial of service attack. This non-answering state is detected by noticing a non-answering server, during repetitive *DSClient* validation requests. Combining the Ethernet resetting action with a watchdog, full system functionality can be always restored, without noticeable service reduction. User credentials are first checked for tentative local validation. If the current credentials are not present in the local table, a tentative central server validation follows. The *FreeBSD* server implements a UDP service in a system communication port, receiving the validation requests from the set of all distributed *DSClient* modules. The presented credentials are matched with those on the database and an appropriate answer is generated, through an UDP packet sent to the same *DSClient* system port.

The information provided by the *DSClient* modules is the following: *Ibutton* or *RFID* Card number, local time counter (nanosecond precision), number of valid HID or *Ibutton* readings, number of UDP requests without server answer, number of times the door was open, number of times access was not permitted, actual IP address of the module and some information associated with the security techniques. If local validation was not successful, the same information is sent to the server for registering and administration purposes.

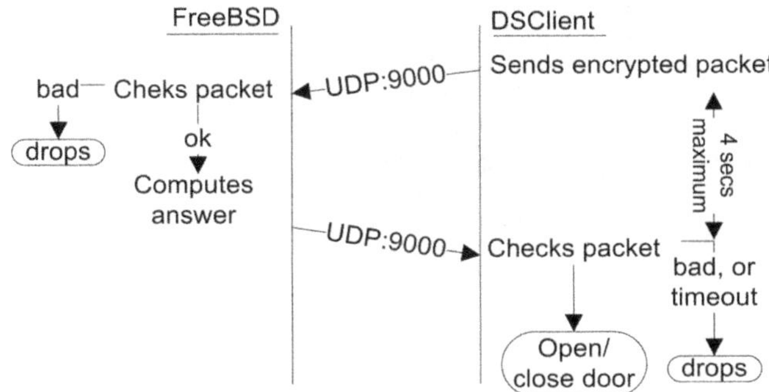

Fig. 5. Network flow for UDP packets, between a *DSClient* module and the database server, for central server validation.

In a first step, the FreeBSD server decrypts the UDP packet in order to validate its origin and credentials. If the packet is not valid it is immediately discarded and no answer is generated. A validated packet generates an UDP answer packet with the following information: pulse width to activate the electric locker (milliseconds), pulse width to activate the audio tone or BEEP (milliseconds), access authorization or access denial, date and time of authorization, and some other information associated with the security techniques.

The *DSClient* module, when receiving a server generated answer, verifies if it corresponds to its last request through the packet identification technique described in the in Section 3. If it does, the answer is validated if it was received in a time window of ***n*** seconds. Otherwise the answer is discarded. The information flow for packet exchange between *DSClient* modules and the database server is illustrated in Figure 5.

A total of three hardware prototypes for the *DSClient* module were built and tested. Two are the ones based on the Microchip microcontrollers and described above. The third is based on the ARM architecture. The Microchip versions were programmed using the MPLAB-C18 Tool [23]. The ARM based version was programmed using the GCC compiler targeting the ARM architecture [24]. List 1 shows the encrypted packet reception in the *FreeBSD* system.

3.2 An application to the educational environment

The described system, thanks to its distributed characteristics and modular implementation, has the flexibility for a large number of possible applications using *RFID* Tags or *Ibutton* technologies. Furthermore, it is highly hardware and software scalable, while exhibiting

```
int main(void)
{   struct sockaddr_in si_me,
si_other,si_pic;
  int          s,          i,
slen=sizeof(si_other),sz;
  unsigned char buf[BUFLEN];
  unsigned char lv_ip[50];
  unsigned              char
lv_rfid[80],lv_mac[50];
  int indice_crypt,lv_abre;
  int last_ind_checksum;
  unsigned long lv_ncard;
  struct timeb timep;
  struct timespec lv_timep;
  time_t *ptime_t;
  unsigned              char
lv_byte_pck_id;
  init_crypt_default();
  reset_default_passwd();
  indice_crypt=save_indice();
  if     ((s=socket(AF_INET,
SOCK_DGRAM,
IPPROTO_UDP))==-1)
diep("socket");
  memset((char *) &si_me, 0,
sizeof(si_me));
  si_me.sin_family         =
AF_INET;
  si_me.sin_port           =
htons(PORT);
  si_me.sin_addr.s_addr    =
htonl(INADDR_ANY);
  if      (bind(s,    &si_me,
sizeof(si_me))==-1)
diep("bind");
  if         (connect_bd()==0)
printf("Error DB System\n");
  sz=28;
  if (!pic_decrypt(teste,sz)) {
        printf("Crypt     Error:
%d bytes\n",sz);
  }
```

```
  while (1) {
    slen=sizeof(si_other);
    if   ((sz=recvfrom(s,   buf,   BUFLEN,   0,   &si_other,   &slen))==-1)
diep("recvfrom()");
    if (!pic_decrypt(&buf[0],sz)) {
        printf("Crypt Error: %d bytes\n",sz);
        continue;
    }
    show_packet(buf,44,1,',',1);
    lv_ncard = *((unsigned long *) &buf[7+14]);
    snprintf(lv_rfid,80,"%d",lv_ncard);
    printf("RFID %s\n",lv_rfid);
snprintf(lv_ip,50,"%d.%d.%d.%d",buf[7],buf[8],buf[9],buf[10];
    lv_abre=ask_DBsystem(lv_rfid,lv_ip,1);
    reset_default_passwd();
    buf[4]=indice_crypt;
    buf[18]=lv_abre;
    buf[19]=lv_abre;
    my_crypt(&buf[0],5,&buf[0]);
    restore_indice(indice_crypt);
    my_crypt(&buf[5],last_ind_checksum+2-5,&buf[5]);
give_me_checksums_crypt(&buf[last_ind_checksum],&buf[last_ind_checksum    +
1]);
    indice_crypt=save_indice();
    show_packet(buf,32,1,',',0);

    if (sendto(s, buf, last_ind_checksum +2, 0, &si_pic, slen)==-1) diep("sendto()");
} // While loop
```

List 1. FreeBSD daemon receiving encrypted packets from Embedded *DSClient*.

very robust security characteristics [25]. Its robust security implementation allows for the use in sensitive applications. Based on the advanced configuration and administration of the system database, efficient and powerful information systems can be envisaged, with enough flexibility for a high number of secure distributed automation applications.

A field implementation of the described system is currently in service in the Electrical Engineering Department – *"Instituto Superior de Engenharia de Coimbra"* (Figure 6). A total of sixteen rooms are monitored and have access control installed. These include a general use printing room, a student project room, one general purpose classroom and ten specialized laboratories. Three experimental systems are also installed in other school departments, one in the Mechanical Engineering Department and two in the Physics and Mathematics Department. Common room access is the responsibility of the Head of Department while laboratories have dedicated administrators which are also responsible for the general use of the specific laboratory. Automated access control allows for high flexibility, maximizing resource availability and usage, while keeping a high degree of security and individual responsibility. A potential installation of 150 distributed modules exists.

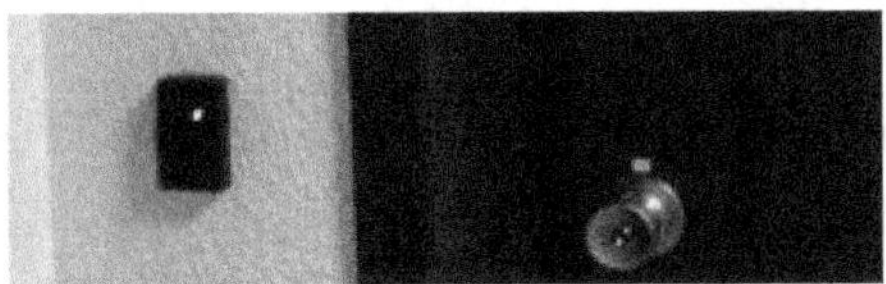

Fig. 6. Laboratory application example: Electrical Engineering Department - *Instituto Superior de Engenharia de Coimbra.*

The current implementation is being expanded to all department rooms to allow global management applications that can support most of the academic activities. Work in progress addresses fully registration of student attendance, permitting precise and dynamic adjustment in the number and time-allocation of laboratory classes. Early identification and active signalling of students with specific attendance difficulties can trigger timely and effective pedagogic correction actions by the course director.

Other functionalities can be added to the system such as the local management of Campus transactions. These can include student restaurants and bars, bookstore, academic fees, library registering and fine management, post-office, etc. This is a more security sensitive application area [25]. Some of these services are already deployed using other platforms.

Since there is a working Campus Access System, installed at *Instituto Superior de Engenharia de Coimbra,* which is managed by a private contractor (Figure 7), it is of most interest to interconnect both access networks and information processing applications, in order to maximize capabilities and comply with common security policies.

Fig. 7. Campus Access control - *Instituto Superior de Engenharia de Coimbra.* Installed car park and building access, by a security contractor using HID RFID technology.

3.3 Quality of service

Preliminary simple testing was performed, targeting the evaluation of the quality of service that can be achieved. The main concerns addressed initially were those related to sharing the network infrastructure with existing network services in a UDP transmission scenario.

The Electrical Engineering Department is a three store building with a two-level tree, 100 Mbps network infrastructure, based on 20 main switches (24 port) and a 1 Gbps fiber connection to the School backbone. About 240 permanently connected personal computers and 2 network servers are installed in offices, classrooms and laboratories. A total of 650 class hours are allocated each week for the duration of 15 week semesters. A set of 16 devices is fully operational at the present time. Two preliminary tests were conducted: rate of lost packets and denial of service through severe network congestion.

One semester of access statistics was registered for the installed devices. A rate of 1% of lost packets was measured in normal working conditions. This corresponds to extreme congestion situations and Ethernet chip limitations. In these cases the identification card has to be presented twice for the validation of credentials.

To assess the performance of the service in continuous high traffic environments, a second test was performed using the transmission of multicast video with controlled bitrate. A video server and a set of 8 video clients were connected, one in the same switch as the video server, and 7 on different switches. The video was sent in UDP multicast at 2, 4, 6, 8, 10 and 12 Mbps constant bitrates. Multicast traffic was not filtered for the switches where the HID readers were installed, reaching equally all ports.

It was observed that the rate of lost packets remained very low (in the order of 1%) for all 10Mbps *DSClient* modules, until it dropped drastically for some of them. This drop corresponded to the video bitrate reaching 10 Mbps at the same switch and port where the HID reader was connected. This is because 10 Mbps is the upper limit operating bitrate for the *DSClient* Ethernet chip. The 100Mbps *DSClient* Modules were unaffected under 12 Mbps constant bitrate. Further testing is planned for different traffic profiles, network setup and a more comprehensive set of statistics.

4. Integrated information system for course management

This section presents an Integrated Information System for the management of Technology Specialization Courses (TSC). These courses are subject to a stringent set of legal requirements that regulate the scientific, pedagogic and functioning components. To meet these requirements the availability of an organizational support structure is essential.

The developed information system accepts high-level definitions introduced by the Course Director, such as the teaching service allocation, the course calendar and schedule, as well as the individual student profile. Information relating to each class such as summary, individual student attendance, punctuality, participation and progress is dynamically managed by the teacher in each Training Unit.

Global information is continuously available online. Weekly reports are generated that allow the coordination of the course as well as the automatic sending of information required to generate all legal documentation.

According to Portuguese Law - Dec.-Lei n.º 88/2006, May 23 [26], TSC are post-secondary, non-higher education training courses, that can be taught at Higher Education Institutions or with their collaboration. According to Dec.-Lei n.º 782/2009, July 23 [26], since the 1st of October 2010, TSC are classified with the skill level 5 on a {1-8} scale, according to the European Qualifications Framework for life long learning [27]. On the other hand, in the registration process they are as qualification level 4, on a {1 -5} scale, according to the Decision n.º 85/368/EEC, published in the Official Journal of the European Communities, n.º L199, 31 July 1985. In both cases, TSC are described as a Qualification at a post-secondary non-higher education level, where credits can be gathered for further higher studies.

In accordance with the applicable law, TSC are organized by time editions with very different rules from those normally applicable to BSc and Master Courses in terms of organization, assessment and attendance. This requires the teaching Institutions to strongly adapt their steady mechanisms commonly used for course management. Thus, in addition to the registration of the final classifications and updating of student individual records, Dec.-Lei Law n.° 88/2006 also establishes the need to create, update and register on file:

- Records for the presence and punctuality of the students;
- The summary for each lesson;
- Justifications for not being present, validated by the TSC Director;
- Information about each assessment element, including individual marks.

In this context, for each training unit, it is necessary to maintain an updated file with all the mentioned items as well as educational support material. For each student, in addition to the final assessment results, it is necessary to organize a personal file containing the relevant classification information and his personal and professional profile. In addition, it is mandatory, on a monthly basis, to inform the relevant government agency on the actual number of students with effective class attendance.

Overall, course management is a very demanding, data-intensive distributed task. It must be automated in order to guarantee that valuable human resources are used in the most noble activity that is the teaching itself.

Information technologies are a very powerful tool for the efficient management of activities that require the processing of large amounts of data in an intensive and distributed manner. There are however security and confidentiality issues, including the management of the access to third parties and to individuals with administrative privileges.

4.1 Global architecture

An embedded system is used as the basis component of a distributed information system, specially developed to manage Technology Specialization Courses (TSC). In these courses, full control of student progress and student presence in classes is extremely important. The distributed information system for course management includes the functionality to record student attendance in class by using a specially developed module which is based on the Linux Embedded operating system [28] running on a ARM processor. This module permits to read fingerprints and RFID tags for student identification and further network transmission of relevant information - this module is hereafter named Embedded Identification Module (EIM).

The Embedded Identification Module is integrated in the whole course management information system as illustrated in Figure 8. The system consists of four hardware and software modules connected via TCP/IP over Ethernet: the Teacher Application, the Central Server, the Embedded Identification Module and the Management Interface.

The Teacher Application, developed in Microsoft Access (MS-Access) [29], is the teacher interface with the central server. It is based on a local database with forms allowing the management of information about class summaries, attendance, punctuality, participation and individual and collective progress. This application also permits the generation of local reports, by exporting in MS Excel format, information containing class syllabus, partial and

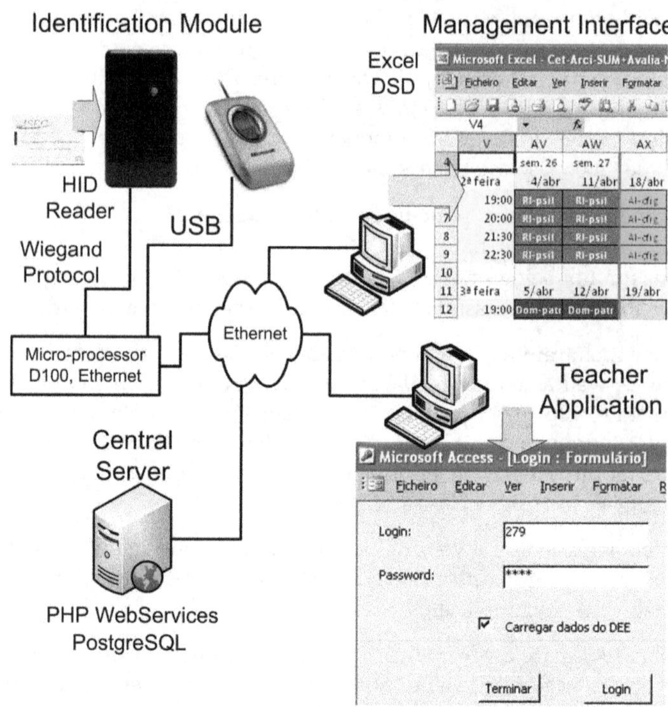

Fig. 8. Architecture of the integrated system: Teacher Application (MS-Access, Local); Central Server (Global Database); Management Interface and Embedded Identification Module (RFID, Fingerprint, Local).

final classifications. It also allows the browsing of the planning and schedule for past and future classes. The application requires a *login* and *password* to identify the teacher.

The Teacher Application receives from the central server, managed by the TSC Director, the teaching service allocation, the course schedule and calendar as well as the student individual profile. Later, it sends back the information on class operation. This information will be the basis for the server generated global reports and to the final documentation about the course operation. The interconnection between the Teacher Application and the Central Server is achieved through a Website using WebServices technology [30].

The Embedded Identification Module communicates with the Teacher Application and with the Central Server. In the Teacher Application the user selects a search in the local network to find the Embedded Identification Module IP. The target test hardware for fingerprint validation uses a commercial router, the D100 from *Huwuei*, which is a very inexpensive hardware, with specific Linux-based firmware developed by the authors (see Figure 9). This router has an USB port allowing the connection of the fingerprint reader, a *Microsoft* model in this application. A custom Broadcom Chipset board is being developed for further use.

The fingerprint image acquisition is based on software derived from the *libfprint* library. The images are taken from the fingerprint reader, having been turned off the proprietary encryption mechanism of the device. The images are then processed to obtain the unique characteristics of each fingerprint. This unique features, consisting in a set of distances, are recorded in a USB-Pen attached to the D100, using an encryption mechanism. The data from each fingerprint is assigned an identification number. This number identifies the person in the central PostgreSQL database.

To build the Linux Embedded firmware, the *buildroot, busybox* and *u-boot* projects have contributed as a starting point - for more details see [12].

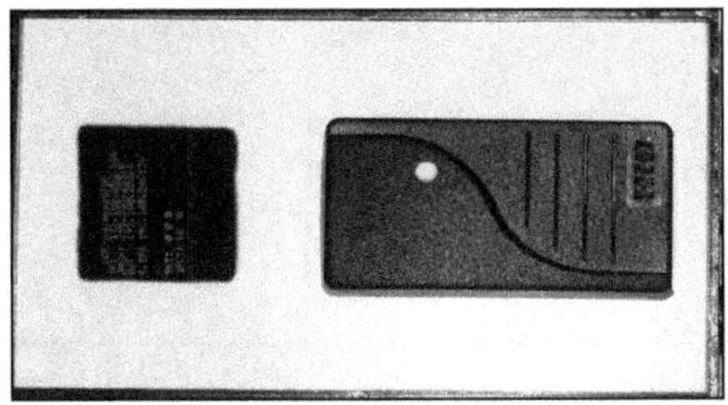

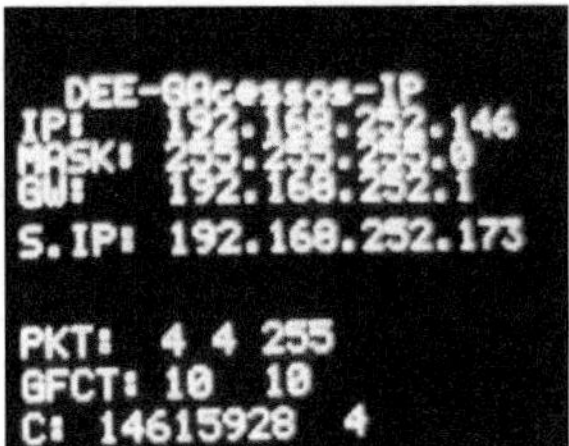

Fig. 9. EIM - System to read HID-RFID Cards.

When using RFID authentication only, the system uses an ARM processor similar to the device explained in Section 3 - see Figure 1 for a hardware illustration and Figure 9 for an enclosure and test overview. The mechanism to send data to the central database is also similar to the method proposed for the RFID authentication method described in Section 3.

The Central Server is based on an Apache server [21] and a PostgreSQL database [20] installed on a FreeBSD operating system [21]. WebServices implemented in PHP are used as communication technology [21]. The teacher service allocation, the course calendar and course schedule, validation of missed class and the individual student profile, all are entered and updated by the TSC Director, using a Management Interface. This Management Interface uses MS-Excel, Visual Basic for Applications (VBA) [31] and WebServices to communicate with the Central Server.

The Central Server registers the information generated and validated locally by each teacher when using the Teacher Application, maintaining a global database. From this global database, the elements needed to the organization, operation and supervision of the course, in accordance with the legal requirements, are automatically generated and forwarded to the interested parties. Thus, the system ensures the data recording, edition and validation locally in the Teacher Application, with subsequent submission, registration and processing in the Central Server.

4.2 Teacher Application

The Teacher Application was developed in Microsoft Access allowing localized and autonomous management of information and, through a mechanism of communication and synchronization, the periodic transmission of teacher validated information to the Central Server. The local database in MS-Access consists of seventeen separate tables that are presented in Figure 10 - left. From the global set of tables, eleven are interconnected according to the structure in Figure 10 - right.

The Teacher Application communicates with the Central Server via WebServices. A set of functions in VBA and a set of forms were developed for this purpose. For interaction via

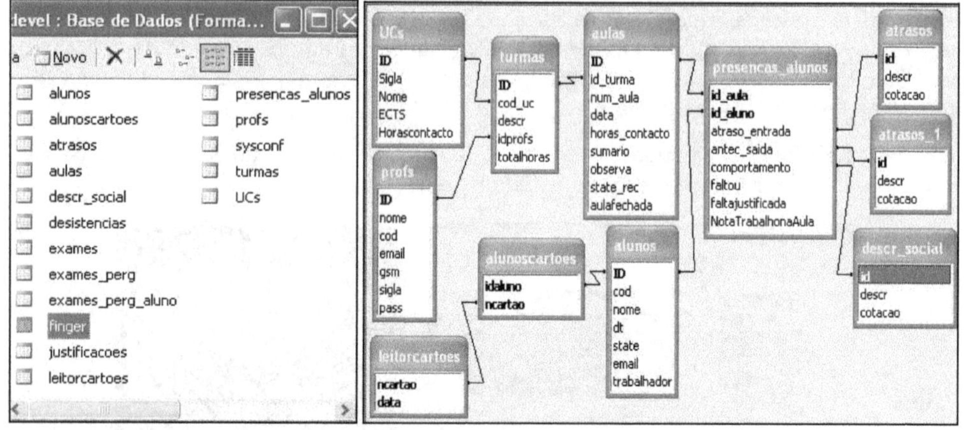

Fig. 10. Left: Structure of the local database in MS-Access. Right: Interconnection between the main tables.

WebServices with the PostgreSQL database on the central server, a developed VBA class *TSCARCIws* exchanges information through a specific address on the Intranet, whose functions are presented in Figure 11 - left.

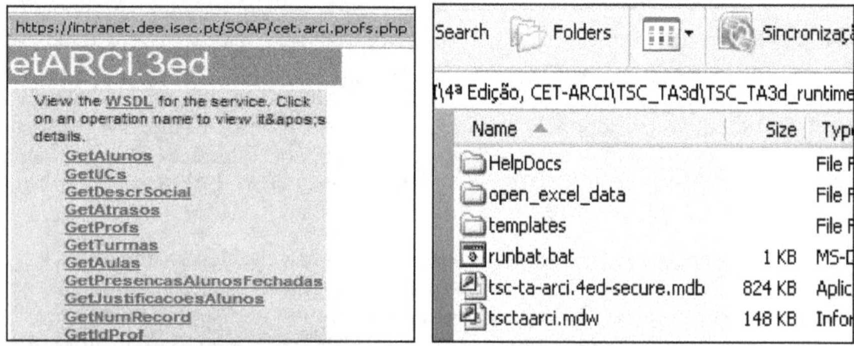

Fig. 11. Left: WebServices developed for communication between MS-Access and the PostgreSQL. Right: Developed application structure in MS-Access.

In terms of the local organization of files that support the implementation of the Teacher Application, the structure is shown in Figure 11 - right. In the templates folder is a spreadsheet developed in Excel, for which the application exports the information. This spreadsheet allows managing all the assessments for each training unit.

Each teacher is assigned a *username* and a *password* to access the system. After login, the teacher may choose to update the local database from the Central Server, which is mandatory the first time, or in a regular access, can use the application only locally with previous downloaded data.

When updating the local database with new information from the Central Server, the local information that has already been published is not modified. In both modes, local use only or server update, teacher lessons will be available for browsing and summary writing. After teacher identity validation, the Main Menu illustrated in Figure 12 will be available. The options shown in Figure 12 allow managing all information concerning the specific TSC training unit, namely: Edit summaries, consulting old class data, send data to the Central Server, report generation and deleting of the local database.

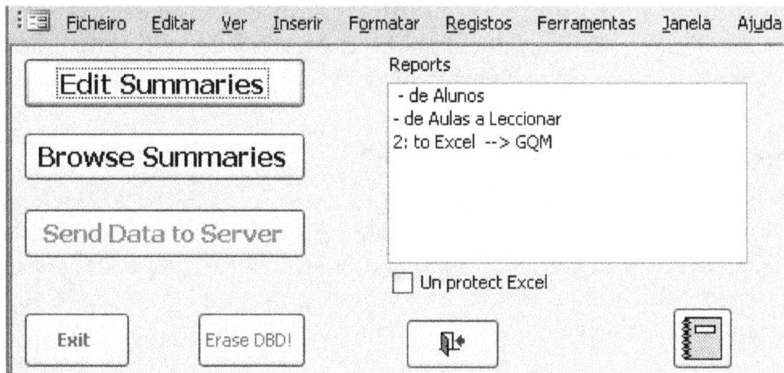

Fig. 12. Teacher Application Main menu. Editing and Browsing Summaries, Presence Management, Sending data to the Central Server and Reporting.

Figure 13 shows the interface for summaries, assiduity, punctuality, participation and for student assessment. This information is transmitted to the Central Server only after the teacher indicates that the class reports are final. After validation and transmission, classes are marked as delivered and are signalled with a green background in the summaries interface, as can be seen in Figure 13 - right.

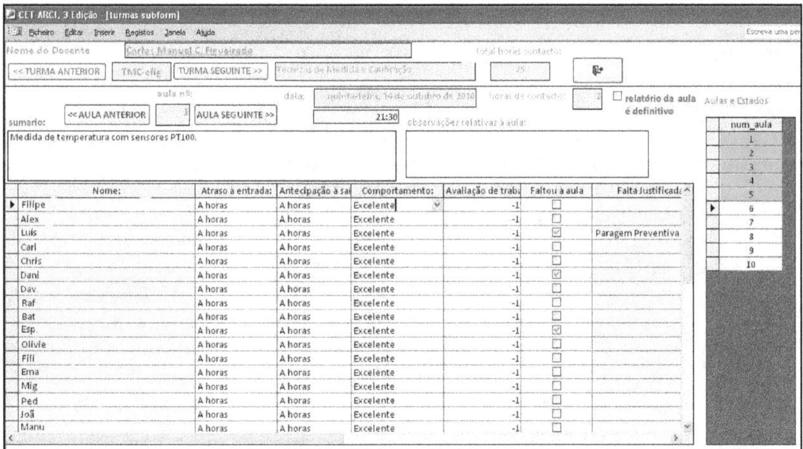

Fig. 13. Teacher Application. Summaries edition.

Data transmission to the Central Server includes data integrity check to detect transmission errors. Data transmitted without errors assumes a definitive state and can no longer be changed locally. Later edition is only possible for specific classes with the intervention of the TSC Director by setting an authorization in the Management Interface.

Export option for specific training units can be generated as a set of spreadsheets for assiduity, participation, exam and final classifications. Class summaries, absence justifications and student progress can also be exported.

The Teacher Application performs the main functionality of the system, since it is the liaison between the Embedded Identification Module, the Central Server and the teachers themselves. In addition to the functions already described, the Teacher Application allows to connect to the Embedded Identification Module. This identification module will be described in the next section and its job is to read RFID tags and fingerprints.

4.3 Embedded identification module operation

Each student in the class is identified by the presentation of an HID RFID card or by his fingerprint. The association between the student and his RFID identification number is performed in the PostgreSQL database using the Central Server Management Interface. The card reader system, illustrated in Figure 9, was programmed using C language and embedded in a microcontroller with ARM architecture [22, 23].

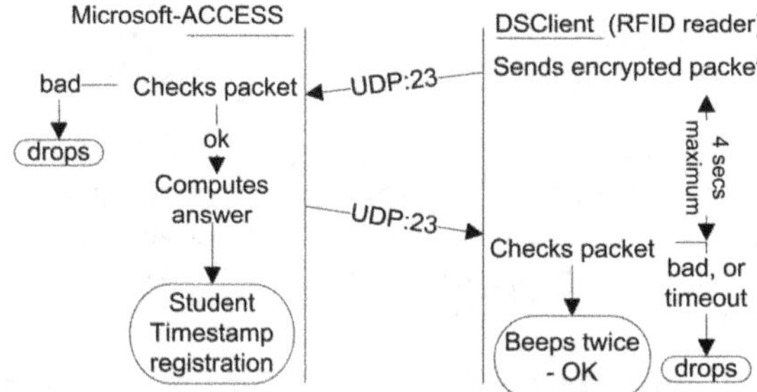

Fig. 14. Communication between the Teacher Application and the EIM.

The exchange of information between the Teacher Application and the Embedded Identification Module (EIM) is encrypted and carried through the UDP protocol. Figure 14 shows a diagram representing the bidirectional communication between the two systems.

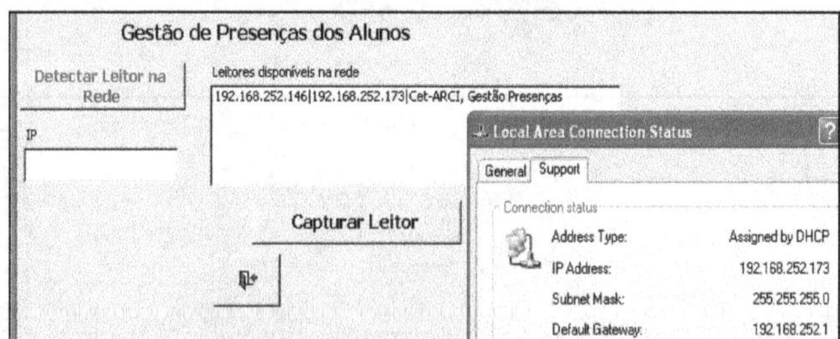

Fig. 15. Operation of the Teacher Application in capture mode. Searches in the local network for EIM devices and informs them where to forward packets.

For classroom operation, the teacher uses the Teacher Application to search for identification modules in the local room network using broadcast messages. After getting a response, the connected equipment is captured using the interface shown in Figure 15.

```
, Captures the EIM module
Private Sub EIM_Capture_command()
   Dim lv_i As Integer, cod_leitor As String
   Dim myItens, lip
   ...
   cod_leitor = Lista4.ItemData(lv_i)
   myItens = Split(cod_leitor, "|")
   lip = Winsock3.LocalIP
   gv_ip_leitor_HID = myItens(0)
   If lip <> myItens(1) Then
      Winsock3.RemoteHost = myItens(0)
      lip_parts = Split(lip, ".")
      Call clean_list
      Winsock3.SendData          Chr(253)          +
Chr(Val(lip_parts(0))) + Chr(Val(lip_parts(1))) + _
          Chr(Val(lip_parts(2))) + Chr(Val(lip_parts(3)))
      Winsock3.RemoteHost = "0.0.0.0"
      Exit Sub
   End If
   Call Change_Form_attendance_record
End Sub

Private Sub Winsock3_DataArrival(ByVal bytesTotal As
Long)
   Dim buff As Meus_DADOS
   Dim strData As String

   Winsock3.GetData strData, bytesTotal
   If (bytesTotal > 20) And (bytesTotal = Len(strData))
Then
      If bytesTotal = 84 Then
         If                    descodifica(strData,
CStr(Winsock3.RemoteHostIP)) = 3 Then
            'changes Screen
            Call Change_Form_attendance_record
         End If
      End If
   End If
End Sub
```

```
Private Function Decode_EIM_data(str As String, rip As
String) As Integer
   Dim ip As String, app As String, mac As String
   Dim lim As Integer, i As Integer, lip As String
   Dim anyDate() As Byte

   anyDate = StrConv(str, vbFromUnicode)
   Decode_EIM_data = 0
   If (anyDate(2) <> &H2) Then
      Exit Function
   End If
   If Not ((anyDate(0) = &HFE) Or (anyDate(0) = 252))
Then
      Exit Function
   End If
   ip = CStr(anyDate(5)) + "." + CStr(anyDate(6)) + "." +
CStr(anyDate(7)) + "." + CStr(anyDate(8))
   lim = 20
   While (anyDate(lim) And (lim < 82)) <> 0
         lim = lim + 1
   Wend
   app = Mid(str, 20, lim - 20 + 1)
   mac = Hex(anyDate(9)) + ":" + Hex(anyDate(10)) + ":"
+ Hex(anyDate(11)) + ":" + _
        Hex(anyDate(12)) + ":" + Hex(anyDate(13)) + ":" +
Hex(anyDate(14))
   Lista4.AddItem (rip + "|" + ip + "|" + app)
   If (anyDate(0) = &HFE) Then
         Decode_EIM_data = 2
   Else
         lip = Winsock3.LocalIP
         If lip <> ip Then
            MsgBox "Error Capturing EIM Device"
         Else
            Decode_EIM_data = 3
         End If
   End If
End Function
```

List 2. VBA code for EIM capture by sending a broadcast message announcing the Teacher Application network IP.

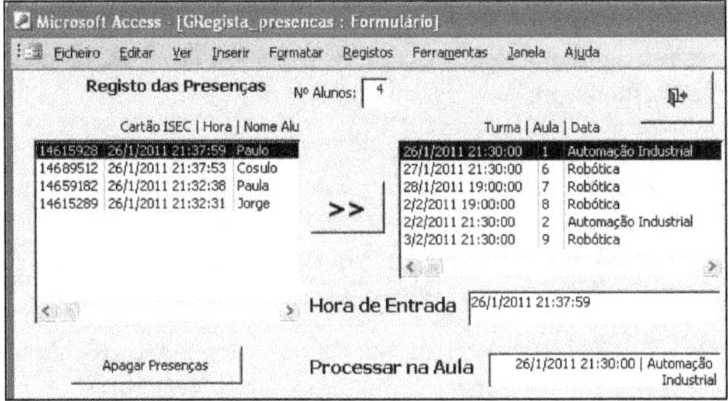

Fig. 16. After the Teacher Application captures the EIM, students should approach their RFID card to the EIM to identify themselves and record time-of-entry.

After the EIM has been captured, students entering the classroom approach the HID card to the EIM, identifying them and recording the time-of-entry as illustrated in Figure 16. Time-of-entry is later used for presence related information in accordance with a start time reference defined by the TSC Director.

As an alternative to the HID reader, the identification from the fingerprint reader can be used. A Microsoft Fingerprint Reader with USB interface is used. The sensor is interfaced with a microcontroller containing embedded Linux, where the image processing algorithms leading to the identification are programmed.

For confidentiality reasons, associated with the collection and processing of biometric data, the entire processing software shall be contained and secured in the microcontroller. For identification, only a unique index is provided. Fingerprints are stored in-device, on an SD card, encrypted and associated to a student identification index. The widespread and final use of this sensor will be implemented only after all legal requirements associated with the protection of personal data are guaranteed.

4.4 Implementation details

For the RFID reader, the EIM is implemented with an ARM Cortex-M3 processor. All the programming tools for this microcontroller have been developed based on the GNU GCC *toolchain* for ARM Cortex-M3 version 4.3.3, *Binutils-2.19.1* and *newlib-1.18.0* under *Gygwin* with *lwip* TCP Stack. Information about setting up a free GCC *toolchain* is available from [13].

For the Fingerprint reader, as presented in Section 4.1, the D100 router from *Huwaei* with specific Linux-based firmware was used as test platform for the Broadcom Chipset.

By default, the EIM sends data to the Central Server (FreeBSD) but the Teacher Application can capture the device through a broadcast packet, informing the EIM where to send its data packets, that is to the Teacher Application. List 2 shows the VBA code that triggers the capture of the EIM device in the local network.

After the EIM has been informed where to send its UDP packets with RFID information, the Teacher Application waits for this information through a socket data reception event. List 3 shows the Teacher Application (MS-Access) code for encrypted packet reception. List 4 shows the firmware for the main state machine while a similar state machine is also used to control Ethernet communications as presented in Fig. 15.

Figure 17 shows the Common Firmware Environment (CFE) available from Broadcom. It is the first code that is executed when the router boots. It performs functions such as system initialization, setting up a basic environment, optionally providing a command line interface and loading and executing a kernel image. After this first code Linux will boot if it was initially programmed in the flash memory of the router.

Figure 18 illustrates the fingerprint test hardware setup, and results from the image processing algorithm, based on Linux Embedded. This system is compatible with the communication protocol used by the ARM RFID system. A custom board based on the Broadcom Chipset will be used for the long-term application.

```
Private Sub Winsock_readhid_DataArrival(ByVal bytesTotal As Long)
  Dim strData As String, arrayOUT() As Byte
  Dim anyDate() As Byte, nrdif_card As Long
  Dim rslt As Boolean, last_ind_checksum As Long
  Dim TIME_BEEP_10MS As Integer
  Dim TIME_LED_ON As Integer, lv_open As Integer

  If bytesTotal <= 0 Exit Sub
  Winsock_lehid.GetData strData, bytesTotal
  anyDate = StrConv(strData, vbFromUnicode)
  If (bytesTotal > 0) And (bytesTotal = Len(strData)) Then
    rslt = gv_crypt_class.pic_decrypt(anyDate, bytesTotal)
    If rslt Then ' MSG ok, sends answer
      nrdif_card = anyDate(7 + 14 + 3)
      nrdif_card = nrdif_card * 256
      nrdif_card = nrdif_card + anyDate(7 + 14 + 2)
      nrdif_card = nrdif_card * 256
      nrdif_card = nrdif_card + anyDate(7 + 14 + 1)
      nrdif_card = nrdif_card * 256
      nrdif_card = nrdif_card + anyDate(7 + 14 + 0)
      ' --------- packet to answer EIM
      TIME_BEEP_10MS = 100
      TIME_LED_ON = 50
      lv_open = 0
      last_ind_checksum = 30
      anyDate(14) = anyDate(0)
      anyDate(0) = Int((6 * Rnd) + 1)
      anyDate(2) = TIME_BEEP_10MS
      anyDate(18) = lv_open
      anyDate(20) = TIME_LED_ON
      anyDate(21) = anyDate(20)
      last_ind_checksum = last_ind_checksum + 2
      ReDim arrayOUT(last_ind_checksum - 1)
      For lv_open = 0 To last_ind_checksum - 1
        arrayOUT(lv_open) = anyDate(lv_open)
      Next
      Call gv_crypt_class.pic_crypt(arrayOUT, last_ind_checksum - 2)
      Winsock_readhid.RemoteHost = gv_ip_leitor_HID
      Winsock_readhid.SendData arrayOUT
      Call insert_in_bd_EIM_hid_RFID(nrdif_card)
    End If
  End If
End Sub
, VBA crypt_c class
, .... Other fuctions not listed
Public Sub reset_class()
   indice = 0 'Indice na password
   Call init_crypt_default
   Call reset_default_passwd
   indice_crypt = save_indice()
   gv_lv_ind2crypt = save_indice()
End Sub

Function pic_decrypt(ByRef buf() As Byte, sz As Long) As Boolean
   Dim ind As Integer, ch0 As Byte, ch1 As Byte

   Call reset_default_passwd
   Call my_decrypt(buf, 5, buf, 0)
   ind = buf(4)
   Call restore_indice(ind)
   Call my_decrypt(buf, sz - 7, buf, 5)
   Call give_me_checksums(ch0, ch1)
   If ((ch0 = buf(sz - 2)) And (ch1 = buf(sz - 1))) Then
      pic_decrypt = True
   Else
      pic_decrypt = False
   End If
End Function

Function pic_crypt(ByRef buf() As Byte, sz As Long) As Boolean
   Dim ind As Integer, ch0 As Byte, ch1 As Byte

   Call reset_default_passwd
   buf(4) = gv_lv_ind2crypt
   Call my_crypt(buf, 5, buf, 0)
   Call restore_indice(gv_lv_ind2crypt)
   Call my_crypt(buf, sz - 5, buf, 5)
   Call give_me_checksums_crypt(ch0, ch1)
   gv_lv_ind2crypt = save_indice()
   buf(sz) = ch0
   buf(sz + 1) = ch1
   pic_crypt = True
End Function
```

List 3. MS-Access receiving encrypted packets from the EIM.

```
// Loop forever.
gv_state_grafcet=0;
gv_udp_link.state=0;
gv_serverip=0x8B14A8C0; // 192.168.20.139

show_my_ip();
gv_leitura_cartao=gv_gpio_out_on=0;
while(1) {
   clock = HID_Clock;
   data = HID_Data << 1;
   ulData= (clock) | ( data );
   If (Fingerprint_ID!=0) ulData= Fingerprint_ID;
   if (gv_state_grafcet>0) show_packets_out();
   switch (gv_state_grafcet) {
   case 0: // waiting DHCP for an IP
         ulIPAddress = lwIPLocalIPAddrGet();
         if (gv_udp_link.state==50) {
               gv_udp_link.state=10;
               if (gv_answer==0) {
                     gv_state_grafcet=40;
                     lv_t_secs =g_ulSystemTimeSeconds+1;
                     GPIOPinWrite(PgpioBASE, BEEPgpioPIN, 1);
                     lv_conta_iter=0;
               } else {
                     lv_t_secs =g_ulSystemTimeSeconds+2;
                     gv_state_grafcet=30;
                     GPIOPinWrite(PgpioBASE, PgpioPIN, 1);
                     gv_gpio_out_on =0;
               }
         }
         break;
   case 30: // set GPIO out on for a while
```

```
    if (ulIPAddress!=0) {
        gv_state_grafcet=10;
        gv_udp_link.state=0;
        lv_t_secs=g_ulSystemTimeSeconds+2;
    }
    break;
case 10: // RFID or fingerprint valid read?
    if (ulData&1!=3) if (Le_cartao()) {
        nleituras_cartao++;
        show_state(gv_ncartao,nleituras_cartao);
        gv_state_grafcet=20;
        gv_gpio_out_on =0;
        break;
    }
    if (gv_gpio_out_on!=0) {
        gv_gpio_out_on =0;
        GPIOPinWrite(PgpioBASE,PgpioPIN, 1);
        gv_state_grafcet=30;
    }
    break;
case 20: // sends RFID card or fingerprint id
    udp_protocol_ask((UDP_LINK *)&gv_udp_link);
    if (gulSystemTSecs > lv_time_seconds) {
        GPIOPinWrite(PgpioBASE, PgpioPIN, 0);
        gv_gpio_out_on =0;
        gv_state_grafcet=10;
    }
    break;
case 40: // Beeps (another GPIO out line)
    if (gulSystemTSecs > lv_time_seconds) {
        lv_t_secs =g_ulSystemTimeSeconds+1;
        gv_state_grafcet=50;
        GPIOPinWrite(PgpioBASE, BEEPgpioPIN, 0);
        if (lv_conta_iter>1) gv_state_grafcet=10;
    }
case 50: // Beeps (another GPIO out line)
    if (gulSystemTSecs > lv_time_seconds) {
        lv_conta_iter++;
        lv_t_secs = gulSystemTSecs +1;
        gv_state_grafcet=40;
        GPIOPinWrite(PgpioBASE, BEEPgpioPIN, 1);
    }
    break;
}
```

List 4. ARM-embedded program or Linux embedded daemon – Principal state machine.

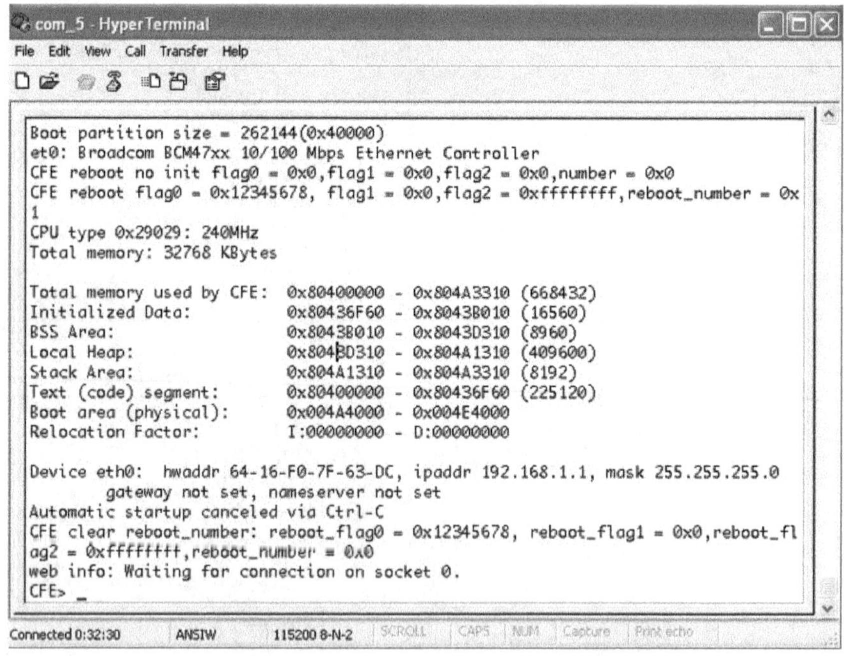

Fig. 17. The Common Firmware Environment (CFE) from Broadcom.

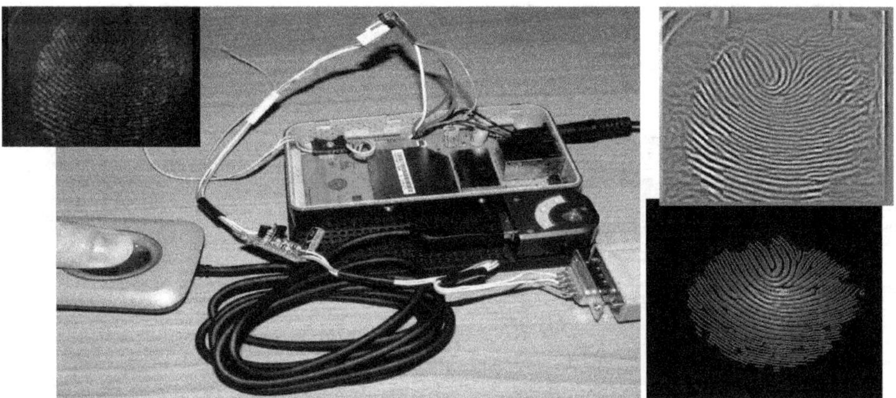

Fig. 18. Left: Test hardware - Huwaei D100 router with Linux Embedded for fingerprint acquisition. Right: An example of a fingerprint and its processing.

4.5 Central server and management interface

The Central Server main function is to register and maintain the final course information in a central database. This information, associated with the management of the TSC, includes high level general information and specific information for each training unit. The server software also allows to automatically generate all the legally required documents for the operation of the course. *E-mail* alerts are also created and addressed to teachers who have not timely updated data in the Teacher Application. A further weekly report is generated and *e-mailed* to the TSC Director with information on the presence, punctuality, participation and progress of the students. This information allows an efficient supervision of the course operation. In addition, it permits to fulfill the legal information communication requirements such as the exact and actual number of students attending the course.

In terms of implementation technology, the Central Server is based on an Apache Server and on a PostgreSQL database. These software packages are installed on a FreeBSD operating system and use WebServices implemented in PHP as communication technology. In order to ensure maximum consistency and simplify synchronization between the local and central databases, the PostgreSQL tables in the Central Server and the MS-Access tables in the Teacher Application are identical.

The TSC Director, through the Management Interface, defines in the Central Server the common elements and top-level requirements for the course operation. The interface can be accessed through the Intranet or Internet and allows the introduction of all relevant information as for example the Teacher Service Allocation. This interface uses Excel spreadsheets, VBA programming and WebServices to communicate with the Central Server.

Figure 19 presents an example of the Teacher Service Allocation and the course schedule for a set of training units. It also presents the VBA source code used to search in Excel spreadsheets for the Teacher Service Allocation, generating the SQL commands that are sent through WebServices to the PostgreSQL database.

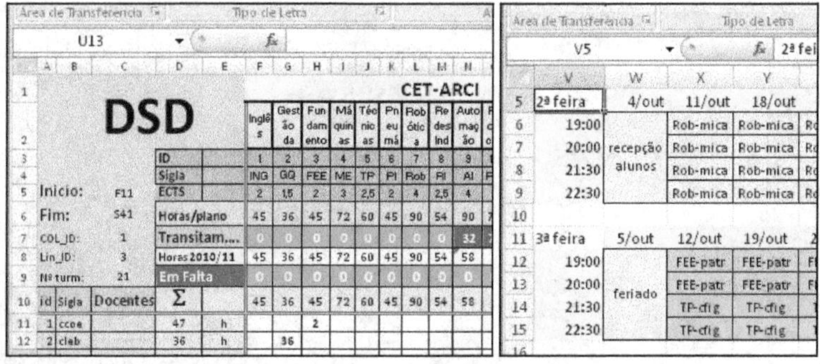

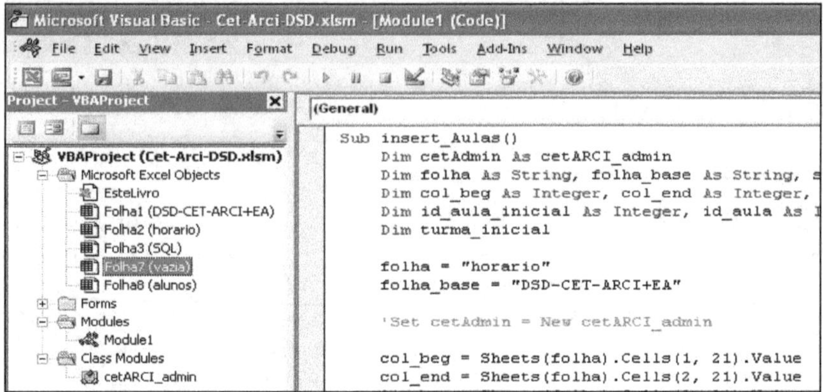

Fig. 19. Excel spreadsheet: Time and the Teacher Service Allocation for the course together with VBA programming using WebServices.

5. Discussion and conclusions

In this chapter we intended to present successful applications using networked embedded systems. For this purpose we described a network architecture and two application examples in the educational area, which are full implemented and successfully deployed. The first application consists in a campus automated access control and access management system while the second implements a full-featured distributed course management tool, tailored for a specific scientific environment. Both applications are in operation at the Electrical Engineering Department of the *Instituto Superior de Engenharia de Coimbra.*

Distributed control modules exhibit high programming flexibility, with the possibility of local and remote programming. The modules are very reliable and have powerful processing and interfacing capabilities. Furthermore, they are highly hardware and software scalable, while exhibiting very robust security characteristics [25]. Open Source Software, both in the distributed modules and in the central database, guarantees flexibility and high evolution potential.

Real-Time Operating Systems (RTOS) are candidates for both applications described in this chapter and work is in progress to use FreeRTOS as a basic development environment for the ARM processor. Despite the fact that these are not real-time intensive applications,

RTOS can greatly facilitate system development because multiple tasks can be programmed as if they were unique.

In this chapter we presented and detailed a set of engineering choices that can be used to develop successful networked embedded systems applications. These choices include network and communication architecture, hardware, development and programming tools for the embedded modules as well as communication technology and server operating system and basis software.

As a general conclusion we can state that networked embedded systems exhibit a great potential to serve as remote intelligent modules in high performance distributed applications such as those that can be developed for the educational and industrial fields. Furthermore, it was demonstrated that it is possible to create advanced networked distributed applications using Open Source Software for the system infrastructure.

6. References

[1] G. Pottie, W. Kaiser, *Principles of Embedded Networked Systems Design*, Cambridge University Press, 2005.

[2] Embedded Design, Available from www.embedded.com and www.linuxdevices.com, last visit on 24th September 2011.

[3] Fonseca, I.; Lopes, F.; "*An embedded system and an architecture for access control and access management: An application to the educational environment*", Information Systems and Technologies (CISTI), 2010 5th Iberian Conference on , vol., no., pp.1-5, 16-19 June 2010, Available from ieeexplore.ieee.org/stamp/stamp.jsp?tp=&arnumber=5556614&isnumber=555659, last visit on 2nd October 2011.

[4] Fonseca, I; Coelho Teixeira, C.; Lopes, F.; "Sistema de Informação Integrado para a Gestão de Cursos de Especialização Tecnológica", Information Systems and Technologies (CISTI), 2011 6th Iberian Conference.

[5] Hongtao Zeng, Jiang Guo, Zhihuai Xiao, *Real time embedded maintenance system of hydro generator excitation system*, International Conference on Condition Monitoring and Diagnosis, CMD 2008, Beijing, China, April 21-24.

[6] Ambient Assisted Living, Available from www.aal-europe.eu, last visit on 24th September 2011.

[7] S. S. Iyengar and R.. R. Brooks, Eds, *Distributed Sensor Networks*, Chapman & Hall, 2005

[8] Philip J. Koopman, Jr, *Embedded System Design Issues*, Proceedings of the International Conference on Computer Design (ICCD 96), Available from www.ece.cmu.edu/~koopman/iccd96/iccd96.html, last visit on 2nd October, 2011.

[9] Seventh Framework Programme, European Network of Excellence on Embedded Systems Design, Available from www.artist-embedded.org/artist/State-of-the-Art,715.html, last visit on 2nd October, 2011.

[10] Krishna Kavi, Robert Akl, Ali Hurson, *Real-Time Systems: An Introduction And The State-Of-The-Art*,Wiley Encyclopedia of Computer Science and Engineering, 2008, Available from csrl.unt.edu/~kavi/Research/encyclopedia-realtime.pdf, last visit on 2nd October 2011.

[11] Ramesh Yerraballi, University of Texas, Real-Time Operating Systems: An Ongoing Review, Available from citeseerx.ist.psu.edu/viewdoc/download?doi=10.1.1.111.5799&rep=rep1&type=pdf, last visit on 2nd October 2011.

[12] Michael Opdenacker, *Embedded Linux From Scratch... in 40 minutes!*, Available from free-electrons.com.

[13] *GCC toolchain for ARM*, Available from www.microbuilder.eu/projects/LPC1343ReferenceDesign/LPC1343Toolchain.asx and www.microbuilder.eu/Tutorials/SoftwareDevelopment/BuildingGCCToolchain.aspx, last visit on 24th September 2011.

[14] Karim Yaghmour, Jon Masters,Gilad BenYossef, Philippe Gerum, Michael Opdenacker, *Building Embedded Linux Systems*, O'Reilly, August 2008.

[15] Hiroyuki Tomiyama, Shinya Honda, Hiroaki Takada, *System-Level Design Tools and RTOS for Multiprocessor SoCs*, MPSoC 2004, Available from www.yxi.com/applications/Tomiyama.pdf, last visit on 2nd October 2011.

[16] Fernanda Coutinho, Inácio Sousa Fonseca, *Local Security System Using CAN*, CAN Newsletter, December 2001, EUA.

[17] Evan Welbourne, Magdalena Balazinska, Gaetano Borriello, Waylon Brunette, *Challenges for Pervasive RFID-Based Infrastructures*, Fifth IEEE International Conference on Pervasive Computing and Communications, New York, USA, March 2007.

[18] Hugo Oliveira, Tiago Oliveira, *Controlador de Acessos Modular Baseado em Tecnologia de Cartões de Proximidade*, In Portuguese, Relatório de fim de curso, Ano 2004, Escola Superior de Tecnologia de Setúbal.

[19] Commercial Security Systems, Available from www.idonic.com and www.bioglobal.pt, last visit on 24th September 2011.

[20] PostgreSQL Global Development Group, Available from www.postgresql.org, last visit on 24th September 2011.

[21] Apache Web Server and PHP language, Available from www.apache.org and www.php.net, last visit on 24th September 2011.

[22] FreeBSD Unix System, Available from www.freebsd.org, last visit on 24th September 2011.

[23] Microchip Technology, Available from www.microchip.com, last visit on 24th September.

[24] Gnu Arm ToolChain, Available from www.gnuarm.com, last visit on 24th September 2011.

[25] Chen X., Makki K., Yen K., Pissinou N., *Sensor network security: a survey*, IEEE Communications Surveys & Tutorials, Volume 11, Issue 2, Pages:52 - 73, 2009.

[26] Portugal, "*Diário da República*", Available from www.dre.pt, last visit on 4th September 2010.

[27] Recomendação 2008/C111/01/CE do Parlamento Europeu e do Conselho, "*Quadro Europeu de Qualificações para a aprendizagem ao longo da vida*", 23 de Abril de 2008.

[28] Building a Linux Embedded system, Available from http://www.linuxfordevices.com/c/a/Linux-For-Devices-Articles/Tutorial-Improving-an-embedded-Linux-system, last visit on 24th September 2011.

[29] Microsoft, *Access Developer Center*, Available from msdn.microsoft.com/en-us/office/aa905400, last visit on 4th Sep. 2011.

[30] W3C Web of Services, *WebServices*, Available from www.w3.org/standards/webofservices, last visit on 24th September 2011.

[31] Teresa Hennig, Rob Cooper, Geoffrey L. Griffith and Armen Stein, *Access 2007 VBA Programmer's Reference*, Wiley Publishing 2007.

6

An Agent-Based System for Sensor Cloud Management

Yu-Cheng Chou, Bo-Shiun Huang and Bo-Jia Peng
Chung Yuan Christian University
Taiwan

1. Introduction

An embedded sensor network is a network of embedded computers deployed in the physical world that interacts with the environment. Each embedded computer, commonly referred to as a sensor node, is a physically small and relatively inexpensive computer that has one or more sensors. These sensor nodes are often networked, allowing them to communicate and cooperate with each other to monitor the environment[1]. In recent years, embedded sensor networks have been gaining increasing attention, both from the academia and industry, because of their potential to be a novel and practical solution across multiple areas such as industrial automation, asset management, environmental monitoring, transportation business, and healthcare. Typically, an embedded sensor network is controlled by its own applications that can access the sensor nodes within the network. On the other hand, the sensor nodes cannot be easily accessed by applications outside of the network. Moreover, even within the same network, different applications might encounter a race condition when they are trying to access a sensor node simultaneously. Existing research works of embedded sensor networks focus on data processing[2], routing[3, 4], power management[5], clock synchronization[6-8], localization[9, 10], operating system[11, 12], and programming[13, 14]. However, not much research has been done with a focus on the management of sensor nodes.

In the past few years, Cloud computing[15] has emerged as a new computing paradigm to provide reliable resources, software, and data on demand. As for resources, essentially, Cloud computing services provide users with virtual servers. Users can utilize virtual servers without concerning about their locations and specifications. With such an inspiration, this project proposes a system, Sensor Agent Cloud, where users can access the sensor nodes without worrying about their locations and detailed specifications.

Sensor Agent Cloud virtualizes a physical sensor node as a virtual "sensor agent". Users can use and control sensor agents with standard functions. Dynamically grouped sensor agents are provisioned in response to the users' requests. Users can destroy their sensor agents when they are not needed. Monitoring sensor agents is used to maintain the quality of service. Sensor Agent Cloud also provides a user interface for registering / deleting sensor nodes, requesting for provisioning / destroying sensor agents, controlling / monitoring sensor agents, and registering / deleting users.

Each sensor agent operates on behalf of its user. The mandatory coordination of these sensor agents, which might belong to different users and try to access the same sensor node, is related to the system management. Therefore, Sensor Agent Cloud shall be self-managing. In other words, Sensor Agent Cloud shall be an autonomic system. For a system to be self-managing, there must be an automated method to collect the details of the system, to analyze the details to determine whether any changes need to be made, to create a plan that specifies the necessary changes, and to perform the created plan[16, 17]. An autonomic system shall possess one of the following four autonomic properties, recognized as the four fundamental areas of self-management:

- *Self-configuring* property that enables the system to adapt to unpredictable conditions by automatically changing its configuration, such as adding or removing new components or resources, or installing software changes without disrupting the services provided by itself.
- *Self-healing* property that can prevent and recover from failure by automatically discovering, diagnosing, circumventing, and recovering from issues that might cause service disruptions.
- *Self-optimizing* property that enables the system to continuously tune itself, that is, proactively to improve on existing processes and reactively in response to environmental conditions.
- *Self-protecting* property that detects, identifies, and defends against viruses, unauthorized access, and denial-of-service attacks. Self-protection also can include the ability to protect itself from physical harm.

Therefore, it is expected that our proposed Sensor Agent Cloud, enabling users to easily access various kinds of sensor nodes residing in different embedded sensor networks, can enhance the applicability and usability of embedded sensor networks in many application areas.

The remainder of the chapter will be organized as follows. Section 2 introduces related works in this regard. Section 3 describes design considerations of Senor Agent Cloud. System architecture and implementation will be presented in Sections 4 and 5, respectively. Section 6 illustrates a prototype sensor node. A proof-of-concept, real-world application will be used in Section 7 to validate the Sensor Agent Cloud. Conclusions and future work will be discussed in Section 8.

2. Related works

There have been a few studies focusing on the management of physical sensors. OGC (Open Geospatial Consortium)[18] defined a language called Sensor Modeling Language (SensorML)[19] that provides standard models and an XML encoding for physical sensors' description and measurement processes. SensorML can represent the metadata for any physical sensors (such as the type, the location, and the accuracy).

Although there are many kinds of physical sensors, no applications need to use all of them. Each application only needs sufficient physical sensors that meet its requirements. A publish / subscribe mechanism is used to select physical sensors[20, 21]. When there are multiple sensor networks, each sensor network publishes sensor data and metadata that describe the type physical sensors. Each application subscribes to one or more sensor networks in order to receive a real-time data stream from the physical sensors. Such publish / subscribe mechanism allows each application to select only the type of physical sensors where it collects data.

Users shall check whether the physical sensors are available and detect physical sensors' faults in order to maintain the quality of data coming from physical sensors. FIND[22] provides a novel approach to detect physical sensors with faulty data. FIND ranks the physical sensors based on their sensing readings and their physical distances from an event. FIND considers a physical sensor to be faulty when there is a significant mismatch between the sensor data rank and the distance rank.

3. Design considerations of sensor agent cloud

An overview of Sensor Agent Cloud is shown in Figure 1. The bottom layer of Sensor Agent Cloud is the sensor node layer that contains various kinds of physical sensor nodes. The next layer is the sensor agent group layer that contains sensor agent groups consisting of virtual sensor agents. The next layer is the regulation layer that is responsible for monitoring, provisioning, and control of sensor agent groups. The top layer is the user interface layer through which users can access their sensor agent groups. The user interface includes functions and a GUI web page. A sensor agent group requested by a user is automatically provisioned by Sensor Agent Cloud. Users can control and monitor their sensor agents via customized programs or a Web browser.

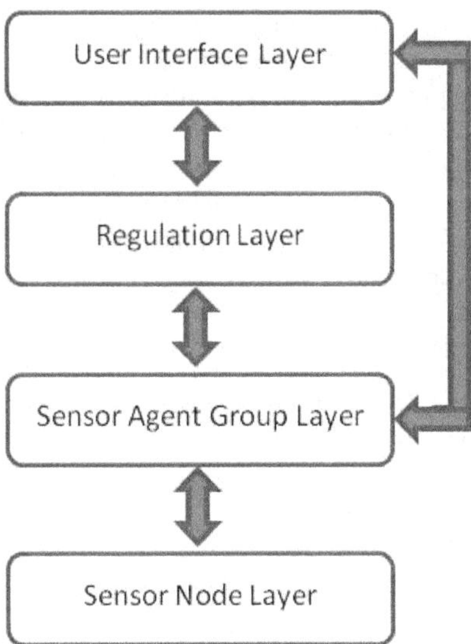

Fig. 1. Overview of Sensor Agent Cloud.

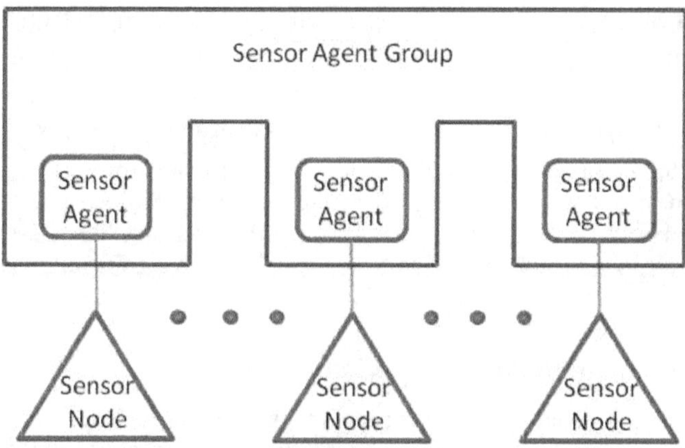

Fig. 2. Relationships among sensor node, sensor agent, and sensor agent group.

The design considerations of Sensor Agent Cloud are illustrated as follows.

1. **Virtualization**: There are various kinds of physical sensor nodes scattered in different locations and networks. The main idea of this project is that, through sensor agent groups, users are able to use physical sensor nodes without worrying about their locations and specifications. Figure 2 describes the relationships among sensor agent groups, sensor agents, and physical sensor nodes. Each sensor agent corresponds to one sensor node. A sensor agent group is created from one or more sensor agents. Users can create sensor agent groups and use sensor agents included in the groups as if they own the physical sensor nodes. For example, they can activate or inactivate their sensor agents, check their status, and set the data collection frequency. The advantage of adopting virtualization is to avoid race conditions that would otherwise occur when multiple users are trying to access or control the same physical sensor node.
2. **Standardization**: Different kinds of sensor nodes have different specifications. Each sensor node provides its own functions for control and data collection. A standard mechanism allows users to access sensor nodes without considering about their different specifications. A set of standard functions are defined for sensor agents, so that users can access sensor agents through standardized functions. A translation mechanism is designed to translate standard functions for the sensor agents into specific functions for different kinds of sensor nodes.

   Standardization also needs to reflect from the aspects of programming and communication languages. Sensor Agent Cloud adopts C programming language and XML-based agent communication language specified in the IEEE FIPA (Foundation for Intelligent Physical Agents) standard. C is an internationally standardized language with a large user base. C has both high-level and low-level functionalities to accommodate the diversity of scientific and engineering applications. Therefore, a huge amount of existing C resources can be used to define a set of standard functions in Sensor Agent Cloud for sensor agent access.

   Since Sensor Agent Cloud employs agents, a standard for agent technology shall be adopted as well. The IEEE FIPA [23] is an international agent standard. The majority of actively maintained Java-based or C-based multi-agent platforms, such as JADE and Mobile-C[24, 25], are IEEE FIPA compliant platforms. Additionally, members of the IEEE FIPA standard include researchers and experts from many academic institutions and industrial companies. Therefore, by adopting the IEEE FIPA standard, Sensor Agent Cloud is able to interoperate with a growing number of FIPA compliant agent platforms.

3. **Automation**: As mentioned in Section 1, for a system to be self-managing, automation is mandatory to keep the human interference to the minimum. Automation therefore improves the service delivery time and reduces the cost. Sensor Agent Cloud provides templates for sensor agents and sensor agent groups. When a user completes a template for a sensor agent group, Sensor Agent Cloud dynamically and automatically provisions the sensor agent(s) in the sensor agent group specified in the template. Sensor Agent Cloud supports on-demand service delivery as well as the full lifecycle of service delivery, starting from the registration of physical sensor nodes, creation of templates for senor agents, request, provision, use, and release for sensor agents, and deregistration (removal) of physical sensor nodes. These services are automatic and delivered without human interference.
4. **Monitoring**: An application is unable to perform properly and correctly when necessary sensor data cannot be obtained from sensor agents. Therefore, an application owner or user shall be able to check whether or not the sensor agents are still available and monitor the status of the sensor agents for maintaining the quality of service. Users can perform the checking and monitoring operations through Sensor Agent Cloud's monitoring mechanism.
5. **Clustering**: There might be a variety of different physical sensor nodes existing in a network. However, an application is unlikely to use all of them. An application essentially uses certain types of sensor nodes. Sensor Agent Cloud provides virtual sensor agent groups. Users can control each virtual sensor agent group. For instance, a user can set the access control and the frequency of data collection for a virtual sensor group. Sensor Agent Cloud provides templates for typical sensor agent groups. But a user can also create new sensor agent groups by incorporating his/her desired sensor agents.
6. **Participant Role**: Three different roles for participants are defined in Sensor Agent Cloud.
   a. *Sensor Node Owner*: A sensor node owner possesses physical sensor nodes. A sensor node owner allows others to use his/her sensor nodes through Sensor Agent Cloud. A sensor node owner registers his/her sensor nodes along with their properties to Sensor Agent Cloud. On the other hand, a sensor node owner deregisters the sensor nodes when he/she is not willing to share them anymore.
   b. *Sensor Agent Cloud Administrator*: A Sensor Agent Cloud Administrator manages the Sensor Agent Cloud system. An administrator manages the required computing resources for sensor agents, monitoring mechanism, and user interface. An administrator also needs to provide templates for sensor agents and some typical sensor agent groups.
   c. *End-User*: An end-user has one or more applications that use the sensor data. Through templates, an end-user requests the use of sensor agent groups that satisfy the requirements of his/her applications. Basic and typical templates are provided

by Sensor Agent Cloud administrators. An end-user can also create a new template for a sensor agent group by incorporating multiple templates of sensor agents or by modifying the existing template of a sensor agent group. End-users can share their own templates among other end users. An end-user can control his/her sensor agents through programs with standard functions or via a Web interface provided by Sensor Agent Cloud. An end-user can monitor the status of sensor agents. When sensor agents become not needed, an end-user can release them.

4. System architecture of Sensor Agent Cloud

The system architecture of Sensor Agent Cloud is shown in Figure 4. The functions of main components are described as follows.

User Interface Layer	Regulation Layer			Sensor Agent Group Layer	Sensor Node Layer
Portal Server	Autonomic Manager		Monitoring Server	Sensor Agent Group	Sensor Node
GUI Portal	Provisioning	Resource Management	Monitoring		

Fig. 3. System architecture of Sensor Agent Cloud.

1. Portal server: When a user logs into the portal from a Web browser, the user's role - sensor node owner, Sensor Agent Cloud administrator, or end-user, determines the operations available to the user. For an end-user, the portal server shows menus for logging in, logging out, requesting for provisioning or destroying sensor agent groups, monitoring sensor agents, controlling sensor agents, and creating templates for sensor agent groups. For a sensor node owner, the portal server gives menus for logging in, logging out, registering sensor nodes, and deleting sensor nodes. For a Sensor Agent Cloud administrator, the portal server gives menus for creating, modifying, and deleting templates for sensor agents and sensor agent groups. Other menus shown to a Sensor Agent Cloud are used to register or delete virtual servers, to manage end-users and sensor node owners, and to check the status of virtual servers. All of the menus for end-users and sensor node owners are available to a Sensor Agent Cloud administrator.
2. Autonomic Manager: The autonomic manager provisions sensor agent groups for requests from the portal server. It contains a workflow engine and predefined workflows. It executes the workflows in a proper order. First, it checks and reserves the computing resource pool when it receives a request for provisioning. It retrieves the templates for sensor agents and sensor agent groups, and then provisions the requested sensor agent groups including sensor agents on the existing or a new virtual server. It also provides virtual servers with monitoring agents. After provisioning, the autonomic manager updates the information of the sensor agent groups.
3. Sensor Agent Group: A sensor agent group is automatically provisioned on a virtual server by the autonomic manager. Each sensor agent group is possessed by an end-user and contains one or more sensor agents. End-users can control the sensor agents. For instance, they can activate or inactivate their sensor agents, set their frequency of data collection, and check their status. Sensor agent groups can be controlled directly or via a Web browser.

4. Monitoring Server: The monitoring server receives the data about sensor agents from the monitoring agents residing in the virtual servers. It stores the received data in a database. The monitoring information for sensor agents can be accessed through a Web browser. Sensor Agent Cloud administrators are able to monitor the status of the monitoring servers as well.

5. Implementation blueprint of Sensor Agent Cloud

Figure 4 shows the implementation blueprint of Sensor Agent Cloud. As shown in Figure 4, the autonomic manager is planned to be implemented as a portal server as well.

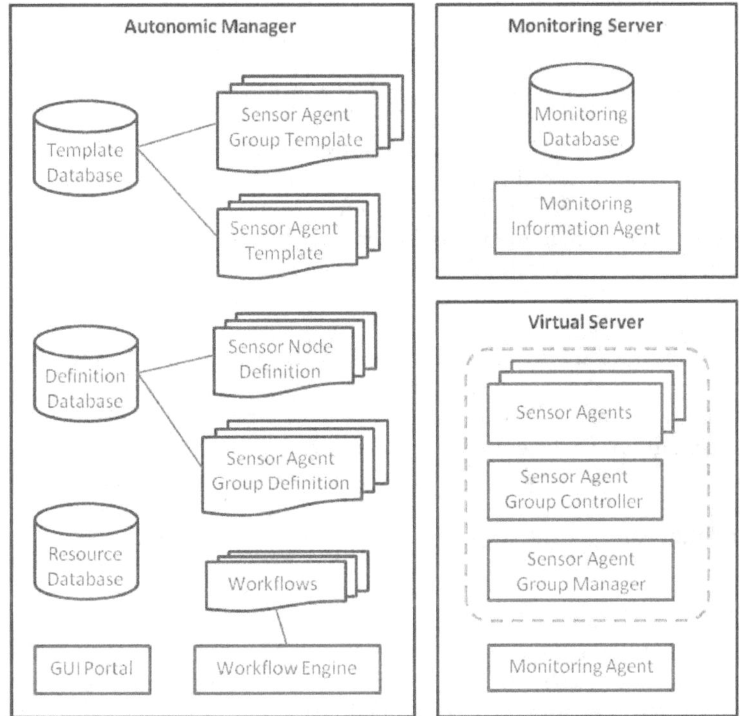

Fig. 4. Implementation blueprint of Sensor Agent Cloud.

There are three databases maintained by the autonomic manager. The definition database stores definitions of the sensor nodes and the provisioned sensor agent groups. Definitions of sensor nodes describe sensor nodes' properties, such as the owner's ID and the type of sensor data. Definitions of sensor agent groups describe the provisioned sensor agent group, such as sensor agent group's ID, end-user's ID, and virtual server's ID. The template database stores the templates for the sensor agents and sensor agent groups. A sensor agent template contains C functions and the data mapping rule. A sensor agent group's template defines the links to templates of included sensor agents and the creator's ID. The workflow engine contains the workflows for each task, such as provisioning sensor agent groups, registering sensor nodes, and controlling sensor agents. The resource database stores the IT resource pool's definition that describes the data regarding the autonomic manager, monitoring server, and virtual servers, such as IP address, host name, specifications, and usage. The monitoring information agent receives the data from monitoring agents residing in virtual servers and stores in the database. Each virtual server has a monitoring agent, a sensor agent group manager, a sensor agent group controller, and one or more sensor agents. The sensor agent group controller has methods for controlling sensor agents, such as activating or inactivating them, and specifying their frequency of data collection. The methods are called by the workflow for controlling sensor agents. The end-user's application can also call the methods directly. Each sensor agent contains a standard method for accessing its corresponding physical sensor node's specification. An application can get data originating from sensor nodes through standard methods contained in sensor agents.

The flow for provisioning a sensor agent group is illustrated as follows.

1. An end-user logs in the GUI portal on a Web browser.
2. The autonomic server gets the list of templates for sensor agents and sensor agent groups from the Template Database and shows the list to the user.
3. The user requests for selecting and provisioning a sensor agent group.
4. The autonomic manager calls the workflow engine with the user's ID and the template's ID for the requested sensor agent group.
5. The workflow engine executes the workflow for provisioning the sensor agent group.
6. The workflow updates IT resource pool for reservation and gets the virtual server's information.
7. The workflow gets the sensor agent group's template by ID and the sensor agents' templates from the links inside the sensor agent group's template.
8. The workflow creates and sends sensor agents, a sensor agent group controller, and a sensor agent group manager to the virtual server.
9. The workflow adds the definition of the new sensor agent group to the Definition database.
10. The workflow informs the user of the completion of provisioning.

6. A Prototype sensor node

The fundamental building block of the proposed Sensor Agent Cloud is a sensor node that supports agents, C language, and IEEE FIPA standard. Thus, a prototype sensor node supporting those three features is presented in this section.

With regard to software, Mobile-C[24, 25], an embeddable multi-agent agent platform supporting C/C++ mobile agents, is employed in Sensor Agent Cloud as the sensor node agency and client agency, as shown in Figure 5. Among the Mobile-C modules shown in Figure 5, by default, the three FIPA mandatory modules, the Agent Management System (AMS), Agent Communication Channel (ACC), and Directory Facilitator (DF), are initialized when Mobile-C is started. The AMS is related to the creation, registration, execution, migration, persistence, and termination of a mobile agent. The ACC is related to the inter-agency mobile agent transport and inter-agent communication. The DF is related to yellow page activities. The Agent Security Manager (ASM) is responsible for maintaining the security policies for an agency. Here, mobile agents are assumed authorized mobile agents. Thus, the ASM is not required to be initialized in Mobile-C. By default, the ASM is not initialized when Mobile-C is started.

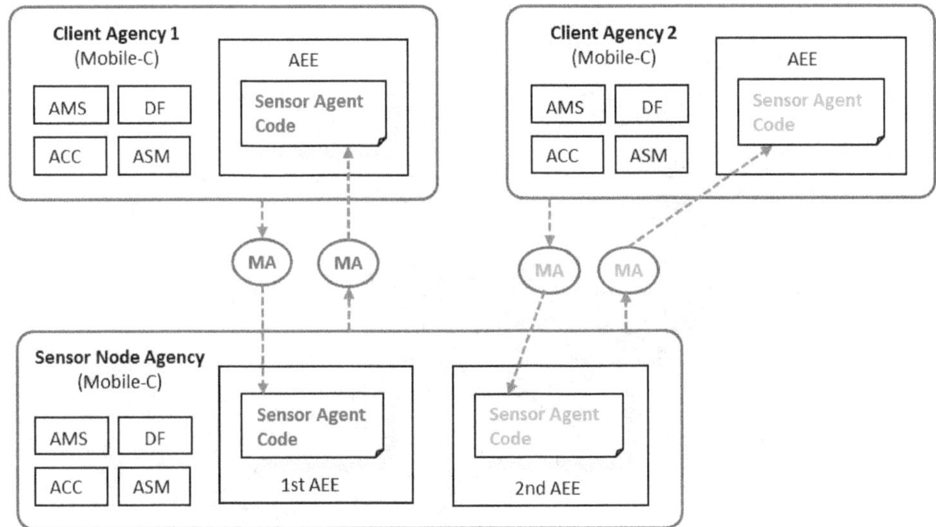

Fig. 5. Sensor node agency and client agency in Sensor Agent Cloud.

Fig. 6. VIA ARTiGO A1100 computer of the prototype sensor node.

Fig. 7. FLAG PSoC development system of the prototype sensor node.

A mobile agent has an XML structure where a C/C++ sensor agent code is embedded[26]. As shown in Figure 5, after a mobile agent is created at a client agency, it will migrate to a specified sensor node agency. When a mobile agent arrives at a sensor node agency, an Agent Execution Engine (AEE) will be automatically created to run the sensor agent code. Once the execution of the sensor agent code is finished, the result will be carried by the original mobile agent back to its home client agency. Similarly, when such a mobile agent arrives at its home client agency, an AEE will be created to run the sensor agent code, which typically displays the result required by a user. Ch[27], a C/C++ interpreter, is the AEE of Mobile-C.

With regard to hardware, the prototype sensor node consists of a VIA ARTiGo A1100[28] and a FLAG Programmable System on Chip (PSoC) development system[29], as shown in Figures 6 and 7. The VIA ARTiGO A1100 has a size of 14.6 cm x 9.9 cm x 5.2 cm, and has key features including a 1.2GHz VIA Nano processor, hardware accelerated video decoding, multiple I/O ports, and Gigabit Ethernet and wireless networking. The FLAG PSoC development system is composed of a PSoC development board (FLAG-1605A) with a Cypress programmable chip (CY8C29466-24PXI), a TCP/IP network module (FLAG-N001), an LCD module, and a temperature and humidity sensor module (FLAG-1613A).

7. Dynamic sensor node data retrieval

This section uses an application of dynamic sensor node data retrieval to validate the fundamental building block of Sensor Agent Cloud, the sensor node, in terms of its ability to execute sensor agent codes to obtain user-desired information.

Figure 8 shows the diagram for the dynamic sensor node data retrieval application. The communication between the PSoC development board and TCP/IP network module is through a Universal Asynchronous Receiver/Transmitter (UART). The Peer-to-Peer (P2P) communication is the communication method between the TCP/IP network module and ARTiGO computer. Moreover, the wireless network communication is the communication method between the ARTiGO computer and a remote desktop computer.

In the PSoC development board, there is a sensor data transmitter program that continuously waits for three seconds, reads the real-time temperature and humidity data from the sensor module, displays the data on the LCD module, and sends the data to the ARTiGO computer through the TCP/IP network module, as shown in Figure 9.

A sensor data receiver program and a sensor node agency are running in the ARTiGO computer. The sensor data receiver program continuously receives the real-time data from the PSoC development board and saves the data into a database, as shown in Figure 10. Here, the database is implemented as a text file for simplicity's sake.

In the sensor node agency, an AEE will be created to run the sensor agent code of an arrived mobile agent. Such a mobile agent has two tasks, each of which corresponds to a sensor agent code. The first sensor agent code will be executed on the ARTiGO computer, which is to access the database and perform calculations on the data to obtain the desired result, the average temperature and humidity, as shown in Figure 11. The result will be carried by the original mobile agent back to its source location, the client agency, where an AEE will be created to run the second sensor agent code to display the average temperature and humidity, as shown in Figure 12.

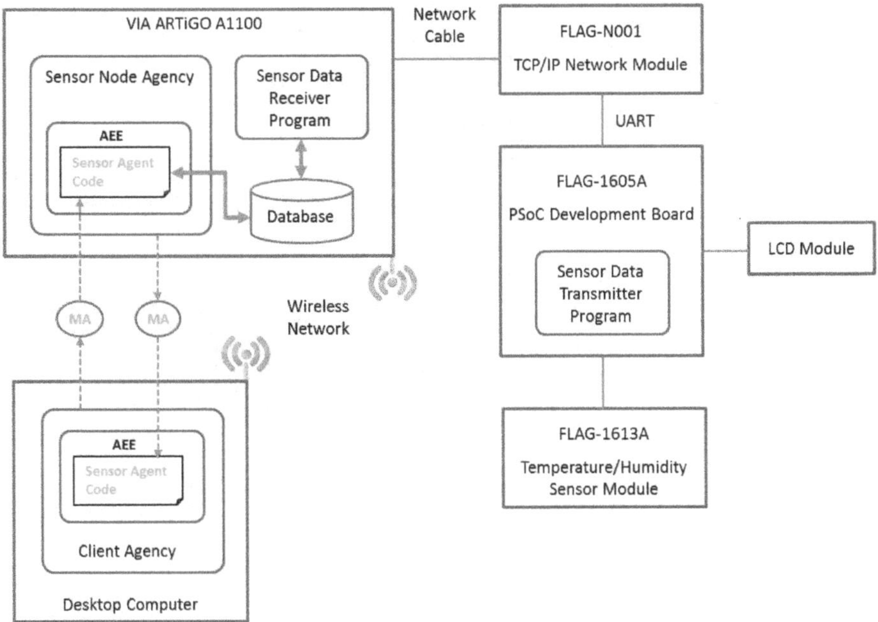

Fig. 8. Dynamic sensor node data retrieval application diagram.

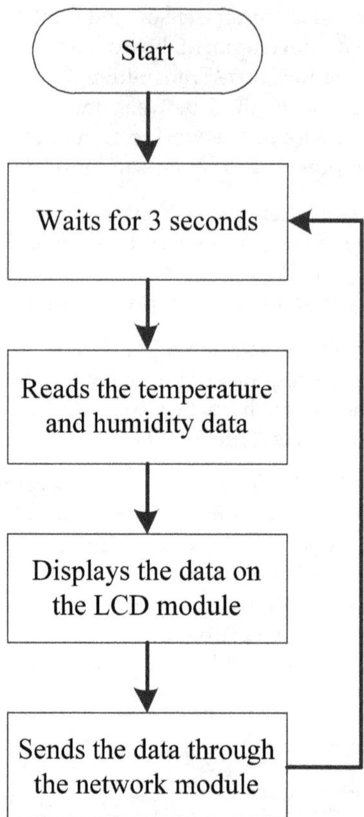

Fig. 9. Simplified flowchart of the sensor data transmitter program.

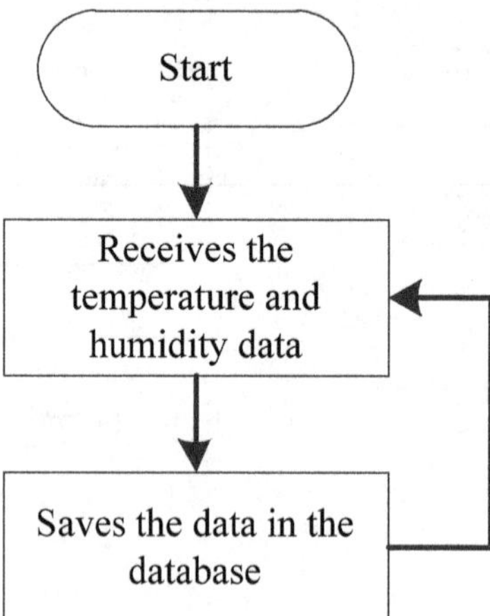

Fig. 10. Simplified flowchart of the sensor data receiver program.

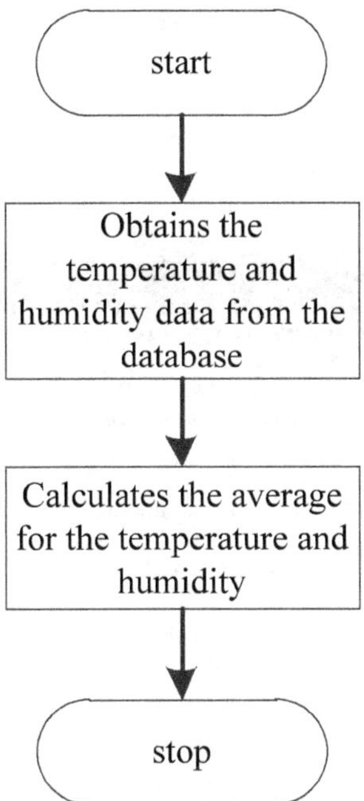

Fig. 11. Simplified flowchart of the 1st sensor agent code carried by the mobile agent.

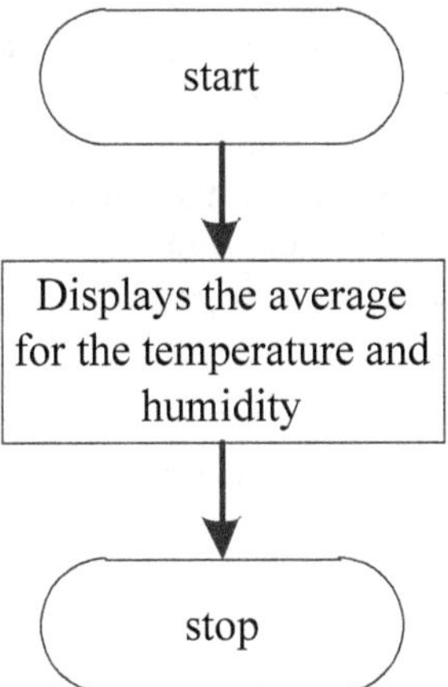

Fig. 12. Simplified flowchart of the 2nd sensor agent code carried by the mobile agent.

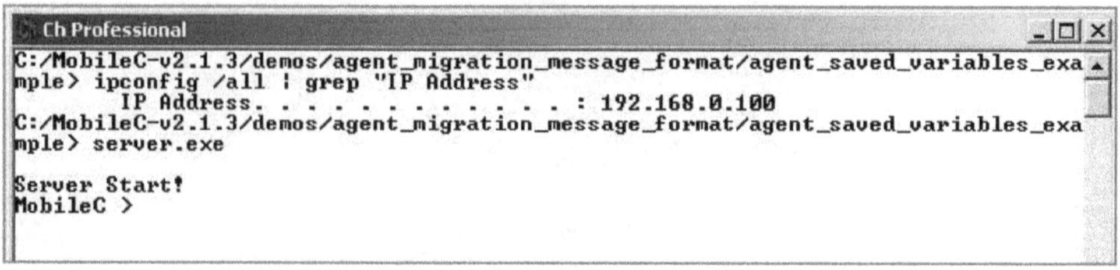

```
Ch Professional
C:/MobileC-v2.1.3/demos/agent_migration_message_format/agent_saved_variables_exa
mple> ipconfig /all | grep "IP Address"
        IP Address. . . . . . . . . . . . : 192.168.0.100
C:/MobileC-v2.1.3/demos/agent_migration_message_format/agent_saved_variables_exa
mple> server.exe

Server Start!
MobileC >
```

Fig. 13. Screenshot of the sensor node agency, server.exe.

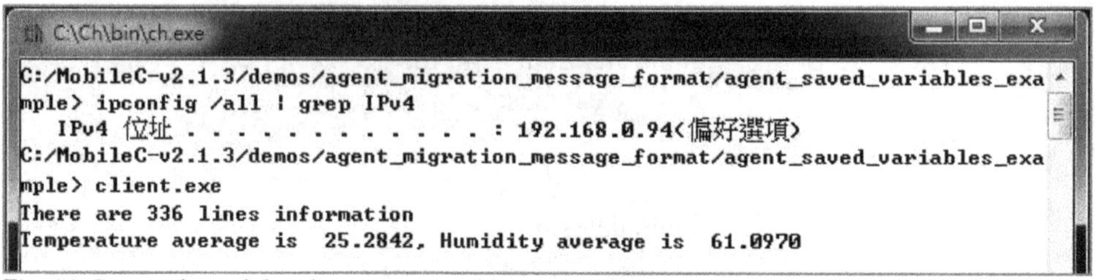

```
C:\Ch\bin\ch.exe
C:/MobileC-v2.1.3/demos/agent_migration_message_format/agent_saved_variables_exa
mple> ipconfig /all | grep IPv4
   IPv4 位址 . . . . . . . . . . . . : 192.168.0.94(偏好選項)
C:/MobileC-v2.1.3/demos/agent_migration_message_format/agent_saved_variables_exa
mple> client.exe
There are 336 lines information
Temperature average is  25.2842, Humidity average is  61.0970
```

Fig. 14. Screenshot of the client agency, client.exe.

Figures 13 and 14 illustrate the screenshots for the sensor node agency and client agency, respectively. The IP address of the VIA ARTiGO A1100 where the sensor node agency is running is 192.168.0.100, as shown in Figure 13. The IP address of the remote desktop computer where the client agency is running is 192.168.0.94, as shown in Figure 13. Moreover, there are totally 336 lines of information, each of which corresponds to one set of temperature and humidity data. The average temperature and humidity are 25.2842 °C and 61.097%, respectively.

8. Conclusion and future work

This paper presents the architecture and implementation blueprint for a cloud-based autonomic system for sensor nodes management, called Sensor Agent Cloud. The implementation of a prototype sensor node for the Sensor Agent Cloud is also presented. An application of dynamic sensor node data retrieval is used to validate the Sensor Agent Cloud's building block, the sensor node, in terms of its ability to execute sensor agent codes to obtain user-desired information. However, the entire system is still under development. Therefore, the future work is to fully implement the Sensor Agent Cloud and compare it with other representative sensor-cloud systems.

9. Acknowledgment

This research is supported by the National Science Council, Taiwan, under grant NSC 100-2221-E-033-080.

10. References

[1] J. Heidemann and R. Govindan, "An Overview of Embedded Sensor Networks," USC/Information Sciences Institute, 2004.

[2] S. R. Madden and M. J. Franklin, "Fjording the Steam: An Architecture for Queries Over Streaming Sensor Data," in The 18th International Conference on Data Engineering, 2002.

[3] M. H. Alizai, O. Landsiedel, J. A. B. Link, S. Goetz, and K. Wehrle, "Bursty Traffic over Bursty Links," 2009.

[4] O. Gnawali, R. Fonseca, K. Jamieson, D. Moss, and P. Levis, "Collection Tree Protocol," in The 7th ACM Conference on Embedded Networked Sensor Systems, 2009.

[5] R. Katsuma, Y. Murata, N. Shibata, K. Yasumoto, and M. Ito, "Extending k-Coverage Lifetime of Wireless Sensor Networks Using Mobile Sensor Nodes," in The 5th IEEE International Conference on Wireless and Mobile Computing, Networking and Communications, 2009.

[6] J. Koo, R. K. Panta, S. Bagchi, and L. Montestruque, "A Tale of Two Synchronizing Clocks," in The 7th ACM Conference on Embedded Networked Sensor Systems, 2009.

[7] C. Lenzen, P. Sommer, and R. Wattenhofer, "Optimal Clock Synchronization in Networks," in The 7th ACM Conference on Embedded Networked Sensor Systems, 2009.

[8] A. Rowe, V. Gupta, and R. Rajkumar, "Low-Power Clock Synchronization using Electromagnetic Energy Radiating from AC Power Lines," in The 7th ACM Conference on Embedded Networked Sensor Systems, 2009.

[9] K. Matsumoto, R. Katsuma, N. Shibata, K. Yasumoto, and M. Ito, "Extended Abstract: Minimizing Localization Cost with Mobile Anchor in Underwater Sensor Networks," in The Fourth ACM International Workshop on UnderWater Networks, 2009.

[10] Z. Zhong and T. He, "Achieving Range-Free Localization Beyond Connectivity," in The 7th ACM Conference on Embedded Networked Sensor Systems, 2009.

[11] J. Hill, R. Szewczyk, A. Woo, S. Hollar, D. Culler, and K. Pister, "System Architecture Directions for Networked Sensors," in International Conference on Architectural Support for Programming Languages and Operating Systems, 2000.

[12] K. Klues, C. Liang, J. Paek, R. Musaloiu-E, P. Levis, A. Terzis, and R. Govindan, "TOSThreads: Thread-Safe and Non-Invasive Preemption in TinyOS," in The 7th ACM Conference on Embedded Networked Sensor Systems, 2009.

[13] J. S. Miller, P. Dinda, and R. Dick, "Evaluating a BASIC Approach to Sensor Network Node Programming," in The 7th ACM Conference on Embedded Networked Sensor Systems, 2009.

[14] T. I. Sookoor, T. W. Hnat, P. Hooimeijer, W. Weimer, and K. Whitehouse, "Macrodebugging: Global Views of Distributed Program Execution," in The 7th ACM Conference on Embedded Networked Sensor Systems, 2009.

[15] A. Weiss, "Computing in the Clouds," netWorker, vol. 11, pp. 16-25, 2007.

[16] IBM, "IBM Autonomic Computing White Paper - An Architectural Blueprint for Autonomic Computing," 2005.

[17] J. O. Kephart and D. M. Chess, "The vision of autonomic computing," IEEE Computer, vol. 36, pp. 41-50, 2003.

[18] "OGC: Open Geospatial Consortium," http://www.opengeospatial.org/.

[19] "SensorML: Sensor Modeling Language," http://vast.uah.edu/SensorML/.

[20] M. Gaynor, M. Welsh, S. Moulton, A. Rowan, E. LaCombe, and J. Wynne, "Integrating Wireless Sensor Networks with the Grid," IEEE Internet Computing, 2004.

[21] J. Shneidman, P. Pietzuch, J. Ledlie, M. Roussopoulos, M. Seltzer, and M. Welsh, "Hourglass: An Infrastructure for Connecting Sensor Networks and Applications," Harvard University, 2004.

[22] S. Guo, Z. Zhong, and T. He, "FIND: Faulty Node Detection for Wireless Sensor Networks," in Proceedings in the 7th ACM Conference on Embedded Networked Sensor Systems, 2009, pp. 253-266.

[23] "FIPA: The Foundation for Intelligent Physical Agents," http://www.fipa.org/repository/standardspecs.html.

[24] B. Chen, H. H. Cheng, and J. Palen, "Mobile-C: A Mobile Agent Platform for Mobile C/C++ Code," Software - Practice & Experience, vol. 36, pp. 1711-1733, 2006.

[25] Y.-C. Chou, D. Ko, and H. H. Cheng, "An Embeddable Mobile Agent Platform Supporting Runtime Code Mobility, Interaction and Coordination of Mobile Agents and Host Systems," Information and Software Technology, vol. 52, pp. 185-196, 2010.

[26] B. Chen, D. D. Linz, and H. H. Cheng, "XML-Based Agent Communication, Migration and Computation in Mobile Agent Systems," Journal of Systems and Software, vol. 81, pp. 1364-1376, 2008.

[27] H. H. Cheng, "Ch: A C/C++ Interpreter for Script Computing," C/C++ User's Journal, vol. 24, pp. 6-12, 2006.

[28] "VIA ARTiGO A1100 PC Kit," http://www.via.com.tw/en/products/embedded/artigo/a1100/index.jsp.

[29] "FLAG Programmable System on Chip (PSoC) Development System," http://www.flag.com.tw/book/bookinfo.asp?bokno=E8773.

7

A VLSI Architecture for Output Probability and Likelihood Score Computations of HMM-Based Recognition Systems

Kazuhiro Nakamura[1], Ryo Shimazaki[1], Masatoshi Yamamoto[1],
Kazuyoshi Takagi[2] and Naofumi Takagi[2]
[1]*Nagoya University*
[2]*Kyoto University*
Japan

1. Introduction

Due to their effectiveness and efficiency for user-independent recognition, hidden Markov models (HMMs) are widely used in applications such as speech recognition (word recognition, connected word recognition and continuous speech recognition), lip-reading and gesture recognition. Output probability computations (OPCs) of continuous HMMs and likelihood scorer computations (LSCs) are the most time-consuming part of HMM-based recognition systems.

High-speed VLSI architectures optimized for recognition tasks have been developed for the development of well-optimized HMM-based recognition systems (Mathew et al., 2003a;b; Nakamura et al., 2010; Yoshizawa et al., 2004; 2006; Kim & Jeong, 2007). Yoshizawa *et al.* investigated a *block-wise parallel processing* (*BPP*) for OPCs and LSCs, and proposed a high-speed VLSI architecture for word recognition (Yoshizawa et al., 2002; 2004; 2006). Nakamura *et al.* investigated a BPP, *store-based block parallel processing* (*StoreBPP*), for OPCs, and proposed a high-speed VLSI architecture for OPCs (Nakamura et al., 2010). As for OPCs and LSCs with StoreBPP, Viterbi scorer for the StoreBPP architecture is required, but not presented yet. An easy application of a Viterbi scorer to the StoreBPP architecture requires many registers and reduces the advantage of using StoreBPP. Different BPPs require different architectures of Viterbi scorer. Viterbi scorer which is suitable for StoreBPP is required for the development of well-optimized future HMM-based recognition systems.

In this chapter, we firstly show *fast store-based block parallel processing* (*FastStoreBPP*) for OPCs and LSCs, and present a Viterbi scorer which supports FastStoreBPP. FastStoreBPP exploits full performance of StoreBPP by doubling the bit length of the input to OPCs and LSCs, e.g., from 8-bit to 16-bit. We demonstrate a high-speed VLSI architecture that supports FastStoreBPP. We secondly show *multiple store-based block parallel processing* (*MultipleStoreBPP*) for OPCs and LSCs, and present a Viterbi scorer which supports MultipleStoreBPP. MultipleStoreBPP has high performance scalability by further extending the bit length of the input to OPCs and LSCs, e.g., from 8-bit to 32-bit.

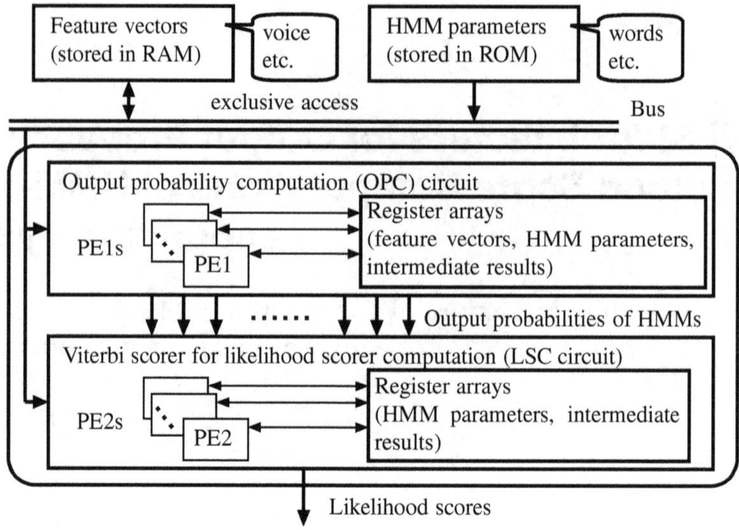

Fig. 1. Basic structure of HMM-based recognition hardware.

Compared with the StreamBPP (Yoshizawa et al., 2002; 2004; 2006) architecture, our FastStoreBPP and MultipleStoreBPP architectures have fewer registers and requires less processing time. From a VLSI architectural viewpoint, a comparison shows the efficiency of the MultipleStoreBPP architecture through its efficient use of processing elements (*PE*s).

The remainder of this chapter is organized as follows: the structure of HMM-based recognition systems is described in Section 2, the FastStoreBPP architecture is introduced in Section 3, the MultipleStoreBPP architecture is introduced in Section 4, the architectures are evaluated in Section 5, and conclusions are presented in Section 6.

2. HMM-based recognition systems

2.1 HMM-based recognition hardware

Figure 1 shows the basic structure of the relevant part of HMM-based recognition hardware (Mathew et al., 2003a;b; Nakamura et al., 2010; Yoshizawa et al., 2002; 2004; 2006; Kim & Jeong, 2007). The OPC circuit and the Viterbi scorer for LSC work together as a recognition engine. The inputs to the OPC circuit are feature vectors of several dimensions and HMM parameters. These values are stored in RAM and ROM respectively, as shown in Fig. 1. The RAM, ROM, OPC circuit and Viterbi scorer interconnect via a single bus, and memory accesses are exclusive. The OPC circuit produces HMM output probabilities. The inputs to the Viterbi scorer are these results and HMM parameters. The Viterbi scorer computes likelihood scores using the Viterbi algorithm. In HMM-based recognition systems, the most time-consuming task is OPCs and LSCs, and the OPC circuit and the Viterbi scorer accelerate these computations. The OPC circuit and the Viterbi scorer have several register arrays and *PE*s for efficient high-speed parallel processing. Feature vectors, HMM parameters and intermediate results are effectively shared between *PE*s as shown in Fig. 1. More details can be found in (Nakamura et al., 2010; Yoshizawa et al., 2002; 2004; 2006).

2.2 OPC of HMMs and LSC with Viterbi algorithm

Let $\mathbf{O}_1, \mathbf{O}_2, ...,$ and $\mathbf{O}_T$ be a sequence of P-dimensional input feature vectors to HMMs, where $\mathbf{O}_t = (o_{t1}, o_{t2}, ..., o_{tP})$, $1 \leq t \leq T$. T is the number of input feature vectors, and P is the dimension of the input feature vector. For any input feature vector $\mathbf{O}_t$, the output probability of N-state continuous HMMs at the j-th state is given by

$$\log b_j(\mathbf{O}_t) = \omega_j + \sum_{p=1}^{P} \sigma_{jp}(o_{tp} - \mu_{jp})^2 \tag{1}$$

where ω_j, σ_{jp} and μ_{jp} are the parameters of the Gaussian probability density function which are precomputed and stored in ROM. The OPC circuit computes $\log b_j(\mathbf{O}_t)$ based on Eq. (1), where $1 \leq j \leq N$ and $1 \leq t \leq T$. All HMM parameters ω_j, σ_{jp}, and μ_{jp} are stored in ROM and the input feature vectors are stored in RAM. The values of T, N, P, and the number of HMMs V differ for each recognition system. For isolated word recognition systems, T, N, P, and V are 86, 32, 38, and 800, respectively (Yoshizawa et al., 2004; 2006), and for another word recognition system, T, N, P, and V are 89, 12, 16 and 100 (Yoshizawa et al., 2002).

For output probabilitie $\log b_j(\mathbf{O}_t)$, where $1 \leq j \leq N$ and $1 \leq t \leq T$, the log-likelihood score $\log S^*$ is given by

$$\log \delta_1(j) = \log \pi_j + |\log b_j(\mathbf{O}_1)|, \tag{2}$$

$$\log \delta_t(j) = \min[\log \delta_{t-1}(j-1) + |\log a_{j-1,j}|, \log \delta_{t-1}(j) + |\log a_{j,j}|] + |\log b_j(\mathbf{O}_t)|, \tag{3}$$

$$\log S^* = \min_{1 \leq j \leq N} [\log \delta_T(j)]. \tag{4}$$

All HMM parameters $\log \pi_j$, $\log a_{j-1,j}$, and $\log a_{j,j}$ are stored in ROM, and the Viterbi scorer computes $\log \delta_t(j)$ based on Eqs. (2) and (3). A flowchart of OPCs and LSCs is shown in Fig. 2 (Yoshizawa et al., 2004; 2006). All HMM output probabilities are obtained by $P \cdot N \cdot T \cdot V$ times the partial computation of $\log b_j(\mathbf{O}_t)$ calls. Partial computation of $\log b_j(\mathbf{O}_t)$ performs four arithmetic operations, an addition, a subtraction and two multiplications in Eq. (1). All likelihood scores are obtained by $N \cdot T \cdot V$ times the partial computation of $\log \delta_t(j)$ calls. Partial computation of $\log \delta_t(j)$ performs three additions in Eq. (3). The OPC circuit and the Viterbi scorer accelerate these computations. More details can be found in (Yoshizawa et al., 2002; 2004; 2006).

2.3 Block parallel processing for OPCs and LSCs

BPP for OPCs and LSCs was proposed as an efficient high-speed parallel processing method for HMM-based isolated word speech recognition (Yoshizawa et al., 2002). In BPP, the set of input feature vectors is called a *block*, and HMM parameters are effectively shared between the different input feature vectors for OPC. In recent years, two types of BPP are classified according to input data flow: *StreamBPP* and *StoreBPP* (Nakamura et al., 2010).

A block can be considered as a $M \cdot P$ matrix whose elements are $o_{t'p}$, where $1 \leq t' \leq M\ (\leq T)$ and $1 \leq p \leq P$. *StreamBPP* performs arithmetic operations on the input stream $o_{11}, o_{12}, ..., o_{1P}$, $o_{21}, o_{22}, ..., o_{2P}, ..., o_{M1}, o_{M2}, ..., o_{MP}$ (Yoshizawa et al., 2006). StreamBPP performs N OPCs in parallel with N *PE1*s (Fig. 1) and obtains N output probabilities $\log b_1(\mathbf{O}_t), \log b_2(\mathbf{O}_t), ...,$ and $\log b_N(\mathbf{O}_t)$ simultaneously. These N output probabilities are obtained every P clock cycles

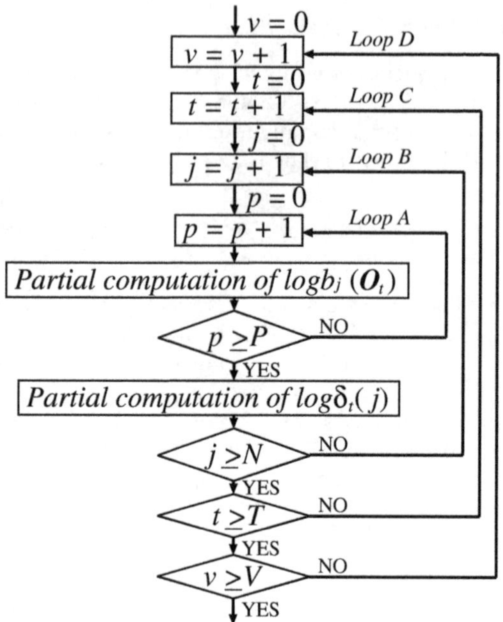

Fig. 2. Flowchart of OPCs and LSCs.

and they are fed to the Viterbi scorer for LSCs. An Viterbi scorer that supports the OPCs and LSCs in StreamBPP was presented in (Yoshizawa et al., 2006), where N LSCs are performed with N *PE2*s (Fig. 1). In the Viterbi scorer, N intermediate scores $\log \delta_t(1)$, $\log \delta_t(2)$, ..., and $\log \delta_t(N)$ are computed simultaneously.

A block can be considered as a set of M input feature vectors whose elements are $\mathbf{O}_{t'}$ where $1 \leq t' \leq M$ $(\leq T)$. *StoreBPP* performs arithmetic operations to locally stored input feature vectors $\mathbf{O}_1$, $\mathbf{O}_2$, ..., and $\mathbf{O}_M$ (Nakamura et al., 2010). StoreBPP performs $\lceil M/2 \rceil$ OPCs in parallel with $\lceil M/2 \rceil$ *PE1*s (Fig. 1) and obtains M HMM output probabilities $\log b_j(\mathbf{O}_{t'+1})$, $\log b_j(\mathbf{O}_{t'+2})$, ..., and $\log b_j(\mathbf{O}_{t'+M})$. These M HMM output probabilities are obtained every $2 \cdot P$ clock cycles and they are fed to the Viterbi scorer for LSCs. Different BPPs require different Viterbi scorer architectures. In StoreBPP, a Viterbi scorer that supports the OPCs, where M HMM output probabilities are computed simultaneously, is required, but the Viterbi scorer for the StoreBPP was not addressed in (Nakamura et al., 2010). An easy introduction of the Viterbi scorer to StoreBPP requires many registers, which reduces the advantage of the StoreBPP architecture.

3. VLSI architecture for OPCs and LSCs with fast store-based block parallel processing

3.1 Fast store-based block parallel processing

A two-step process was adopted in StoreBPP to compute M HMM output probabilities $\log b_j(\mathbf{O}_{t'+1})$, $\log b_j(\mathbf{O}_{t'+2})$, ..., and $\log b_j(\mathbf{O}_{t'+M})$, where half of the output probabilities are computed simultaneously with $\lceil M/2 \rceil$ *PE1*s (Nakamura et al., 2010). The $\lceil M/2 \rceil$

computations which are performed in parallel and a ROM access are performed simultaneously in StoreBPP, where two HMM parameters $-\mu_{j,p+1}$ and $\sigma_{j,p+1}$ are required for next OPC. Because it takes two cycles to read two HMM parameters from ROM, it was appropriate to use a two-step process in StoreBPP.

StoreBPP performs $\lceil M/2 \rceil$ OPCs in parallel by using a register array of size M, where M is the size of block (Nakamura et al., 2010). We improve StoreBPP by reducing the required register size for performing M OPCs in parallel. We modify the parallel computation of $\lceil M/2 \rceil$ OPCs by doubling the bit length of the input to OPC. By this bit length extension, two HMM parameters can be read simultaneously. We call the modified parallel processing *fast store-based block parallel processing* (*FastStoreBPP*), and we show a pipelined Viterbi scorer that supports FastStoreBPP. It performs M OPCs in parallel by using a register array of size M.

A flowchart of our FastStoreBPP is shown in Fig. 3. The flowchart consists of two tasks, *M-parallel OPC* and *$\lceil M/P \rceil$-stage pipelined LSC*. In Fig. 3, the M-parallel OPC and $\lceil M/P \rceil$-stage pipelined LSC are framed by dashed and double dashed lines, respectively. The M-parallel OPC performs M OPCs in parallel with M $PE1$s. The $\lceil M/P \rceil$-stage pipelined LSC performs LSC in serial with $\lceil M/P \rceil$ $PE2$s and $\lceil M/P \rceil$ registers. Loops A′, B′, and D′ correspond to Loops A, B, and D (Fig. 2), where M HMM output probabilities and M intermediate scores are computed with M $PE1$s and $\lceil M/P \rceil$ $PE2$s. Loop C1 is based on StoreBPP, where Loop C (Fig. 2) is partially expanded in Fig. 3.

$PE1_1$, $PE1_2$, ..., and $PE1_M$ (Fig. 3) represent M processing elements which perform partial computations $\log b_j(\mathbf{O}_{t'+1}), \log b_j(\mathbf{O}_{t'+2}), ...,$ and $\log b_j(\mathbf{O}_{t'+M})$ using Eq. (1). M HMM output probabilities $\log b_j(\mathbf{O}_{t'+1})$, $\log b_j(\mathbf{O}_{t'+2})$, ..., and $\log b_j(\mathbf{O}_{t'+M})$ are simultaneously obtained every P cycles by Loop A′. The modified M OPCs are performed in parallel and a ROM access $-\mu_{j,p+1}$ and $\sigma_{j,p+1}$ are performed simultaneously in Loop A′. The two HMM parameters are read from ROM simultaneously. These values are needed for next computation in Loop A′.

Next, the M HMM output probabilities $\log b_j(\mathbf{O}_{t'+1})$, $\log b_j(\mathbf{O}_{t'+2})$, ..., and $\log b_j(\mathbf{O}_{t'+M})$ are fed to $\lceil M/P \rceil$-stage pipelined LSC (Fig. 3) which is a new Viterbi scorer introduced for FastStoreBPP. $PE2$s represent $\lceil M/P \rceil$ processing elements for computing M intermediate scores $\log \delta_{t'+1}(j), \log \delta_{t'+2}(j), ...,$ and $\log \delta_{t'+M}(j)$ using Eqs. (2) and (3). In our FastStoreBPP, Loops E_1, E_2, ..., and $E_{\lceil M/P \rceil}$ (Fig. 3) perform LSC, where the i-th intermediate score $\log \delta_{t'+i}(j)$ is computed by Loop $E_{\lceil i/P \rceil}$. Each Loop $E_{i'}$, where $1 \leq i' \leq \lceil M/P \rceil - 1$, has a $PE2$ and computes P intermediate scores sequentially, where P clock cycles are required for the computation. Loop $E_{\lceil M/P \rceil}$ has a $PE2$ and computes $M - P \cdot (\lceil M/P \rceil - 1)$ intermediate scores sequentially by using $M - P \cdot (\lceil M/P \rceil - 1)$ clock cycles. All Loop Es are pipelined in FastStoreBPP, where the last intermediate score $\log \delta_{t'+i' \cdot P}(j)$, obtained by Loop $E_{i'}$, $1 \leq i' \leq \lceil M/P \rceil - 1$, is fed to the next stage Loop $E_{i'+1}$. Loop A′ and Loop $E_{i'}$s, $1 \leq i' \leq \lceil M/P \rceil$, proceed simultaneously, where each Loop $E_{i'}$ finishes its computation before the next M output probabilities are obtained by Loop A′.

3.2 FastStoreBPP architecture for OPCs and LSCs

Our FastStoreBPP architecture that supports FastStoreBPP is shown in Fig. 4, where we assume $M \leq P$ and hence $\lceil M/P \rceil = 1$. The FastStoreBPP architecture consists of an OPC circuit and a Viterbi scorer. The architecture has two register arrays (Reg$\mathbf{O}$ and Regω),

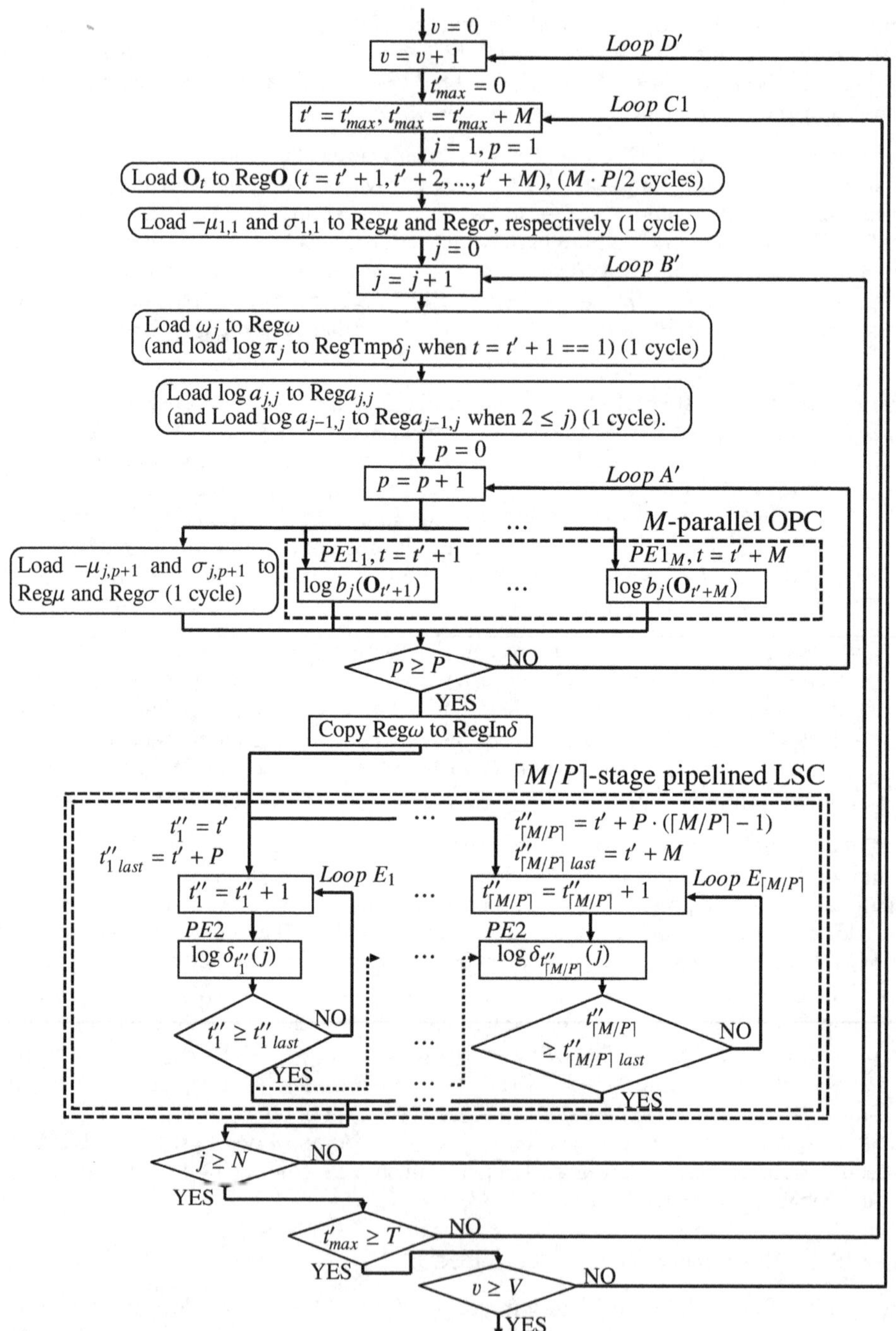

Fig. 3. Flowchart of OPCs and LSCs with FastStoreBPP.

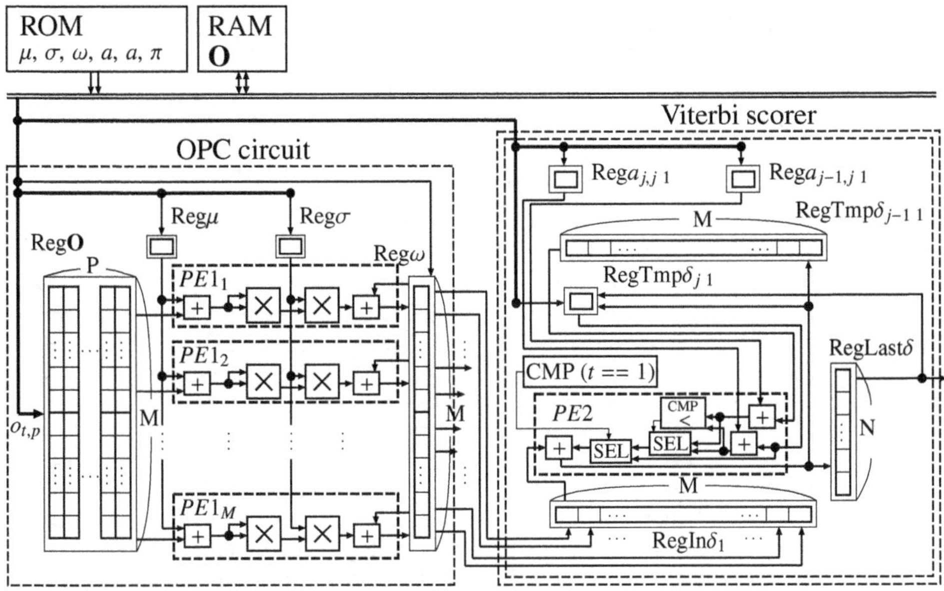

Fig. 4. FastStoreBPP architecture for OPCs and LSCs ($M \leq P$).

two registers (Regμ and Regσ), and M $PE1$s for OPCs. Each $PE1$ consists of two adders and two multipliers, which are used for computing $\omega_j + \sum_{p=1}^{P} \sigma_{jp}(o_{tp} - \mu_{jp})^2$. $PE1_i$ in the FastStoreBPP architecture, the StreamBPP architecture (Yoshizawa et al., 2006), and the StoreBPP architecture (Nakamura et al., 2010) are identical but differ in number. In addition, the architecture has three register arrays (RegInδ_1, RegLastδ, and RegTmp$\delta_{j-1\,1}$), three registers (Reg$a_{j,j\,1}$, Reg$a_{j-1,j\,1}$, and RegTmp$\delta_{j\,1}$), and a $PE2$ for LSCs. $PE2$ consists of three adders, two selectors and two comparators, which are used for LSC based on Eqs. (2) and (3). $PE2$ in the FastStoreBPP architecture and the StreamBPP architecture (Yoshizawa et al., 2006) are identical but differ in number.

OPC starts by reading M input feature vectors $\mathbf{O}_{t'+1}$, $\mathbf{O}_{t'+2}$, ..., and $\mathbf{O}_{t'+M}$ from RAM and storing them in Reg**O** in OPC circuit (Fig. 4) based on Loop C1 (Fig. 3). $M \cdot P/2$ cycles are required for reading M input feature vectors. Then, the HMM parameters of v-th HMM are read from ROM, which are $-\mu_{11}$, σ_{11}, and ω_1, and stored in Regμ, Regσ, and Regω, respectively, based on Loop C1 and Loop B$'$ (Fig. 3). For the stored input feature vectors, M intermediate results of M OPCs are simultaneously computed with the stored HMM parameters by using M $PE1$s (Fig. 4) based on Loop A$'$ (Fig. 3).

The stored HMM parameters are shared by all $PE1$s, and the obtained M intermediate results are stored in Regω. At the same time, two HMM parameters $-\mu_{jp+1}$ and σ_{jp+1} of v-th HMM are read from ROM and stored in Regμ and Regσ, respectively, where the values are overwritten. The HMM parameters are used in next M computations which are performed in parallel with M $PE1$s based on Loop A$'$ (Fig. 3).

M HMM output probabilities are simultaneously obtained every P cycles by M $PE1$s, which are $\log b_j(\mathbf{O}_{t'+1})$, $\log b_j(\mathbf{O}_{t'+2})$, ..., and $\log b_j(\mathbf{O}_{t'+M})$ of v-th HMM based on Loop A$'$ (Fig. 3).

The results are copied from Regω to RegInδ_1 to start LSCs $\log \delta_{t''+1}(j)$, $\log \delta_{t''+1}(j)$, ..., and $\log \delta_{t''+M}(j)$ and the next M OPCs for the $(j+1)$-th state of v-th HMM $\log b_{j+1}(\mathbf{O}_{t'+1})$, $\log b_{j+1}(\mathbf{O}_{t'+2})$, ..., and $\log b_{j+1}(\mathbf{O}_{t'+M})$ based on Loop B$'$ (Fig. 3). $M \cdot N$ HMM output probabilities of v-th HMM are obtained by Loop B$'$ (Fig. 3). $M \cdot N \cdot T$ HMM output probabilities of v-th HMM are obtained by Loop C1 (Fig. 3). $M \cdot N \cdot T \cdot V$ HMM output probabilities of all HMM are obtained by Loop D$'$ (Fig. 3).

Viterbi scorer, denoted by double -dashed lines in (Fig. 4), performes $\lceil M/P \rceil$-stage pipelined LSC, denoted by double -dashed lines in Fig. 3. LSC starts by reading HMM parameters of v-th HMM, $\log \pi_1$ and $\log a_{1,1}$, from ROM and storing them in RegTmp$\delta_{j\,1}$ and Reg$a_{j,j\,1}$, respectively based on Loop B$'$ (Fig. 3). Then, an intermediate score $\log \delta_1(1)$ is computed by $PE2$ with the HMM parameter, $\log \pi_1$, and the HMM output probability $\log b_1(\mathbf{O}_1)$ obtained using Eq. (1). The obtained intermediate score is stored in both RegTmp$\delta_{j\,1}$ and RegTmp$\delta_{j-1\,1}$ (Fig. 4). RegTmp$\delta_{j\,1}$ stores an intermediate score that is needed in the next computation in Loop E$_1$ (Fig. 3). RegTmp$\delta_{j-1\,1}$ stores M intermediate scores $\log \delta_{t'+1}(j)$, $\log \delta_{t'+2}(j)$, ..., and $\log \delta_{t'+M}(j)$, which is needed in the next LSC for the $(j+1)$-th state of the HMM in Loop B$'$. After the computation of $\log \delta_1(1)$, $M-1$ intermediate scores $\log \delta_2(1)$, $\log \delta_3(1)$, ..., and $\log \delta_M(1)$, are sequentially computed by $PE2$ using Eq. (3). In sequential computation, the last obtained intermediate score $\log \delta_M(1)$ is stored in RegTmp$\delta_{j-1\,1}$ and RegLastδ (Fig. 4). RegLastδ stores N intermediate scores that are the last obtained intermediate scores by Loop E$_1$ during Loop B$'$ (Fig. 3). These intermediate scores are $\log \delta_{t'+M}(1)$, $\log \delta_{t'+M}(2)$, ..., and $\log \delta_{t'+M}(N)$ of v-th HMM, which are required when starting LSC with new M HMM output probabilities $\log b_j(\mathbf{O}_{t'+M+1})$, $\log b_j(\mathbf{O}_{t'+M+2})$, ..., and $\log b_j(\mathbf{O}_{t'+2\cdot M})$ at the first computation in Loop E$_1$ (Fig. 3), given as $\log \delta_{t'+M+1}(1)$, $\log \delta_{t'+M+1}(2)$, ..., and $\log \delta_{t'+M+1}(N)$. A required intermediate score is read from RegLastδ and is stored in RegTmp$\delta_{j\,1}$ before computation. Reg$a_{j-1,j\,1}$ (Fig. 4) stores an HMM parameter $\log a_{j-1,j}$ of v-th HMM, which is used for computing $\log \delta_t(j)$ based on Eq. (3), when $2 \leq t$ and $2 \leq j$.

Our Viterbi scorer, which support FastStoreBPP, was presented in Fig. 4, where $M \leq P$ and $\lceil M/P \rceil = 1$. Our $\lceil M/P \rceil$-stage pipelined Viterbi scorer, which supports $P < M$ and $1 < \lceil M/P \rceil$, is shown in Fig. 5. The Viterbi scorer in Fig. 4 is an instance of the generalized $\lceil M/P \rceil$-stage pipelined Viterbi scorer where $\lceil M/P \rceil = 1$. The $\lceil M/P \rceil$-stage pipelined Viterbi scorer consists of RegLastδ and $\lceil M/P \rceil$ sub Viterbi scorers. The i-th stage, i.e., i-th sub Viterbi scorer consists of two register arrays (RegInδ_i and RegTmp$\delta_{j-1\,i}$), three registers (RegTmp$\delta_{j\,i}$, Reg$a_{j,j\,i}$ and Reg$a_{j-1,j\,i}$) and a $PE2$. Each RegInδ_i consists of $i \cdot P$ registers, where $i = 1$, $i = 2$, ..., $\lceil M/P \rceil - 1$. RegIn$\delta_{\lceil M/P \rceil}$ consists of $\lceil M/P \rceil \cdot (M \bmod P)$ registers. In each RegInδ_i, rows are shifted upward every P clock cycles. Each RegTmp$\delta_{j-1\,i}$ consists of P registers, where $i = 1$, $i = 2$, ..., and $\lceil M/P \rceil - 1$. RegTmp$\delta_{j-1\,\lceil M/P \rceil}$ consists of M mod P registers. HMM parameters in Reg$a_{j,j\,i}$ and Reg$a_{j-1,j\,i}$ are copied every P clock cycles to Reg$a_{j,j\,i+1}$ and Reg$a_{j-1,j\,i+1}$, respectively, where $i = 1$, $i = 2$, ..., and $\lceil M/P \rceil - 1$. The last obtained intermediate score by $PE2$ based on Loop E$_i$ (Fig. 3), where $i = 1$, $i = 2$, ..., and $\lceil M/P \rceil - 1$, is stored in RegTmp$\delta_{j-1\,i}$ and RegTmp$\delta_{j\,i+1}$ every P clock cycles based on $\lceil M/P \rceil$-state pipelined LSC (Fig. 3). The last obtained intermediate score by $PE2$ based on Loop E$_{\lceil M/P \rceil}$ (Fig. 3) is stored in RegTmp$\delta_{j-1\,\lceil M/P \rceil}$ and RegLastδ every P clock cycles during Loop B$'$ (Fig. 3). The stored intermediate scores are required when starting LSC with new M output probabilities at the first computation by Loop E$_1$ (Fig. 3). The required intermediate score is read from RegLastδ and stored in RegTmp$\delta_{j\,1}$ before computation.

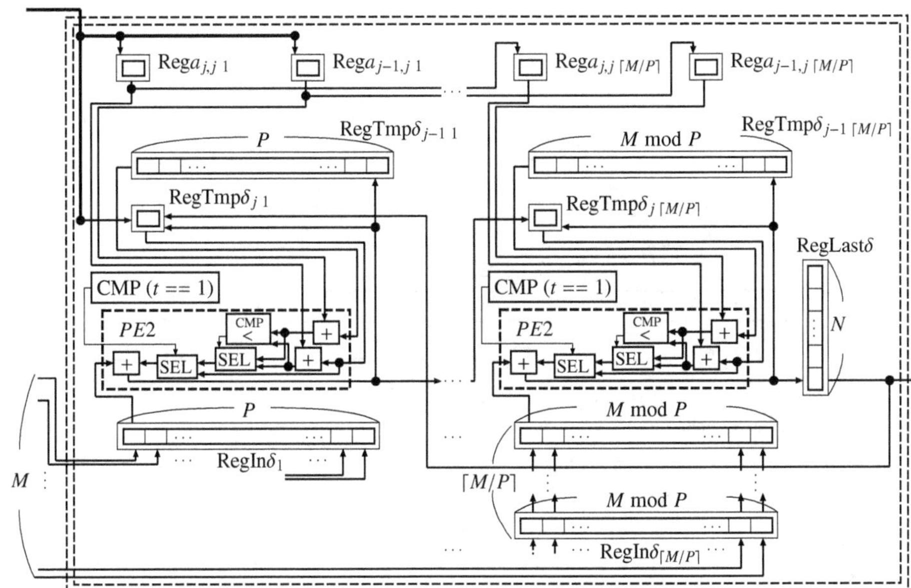

Fig. 5. Pipelined Viterbi scorer for the FastStoreBPP architecture.

4. VLSI architecture for OPCs and LSCs with multiple store-based block parallel processing

FastStoreBPP is obtained from StoreBPP by doubling the bit length of the input to OPC for reading two HMM parameters simultaneously.

We further extend the bit length of the input to OPC and we obtain *multiple store-based block parallel processing* (*MultipleStoreBPP*).

4.1 Multiple store-based block parallel processing

StoreBPP performs $M/2$ OPCs in parallel by using a register array of size M and $M/2$ $PE1$s, where $M/2$ OPCs are performed by a single HMM (Nakamura et al., 2010). We improve StoreBPP and further reduce the required register size for performing OPCs in parallel. We modify $M/2$-*parallel OPC*, where $M/2$ OPCs are performed in parallel, to deal with multiple HMMs by further extending the bit length of the input to OPC. By this bit-length extension, $L' \cdot M'/2$ OPCs are performed in parallel, where L' HMM parameters can be read from ROM simultaneously. We call the modified parallel processing *MultipleStoreBPP*. Our MultipleStoreBPP performs $M'/2$-*parallel OPC*, where $M'/2$ OPCs are performed in parallel, to L' HMMs and $L' \cdot M'/2$ OPCs are performed in parallel by using a register array of size M'.

A flowchart of our MultipleStoreBPP is shown in Fig. 6. Loops D2$'$, C1$'$, B$''$, and A$''$ in Fig. 6 are based on StoreBPP. In our MultipleStoreBPP, Loop D$'$ (Fig. 3) is partially expanded as shown in Fig. 6 for performing $L' \cdot M'/2$ OPCs in parallel in Loop A$''$. By the expansion, input feature vectors are effectively shared between different $M'/2$-parallel OPCs.

The flowchart consists of L' $M'/2$-parallel OPCs and L' $\lceil M'/(2 \cdot P) \rceil$-stage pipelined LSCs. Each $M'/2$-parallel OPC and $\lceil M'/(2 \cdot P) \rceil$-stage pipelined LSC are denoted by dashed and

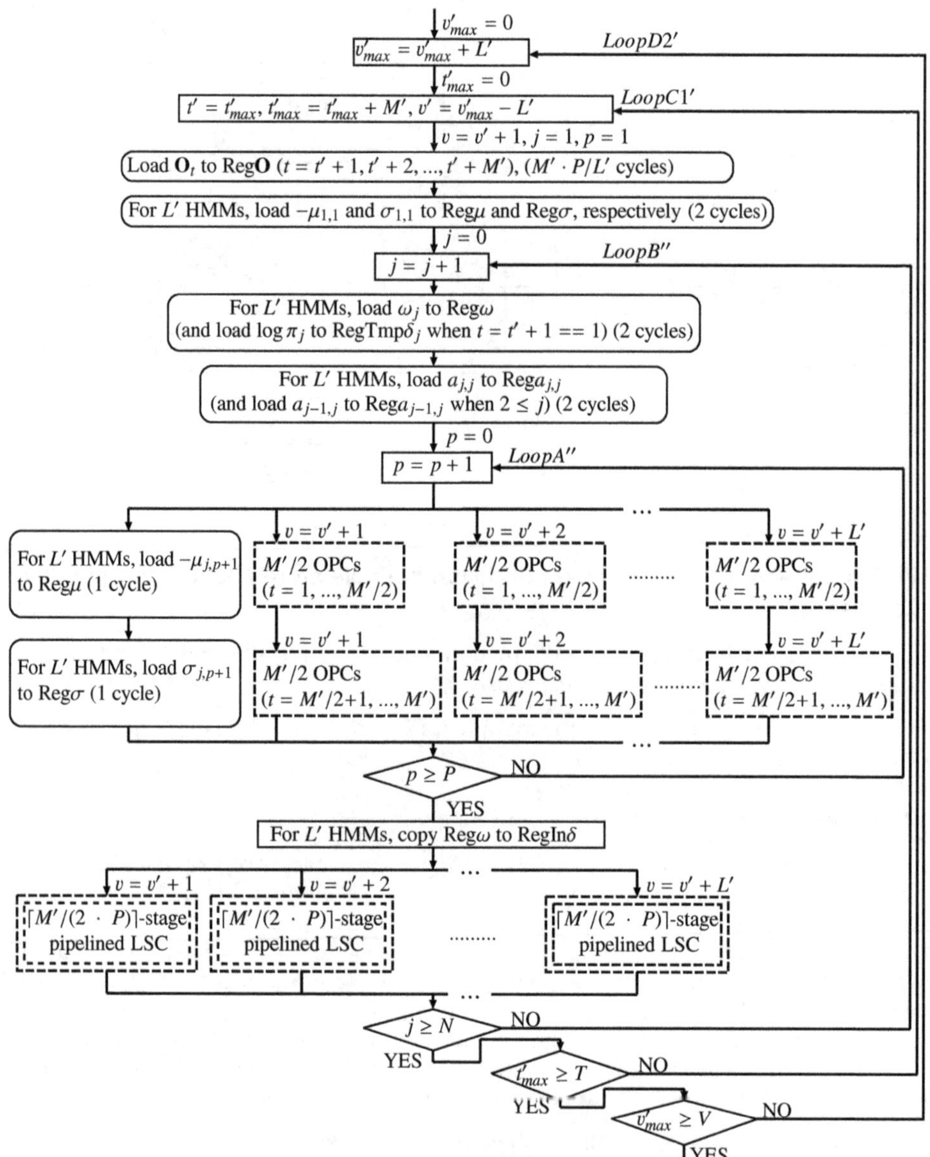

Fig. 6. Flowchart of OPCs and LSCs with MultipleStoreBPP.

double-dashed lines, respectively, in Fig. 6. Each $M'/2$-parallel OPC performs $M'/2$ OPCs in parallel with the same $PE1$s used in StoreBPP and FastStoreBPP, but differ in number. Each $\lceil M'/(2 \cdot P) \rceil$-stage pipelined LSC computes likelihood scores based on $\lceil M/P \rceil$-stage pipelined LSC denoted by double-dashed lines in Fig. 3 with the same $PE2$s used in FastStoreBPP, but differ in number. Loops A$'$ and B$'$ (Fig. 3) correspond to Loops A$''$ and B$''$, respectively. By Loop A$''$, the output probabilities of L' HMMs, $(v'+1)$-th to $(v'+L')$-th HMMs, are computed with $L' \cdot M'/2$ $PE1$s. These output probabilities are simultaneously obtained every P clock cycles by Loop A$''$. In Loop A$''$, firstly, L' $M'/2$-parallel OPCs and ROM access $-\mu_{j,p+1}$ of L' HMMs are performed simultaneously. Secondly, L' $M'/2$-parallel OPCs and ROM access $\sigma_{j,p+1}$ of L' HMMs are performed simultaneously. $2 \cdot L'$ HMM parameters are read from ROM using two cycles. These HMM parameters are needed for next computation in Loop A$''$. Then, the obtained $L' \cdot M'/2$ output probabilities are fed to L' LSCs, where each LSC is the same Viterbi scorer as that introduced for FastStoreBPP, as shown in Fig. 3. These L' LSCs support LSC of $(v'+1)$-th to $(v'+L')$-th HMMs. Loop A$''$ and L' LSCs proceed simultaneously.

4.2 MultipleStoreBPP architecture for OPCs and LSCs

Our MultipleStoreBPP VLSI architecture is shown in Fig. 7, where we assume $M' \leq 2 \cdot P$ and hence $\lceil M'/(2 \cdot P) \rceil = 1$. The MultipleStoreBPP architecture consists of L' OPC circuits and L' Viterbi scorers. The architecture has $2 \cdot L' + 1$ register arrays (Reg$\mathbf{O}$, Regσ and Regω), L' registers (Regμ), and $L' \cdot M'/2$ $PE1$s for OPCs of L' HMMs. Each $PE1$ consists of two adders and two multipliers, which are used for computing $\omega_j + \sum_{p=1}^{P} \sigma_{jp}(o_{tp} - \mu_{jp})^2$. $PE1$s in our MultipleStoreBPP and FastStoreBPP architectures, Yoshizawa et al. (2006), and Nakamura et al. (2010) are identical but differ in number. In addition, the architecture has $3 \cdot L'$ register arrays (RegInδ_1, RegLastδ, and RegTmp$\delta_{j-1\,1}$), $3 \cdot L'$ registers (Reg$a_{j,j\,1}$, Reg$a_{j-1,j\,1}$, and RegTmp$\delta_{j\,1}$), and L' $PE2$s for LSCs of L' HMMs. $PE2$ consists of three adders, two selectors and two comparators, which are used for LSC on the basis of Eqs. (2) and (3). $PE2$s in our MultipleStoreBPP and FastStoreBPP architectures and Yoshizawa et al. (2006) are identical but differ in number.

OPC starts by reading M' input feature vectors $\mathbf{O}_{t'+1}$, ..., and $\mathbf{O}_{t'+M'}$ from RAM and storing them in Reg$\mathbf{O}$ in OPC circuit$_1$ (Fig. 7) based on Loop C1$'$ (Fig. 6). $M' \cdot P/L'$ cycles are required for reading M' feature vectors. Then, the HMM parameters of L' HMMs, i.e., $(v'+1)$-th to $(v'+L)$-th HMMs, are read from ROM, which are $-\mu_{11}$, σ_{11} and ω_1, and stored in Regμ, Regσ, and Regω, respectively, based on Loop C1$'$ and Loop B'' (Fig. 6). For half of the stored input feature vectors, $\mathbf{O}_{t'+1}$, ..., and $\mathbf{O}_{t'+M'/2}$, $L' \cdot M'/2$ intermediate results of L' OPCs are simultaneously computed with the stored HMM parameters by using $L' \cdot M'/2$ $PE1$s (Fig. 7) based on Loop A$''$ (Fig. 6). Then, for the other half of the stored input feature vectors, $\mathbf{O}_{t'M'/2+1}$, ..., and $\mathbf{O}_{t'+2 \cdot M'}$, $L' \cdot M'/2$ intermediate results of L' OPCs are simultaneously computed with the stored HMM parameters by using $L' \cdot M'/2$ $PE1$s (Fig. 7) based on Loop A$''$ (Fig. 6). The stored M' input feature vectors are effectively shared by all OPC circuits.

In each OPC circuit, denoted by dashed line in Fig. 7, the two HMM parameters, $-\mu_{jp}$ and σ_{jp} are shared by all $PE1$s, and the obtained first $M'/2$ intermediate results and the second $M'/2$ intermediate results are stored in Regω using two cycles. At the same time, the two HMM parameters $-\mu_{jp+1}$ and σ_{jp+1} are read from ROM and stored in Regμ and Regσ, respectively,

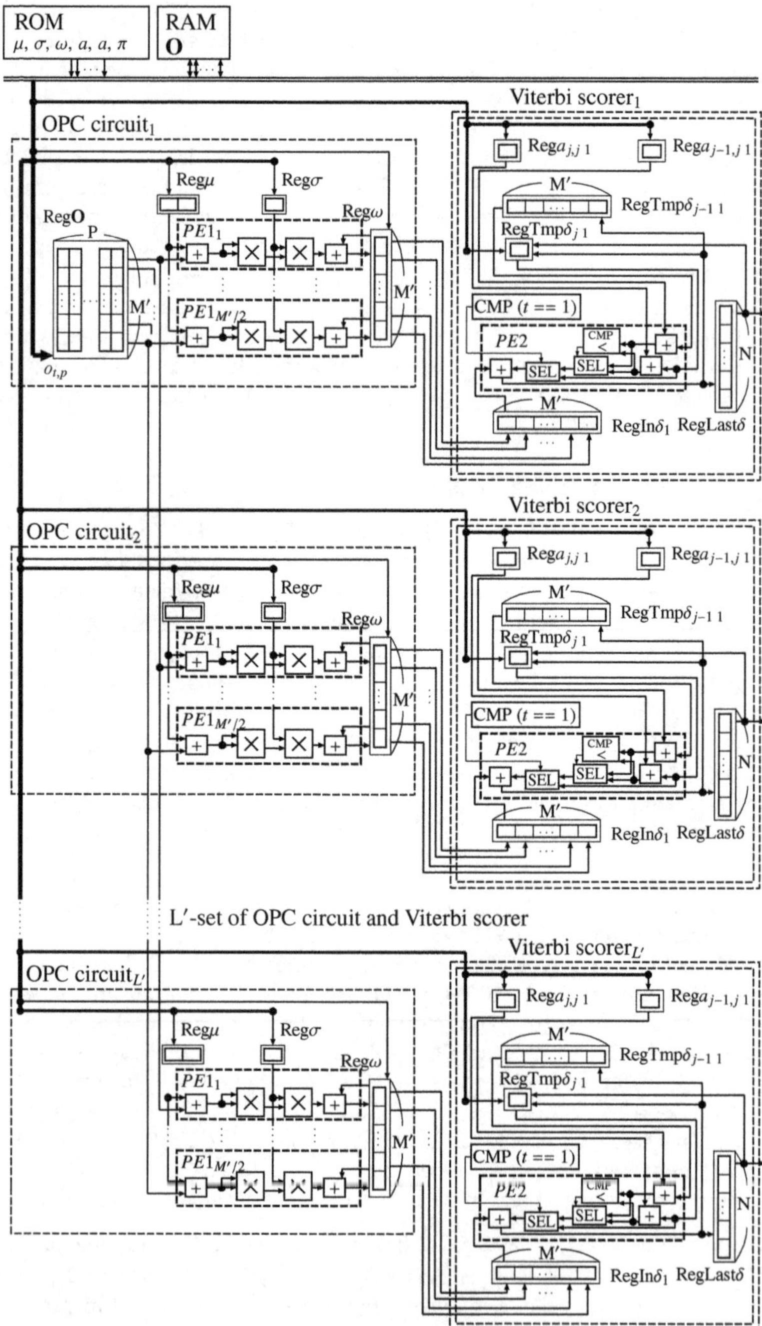

Fig. 7. MultipleStoreBPP architecture for OPCs and LSCs.

using two clock cycles. The HMM parameters are used in the next M'-parallel computation in the OPC circuit.

$L' \cdot M'$ output probabilities are simultaneously obtained every $2 \cdot P$ clock cycles by L' OPC circuits, which are $\log b_j(\mathbf{O}_{t'+1})$, ..., and $\log b_j(\mathbf{O}_{t'+M'})$ of L' HMMs based on Loop A$''$ (Fig. 6). The results are copied from Regω to RegInδ_1 for starting LSCs of L' HMMs and next OPCs for $(j+1)$-th states of L' HMMs $\log b_{j+1}(\mathbf{O}_{t'+1})$, ..., and $\log b_{j+1}(\mathbf{O}_{t'+M'})$ based on Loop B$''$ (Fig. 6). $L' \cdot M' \cdot N$ output probabilities of L' HMMs are obtained by Loop B$''$ with the same M' input feature vectors $\mathbf{O}_{t'+1}$, ..., and $\mathbf{O}_{t'+M'}$.

Each Viterbi scorer, denoted by double-dashed lines in Fig. 7, performs $\lceil M'/(2 \cdot P) \rceil$-stage pipelined LSC, denoted by double-dashed lines in Fig. 3. LSC starts by reading HMM parameters of L' HMMs, $\log \pi_1$ and $\log a_{1,1}$, from ROM and storing them in RegTmp$\delta_{j\,1}$ and RegTmp$a_{j,j\,1}$ based on Loop B$''$ (Fig. 6). Then, in each Viterbi scorer, an intermediate score $\log \delta_1(1)$ is computed by $PE2$ with the HMM parameter and the output probability obtained using Eq. (1). The obtained intermediate score is stored in both RegTmp$\delta_{j\,1}$ and RegTmp$\delta_{j-1\,1}$ (Fig. 7). RegTmp$\delta_{j\,1}$ stores an intermediate score that is needed in the next computation in Loop E$_1$ (Fig. 3). RegTmp$\delta_{j-1\,1}$ stores M' intermediate scores $\log \delta_{t'+1}(j)$, ..., and $\log \delta_{t'+M'}(j)$, which is needed in the next LSC for the $(j+1)$-th state of the HMM in Loop B$''$. After the computation of $\log \delta_1(1)$, $M'-1$ intermediate scores $\log \delta_2(1)$, ..., and $\log \delta_{M'}(1)$ are sequentially computed by $PE2$ on the basis of Eq. (3). In sequential computation, the last obtained intermediate score $\log \delta_{M'}(1)$, is stored in RegTmp$\delta_{j-1\,1}$ and RegLastδ (Fig. 7). RegLastδ stores N intermediate scores that are the last obtained intermediate scores by Loop E$_1$ during Loop B$''$. These intermediate scores are $\log \delta_{t'+M'}(1)$, ..., and $\log \delta_{t'+M'}(N)$ of v-th HMM, which are required when starting LSC with new M' output probabilities $\log b_j(\mathbf{O}_{t'+M'+1})$, ..., and $\log b_j(\mathbf{O}_{t'+2\cdot M'})$ at the first computations in Loop E$_1$, given as $\log \delta_{t'+M'+1}(1)$, ..., and $\log \delta_{t'+M'+1}(N)$. A required intermediate score is read from RegLastδ and is stored in RegTmp$\delta_{j\,1}$ before computation. Reg$a_{j-1,j\,1}$ (Fig. 7) stores an HMM parameter $\log a_{j-1,j}$, which is used for computing $\log \delta_{t'}(j)$ on the basis of Eq. (3) when $2 \leq t'$ and $2 \leq j$.

Our Viterbi scorers, which support MultipleStoreBPP, were presented in Fig. 7 as Viterbi scorer$_i$, where $M' \leq 2 \cdot P$ and $\lceil M'/(2 \cdot P) \rceil = 1$. Our $\lceil M'/(2 \cdot P) \rceil$-stage pipelined Viterbi scorer, which supports $2 \cdot P < M'$ and $1 < \lceil M'/(2 \cdot P) \rceil$, is shown in Fig. 8. The Viterbi scorers shown in Fig. 7 are instances of the generalized $\lceil M'/(2 \cdot P) \rceil$-stage pipelined Viterbi scorer where $\lceil M'/(2 \cdot P) \rceil = 1$. The $\lceil M'/(2 \cdot P) \rceil$-stage pipelined Viterbi scorer consists of a register array RegLastδ and $\lceil M'/(2 \cdot P) \rceil$ sub Viterbi scorers. The i-th stage, i.e., i-th sub Viterbi scorer consists of two register arrays (RegInδ_i and RegTmp$\delta_{j-1\,i}$), three registers (RegTmp$\delta_{j\,i}$, Reg$a_{j,j\,i}$, and Reg$a_{j-1,j\,i}$), and a $PE2$. Each RegInδ_i consists of $i \cdot P$ registers, where $i = 1$, ..., and $\lceil M'/(2 \cdot P) \rceil - 1$. RegIn$\delta_{\lceil M'/(2 \cdot P) \rceil}$ consists of $\lceil M'/(2 \cdot P) \rceil \cdot (M' \bmod (2 \cdot P))$ registers.

In each RegInδ_i, rows are shifted upward every P clock cycles. Each RegTmp$\delta_{j-1\,i}$ consists of P registers, where $i = 1$, ..., and $\lceil M'/(2 \cdot P) \rceil - 1$. RegTmp$\delta_{j-1\,\lceil M'/(2 \cdot P) \rceil}$ consists of $M' \bmod (2 \cdot P)$ registers. HMM parameters in Reg$a_{j,j\,i}$ and Reg$a_{j-1,j\,i}$ are copied every P cycles to Reg$a_{j,j\,i+1}$ and Reg$a_{j-1,j\,i+1}$, respectively, where $i = 1$, ..., $\lceil M'/P \rceil - 1$. The last obtained intermediate score by $PE2$ based on Loop E$_i$ (Fig. 3), where $i = 1$, ..., and $\lceil M'/(2 \cdot P) \rceil - 1$, is stored in RegTmp$\delta_{j-1\,i}$ and RegTmp$\delta_{j\,i+1}$ every P cycles based on $\lceil M'/(2 \cdot P) \rceil$-stage pipelined LSC (Fig. 3). The last obtained intermediate score by $PE2$ based

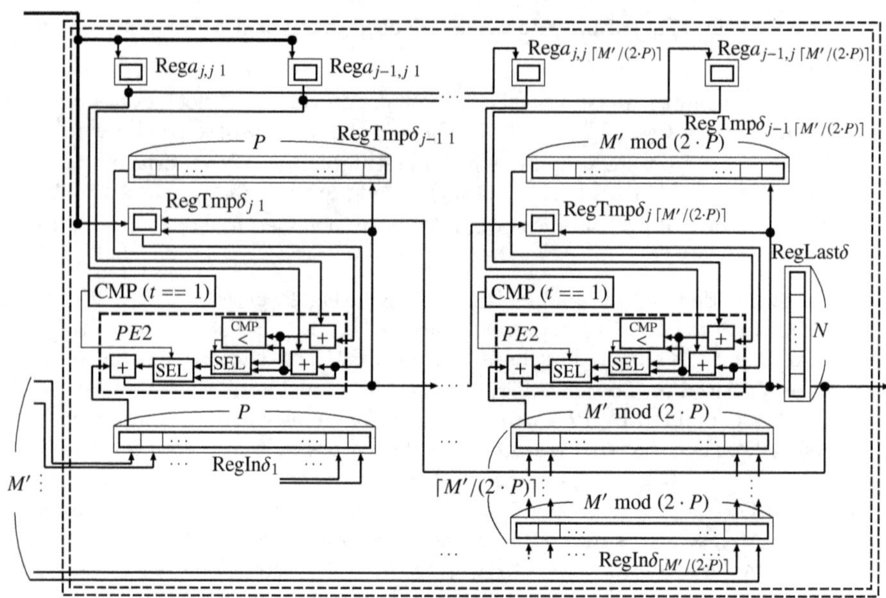

Fig. 8. Pipelined Viterbi scorer for the MultipleStoreBPP architecture (Viterbi scorer$_i$, $i = 1, \ldots, L'$).

on Loop $E_{\lceil M'/(2\cdot P)\rceil}$ (Fig. 3) is stored in RegTmp$\delta_{j-1\,\lceil M'/(2\cdot P)\rceil}$ and RegLastδ every P cycles during Loop B$''$ (Fig. 6). The stored intermediate scores are required when starting LSC with new M' output probabilities for first computation in Loop E_1 (Fig. 3). The required intermediate score is read from RegLastδ and stored in RegTmp$\delta_{j\,1}$ before computations.

5. Evaluation

We compared StreamBPP Yoshizawa et al. (2004; 2006), StoreBPP Nakamura et al. (2010), FastStoreBPP (Figs. 3, 4, and 5), and MultipleStoreBPP (Figs. 6, 7, and 8) VLSI architectures.

Table 1 shows the register size of MultipleStoreBPP, FastStoreBPP, StoreBPP, and StreamBPP architectures, where x_μ, x_σ, x_ω, x_o , x_a, and x_f represent the bit length of μ_{jp}, σ_{jp}, ω_j, o_{tp}, a_{jj}, and the output of $PE1$, respectively. N, P, and M are the number of HMM states, the dimension of the input feature vector, and the number of input feature vectors in a block, respectively. M' and L' are the number of input feature vectors in a block with MultipleStoreBPP and the number of HMMs whose output probabilities are simultaneously computed by Loop A$''$ (Fig. 6) with MultipleStoreBPP, respectively. OPC and Viterbi scorer represent the register size of the OPC circuit and Viterbi scorer, respectively.

Table 2 shows the processing time for computing output probabilities of V HMMs and likelihood scores with MultipletStoreBPP, FastStoreBPP, StoreBPP, and StreamBPP architectures, where L is the number of HMMs whose output probabilities are computed using the same input feature vectors with StoreBPP Nakamura et al. (2010). OPC and the Viterbi scorer represent the number of clock cycles for OPC and additional cycles for LSC, respectively.

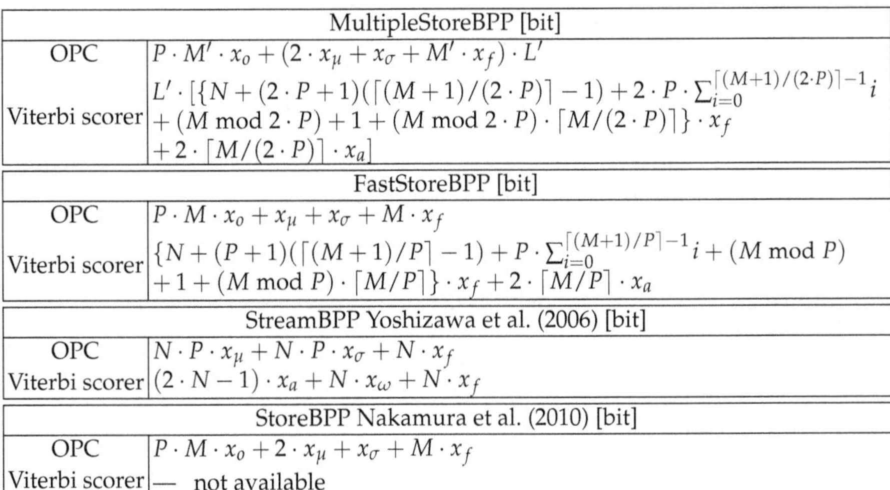

MultipleStoreBPP [bit]	
OPC	$P \cdot M' \cdot x_o + (2 \cdot x_\mu + x_\sigma + M' \cdot x_f) \cdot L'$
Viterbi scorer	$L' \cdot [\{N + (2 \cdot P + 1)(\lceil (M+1)/(2 \cdot P) \rceil - 1) + 2 \cdot P \cdot \sum_{i=0}^{\lceil (M+1)/(2 \cdot P) \rceil - 1} i$ $+ (M \bmod 2 \cdot P) + 1 + (M \bmod 2 \cdot P) \cdot \lceil M/(2 \cdot P) \rceil\} \cdot x_f$ $+ 2 \cdot \lceil M/(2 \cdot P) \rceil \cdot x_a]$
FastStoreBPP [bit]	
OPC	$P \cdot M \cdot x_o + x_\mu + x_\sigma + M \cdot x_f$
Viterbi scorer	$\{N + (P+1)(\lceil (M+1)/P \rceil - 1) + P \cdot \sum_{i=0}^{\lceil (M+1)/P \rceil - 1} i + (M \bmod P)$ $+ 1 + (M \bmod P) \cdot \lceil M/P \rceil\} \cdot x_f + 2 \cdot \lceil M/P \rceil \cdot x_a$
StreamBPP Yoshizawa et al. (2006) [bit]	
OPC	$N \cdot P \cdot x_\mu + N \cdot P \cdot x_\sigma + N \cdot x_f$
Viterbi scorer	$(2 \cdot N - 1) \cdot x_a + N \cdot x_\omega + N \cdot x_f$
StoreBPP Nakamura et al. (2010) [bit]	
OPC	$P \cdot M \cdot x_o + 2 \cdot x_\mu + x_\sigma + M \cdot x_f$
Viterbi scorer	— not available

Table 1. Register size.

MultipleStoreBPP [cycle]	
OPC	$\lceil V/L' \rceil \{\lceil P \cdot M'/L' \rceil + (1 + 2 \cdot P) \cdot N\} \lceil T/M' \rceil$
Viterbi scorer	$\lceil V/L' \rceil \{2 \cdot N \cdot \lceil T/M' \rceil + N\}$
FastStoreBPP [cycle]	
OPC	$V \cdot \{P \cdot \lceil M/2 \rceil + (1 + P) \cdot N\} \lceil T/M \rceil$
Viterbi scorer	$V \cdot \{N \cdot \lceil T/M \rceil + N\}$
StreamBPP Yoshizawa et al. (2006)[cycle]	
OPC	$V \cdot (2 \cdot N \cdot P + N + P \cdot T)$
Viterbi scorer	$V \cdot (3 \cdot N - 1)$
StoreBPP Nakamura et al. (2010) [cycle]	
OPC	$\lceil V/L \rceil \{P \cdot M + (1 + 2 \cdot P) \cdot L \cdot N\} \lceil T/M \rceil$
Viterbi scorer	— not available

Table 2. Processing times.

Table 3 shows the register size, processing time, and the number of *PEs* for computing output probabilities of 800 HMMs and likelihood scores, where it is assumed that $N = 32$, $P = 38$, $T = 86$, $x_\mu = 8$, $x_\sigma = 8$, $x_f = 24$, $x_o = 8$, $x_a = 8$, and $V = 800$. These values are the same as those used in a recent circuit design for isolated word recognition Nakamura et al. (2010); Yoshizawa et al. (2004; 2006). In addition, we assume that $M' = 12$, $L' = 4$ for the MultipleStoreBPP architecture. Futhermore, ratios compared with StreamBPP are shown in Table 3. Compared with the StreamBPP architectures, the MultipleStoreBPP architecture has fewer registers (48% = 10,432/21,752) and requires less processing time (91% = 4,233,600/4,661,600). The number of *PE*2s in MultipleStoreBPP and FastStoreBPP are less than that in StreamBPP.

Figure 9 shows the processing time, and the number of *PE*s in MultipleStoreBPP, FastStoreBPP, and StreamBPP architectures, and the value of M, where $M = M' \cdot L'/2$ for MultipleStoreBPP.

	Reg. size [bit]	Proc. time [cycle]	#PEs	
			PE1	PE2
MultipleStoreBPP $(M', L') = (12, 4)$	10,432 (48%)	4,233,600 (91%)	24 (75%)	4 (13%)
FastStoreBPP $(M = 24)$	9,848 (45%)	5,580,800 (120%)	24 (75%)	1 (3%)
StreamBPP	21,752 (100%)	4,661,600 (100%)	32 (100%)	32 (100%)

Table 3. Evaluation of the MultipleStoreBPP, FastStoreBPP, and StreamBPP performance.

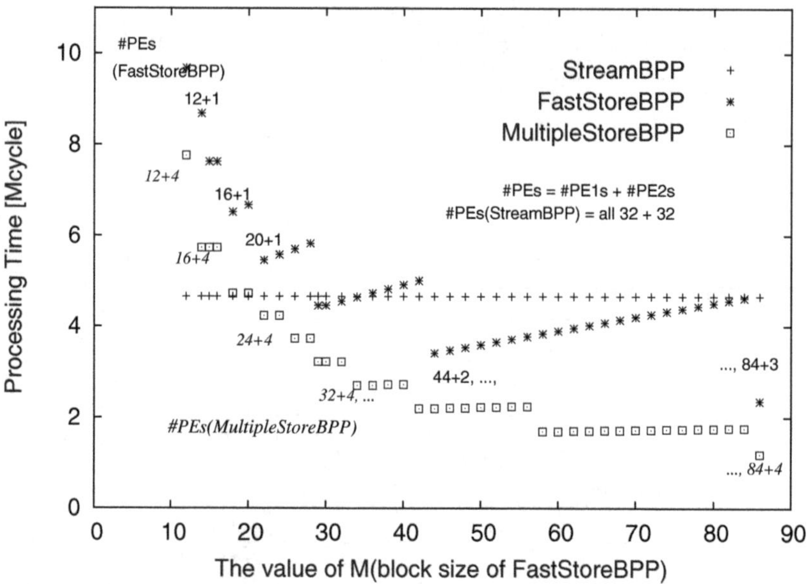

Fig. 9. Processing time, the number of PEs and value of M.

This graph shows that the processing time of MultipleStoreBPP is less than that of FastStoreBPP architecture. It is also less than that of the StreamBPP architecture when M is greater than 22.

Figure 10 shows the register size of MultipleStoreBPP, FastStoreBPP, and StreamBPP architectures as well as the value of M (block size). This graph shows that the register size of MultipleStoreBPP is less than those of FastStoreBPP, and StreamBPP architectures when M is greater than 36 and less than 74.

Table 4 shows the circuit area, clock period, and power dissipation of the OPC and LSC circuits based on the MultipleStoreBPP and FastStoreBPP architectures, which are derived from the report of the Synopsys Design Compiler (Ver. B-2008.09-SP5), where the target technology is the 90nm technology (STARC 90nm) and the report on power dissipation is obtained with report_power command after logic synthesis. In the table, the delay and area represent the

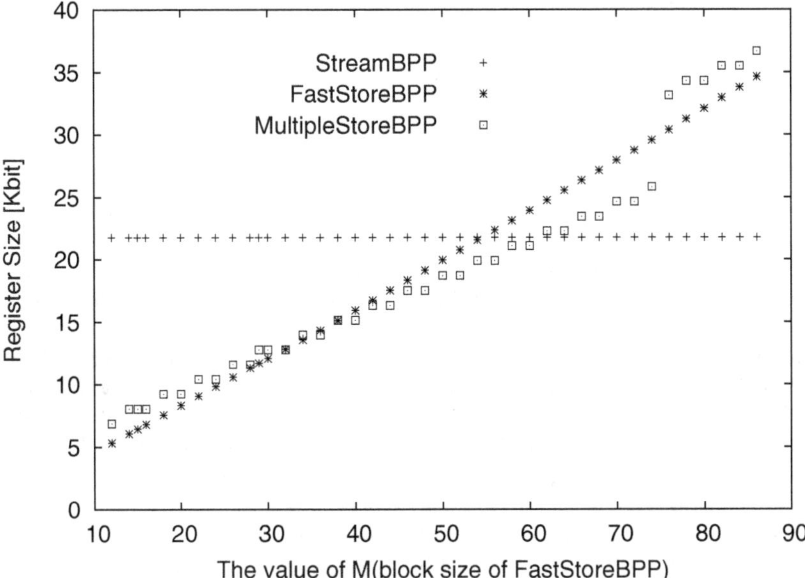

Fig. 10. Register size and the value of M.

Arch.	area [μm^2]	delay [ns]	power [mW]
MultipleStoreBPP ($\#PE1 = 44,\ M' = 22,\ L' = 4$)	1,042,492	2.8	4.5
FastStoreBPP ($\#PE1 = 32,\ M = 32$)	849,955	2.7	3.5
FastStoreBPP ($\#PE1 = 44,\ M = 44$)	1,155,595	2.7	4.8

Table 4. Area, delay and power of OPC and LSC circuits.

minimum clock period and area of the circuit, respectively. Power represents the power dissipation of the circuit whose operating clock frequency is 11 MHz, and for an 800-word real-time isolated word recognition, recognition in 0.2 s is achieved by the MultipleStoreBPP architecture for $T = 86$, a 1-s speech, $V = 800$, $N = 32$, $P = 38$, $M' = 22$ and $L' = 4$. Compared with the FastStoreBPP architecture, the MultipleStoreBPP architecture has lower power and less area, because the MultipleStoreBPP architecture has fewer registers when the number of $PE1$s is 44.

6. Conclusions

We presented MultipleStoreBPP for OPCs and LSCs and presented a new VLSI architecture. MultipleStoreBPP performs parallel-OPCs and pipelined-LSCs for multiple HMMs. Compared with the conventional StoreBPP architecture, the MultipleStoreBPP architecture supports LSC. Furthermore, compared with StreamBPP and FastStoreBPP architectures, the MultipleStoreBPP architecture requires fewer registers and less processing time. In terms of the VLSI architecture the comparison shows the efficiency of the MultipleStoreBPP architecture.

7. Acknowledgements

This work is supported by the VLSI Design and Education Center (VDEC), the University of Tokyo in collaboration with Synopsys, Inc. and the Semiconductor Technology Academic Research Center (STARC).

8. References

B. Mathew; A. Davis & A. Ibrahim. (2003). Perception Coprocessors for Embedded Systems. *Proc. of ESTIMedia*, 109 – 116

B. Mathew; A. Davis & Z. Fang. (2003). A Low-Power Accelerator for the SPHINX 3 Speech Recognition System. *Proc. of Int'l Conf. on Compilers, Architecture and Synthesis for Embedded Systems*, 210 – 219

K. Nakamura; M. Yamamoto; K. Takagi & N. Takagi. (2010). A VLSI Architecture for Output Probability Computations of HMM-Based Recognition Systems with Store-Based Block Parallel Processing, *IEICE TRANS. INF. & SYST.*, Vol. E93-D, No. 2, 300 – 305

S. Yoshizawa; Y. Miyanaga & N. Yoshida. (2002). On a High-Speed HMM VLSI Module with Block Parallel Processing. *IEICE TRANS. Fundamentals*, Vol. J85-A, No. 12, 1440 – 1450

S. Yoshizawa; N. Wada; N. Hayasaka & Y. Miyanaga. (2004). Scalable Architecture for Word HMM-Based Speech Recognition. *Proc. of ISCAS'04*, 417 – 420

S. Yoshizawa; N. Wada; N. Hayakawa & Y. Miyanaga. (2006). Scalable Architecture for Word HMM-based Speech Recognition and VLSI Implementation in Complete System. *IEEE TRANS. ON CIRC. & SYST.*, Vol. 53, No. 1, 70 – 77

Y. Kim & H. Jeong. (2007). A Systolic FPGA Architecture of Two-Level Dynamic Programming for Connected Speech Recognition. *IEICE TRANS. INF. & SYST.*, Vol. E90-D, No. 2, 562 – 568

8

Flexible, Open and Efficient Embedded Multimedia Systems

David de la Fuente, Jesús Barba, Fernando Rincón, Julio Daniel Dondo and Juan Carlos López
School of Computer Engineering Department of Technology and Information Systems
University of Castilla-La Mancha, Ciudad Real
Spain

1. Introduction

Multimedia systems have to deal with the processing of large amount of data in a bounded time window. In order to fulfill the demanded requirements, the critical part of the system functionality has traditionally been implemented using custom hardware. The result is the improvement of both the throughput and the performance of the final system.

The first approaches dealing with hardware-based acceleration were based on the design of custom ASICs (Application Specific Integrated Circuits) or the use of DSPs (Digital Signal Processors). Lately, the emergence of high capacity reconfigurable devices such as FPGAs (Field Programmable Gate Arrays) is encouraging developers to use this technology for the implementation of multimedia embedded systems. Some of the reasons that back up this trend are: short development/prototyping time, the ability to customize hardware, its flexibility, or reconfiguration facilities, just to name a few of them.

Ideally, the development of a multimedia embedded system should be the result of a simple design process, where a set of cores are chained according to a certain execution flow, and later tuned to fit into a certain target platform. To achieve this scenario, a library of platform and vendor independent parameterized components is required. However, nowadays, this is an utopian vision since no standard with such characteristics is available. Each vendor develops their applications and components according to their own needs, without agreeing a common interface nor synchronization mechanisms with other third party actors. As a result, this implies extra difficulties when trying to port working solutions to other platforms. Therefore, a set of standards for developers is necessary in order to assure cross-platforms designs.

Currently, there are some standards for multimedia systems and applications development. However, vendors would rather not assume the cost derived from the adaptation of their products (legacy or new) in order to be compliant with these new norms.

The lack of standardization is the source of ad-hoc solutions whereas the adoption of standards would provide a portable, flexible and reusable answer to the problems that arise in multimedia embedded systems design, and the related applications (i.e. delays in the commercialization of new products, reduced productivity, increment of the development costs, etc.).

In this chapter, a Hw/Sw framework for SoC based embedded multimedia systems is described. In addition to the benefits inherited from the use of the FPGA technology, our solution is also based on the use of OpenMAX standard [1]. This allows building multimedia embedded systems in a reasonable time and, at the same time, being such systems fully reusable and portable.

OpenMAX is an open standard promoted by the Khronos Group [1] which pursuits to reduce the cost and complexity of porting multimedia software to new processors and architectures. Since the OpenMAX standard provides an only software reference implementation, it has been necessary to revisit and redesign all the architectural concepts and protocols of OpenMAX for the heterogeneous embedded systems ecosystem; this means that the proposed framework is intended for hybrid (Hw/Sw) multimedia systems development. Therefore, a flexible and transparent mechanism to manage Hw/Sw interfacing is necessary. Moreover, to cope with the demanded temporal and computational requirements, it is mandatory to keep the overload introduced by the integration infrastructure to a minimum.

The framework described in this work borrows the facilities provided by the Object Oriented Communication Engine (OOCE) [5]. OOCE is an heterogeneous middleware for SoCs. It provides basic and advanced in-chip communication services to transparently handle communication between the software and the hardware parts of an embedded system. In order to meet the performance levels demanded by multimedia systems, in this work we have extended OOCE with new features and some optimizations. The framework also follows a design approach based on MDA (*Model Driver Architecture*, [6]), in order to ease the design workflow (as it is stated in the "MDA manifest" [7]). The main purpose of the framework is then raising the level of abstraction when defining the multimedia system, in order to facilitate the automatization of the design, analysis and verification through the use of executables models.

2. Related works

Multimedia applications have their own requirements that differentiate such applications from other domains. For example: an intensive traffic of data and use of the memory subsystem, a characteristic application model, real time restrictions, etc. These particular features have led the research community to invest a significant amount of effort in projects addressing the specific challenges imposed by the development of multimedia (embedded) systems.

The most widespread solution to improve the throughput relates to to the development of the multimedia platform with hardware acceleration in mind. This solution is mentioned in [8] and [9], which respectively implement the computational cores as coprocessors or heterogeneous reconfigurable engines.

The Cell BroadBand Processor [10], with its characteristic four bus ring, combines a general-purpose Power Architecture core with streamlined coprocessing elements which greatly accelerate multimedia and vector processing applications.

Recently, many-core architectures for graphical applications, such as NVidia GPUs arrays, have gained a great importance mainly due to the availability of CUDA [11], an open software development framework based on a standard widespread language as it is C.

[1] `http://www.khronos.org/`

PeaCE [12] is another alternative to develop Hw/Sw multimedia platforms. PeaCE provides a development flow (from functional simulation to the synthesis process) to multimedia applications with real time constraints.

An important factor of these platforms is how the components in the system communicate. Generally, communication mechanisms are fixed, with a null or limited capability to be customized. Since there are many factors that can affect to the communication performance that should be considered, offering the ability to reorganize the communication channels in run time is essential. This would also be a useful tool for designers that could quickly and easily perform a design space exploration.

For example, Na Ra Yang et al. [13] propose double buffer, open row access and interleaved memory techniques in order to achieve an efficient communication. Another alternative to improve the communication performance is described in [14] which presents a solution based on a time multiplexed memory approach, where the system memory is accessed several times during a single bus cycle. To allow this, the memory and the DMA logic must be operated at a clock frequency which is a multiple of the clock frequency of the microprocessor.

In relationship to the performance analysis of communications in multimedia dedicated platform, in [15] several alternatives for a shared memory data exchange mechanism are compared: point-to-point connection, and based on bus architecture using DMA. In the the final part of the work, they present a performance estimation tool based on a Bus and Synchronization Event Graph (BSE graph) that is used to obtain statistical results.

Concerning the use of MDA techniques for multimedia embedded systems, MARTES (Model-based Approach to Real-Time Embedded Systems development, [16]) is a project whose main goal is the use of UML and SystemC in embedded systems. MARTES has taken some ideas from MDA, particularly, the separation of the application model from the target platform. Ying Wang et al [17] propose an MDA approach combining UML and SystemC in order to promote stepwise semiautomatic conversion from UML specification to executable SystemC code. They intend to build a smooth SoC design flow in which the implementation can be derived directly from the specification.

3. OpenMAX

The OpenMAX standard is an initiative promoted by the Khronos Group that aims to unify the way media components interoperate, in order to reduce the cost and complexity of porting multimedia software to new processors and architectures.

As shown in figure 1, OpenMAX is composed of three layers:

- OpenMAX Application Layer (AL, [2]) provides a standardized interface between an application and the multimedia middleware that provides the services needed to perform an expected API functionality. OpenMAX AL provides application portability with regard to the multimedia interface.
- The OpenMAX Integration Layer (IL, [3]) is an API that provides access to the software components in a system. In this layer, a standardized procedure is defined for the activation, initialization, creation and disposal of components.

  This layer contains three main entities (figure 2):

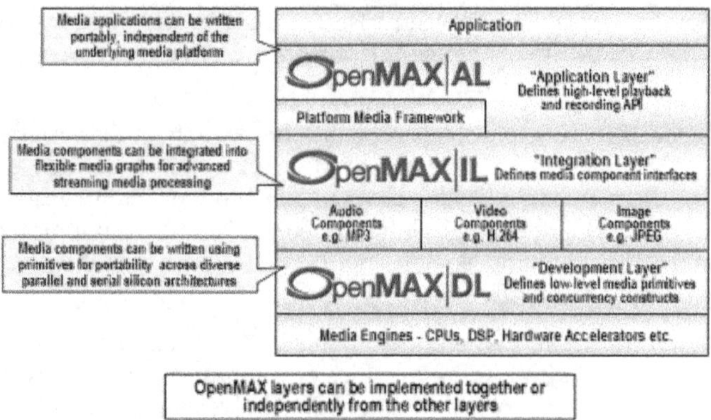

Fig. 1. OpenMAX Portability Library [1]

- The OpenMAX IL Client is the entity that interacts with IL Core. Normally it is a functional piece of a framework or application.
- The OpenMAX IL Core is used for dynamically loading and unloading components and facilitating component communication. Once loaded, the API allows the user to directly communicate with the component, which reduces the system overhead.
- The OpenMAX IL Components (OMX Components) represent individual blocks of functionality. Components can be sources, sinks, codecs, filters, splitters, mixers, or any other data operator.

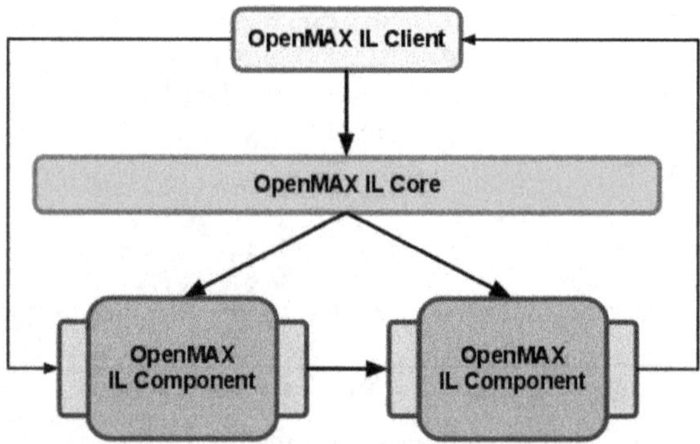

Fig. 2. OpenMAX IL structure

- The OpenMAX Development Layer (DL, [4]) defines a set of low-level multimedia kernels, or media processing building blocks, that might be used to accelerate traditional computational hotspots. The functional scope of the DL API spawns several key domains to mobile multimedia platforms, including the following: signal and image processing, audio coding, image coding, and video coding.

The typical multimedia application topology in OpenMAX depicts a chain of OMX Components that process the data flowing from their inputs to their outputs. OpenMAX offers a standardized component interface for each of the following domains: audio, video and image data.

OMX Components handle data communication through ports. A port is an interface that represents: the connection to other components, the type of streamed data and the *buffers* needed to maintain such connection. In OpenMAX a *buffer* is an entity that holds the information and represents the minimum unit of data that can be exchanged between two OMX Components. One OMX Component sends/receives buffers to/from other OMX Components through output/input ports.

3.1 OpenMAX communication models

Communication between components can take place in three different ways, as it is described in the standard. The designer is free to choose the one best suited to his needs. Therefore, the variety of communication models provided by OpenMAX makes the adaption of applications easier. Briefly, we summarize the three types of communication which are depicted in figure 3:

- *Non-Tunneled*: the communication between components is established through the entity that implements the application control. In figure 3 OMX Components A and B use this scheme.
- *Tunneled*: the communication between components takes place directly. To this end, the standard defines a buffer exchange convention. In figure 3 OMX Components B and C use this scheme.
- *Proprietary*: the communication between components takes place directly but, opposite to the tunneled case, the mechanism is not defined by the standard. In figure 3 OMX Components C and D use this scheme.

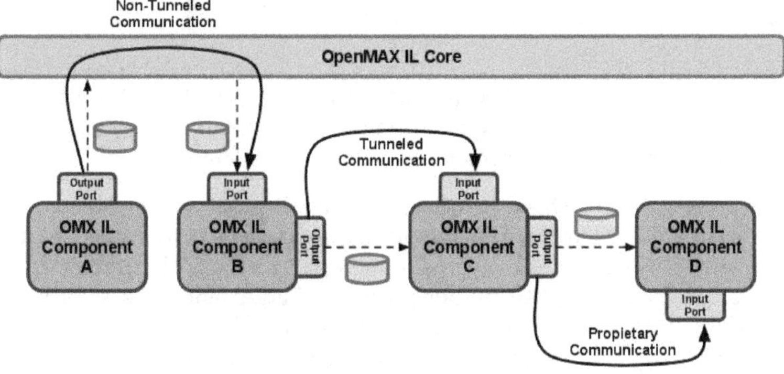

Fig. 3. OpenMAX communication models

3.2 OpenMAX in this project

Lately, the utilization of FPGAs to instantiate components for multimedia system acceleration has grown significantly. Through the use of OpenMAX in embbedded systems, developers can reduce the effort required to design multimedia hardware because: (a) the whole core

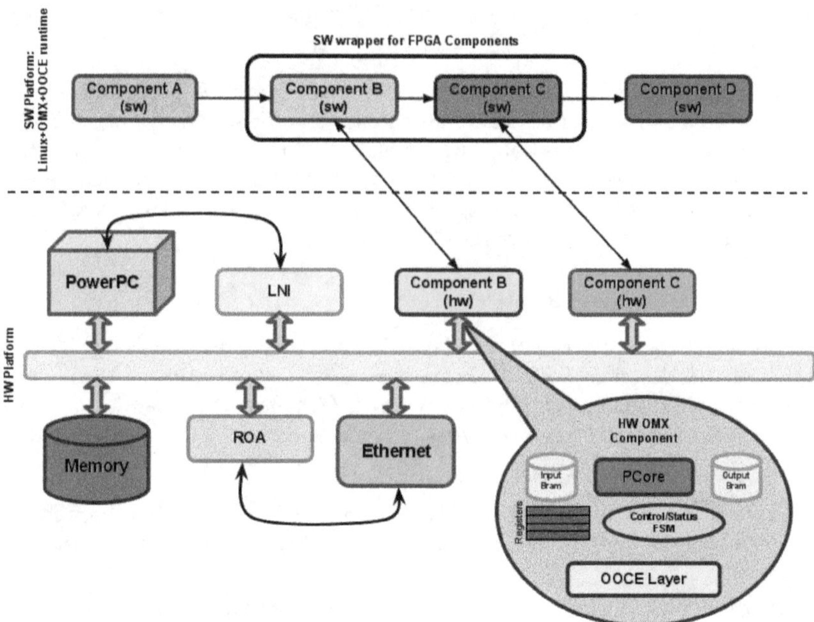

Fig. 4. Example of an implementation of an heterogeneous Hw/Sw multimedia processing chain with Hw OpenMAX Cores

logic can be reused when targeting a new platform (standardized interfaces), (b) it is not necessary to hand write the drivers or code that depends on such components and, (c) communication issues are separated from the processing primitives (same synchronization protocols, standardized communication mechanism, etc.).

However, the standard only specifies the primitives and services which conform the different API layers, always from an only-software point of view. So, the OpenMAX vision has been extended, mainly working at the Integration and Development layers of the standard, to embrace hardware components implementing accelerated multimedia functions.

In Figure 4 a representation of a heterogeneous multimedia processing chain is depicted. Some of the components are implemented, using our approach, as hardware accelerators. In this example, *components B and C* in the chain are mapped to a hardware implementation of an *OpenMAX Core*. Every Hw OMX Component in the FPGA fabric has a software wrapper that implements the *OpenMAX Component class interface* in order to maintain the compatibility with the standard. However, the software wrapper has no responsibility at all in the data transmission process between Hw OMX Components that is actually performed without any software intervention. Synchronization, control and data flow management is performed by the hardware thanks to the *Hardware-to-Hardware Tunneled* invocation semantics provided by the integration infrastructure, which is described in more detail in the next subsection. This has a positive impact in performance since the processor is not mediating in every single data transfer that takes place in the system.

4. Object Oriented Communication Engine

OOCE is a middleware designed to manage the communications in a SoC through message passing. OOCE defines a series of architectural elements that provide a set of basic communication services inspired in the *Distributed Object Paradigm* and the *Remote Method Invocation* (RMI, [18]) semantics. The Distributed Object Model is the basis for an homogeneous communication mechanism, realized through an infrastructure that hides the implementation details from the designer.

In OOCE, every element in the system is an object that can be implemented either in hardware or software. Those objects make use of a set of components and hardware/software artifacts to invoke a functionality from others.

The OOCE infrastructure was designed with these key features in mind:

- Support all communication scenarios that can take place in a SoC. This even includes communication with external objects (outside the chip) through a network interface.
- Provide transparency and a unified view of the communications in the system.
- Facilitate the programmability, making the embedded software development simpler and more productive because of the use of automatic generation tools.
- Be efficient, scalable and fault tolerant, keeping the integration infrastructure overload in minimum levels.
- Be independent from a specific communication protocol or data transport layer.

OOCE is based on the Client/Server communication model with several additions in order to implement RMI semantics. The number and type of the messages exchanged between clients and servers are defined in order to invoke certain functionality in the latter. A message stands for a invocation and embodies: all the necessary information to reach its destiny (header), the parameters and a callback address if necessary (i.e. to deliver the response back to the client). Then, sending a message means to perform one or several transactions over the communication media (e.g., bus writes) with the destination address built from the header information. This communication scheme is common for any communication scenario regardless of the nature (Hw or Sw) of the objects involved. In the case of Hw actors, special adapters to the bus (proxies and skeletons) implementing the FSM which controls this process are generated in an automatic way.

4.1 OOCE workflow

One of the strengths of using OOCE is the capability to design the whole system with a single model (the object model), valid for all the system components regardless their implementation technology. This feature, together with a set of tools that enable the automatic generation of the platform-dependent communication adapters, makes OOCE very practical from the designer's point of view. Hence, each developer must be only focused in what he is really good for (for example, a hardware developer is concerned in writing efficient VHDL code), whilst the responsible of application coding has only to write good algorithms, using any available resource as a regular object.

As it can be seen in figure 5, application experts make homogeneous use of any platform resource in the form of object interfaces. The OOCE middleware provides the developers with the corresponding interface compilers for every technology involved in the system.

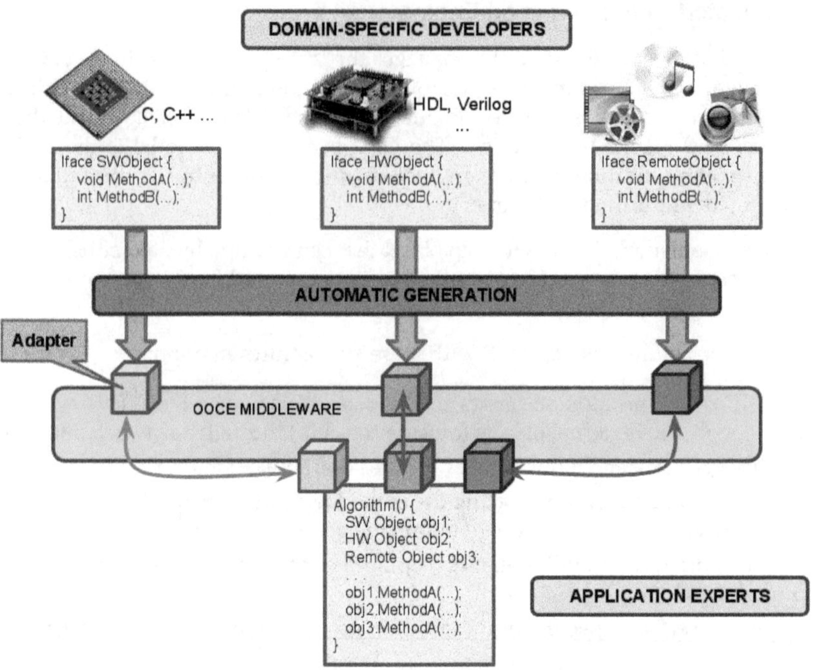

Fig. 5. Separation of roles, unified model and automatic generation in OOCE

Object interfaces are described using an Interface Description Language (IDL). In OOCE the IDL used to this end is Slice (Specification Language of ICE, the Internet Communication Engine, [19]). Once the interfaces have been declared, the interface compiler generates the adapters for each object (proxies and skeletons that are responsible for building/decoding the invocation/response messages). Depending on the nature of the object, the task can be "slice2vhdl" for hardware objects or "slice2<object_language>" for software objects. The generated adapters are optimized to keep the overhead to a minimum. Through this adapters and thanks to OOCE infrastructure each object can communicate in an homogeneous and transparent way with the rest of the object of the system.

As an example of what a hardware object for OOCE actually means, let see figure 6. Here, the entity interface for a hardware module and its skeleton (which connects to the bus) are shown, for example, and interprets the protocol and signals, redirecting the transactions that mean the activation of an operation on the hardware module. If another hardware object needs to execute some functionality from *OBJ A*, a skeleton module will be attached to it (see figure 6 on the right side). The skeleton is the mirror image of *OBJ A*, with the same entity interface. Thus, *OBJ B* will use the point-to-point invocation protocol whereas the actual invocation takes place through the bus. Since both of them are generated in an automatic way from the object interface description, the internal format used to code the messages is completely transparent to the user. Developers should only focus their efforts on implement the functionality of the object respecting its interface.

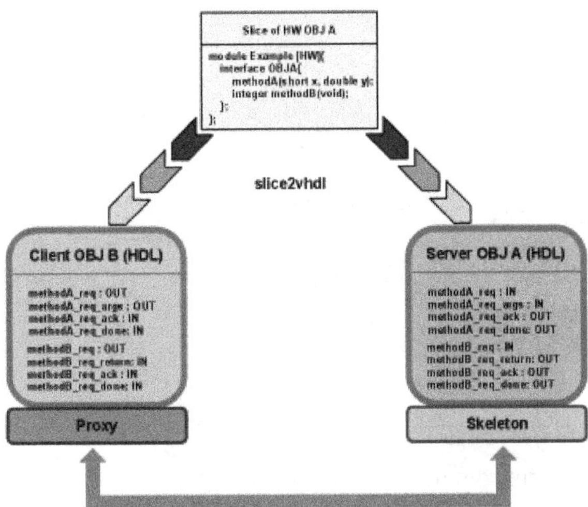

Fig. 6. Automatically Generated Hw Object

4.2 OOCE communication models

As mentioned in the previous subsection, OOCE oversees every transaction between objects in the SoC. The actual methods implemented by the communication systems are characterized by the following features: (a) Hw objects interoperate transparently with the Sw subsystem and conversely; (b) efficient communication mechanisms between any kind of component and; (c) flexibility.

From the whole system point of view, the main advantage is the transparency in the communications between HW/SW objects with a low overhead. In order to achieve this, the system must support three types of communication scenarios: Hw/Hw, Hw/Sw and Sw/Hw. Apart from these three types, OOCE offers the possibility of establishing communication with objects that are outside the chip ("External communication"). Such objects can be regular ICE objects running on a computer or OOCE Hw/Sw objects in a OOCE-compliant SoC.

To establish any communication in the system implies that there must be at least one proxy for each client object that wants to make an invocation, and exactly one skeleton for each server object.

In figure 7 there is an example of a system composed by four OOCE objects: two clients ("Obj4" is a Sw object and "Obj2" is a Hw object) and two servers ("Obj1" in Hw and "Obj3" in Sw). Clients can require the functionality provided either by a Hw or Sw server through their proxies. There is also an external object that is connected with "Obj1" through the Remote Object Adapter (ROA). The three types of communication paths, plus external communication, are represented in the figure.

4.2.1 Hw/Hw communication

This type of communication occurs between two hardware objects that are connected to a common transport architecture. Within the SoC framework we focused on bus interfaces and

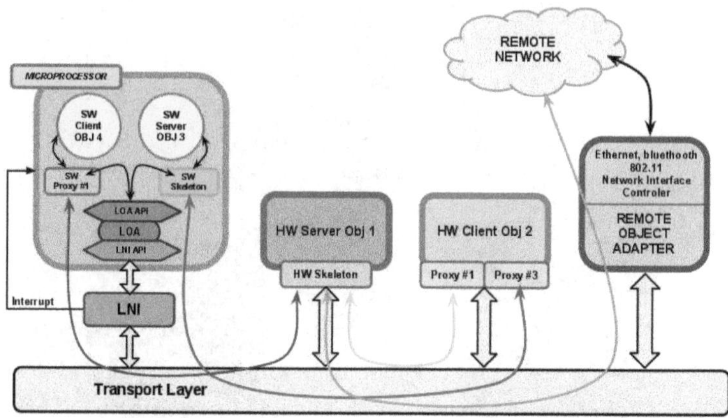

Fig. 7. Example of different communication types in OOCE

hierachies but this approach is flexible and easy to port to other paradigms such as Networks on Chip.

Back to Hw-Hw communication, the elements involved are: (a) A hardware client object, (b) the proxy of the client, (c) a hardware server object and (d) the skeleton of the server. The sequence of generic Hw/Hw invocation steps will be described:

1. The client makes the invocation, activating the corresponding signals of its object interface.
2. The proxy receives the invocation and its parameters and translates them into one or more transactions that are sent through the bus.
3. The skeleton recognizes the address of the transaction, so it reads the data contained in the bus transfer.
4. Finally the skeleton transforms the transaction into an invocation and sends it to the server through the server interface signals.

Figure 7 represents Hw to Hw communication between the client object "Obj2" and the server object "Obj1".

4.2.2 Hw/Sw and Sw/Hw communication

OOCE offers a unique sight of all system objects and a common semantic to their functionality access. In OOCE communication between Hw and Sw objects is done transparently. In order to establish a Hw/Sw communication it is only necessary to incorporate a minimal infrastructure, since the nature of the objects is different, that does not affect the former implementation of the Hw object nor the way the application uses such objects. The elements that have been incorporated to achieve this goal are: the Local Network Interface (LNI) and the Local Object Adapter(LOA).

In this case, the Hw client object invokes through the proxy which generates the corresponding bus transactions. Then, the LNI (which serves as a bridge to the Sw objects that are running in the processor) forwards the traffic whose address is linked to any of the Sw object references.

The LNI has a routing table in which there is information to map physical address (object identifier) to running software processes. The invocation and its parameters are passed to the LOA that finds the proxy/skeleton in charge to process them.

In the figure 7, both types of communication are represented between: (a) the client object "Obj2" and the server object "Obj3" for Hw/Sw communication and (b) the client object "Obj4" and the server object "Obj1" for Sw/Hw communication.

4.2.3 External communication

OOCE allows other entities (typically other OOCE objects in a different SoC or ICE Sw objects) to communicate with internal objects. This service is totally transparent to the internal objects. Again, transparency applied to this scenario means that objects and OOCE associated infrastructure should not change or adapt their behavior to this new scenario. For this reason, OOCE defines a subset of features that are 100% compatible with the ICE commercial middleware. The system data type and encoding rules of OOCE distributed object model are fully compatible with the data coding scheme of ICEP (ICE Protocol). This make it easier, to provide OOCE with the ability to communicate with ICE objects, because it is not necessary to re-encoded the body of the message when it travels from the in chip environment to the external network.

The Remote Object Adapter (ROA) is devoted to adapt the external and internal communication protocol.

4.3 OOCE extension

The need to extend OOCE appears when it is necessary to support the requirements of multimedia systems. Indeed, the first step was to identify the features of the OpenMAX standard that would mean changes or adjustments in the former OOCE architecture. Following, we enumerate the most important ones:

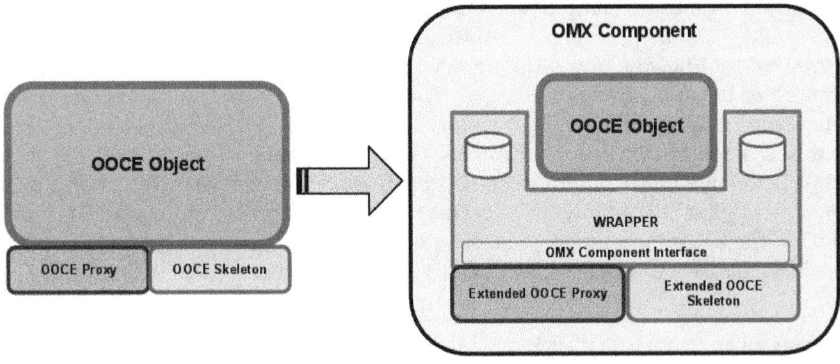

Fig. 8. From object model to component model

- The communication in OOCE (Hw/Hw, Hw/Sw and Sw/Hw) is message oriented, not intended for shared memory communication (data oriented). Therefore, OOCE must allow the components to exchange information through shared memory in a safe way.

- OpenMAX offers three types of communication mechanisms that should be implemented by OOCE, so both proxies and skeletons must be upgraded with new data types and control logic.
- OOCE objects should behave as OMX Components, so it is necessary to provide OOCE objects with a wrapper that implements the part of the OpenMAX Component's functionality that is relevant from a hardware implementation option (e.g., parameter initializaton).
- The logic to manage the communication and the object state must be added.
- The implementation of the OpenMAX methods should not affect the OOCE objects.

In addition, the overhead introduced by the above modifications should be as small as possible.

5. An OMX realization for FPGAs

The solution architecture that we propose is based on FPGA devices (in particular ML507 Virtex-5 Development System). In order to easily port the OpenMAX libraries to this board, an adapted version of a Linux Kernel (Linux-2.6-xlnx.git for XUPV5-LX110T) has been used as the operating system in our prototypes. This allowed us to have the multimedia application implemented entirely in software, as the starting point.

Then, the application components that are candidates for hardware acceleration have to be implemented as Hw OMX Component (described in detail next). At this point is where the extended OOCE comes in, providing the standard compliant Hw/Sw communication mechanism.

So, the bulk of this proposal is the implementation of all communication alternatives between two OMX Components. Communication between two OMX Components that remain implemented in Sw is not treated here since it follows the same principles and mechanism as defined in the standard, and the implementation reference provided by Khronos. So, we concentrate on those scenarios where a Hw version of the OMX Component is present. Every Hw OMX Component needs a software counterpart that interacts with the rest of the OpenMAX middleware and other software components. This is mandatory in order to keep the rest of the application unchanged. Such software wrapper stands for the hardware component and exactly implements the same API required by the standard. The difference is that this is a modified version of the Sw OMX Component, that is, a facade that only redirects to the Hw OMX Component invocations related to the hardware. As an example, the *SetupTunnel* primitive involving two Hw OMX Components is translated by our OMX Component (the software wrapper) into several OOCE invocations to configure the internal registers in the hardware. These registers indicate the base address where data must be written or read.

To illustrate what *transparency* and *easy integration of Hw components* actually mean, let us introduce the listing 1 where an extract of an OpenMAX application example running in a FPGA is represented. The application receives one video frame from the Ethernet interface, it transforms the RGB picture to grey scale, it applies a border detection algorithm and it finally sends the result via Ethernet. The *img_ethreader* and *image_ethsink* components are in charge of the acquisition of the image to be processed by the chain, and the delivery of the result, respectively. These components run in software, whereas the *hw.img_RGB2BW* and *hw.img_sobel* components are implemented in hardware. Nonetheless, there are no distinctions between the use of the hardware components and the software ones since both of them are OMX compatible.

Listing 1. Example of an implementation of an heterogeneous Hw/Sw multimedia processing chain with Hw OpenMAX Cores.

```
int main(int argc, char** argv) {
  /*Getting Components Handler*/
  OMX\_GetHandle(&appPriv->ethreader, ''omx.ext.image.ethreader'', NULL,
                 &readercallbacks);
  OMX\_GetHandle(&appPriv->hwrgb2bw, ''omx.hw.img\_RBG2BW'', NULL,
                 &RGB2BWcallbacks);
  OMX\_GetHandle(&appPriv->hwsobel, ''omx.hw.img\_sobel'', NULL,
                 &hwsobelcallbacks);
  OMX\_GetHandle(&appPriv->ethsink, ''omx.ext.image.ethsink'', NULL,
                 &sinkcallbacks);
  /*Set the size for img Hw OMX Components*/;
  sSize.sWidth.nValue = 640;
  sSize.sHeigth.nValue = 480;
  OMX\_SetConfig(&appPriv->hwrgb2bw, EXT\_OMX\_IndexConfigImgSize,
                 &sSize);
  OMX\_SetConfig(&appPriv->hwsobel, EXT\_OMX\_IndexConfigImgSize,
                 &sSize);
  /*Setting up tunneled communication*/
  OMX\_SetupTunnel(appPriv->hwrgb2bw, 1, appPriv->hwsobel,0);
  /* Change HW OMX Component state */
  OMX\_SendCommand(appPriv->hwrgb2bw, OMX\_CommandStateSet,
                   OMX\_StateIdle, NULL);
  OMX\_SendCommand(appPriv->hwsobel, OMX\_CommandStateSet,
                   OMX\_StateIdle, NULL);
  OMX\_SendCommand(appPriv->hwrgb2bw, OMX\_CommandStateSet,
                   OMX\_StateExecuting, NULL);
  OMX\_SendCommand(appPriv->hwsobel, OMX\_CommandStateSet,
                   OMX\_StateExecuting, NULL);
  ...
  OMX_DeInit();
  return 0;
}
```

Behind the scenes, there is much more to take into account for hardware components. In figure 9, a sequence of messages for a tunneled communication between Hw OMX Components is represented. The diagram shows how the OMX Component, that is used as a wrapper, extends the behavior of standardized messages by adding hardware invocations. For example, when a OMX Component receives the "start execution" by OMX_SendCommand(OMX_CommandStateSet, OMX_StateExecuting) notification, it sends an "active" invocation to Hw OMX Components.

Following in this section, the different communication models will be described, but before this it is important to define: " *What a Hw OMX Component is*".

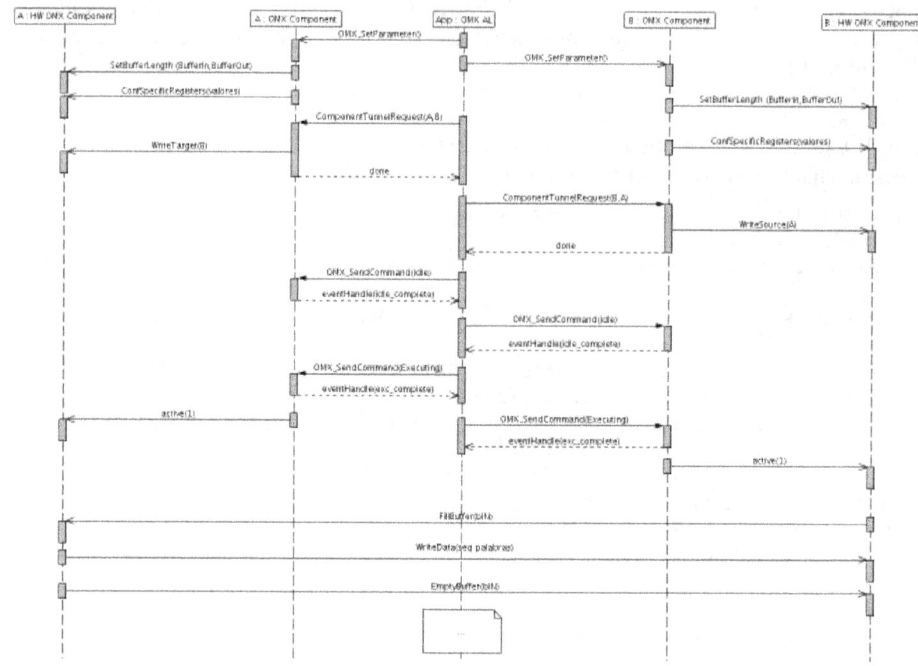

Fig. 9. Init sequence diagram of tunneled communication between two Hw OMX Components

5.1 Hw OMX component

The effort of a multimedia embedded systems developer is too high. The OMX IL hardware adaptation we present in this work helps to reduce this effort enabling the designer to access to standardized procedures, automatic generation, etc.

Since the OMX IL is in the middle of the OMX software stack it bears some of the most important functionalities in OMX (initialization and connection of component as well as resource, communication and synchronization management). Therefore a Hw implementation of the main OMX IL Components will help to raise the throughput of an OMX based multimedia platform.

The Hw OpenMAX Component is the most important component in this layer since it embeds the hardware module that actually implements the multimedia function. That module, the inner one that appears in figure 10, is called *Processing Core* (PCore) and provides hardware acceleration to the corresponding multimedia function in the Development Layer.

As previously mentioned, each Hw OMX Component has an associated software wrapper. This wrapper principally acts as the facade to other OMX framework and application components, with the following goal:

- To act as a bridge for Hw/Sw interfacing operations. This includes, the configuration of the component, or the establishment of the Processing chain, for example. In this case, the standardized OMX Component class would have to be specialized and its methods would

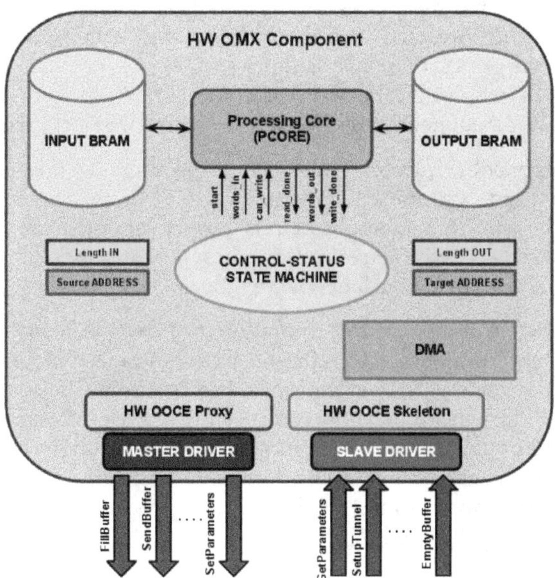

Fig. 10. Hw OMX Component structure

be rewritten to translate software invocations to input/output transactions over the bus through the OOCE middleware.

The OOCE skeleton detects and interprets OOCE messages that encapsulate the invocations addressed to the Hw OMX Component turning them into specific request to the internal units.

The architecture of the Hw OMX Component is thought as the placeholder for the PCore. Getting into details, the PCore has a fixed physical interface to the Hw OMX Component which makes it independent of the bus technology and, therefore, the platform in which it is going to be deployed. Figure 10 shows the structure of a Hw OMX Component mainly dominated by the presence of two local memories, where input and output data are stored. A complete buffer (the minimum data unit to be processed by a Hw OMX Component) must be in the input memory before any other action.

Then, an OMX "EmptyBuffer" operation needs to be received in order to "start" reading the input memory. Another signal, the "can_write" signal, is used to control whether it is possible or not to store data comming from the PCore in the output memory.

The number of data words that PCore has to consume is indicated by "words_in" signal. Once the buffer has been consumed (which means, completely read by the PCore and it activates "read_done" signal) a new one is demanded to the previous component (source_address register stores the address) in the chain ("FillBuffer" OMX operation). Notice that it is not necessary to wait for the Hw OMX Component to finish the processing of one buffer before asking for a new one. This optimization allows to parallelize component's execution with buffer transmission over the on-chip bus.

Once the component finishes the processing of the current buffer and writes the last word in the output memory (PCores activates the "write_done" signal), it transfers the output buffer to the next-in-the-chain component's input memory (addressed by the content of the Target_address register) using a local DMA (Direct Memory Access) engine with a dedicated OOCE proxy. Now, the component is ready again to process the next buffer.

The Hw OMX Component implements two out of the three communication mechanisms described in the standard. Proprietary data exchange is not considered in this work since we believe the best benefit from an application is derived from the use of flexible and open models. As briefly sketched in the above paragraph, synchronization operations are handled separately (by the skeleton) from the data flow (by the internal DMA).

Although the Hw OMX Component can communicate in two different ways, we advocate the use of tunnel communication, which represents a decentralized model, because efficiency is an essential part in dealing with data transmissions in multimedia systems. This model is optimal in hardware since synchronization, control and data flow management are performed without intervention of the software, thanks to the Hardware-to-Hardware invocation semantics provided by the integration infrastructure (OOCE). It is easy to see the tremendous positive impact in performance this method has, since the processor is not mediating in every single data transfer that takes place in the system.

5.2 Hardware-to-Hardware communication model

Hardware-to-Hardware communication is based on the OMX Tunneled communication and is the most efficient communication type available in the standard.

OpenMAX defines a set of methods and primitives that must be observed when a buffer is exchanged between components. The communication meets the producer/consumer pattern and the components involved in the communication exchange "FillBuffer" and "EmptyBuffer" message types.

The goal is to transfer one buffer between two components without the intervention of any other component in the system. The sequence of steps in a Hardware-to-Hardware communication is the following:

1. The input local memory is empty. The component, as a consumer, sends a "FillBuffer" message to the producer component.
2. The consumer waits. The producer writes the buffer in the consumer's input memory and sends a "EmptyBuffer" notification.
3. The consumer receives the "EmptyBuffer" invocation and begins to process the input buffer.
4. As the component processes the buffer, the resulting data are saved in the output memory.
5. When the consumer has read the last word from the buffer (not necessarily processed) it sends a "FillBuffer" notification to the producer again, avoiding unnecessary waiting.
6. When the output buffer is full and the consumer is ready to process The next buffer ("FillBuffer" message, step 1), the local DMA logic transfers the buffer.
7. Finally, the component playing the role of producer sends the "EmptyBuffer" notification.

In figure 11 a Hardware-to-Hardware Tunneled Communication between three Hw OMX Components is represented. The sequence of messages is also described in the picture. The

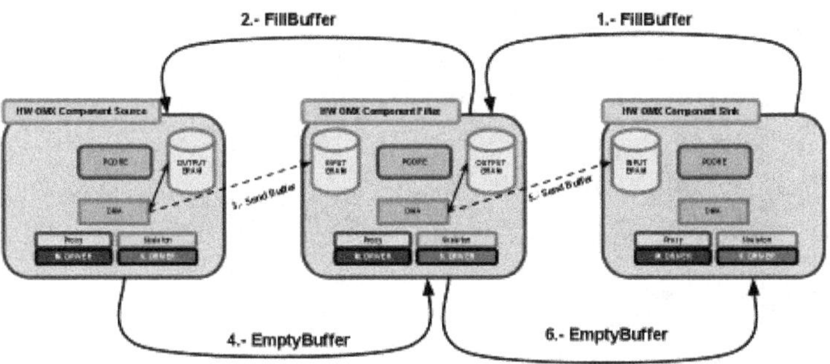

Fig. 11. Sequence of messages in Hw-to-Hw Tunneled Communication

first component in the chain is the *Source Component* which only produces buffers that are fed into the chain (a video streaming producer, ethernet reader or a simple file reader, as examples). The second is a *Filter Component* which plays the role of both a producer and a consumer. The last component in the chain receives the name of *Sink* which only consumes data (typically for storing, transmitting or displaying).

In this kind of systems, in which our work is interested, it is essential to get the maximum performance from the bus because it is the bottleneck in the communication. There is no discussion about the bad suitability of bus-based systems when the application bandwidth exceeds the bus capability. Nonetheless, the scenario we are considering is that where:

- Bus infrastructure is able to absorb the traffic generated by the multimedia application.
- Contention or arbitration issues and unoptimized transfers can result into failure.

Further optimizations have been developed in order to reduce the transmission latency of buffers through the bus and maximize the use of the available bandwidth. With the proposed optimizations, the number of cycles wasted due to punctual bus congestion is reduced, redistributing bus workload using techniques that parallelize and interleave all the transfers between OMX components. This is achieved by means of using the dead times while the component is processing a buffer.

The first optimization (*No Wait Until Fill*) configures the local DMA engine to transfer packets of N-words as soon as they are available in the output memory of the component. In the base configuration (*Wait Until Fill*), the whole output buffer must be in the output memory before the DMA starts transmitting it. The benefit of using this technique is twofold: (1) component's execution and output buffer transfer are overlapped; and (2) several buffer transmissions can take place at the same time (DMA pipelining). The figure 12 represents this optimization, in which the DMA engine sends data when the buffer is being filled without having to wait for its filling.

The second optimization (*multiple buffering*, figure 13) is independent of the DMA transmission configuration chosen. This technique allows to overlap: (1) in consumer mode, the reading of the actual input buffer with the writing of a new input buffer; and (2) in producer mode, the transmission of the actual output buffer with the writing of a new empty output buffer (Wait Until Fill configuration preferred). To this end, the physical address space of one memory is logically divided into N independently managed different regions. Thus, full parallelism is achieved.

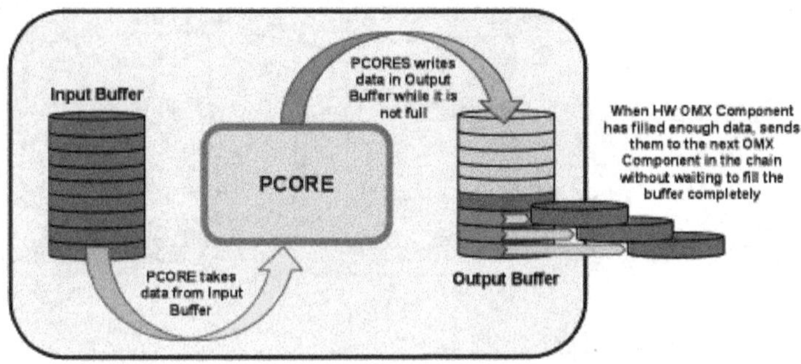

Fig. 12. *No Wait Until Fill* optimization example

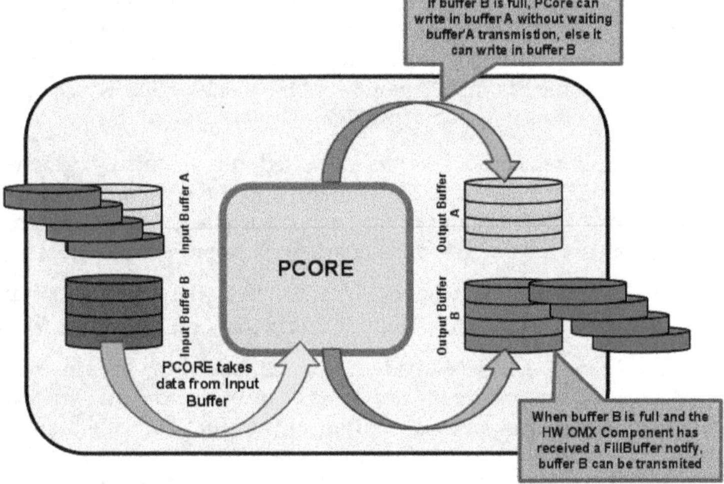

Fig. 13. Multiple Buffering optimization example

Both optimizations are compatible and they can be used simultaneously, but depending on the case their effectiveness might vary.

5.3 Hardware-to-Software communication model

Hardware-to-Software communication is also based in OMX Tunneled communication and it occurs between a Hw OMX Component and a OMX Component (software). This type of communication is not as efficient as Hardware-to-Hardware model, because of the unavoidable presence of software routines, with the associated increase in latency.

A Sw OMX Component reserves an area in memory to store buffers, so the exchanging of buffers takes place between the local memories in Hw OMX Components (Block RAM memory) and the DDR memory in our platform. In this model the DMA engine of a Hw OMX Component writes the buffer content into DDR memory and the synchronization messages are sent/received through the software wrapper used as the facade. It is worth mentioning that, from the Hw OMX Component implementation perspective, there is nothing to change since data transmissions are made through a proxy to memory. Thus, low level details related with the memory technology and the type of connection used are isolated from the the component's logic.

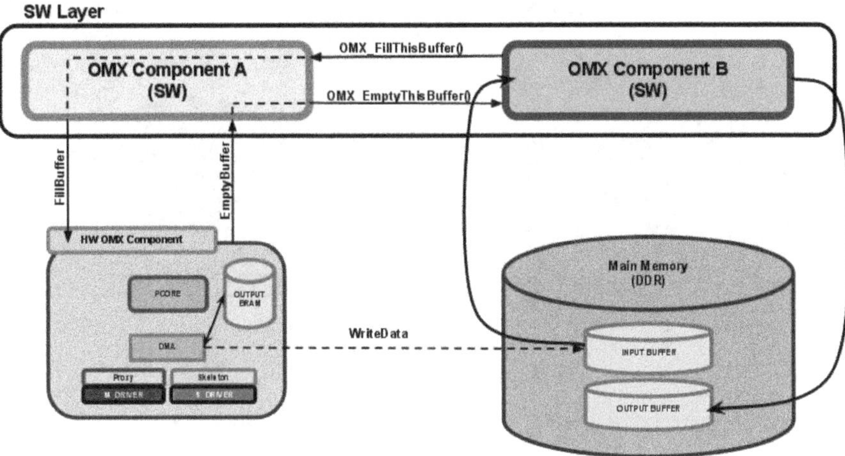

Fig. 14. Hardware-to-Software communication model.

In figure 14, the reader can see an example of Hardware-to-Software Communication model. As shown in the figure, the OMX Component A serves as a wrapper for the Hw OMX Component. This wrapper adapts standard methods into FillBuffer/EmptyBuffer invocations that will be sent or received from/to Hw OMX Component.

5.4 Software-to-Hardware communication model

In this case the Sw OMX Component acts as a producer and the Hw OMX Component as a consumer. The communication is based in the Tunneled OMX protocol too. In order to avoid two main memory accesses (one for writing the output buffer data and another for reading the input buffer data), the output buffer pointer of the Sw OMX Component is mapped to a region in the input local memory of the Hw OMX Component (see figure 15).

This type of communication has a problem in terms of efficiency because in Software-to-Hardware communication data is sent word by word, and burst transactions are not possible, so to use the input buffer of the Hw OMX Component as output buffer of the Sw OMX Component it is essential to get better communication performance.

With regard to the software wrapper for the Hw OMX Component, the implementation of the buffer destination pointer has been slightly changed. The Sw OMX Component still uses a memory reference to *a virtual output buffer* which really forwards memory writes to bus transfers that reach the BRAMs in the Hw OMX Component. This represents an advantage because there is only one copy of the buffer in the system, in contrast to the other models, requiring less memory resources.

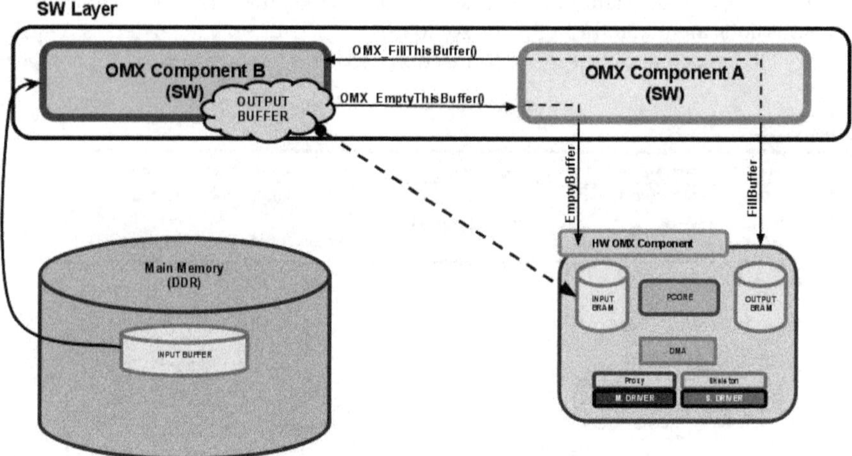

Fig. 15. Software-to-Hardware communication model.

5.5 Multimedia applications modeling for embedded systems using UML

This work aims to model multimedia embedded systems (based on OpenMAX standard) using some of the principles defined in Model Driven Architecture (MDA). For the correct application of MDA, a language that has a precise semantics in the system domain is necessary and it is being developed and is independent of any particular technology. For such a reason, the UML (Unified Modeling Language) has been chosen since it can be specialized or extended for dealing with specific domains or concerns. Moreover, the embedded systems domain needs to accurately express some domain-specific factors as synchronization mechanisms, memory capacity, power consumption or concurrency, for example. Because of this, we adopt MARTE (Modeling and Analysis of Real-Time and Embedded Systems) [20] as the basis to propose a UML profile intended to model embedded multimedia systems: MAME profile (Multimedia Application Modeling for Embedded systems).

MAME integrates OpenMAX in its semantics through the modeling of the main concepts. MAME profile is divided into two sub-profiles:

- *A hardware platform profile* to capture application-independent configuration of the SoC used to deploy the multimedia system. In our case, several prototyping boards from Xilinx have been modeled. This model feeds a set of scripts that generate automatically the infrastructure that enables the system implementation on a specific platform.
- *An OpenMAX profile* for modeling the multimedia applications based on our proposal for a OMX hardware realization. The definition drives the specification of the application through three different levels of abstraction.
    1. GAM Level (General Application Modeling) offers a general view of the whole application (see figure 16). This level reflects the different components that make up the application and concepts related to system architecture as: number of components, media data types, interconnection network, bitrate of the components, etc.
    2. IAM Level (Intermediate Application Modeling) provides a greater level of detail. In this level, the OMX Components are classified into hardware or software,

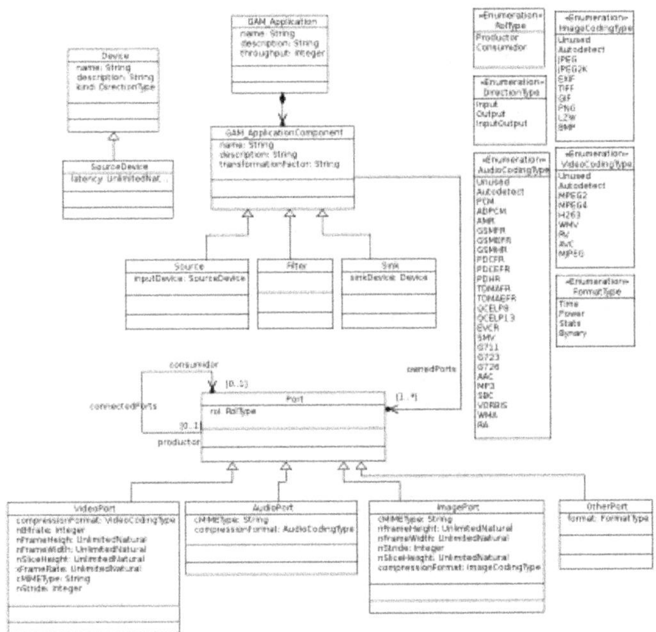

Fig. 16. GAM profile.

characterizing each one differently (see figure 17). The buffer concept is introduced together with the roles of each component.

3. CAM Level (Communication Application Modeling) incorporates the rest of the application attributes that have not been taken into account by the GAM and IAM profiles. It focuses on modeling the communication between the application components (see figure 18). The model supports the different scenarios of communication and optimizations described in previous sections.

5.5.1 Performance analysis of the application

As the result of the application of MDA techniques over both the platform and application models (figure 19), a Platform Specific Model(PSM) is obtained in order to be used to generate:

- An EDK-project with the instances of the necessary Hw OMX components.
- SystemC [21] simulation models that conforms an executable platform that allows testing the performance of the system.

There are two different types of analysis that can be done thanks to the SystemC models and MAME profiles above mentioned:

- Static. System bottlenecks can be detected or predicted through simple evaluations of the attribute values of the entities in the UML models using MAME. The goal is not to have accurate estimations but spot as soon as possible critical parts in the system architecture: memory bandwidth requirements, processing capacity, theoretical throughput, etc.

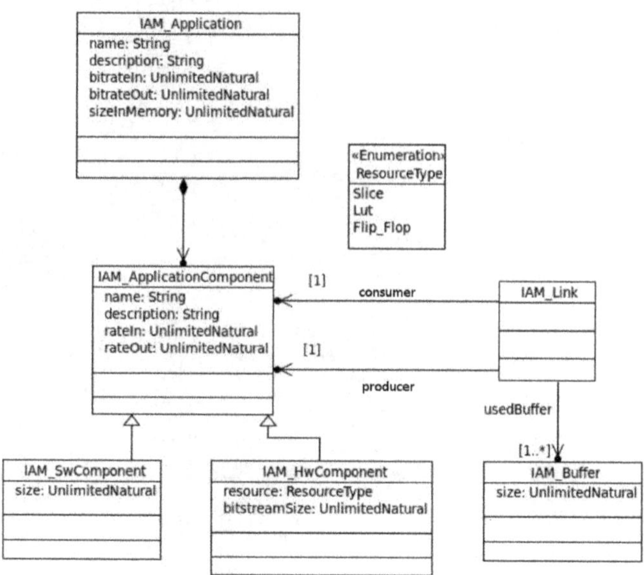

Fig. 17. IAM profile.

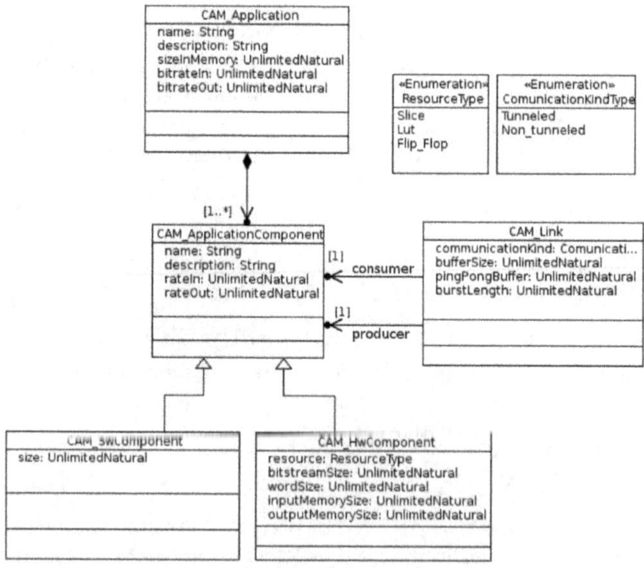

Fig. 18. CAM profile.

- Dynamic. Running the SystemC behavioral models, the developer gets more accurate timed information about the execution of the application. This simulation model allows the user to simulate the behavior of the entire system, offering a flexible mean to play with some component or system configuration parameters (i.e. size of the buffers) and quickly obtain data to:
  - Measure the impact of the application of optimization techniques.
  - Help the designer to explore the design space more efficiently in order to get the maximum performance.
  - Know the average time spent by each component processing or transmitting data and waiting for the bus.
  - Avoid configurations that would lead to bus congestion.
  - Maximize the use of the communication infrastructure and at the same time minimizing the dead times components would be wasting, waiting to be granted by the bus.

  After this analysis, the designer can make the appropriate changes and checks the results running the simulation again.

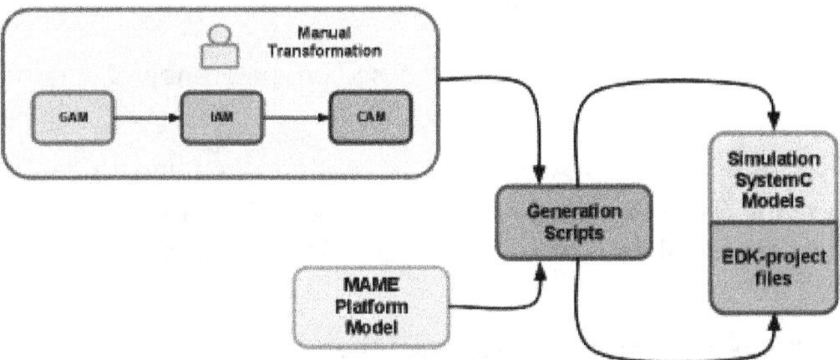

Fig. 19. Automatic generation from MDA application.

6. Experimental results

In order to provide the reader with a glimpse of the benefits and efficiency of the proposed approach, two experiments are dissected in this section. Particularly, we have focused in the analysis of the behaviour "No Wait Until Full" and "Multiple buffering" techniques and how they help to increase the system performance.

For all the experiments, there is a base configuration that comprises:

- 100Mhz clock system.
- 64 bits PLB bus SystemC model provided by GreenSoCs [22].
- 1Kword of local memories for all components.
- A 1Mword input file. The simulations consist in feeding the processing chain (variable components) with synthetic data comming from a file.

For different configurations of the processing chain and parameter values, several simulations have been carried out. It is worth mentioning that in this case we used PLB, but it is almost straightforward to perform new estimations over other platforms just changing the TLM model for the bus.

The first picture (figure 20) attempts to illustrate the benefits obtained by applying the "No Wait Until Full" optimization mechanism (described in section 5.2). As it is expected, the occupancy of the bus increases with the number of components in the processing chain. What is remarkable is how our proposal scales in a linear pattern. The measured transmission times are reduced in 20% (mean value) for the six cases when compared with the "Wait Until Full" strategy.

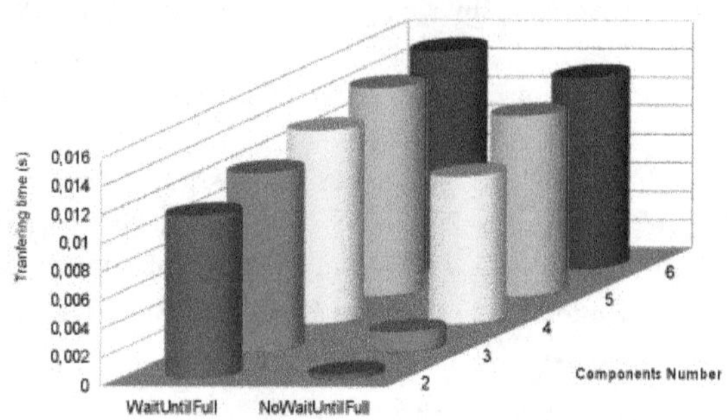

Fig. 20. Comparative chart of transferring time based on the number of components and "No Wait Until Full" optimization.

The second picture (figure 21) represents how the size of the buffer has an influence on the total transmission time. The benefits of the "Multiple buffering" technique are exposed in this experiments and its applicability is delimited, identifying such scenarios where its application makes sense.

Since the size of the local memories is 1Kword, the number of buffers that can be held in it varies (for example, two buffers for a 512 words buffer-size configuration). In this chart, we can see what is the best value for a certain buffer size configuration. To increase the number of buffers means that the control logic also increases, so it is necessary to estimate the cost/performance relation.

From the picture, two lesson can be learnt: (a) in systems with a low overhead regarding the bus bandwidth requirements, the bigger the size of the buffer the better the performance of

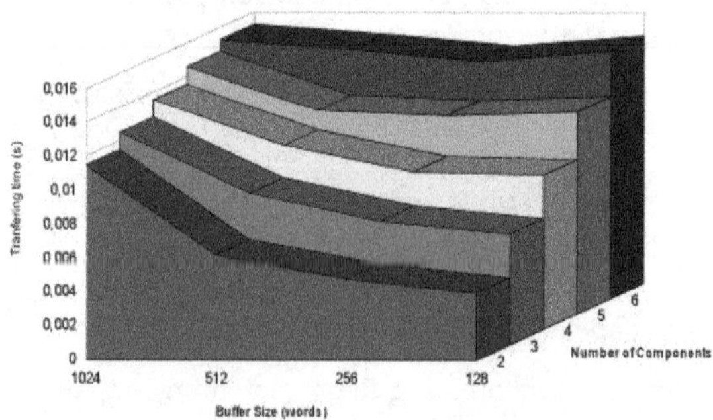

Fig. 21. Comparative chart of transferring time based on the number of components and "Multiple buffering" technique.

the system; whereas (b) in the opposite situation it is better to reduce the size of the buffer since several buffers transmissions can be interleaved, reducing the wait times.

7. Acknowledgment

This research was supported by the Spanish Ministry of Science and Innovation under the project DAMA (TEC2008-06553/TEC), and by the Spanish Ministry of Industry and the Centre for the Development of Industrial Technology under the project ENERGOS (CEN-20091048).

8. References

[1] The Khronos Group.http://www.khronos.org/openmax/

[2] OpenMAX Application Layer Application Programming Interface Specification. Version 1.0. 2007. The Khronos Group Inc.

[3] OpenMAX Integration Layer Application Programming Interface Specification. Version 1.1.1. 2007. The Khronos Group Inc.

[4] OpenMAX Development Layer API Specification. Version 1.0.2. 2005-07. The Khronos Group Inc.

[5] J. Barba, F. Rincon, F. Moya, J.D. Dondo, F.J. Villanueva, D. Villa and J.C. Lopez, *"OOCE: Object-Oriented Communication Engine for SoC Design"* DSD - Euromicro Conference on Digital System Design. Lubeck (Germany), 2007.

[6] Anneke Kleppe, Jos Warmer and Wim Bast. *"MDA. Explained The Model Driven Architecture: Practise and Promise"*. Addison Wesley, 2003

[7] G.Booch et al. An mda manifest. In D. and J. Parodi, editors, The MDA Journal: *"Model Driven Architecture Straight from the Masters"*, pages 133-143. Meghan-Kiffer Press, 2004.

[8] Martijn J. Rutten, Jos T.J. van Eijndhoven, Evert-Jan D.Pol, Egbert G.T. Jaspers, Pieter Van der Wolf, Om Prakash Gangwal and Adwin Timmer. *"Eclipse: A Heterogeneous Multiprocessor Architercture For Flexible Processing"*. Philips Research Laboratories, 2002.

[9] Paul Brelet, Arnaud Grasset, Philippe Bonnot, Frank Ieromnimon and Dimitrios Kritharidis. *"System Level Design for Embedded Reconfigurable Systems using MORPHEUS platform"*. IEEE Annual Symposium on VLSI, 2010.

[10] Kahle J. A., Day M.N., Hofstee H. P., Johns C. R., Maeurer T. R. and Shippy D. *"Introduction to the Cell Multiprocessor"*. IBM Journal of Research and Development. 2005.

[11] Buck, Ian. *"GPU computing with NVIDIA CUDA"*. ACM SIGGRAPH'07. 2007. San Diego (California).

[12] Soonhoi Ha, Sungchan Kim, Youngming Yi, Seongnam Kwon and Young-pyo Joo.*"PeaCE: A Hardware-Software Codesign Environment for Multimedia Embedded Systems"*. ACM Transactions on Design Automation of Electronic Systems, August 2007.

[13] Na Ra Yang, Gilsang Yoon, Jeonghwan Lee, Intae Hwang, Cheol Hong Kim, Sung Woo Chung, Jong Myon Kim, *"Improving the System-on-a-Chip Performance for Mobile Systems by Using Efficient Bus Interface"*. WRI International Conference on Communications and Mobile Computing, 2009.

[14] C. Brunelli, F. Garzia, C. Giliberto, and J. Nurmi, *"A dedicated DMA logic addressing a time multiplexed memory to reduce the effects of the system bus bottleneck"*, in Proc. Field Programmable Logic and Applications'08, 2008.

[15] Lahiri, Kanishka and Raghunathan, Anand and Dey Sujit, *"Fast performance analysis of bus-based system-on-chip communication architectures"*. Proceedings of the 1999 IEEE/ACM international conference on Computer-aided design (ICCAD '99)

[16] Model-Based Approach for Real-Time Embedded Systems development project (MARTES), 2007. http://www.martes-itea.org/
[17] Ying Wang, Xue-Gong Zhou, Bo Zhou, Liang Lianga and Cheng-Lian Peng. *A MDA based SoC Modeling Approach using UML and SystemC*. Computer and Information Technology, CIT '06, 2006.
[18] Remote Method Invocation Home. http://www.oracle.com/
[19] The Internet Communications Engine. http://www.zeroc.com/ice.html
[20] The UML profile for MARTE: Modeling and Analysis of Real-Time and Embedded Systems http://www.omgmarte.org/
[21] Open SystemC Initiative (OSCI). http://www.systemc.org/
[22] The GreenSoCs website. http://www.greensocs.com/

9

Design and Applications of Embedded Systems for Speech Processing

Jhing-Fa Wang[1], Po-Chun Lin[2] and Bo-Wei Chen[1]
[1]*National Cheng Kung University*
[2]*Tung Fang Design University*
Taiwan

1. Introduction

This chapter focuses on speech processing techniques, which involve speech feature extraction, sound localization, speaker identification/verification, and interactive retrieval of spoken documents. Several hardware design issues are discussed in each section. Speech processing applications frequently involve extensive mathematical computation, making resource and power consumption management important. Therefore, this chapter presents not only algorithms but also their corresponding improved solutions to embedded systems, such as fixed-point arithmetic design, field-programmable gate array (FPGA) verification, ARM-based system-on-a-programmable-chip (SoPC) architecture, and other single-chip designs.

The rest of this chapter is organized as follows. Section 2 introduces the feature extraction method that is used in speech processing. Section 3 then describes details of the sound localization technique. Next, Sections 4 and 5 elucidate speaker identification/verification and interactive retrieval of spoken documents. Conclusions are finally drawn in Section 6, along with recommendations for future research.

2. Embedded system design for speech feature extraction

Speech feature extraction is critical in speech processing applications. This section describes in detail frequently used speech features and the design of chips for extracting them. The computational complexity and memory requirement of the associated algorithms are also analyzed in detail to ensure favorable performance. Furthermore, a hybrid approach for fixed-point arithmetic and hardware design is developed to ensure low computational complexity. Finally, a single FPGA development board is considered as a case study to realize the design.

2.1 Methodology

2.1.1 Algorithm for calculating mel-frequency cepstral coefficients

The complete step-by-step process for calculating coefficients is described as follows (Vergin et al., 1996; Wang et al., 2003).

Step 1. Short-time fast Fourier transform (FFT)

$$\begin{cases} Y(m) = \frac{1}{F}\sum_{n=0}^{F-1} z(n)w(n)W_F^{nm} \\ w(n) = \beta(0.5 - 0.5\cos\frac{2\pi n}{F-1}) \end{cases} \tag{1}$$

Step 2. Find the energy spectrum, $X(m) = |Y(m)|^2$.

Step 3. Calculate the energy in each channel:

$$\begin{cases} S[k] = \sum_{j=0}^{F/2-1} W_k(j)X(j) \\ \sum_{j=0}^{F/2-1} W_k(j) = 1 \end{cases} \tag{2}$$

Step 4. Take the logarithm and perform the cosine transform to obtain the Mel-frequency cepstral coefficients (MFCCs),

$$C[n] = \sum_{k=0}^{M-1} \log(S[k])\cos[n(k+0.5)\frac{\pi}{M}] \tag{3}$$

2.1.2 Improved algorithm for calculating mel-frequency cepstral coefficients

Generally, the required computational power and ROM in each frame can be determined clearly according to Table 1 (Wang et al., 2000; Wang et al., 2003). As shown in the table, the total required computational power is quite high due to the redundant operations and memory that stores the required constants. Accordingly, some modifications must be made to reduce the computational load.

The weighted energy spectrum in the Mel-window, $E_{k+1}(j)$, can be obtained by subtracting the weighted energy spectrum $E_k(j)$ from energy spectrum $X(j)$. All of the multiplications in (4) can be replaced by subtraction operations. Therefore, the memory required to store the weight constants for (4) becomes redundant and can be eliminated.

$$E_{k+1}(j) = X(j)\frac{d-(L+D)}{(L+2D)-(L+D)} \tag{4}$$

Additionally, applying the symmetric property of the cosine function to (3) flattens all of the operations and enables related items to be combined in a new formula, given below.

$$C[n] = \sum_{k=0}^{M/2-1} \{log(S[k]) + (-1)^n log(S[M-k-1])\}cos[n(k+0.5)\frac{\pi}{M}] \tag{5}$$

Therefore, the computational complexity of $C[n]$ operations can be re-estimated, and the result is given in Table 2 (Wang et al., 2000; Wang et al., 2003).

	Number of operations and required memory		K=256, M=20, L=12		
	Computational power		Actual computational power		
	C[n]	S[k]	C[n]	S[k]	Total
Addition/subtraction	L(M-1)	M(F/2-1)	12x19=228	20x127=2540	2768
Multiplication	LM	MF/2	12x20=240	20x128=2560	2800
Logarithm	M	0	20	0	20
ROM size (words)	LM	MF/2	12x20=240	20x128=2560	2800

Table 1. Number of operations and the required memory estimated using the original MFCC algorithm.

	Improvement of C[n] calculation		Total improvement			
Operation	Computational power	Improvements (%)	C[n]	S[k]	Total	Improvement (%)
Addition/ subtraction	L(M/2+M/2-1)	0	12x19=228	113	341	87.6
Multiplication	LM/2	50	12x10=120	128	248	91.1
Logarithm	M	0	20	0	20	0
ROM size (words)	LM/2	50	12x10=120	128	228	91.8

Table 2. Improvement of C[n] calculation by rescheduling the original MFCC algorithm and the total improvement provided by the proposed method

The modified procedure in the MFCC algorithm is based mainly on the improved $S[k]$ calculation, as discussed below and shown in Fig. 1 (Wang et al., 2000). Every Mel-window is divided into two blocks with equal bandwidth on the Mel-scale. Because the Mel-windows overlap each other, every block except for the first and last belongs to two Mel-windows.

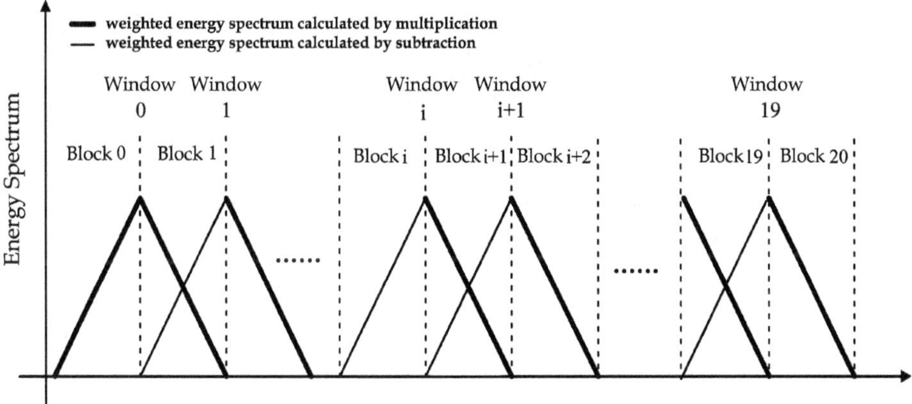

Fig. 1. Modified procedure for calculating $S[k]$.

2.2 Hardware implementation

2.2.1 Fixed-point arithmetic design

The word recognition system is based on the hidden Markov model (HMM). To achieve area-efficiency, MFCC chips are designed using fixed-point arithmetic. The procedure for implementing the fixed-point program is as follows.

Step 1. Partition the algorithm into n modules; this involves calculations of the energy spectrum, channel energy, and MFCCs.
Step 2. Determine the lower bound and upper bound on each module.

The format of fixed-point variables is determined based on the dynamic range of the input variables in the first module. Once this module has been analyzed, the output is fed into the next module and analysis continued until all modules fit the fixed-point data format, as presented in Table 3 (Wang et al., 2003).

	Maximum	Minimum	Abs. minimum	Fixed-point format
Energy spectrum	3121190.0012	0.000311	0.000311	24.8
Energy in each channel	2172253.6092	0.124351	0.124351	24.8
MFCC	214.006766	-75.082199	1.567230	9.7
Logarithm value	5.336967	-0.905350	0.905350	5.11

Table 3. Analysis of dynamic range and determined fixed-point data format.

Step 3. Error measurement for each module

This step evaluates the quantization error by comparing their outputs with the output of the corresponding floating-point routines as shown in Table 4 (Wang et al., 2003).

	Energy spectrum (%)	Energy in each channel (%)	MFCC (%)
Word with vowel phonemes	0.020563623	0.022464977	0.474503142
Word with nasal phonemes	0.028652758	0.035190628	0.481810443
Word with fricative phonemes	0.031959564	0.039397264	0.698307547
Word with stop phonemes	0.052471004	0.057502398	0.454653425
Word with affricate phonemes	0.041492785	0.05067771	0.454107475

Table 4. Average error with the determined fixed-point data format.

Step 4. Performance measurement

The impact of the recognition rate of the fixed-point MFCC algorithm is evaluated at this stage, as shown in Table 5 (Wang et al., 2003).

	User 1(%)	User 2(%)	User 3(%)	User 4(%)	User 5(%)	Average (%)
Floating-point	92.0	90.0	93.0	91.0	93.0	91.8
Fixed-point	91.0	88.0	91.0	88.0	90.0	89.6

Table 5. Comparison of recognition rates achieved using floating-point and fixed-point structure.

2.2.2 Circuit design

The use of improved partitioned look-up tables is another commonly used method to perform such elementary functions as logarithm, square root, and trigonometric functions, for example. Figure 2(a) shows the proposed four-stage pipeline architecture.

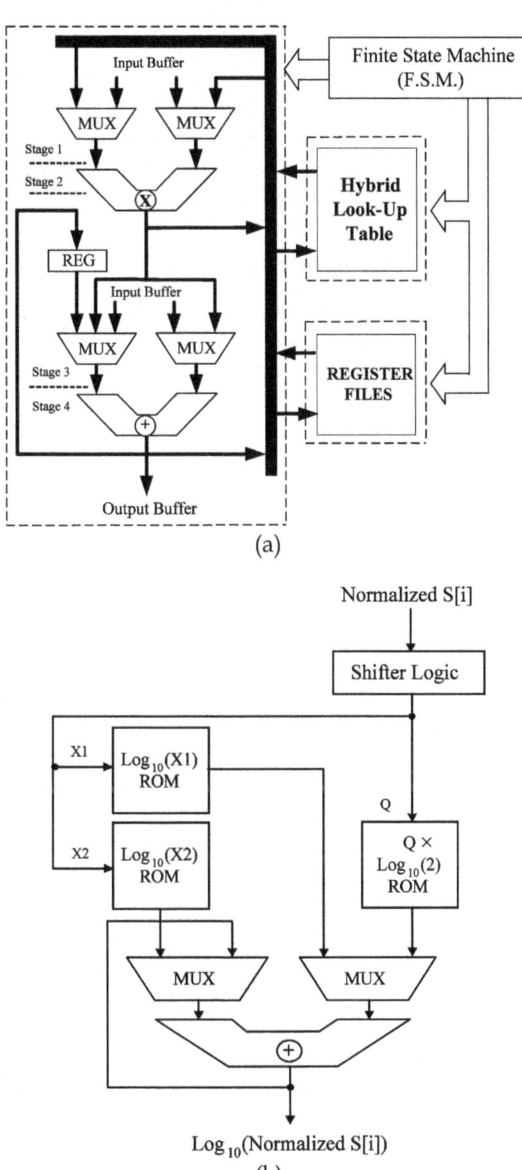

Fig. 2. Circuit design of an embedded system. (a) Architecture of the proposed MFCC chip. (b) Architecture of the look-up table (Wang et al., 2003).

Based on such architecture, only one processing unit is used and all data are processed in pipeline fashion. Figure 2(b) displays the architecture of the improved partitioned table. The shifter logic is used to find the Q value of the minimum left shift and to output the least significant 16 bits, which are the addresses of the two subtables. Only one two-stage pipelined multiplier and adder, which is shared by both the main data path and the look-up table, is used.

At the verification stage, an FPGA board is utilized to implement the MFCC system prototype. First, synthesizable Verilog-HDL descriptions are coded. Synopsys FPGA Express (www.synopsys.com) generates the corresponding netlist files. The Xilinx Flow-Engine completes generating placement, routing, and bit-stream files. The design is implemented successfully in the XC4062XL FPGA chip.

3. Embedded system design for sound localization

This section introduces a sound localization system, which exploits the average magnitude difference function (AMDF), for finding the directions of environmental signal sources. To verify the accuracy of the algorithm, the entire system is implemented on a single FPGA development board using the Quartus II software tool. Then, the System-on-Chip (SoC) design, based on the FPGA code with the 0.18µm CMOS process, is implemented. The experimental results indicate that the proposed system can achieve higher accuracy with reduced complexity and area of the hardware.

3.1 Methodology

Figure 3 presents the overall architecture of the sound localization system, including a sound signal amplifier, an analogue-to-digital (AD) converter, a sound activity detector, and an AMDF module. External acoustic signals are received by a pair of microphones and magnified by an amplifier. The AD converter transforms analogue data to digital data. The sound activity detection block consists of threshold value detection, zero-crossing rate (ZCR), and end-point detection modules. Three methods are utilized to distinguish desired segments from silent periods. Finally, the AMDF module (Wang et al., 2008a; Wang et al., 2009) estimates the delay based on the desired signal segments, and converts the delay into angles. A brief workflow of the system is shown in Fig. 4

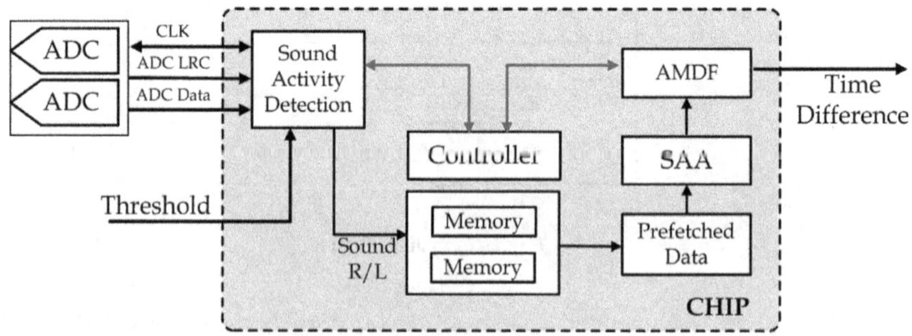

Fig. 3. Overview of the sound localization system (Wang et al., 2011).

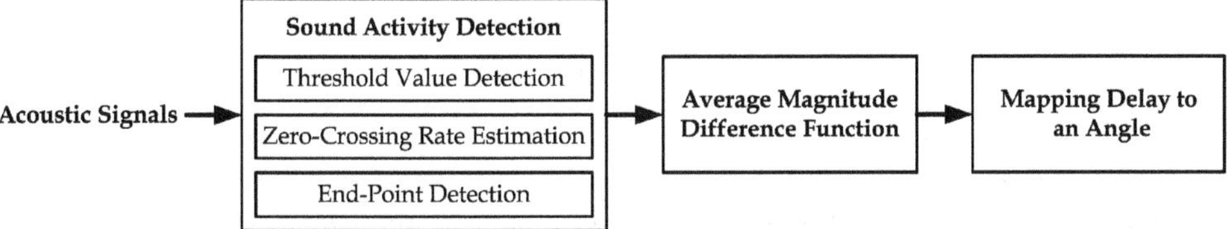

Fig. 4. Workflow of the sound localization system.

3.1.1 Sound activity detection

When the pair of microphones receives the sound signals, the system begins to determine whether the input signal needs to be handled. The detection of sound activity comprises three steps, which are as follows.

- Threshold Value Detection: Whether the amplitude of the input signal exceeds a threshold is determined by this step. If the amplitude exceeds the threshold, then the system begins to store the input signal data in memory.
- Zero-Crossing Rate Estimation: In acoustics, a sound wave has positive and negative values of displacement around the zero amplitude. Zero-crossing rates are calculated by counting the crossings of the baseline over time. The presence of an active ZCR signal can improve threshold value detection.
- End-Point Detection: An end-point beacon is generated when an ongoing input signal falls below the threshold for a preset period.

3.1.2 Direction-of-arrival estimation

Figure 5 displays a microphone array, where $x_1(t)$ and $x_2(t)$ represent the acoustic signals that are received by microphones 1 and 2 respectively; d denotes the distance between these two microphones; θ is the direction between the array and an unknown source, whose signal is represented as $s(t)$. The source is assumed to be far enough from the microphone array so that the acoustic wave-front that impinges upon the microphone array can be approximated as a plane wave. Let microphone 1 be the reference point; the relationship between the received signals and the source signal in the time domain is given by the equation,

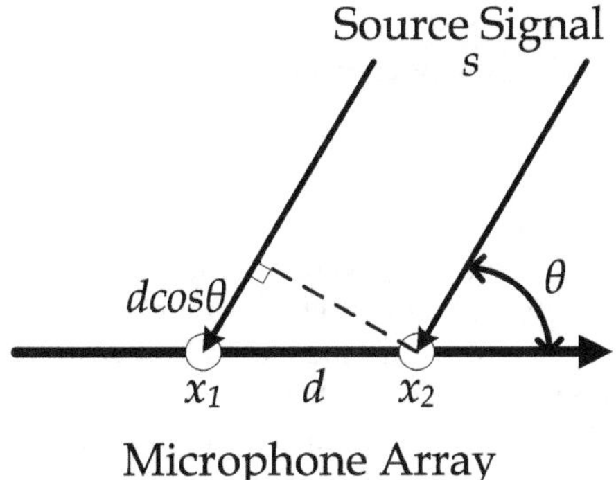

Fig. 5. Direction-of-arrival illustration.

$$\begin{bmatrix} x_1(t) \\ x_2(t) \end{bmatrix} = \begin{bmatrix} s(t) \\ s(t-\tau) \end{bmatrix} \tag{6}$$

where τ is the propagation delay from the source to the microphone. As shown in the figure, after the wave-front impinges on microphone 2, the wave-front takes time "τ" to reach microphone 1. The distance between the wave-front and microphone 1 is $d\cos\theta$ (Chen et al., 2010). Therefore,

$$\tau = \frac{d\cos\theta}{c} \tag{7}$$

where c is the sound velocity. In real-life applications, noise and reverberation may distort wave shapes, potentially affecting the propagation delay. A feasible way to estimate the accurate time delay involves using the AMDF. The AMDF firstly fixes the signal at microphone 1, and then shifts the signal at microphone 2 to calculate the time delay. When both signals are the most similar, the difference between the waves will be minimized. In other words, the τ value is obtained when the correlation between the waveforms of the both microphone signals is maximal. Let N be the total number of windows and i represent the sliding window index. The AMDF can be expressed as

$$\hat{\tau} = \arg\min_{\tau} \frac{1}{N} \sum_{i=1}^{N} \left| x_1^i(t) - x_2^i(t-\tau) \right|. \tag{8}$$

3.2 FPGA implementation

The entire sound localization system (except for the microphone signal amplifiers) was implemented on a single Altera DE2-70 FPGA board. Software design was developed by using the Quartus II software tool. Firstly, on the FPGA board, the AD converter controller used the I²C protocol to control serial input and serial output data. The sound activity detection block was divided into three modules and implemented separately. At the time-delay estimation stage, the AMDF block used conventional basic operational logic elements, such as shift registers, subtraction, absolute value operands, and accumulation, to facilitate the entire design. All blocks implemented the pipeline technique to further accelerate computation. Finally, the output result is displayed on the DE2-70 board using a seven-segment display and LEDs. The system used a total of around 15,600 logic elements (around 188,000 logic gates).

3.3 SoC implementation

After the FPGA simulation and validation were complete, the sound localization system was ported to the chip level. In this system, after an input signal passed through the sound activity detection module, it was stored in the left and right SRAMs respectively. Next, the subtraction/absolute/accumulation (SAA) (Wang et al., 2011) module performed the major operations in the AMDF, including subtraction, taking absolute values, and accumulation. Hence, the AMDF block was able to estimate the time delay using the SAA module and convert it into a direction by accessing a predefined table in the ROM.

However, while running the AMDF, the system must perform the correlation analysis, $\Gamma = \sum_{i=1}^{N} \left| x_1^i - x_2^i \right|$, N times. The variable N is set herein to 64 for convenience of chip implementation. To reach a favorable trade-off between the chip area and performance, the system used a folding technique to realize the SAA architecture (Fig. 6 and (9)). A comparison with the unfolded SAA architecture revealed that the number of adders had been reduced from 127 to eight, and the number of units that performed the absolute value operation had been decreased from 64 to four. The length of the critical paths was effectively minimized, enhancing the clock rate.

$$\Gamma = \begin{cases} \sum_{j=1}^{4} \left| x_1^j(t) - x_2^j(t) \right| + \Gamma_{\text{accumulative}} & \text{when } t = 16j. \\ \sum_{j=1}^{4} \left| x_1^j(t) - x_2^j(t) \right| & \text{when } t = 16j + 1,2,\ldots,15. \end{cases} \quad (9)$$

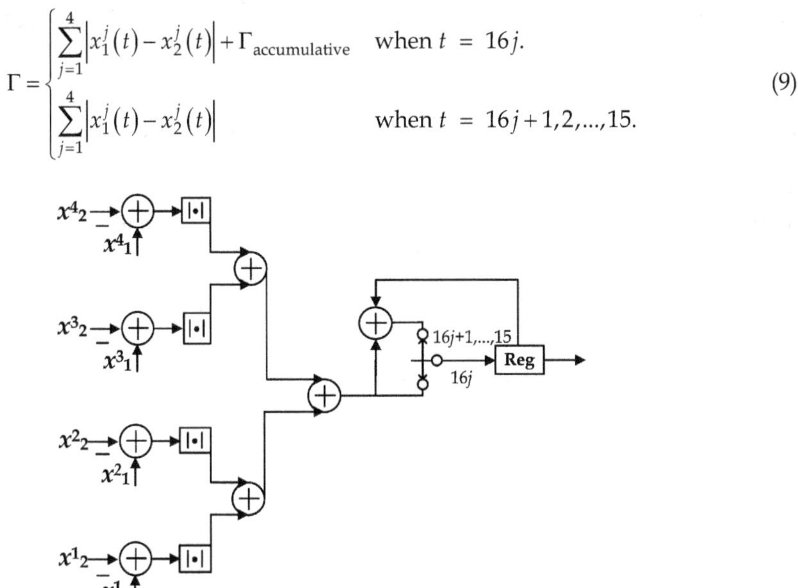

Fig. 6. Folded SAA architecture (Wang et al., 2011).

3.4 Experimental results

The sound localization system was tested with sources in different directions, ranging from 15° to 90° in steps of 15°, at five distances (1-5m). The experimental results indicated that the average accuracy was 80%-90%. The estimation error could be maintained in the range ±5°-±10°. With respect to chip performance, the number of logic gates was reduced to 32,616. Also, the core size and power consumption were minimized (see (Wang et al., 2008a; Wang et al., 2009; Wang et al., 2011) for details).

4. Embedded system design for speaker identification/verification

The field of speaker recognition has existed for five decades (Furui, 2004). Recently, speaker recognition systems have found many applications in the real world. It is highly flexible and convenient for a wide range of daily-life applications. Various approaches, involving neural networks (Clarkson et al., 2001), Gaussian mixture models (GMMs) (Burget et al., 2007), and support vector machines (SVMs) (Cortes et al., 1995), have been adopted for recognizing speakers. Among them, SVM-based speaker recognition has recently attracted much attention.

Based on the idea of the working set, Platt et al. (1998) proposed the use of the sequential minimal optimization (SMO) algorithm, which is a widely used learning algorithm that involves decomposition, to solve the quadratic programming (QP) problem. Basically, the SMO algorithm performs the following two processes repeatedly: 1) selecting a fixed number of Lagrange multipliers, and 2) solving the QP problem of the multipliers until an optimal solution is found. Although the SMO algorithm makes SVM learning feasible when the number of training samples is very large, the number of required computational iterations still results in a heavy computational burden, which makes it unsuitable for use with stand-alone embedded devices.

The operation of the proposed system based on SMO involves a training phase and an identification phase. Since the SMO training algorithm has huge computational load, it is realized as a dedicated, very large-scale integration (VLSI) module, which is a hardware component. The rest processes of the system, such as speech preprocessing, speech feature extraction, and SVM-based voting, are implemented in software. The proposed system has 90% less training time than the embedded C-based ARM processor, and achieves an 89.9% accuracy with the 2010 speaker recognition database of the National Institute of Standards and Technology (NIST). The proposed system was tested and found to be fully functional on a Socle CDK prototype development board (www.socle-tech.com.tw) with an AMBA-based Xilinx FPGA board and an ARM926EJ processor.

4.1 Methodology

4.1.1 Support vector machine

Support vector classification (Cortes et al., 1995) is a computationally efficient means of finding hyperplanes in a high-dimensional feature space. Training an SVM is the equivalent to finding a hyperplane with the maximum margin.

The canonical representation of a decision hyperplane is (10),

$$y_i\left(w^{\mathrm{T}}\phi(x_i)+b\right)\geq 1, \quad i=1,\ldots,N \tag{10}$$

where w is the weights of training instances; b is a constant; y_i is the label of x_i. The optimization problem involves minimizing $\|w\|^2$. In imperfect separation, the optimal hyperplane is obtained by solving the following constrained optimization problem (11),

$$\begin{cases} \min\limits_{w,b,\xi} \dfrac{1}{2} w^T w + C\left(\sum\limits_{i=1}^{N} \xi_i\right) \\ y_i(w\phi(x_i)+b)+\xi_i-1\geq 0, \quad \xi_i \geq 0, 1\leq i\leq N \end{cases} \tag{11}$$

where C is a real-valued cost parameter, and ξ_i is a penalty parameter (slack variable). If $\phi(x_i)=x_i$, the SVM finds a linear separating hyperplane with the maximal margin. An SVM is called a nonlinear SVM when φ maps x_i into a higher-dimensional space. Equation (12) is the Lagrange function for imperfect separation.

$$\begin{cases} \arg\max_{\alpha} \ L_D = \sum_{i=1}^{N} \alpha_i - \frac{1}{2}\sum_{i=1}^{N}\sum_{j=1}^{N} y_i y_j x_i^T x_j \alpha_i \alpha_j \\ \sum_{i=1}^{N} y_i \alpha_i = 0, \quad 0 \le \alpha_i \le C, 1 \le i \le N \end{cases} \tag{12}$$

Basically, (12) is a QP problem and can be solved using the SMO algorithm.

4.1.2 Sequential Minimal Optimization

The basic problem of the SMO algorithm is the need to find hyperplane parameters, w and b, by updating Lagrange parameter a. The SMO algorithm searches through the feasible region of the dual problem and maximizes the objective function by choosing two a terms and jointly optimizes them (with the values of the other a terms fixed) in each iteration. Then, the objective function can be written as (13).

$$\begin{aligned} L_D &= \alpha_1 + \alpha_2 + \text{Constant}_1 \\ &\quad -\frac{1}{2}[y_1 y_1 x_1^T x_1 a_1^2 + y_2 y_2 x_2^T x_2 a_2^2 + 2 y_1 y_2 x_1^T x_2 a_1 a_2 \\ &\quad + 2(\sum_{i=3}^{N} \alpha_i y_i x_i^T)(y_1 x_1 \alpha_1 + y_2 x_2 \alpha_2) + \text{Constant}_2] \end{aligned} \tag{13}$$

Let $\frac{\partial L_D}{\partial \alpha_2} = 0$, yielding (14).

$$\begin{aligned} \alpha_2^{\text{new}} &= \alpha_2^{\text{old}} + \Delta\alpha_2 \\ &= \alpha_2^{\text{old}} + \frac{y_2(E_2^{\text{old}} - E_1^{\text{old}})}{\eta} \end{aligned} \tag{14}$$

where E_1^{old} and E_2^{old} are prediction errors, and η is given by (15).

$$\begin{aligned} \eta &= 2K_{12}\text{-}K_{11}\text{-}K_{22} \\ &= 2x_1^T x_2 - x_1^T x_1 - x_2^T x_2 \\ &= -\|x_2 - x_1\|^2 \end{aligned} \tag{15}$$

Let the minimum and maximum feasible values of a_2 be L and H, respectively. The unconstrained α_2^{new} must be checked to determine whether it is in the feasible range. Then, a clipping function, (16), is used to generate the new constrained $\alpha_2^{\text{new,clipped}}$.

$$\alpha_2^{\text{new,clipped}} = \begin{cases} H, & \text{if } H > \alpha_2^{\text{new}} \\ \alpha_2^{\text{new}}, & \text{if } L \le \alpha_2^{\text{new}} \le H \\ L, & \text{if } \alpha_2^{\text{new}} < L \end{cases} \tag{16}$$

Eventually, α_1^{new} can be obtained from (17).

$$\begin{aligned} \alpha_1^{\text{new}} &= \alpha_1^{\text{old}} + \Delta\alpha_1 \\ &= \alpha_1^{\text{old}} - y_1 y_2 \Delta\alpha_2 \end{aligned} \tag{17}$$

The terms Δa_1 and Δa_2 are used to update the hyperplane parameters w and b according to (18) and (19).

$$\Delta w = \Delta\alpha_1 y_1 x_1 + \Delta\alpha_2 y_2 x_2 \tag{18}$$

$$\begin{aligned} \Delta b &= \frac{1}{2}(b_1 + b_2) \\ &= \frac{1}{2}\left[\left(E_1 + y_1 \Delta\alpha_1 x_1^T x_1\right) + \left(E_2 + y_2 \Delta\alpha_2 x_2^T x_2\right)\right] \end{aligned} \tag{19}$$

4.2 Hardware implementation

The proposed system can perform both speaker training and identification. Based on the complexity analysis in Fig. 7, the SMO training, which takes 90.89% of the training time, is the computational bottleneck. Hence, the SMO is realized in hardware and the rest processes, including preprocessing, feature extraction and voting analysis, are implemented in software. As shown in Fig. 8, the proposed design comprises four blocks, which are the software-based extraction block (SEB), hardware-based training block (HTB), and software-based voting block (SVB). The SEB mainly performs speech preprocessing and speech feature extraction. The HTB executes the SMO algorithm, and the SVB is designed to find the target speaker based on a multiclass SVM. This design can be applied to a fast-trainable system in a stand-alone embedded environment (see (Kuan et al., 2010) for details).

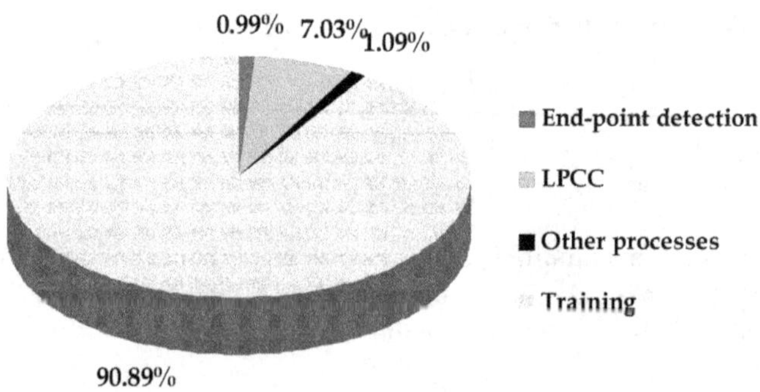

Fig. 7. Complexity analysis for speaker identification.

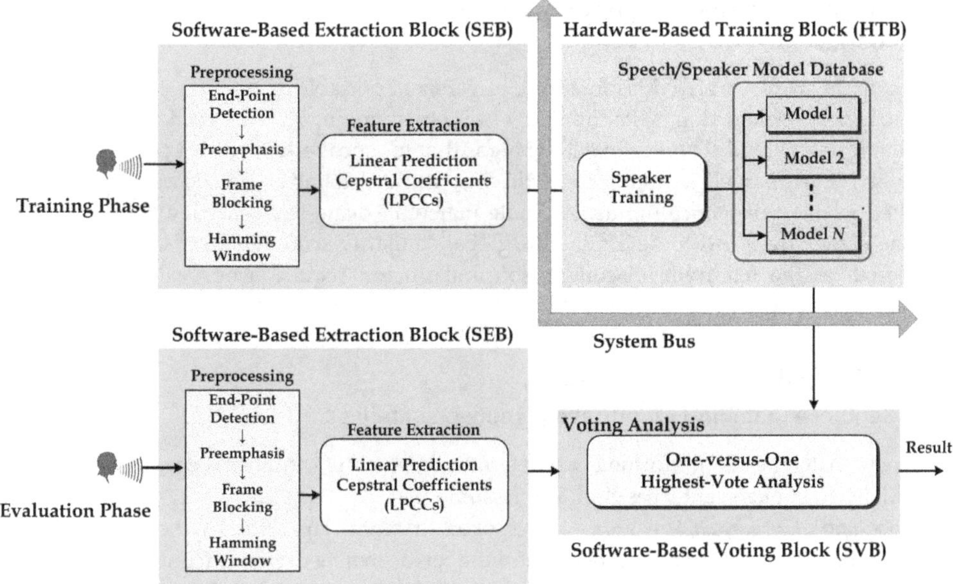

Fig. 8. Proposed hardware/software co-design system for speaker identification

4.3 Experimental results

The NIST 2010 speaker recognition evaluation (SRE10) speech corpus (by nine speakers) was adopted to evaluate the proposed hardware/software co-design framework. Six datasets, including nine speakers' files in SRE10, were used to evaluate a speaker identification system for an entrance security application. The training utterance of each speaker was 10s long. The duration of the testing utterances was 2–6s. The order of the linear predictive cepstral coefficients (LPCCs) was 18.

Figure 9 presents a time-cost comparison between the proposed hardware/software system and the embedded C code system (ARM-ported system). The proposed design had a 90% lower time-cost than the embedded C code one in the case of interest. Details of the evaluation can be found in (Wang et al., 2008b).

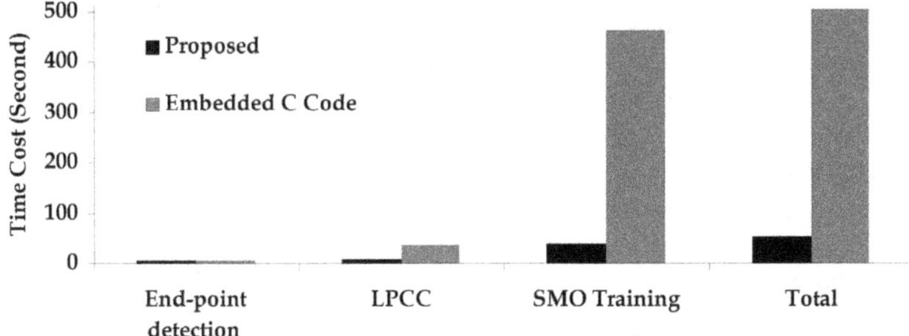

Fig. 9. Performance evaluation based on time cost.

5. Embedded system design for interactive retrieval of spoken documents

Owing to the increasingly widespread use of personal portable devices, an efficient method for retrieving spoken data with limited resources is required. This section proposes an efficient feature-based sentence-matching algorithm for speaker-dependent personal spoken sentence retrieval. Such a system can efficiently retrieve database sentences only partially matched to query sentence inputs. A whole matching plane-based accumulation (WMPB) scheme is then designed to determine the global similarity score. The proposed algorithms are based on the feature-level comparison and do not require acoustical and language models.

5.1 Methodology

5.1.1 Sentence matching for retrieving spoken sentences

Sentence matching is performed to determine the similarity between two sentences. Consider two spoken sentences *A* and *B*: Assume that $A=\{a_1a_2...a_m\}$ is an m-word spoken sentence and $B=\{b_1b_2...b_n\}$ is an n-word spoken sentence. The similarity between *A* and *B* can then be directly determined from the number of matched words (common words) in these two sentences. For example, if spoken sentences *A* and *B* are "I have a meeting in London tomorrow" and "Where is my meeting tomorrow?" respectively, then "meeting" and "tomorrow" are the matched words. Since only subsets of words in sentences are matched, sentence matching is a form of partial matching. This partial sentence-matching concept can be applied to spoken sentence retrieval.

Because this similarity is defined semantically, using a speech recognition system with acoustical and language models to transcribe spoken sentences into semantic texts is intuitive. To develop a language-independent retrieval system with a small required memory and favorable performance for a medium-sized sentence database, feature-level partial matching algorithms that do not use acoustic and language models are proposed herein.

5.1.2 Spoken sentence retrieval based on feature-level partial matching

This subsection presents a new partial matching system that is applied to the feature level. Figure 10 shows the proposed feature-level partial matching. First, the features of the spoken sentence are extracted frame by frame. The feature sequence is then segmented into equally sized matching units that are called feature pattern units (FPUs). Given a query sentence *Q* with *l* FPUs and a database sentence *D* with *k* FPUs, the sentences *Q* and *D* are denoted by $Q = \{q^{\Gamma}_{sub1}q^{\Gamma}_{sub2}...q^{\Gamma}_{subl}\}$ and $D = \{d^{\Gamma}_{sub1}d^{\Gamma}_{sub2}...d^{\Gamma}_{subk}\}$. These equally sized FPUs of the query and database sentences form a matching plane, shown in Fig. 11. Each matching block in the matching plane is associated with an FPU in the query sentence and the database sentence.

Let Ψ be the feature-level similarity function. The global similarity score for *Q* and *D* in the feature-level is calculated

$$\Psi\left[D^F,Q^F\right]=\Psi\left[d^F_{sub1}d^F_{sub2}\dots d^F_{subk},q^F_{sub1}q^F_{sub2}\dots q^F_{subl}\right] \\ =\left\{\sum_{i=1}^{l}\sum_{j=1}^{k}\Psi[d^F_{subj},q^F_{subi}]\right\}\cdot M\left(D^F\right) \tag{20}$$

where $\Psi[d^F_{subj},q^F_{subi}]$ is the local similarity score, which quantifies the similarity between FPUs q^F_{subi} and d^F_{subj}; $M(D^F)=1/k$ represents the normalization factor for different database sentences.

Clearly, $\Psi[d^F_{subj},q^F_{subi}]$ depends on the feature distances between every pair of FPUs, q^F_{subi} and d^F_{subj}. Although $\Psi[d^F_{subj},q^F_{subi}]$ can also be implemented using $\Phi[d^S_{subj},q^S_{subi}]$, however, a distance threshold is required (Itoh, 2001; Itoh & Tanaka 2002). Further, this threshold is difficult to define owing to variation in speech. Without a threshold comparison, an attempt is made herein to find a better similarity score function based on only the feature distances.

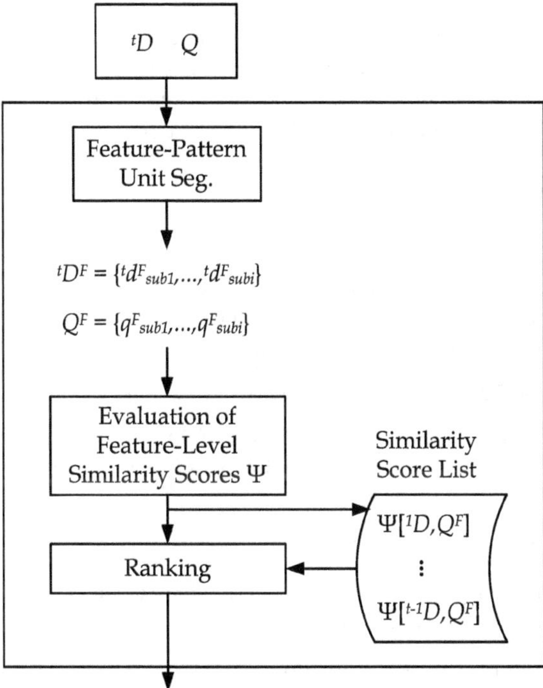

Fig. 10. Proposed feature-level partial matching algorithm.

To test which weighting function performs well, experiments on inverse exponential weighting ($\mathrm{IEW}(X) = 1/e^X$) and inverse distance weighting ($\mathrm{IDW}(X) = 1/X^p$, where p is an integer weighting power) techniques for summing local similarity scores were conducted (see the previous work (Lin & Wang, 2007) for details). Based on this experiment, the IDW function outperformed the IEW function; therefore, IDW was used to evaluate the similarity score. The global similarity score function Ψ is defined as,

$$\Psi\left(D^F,Q^F\right)\equiv\sum_{i=1}^{l}\sum_{j=1}^{k}\mathrm{IDW}\left[\mathrm{distance}\left(d^F_{subj},q^F_{subi}\right)\right]\cdot M\left(D^F\right) \tag{21}$$

where q^F_{subi} denotes the i-th FPU of the query sentence, and d^F_{subj} represents the j-th FPU of the database sentence. The IDW method provides a measure of estimating uncertainty of variables. Moreover, this approach is sufficiently flexible to model the variables in a trend curve (Tomczak, 1998).

5.2 WMPB algorithm

Based on the above description, the proposed spoken sentence retrieval is summarized as follows.

Step 1. Sentence segmentation and feature extraction

Assume that the FPU size is n frames. The length of the overlapping between successive FPUs is $n/2$ frames (Ng & Victor, 2000). A spoken query sentence and a spoken sentence from the database are segmented based on the FPU size, with $n/2$ overlapping frames. The FPU overlap of $n/2$ frames is taken from another work (Itoh, 2001). Moreover, such a setting covers each frame in the query and database sentences; this scheme of redundancy is thought to be advantageous for partial matching. According to Fig. 11, this query sentence has l FPUs and the database sentence has k FPUs.

Step 2. Determination of matching plane

For a query sentence with l FPUs and a database sentence with k FPUs, a 2-D matching plane that contains $l\times k$ matching blocks is created. T matching planes are created if the database contains T sentences. Figure 11 illustrates the creation of the matching planes.

Step 3. Calculation of the similarity score of each matching block

For each matching block, dynamic programming is utilized to calculate the feature distance of the two FPUs. These feature distances are then used to determine local similarity scores using the IDW function.

Step 4. Accumulation of similarity scores

Over the whole matching plane, the similarity scores associated with all of the matching blocks are accumulated to yield a global similarity score.

Step 5. Iterative checking sentences from other databases

Repeat steps 1 to 4 for the other database sentences until all of their global similarity scores are obtained.

Step 6. Ranking of database sentences

Rank the database sentences in accordance with global similarity scores. Because the local similarity scores of all the matching blocks in the matching plane are accumulated to yield a global similarity score, the proposed spoken sentence retrieval method is called the whole matching plane-based (WMPB) algorithm.

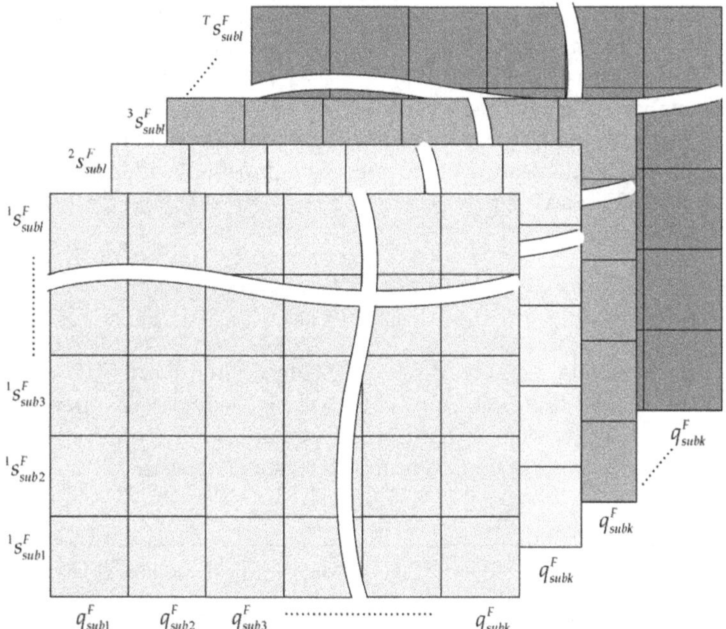

Fig. 11. Example of creation of matching plane.

5.3 Embedded system implementation

The proposed spoken sentence retrieval system was realized in a Pocket PC (HP iPAQ H5550) with a 128 MB RAM and 48 MB flash memory. The Pocket PC uses an Intel PXA255 processor (an XScale micro-architecture based on the ARM V5TE), which is a dedicated portable chip and suitable for handheld devices (www.intel.com). A 16-bit integrated audio codec (AC'97 2.0) was adopted for concurrent real-time speech input/output. The average memory size of one sentence was 142.3 kB with a sampling rate of 8 kHz. The Microsoft embedded complier based on Visual C++ 4.0 was used for the OS of the Pocket PC. Since the PXA255 processor does not support floating-point computation, a fixed-point conversion strategy was conducted to tackle the problem (see (Lin & Wang, 2007)). After the conversion method transformed the partial-matching program into a fixed-point format, the program was burned into the onboard flash memory. The system showed that the program occupied only 140 kB memory, which is appropriate for portable devices.

5.4 Experimental results

The experiments are divided into two phases - the parameter setting phase and the evaluation phase. In the parameter setting phase, experiments are conducted to find the best parameters of the IDW function and the FPU size for the proposed algorithm. Table 6 lists the characteristics of the experimental environment. Some experiments were to evaluate the retrieval performance of the proposed partial matching algorithm. Sentences were spoken naturally by one person without controlling the duration of the words or speaking at a deliberately chosen rate. The query sentences partially matched their related database sentences. Here, matching keywords are defined as the terms that are common to queries and their related database sentences. Table 7 lists the overall statistics concerning the experimental database. The database sentences were ranked by their global similarity scores. The retrieval performance was assessed using the most commonly used measurement, which is non-interpolated mean average precision (mAP) (Baeza-Yates & Ribeiro-Neto, 1999; Lo et al., 2002). The mAP is defined as,

$$\mathrm{mAP} = \frac{1}{L}\sum_{i=1}^{L}\left\{\frac{1}{M}\sum_{j=1}^{M_i}\left\{\frac{1}{N_j}\sum_{k=1}^{N_j}\mathrm{precision}_{N_{Qj}}(k)\right\}\right\} \tag{22}$$

where N_j denotes the total number of relevant sentences for query j; M_i represents the total number of queries in batch i; L is the total number of query batches, and $\mathrm{precision}_{N_{Q_j}}(k)$ is the precision of Q_j when k sentences are retrieved. Finally, Table 8 summarizes the overall statistics for the entire experimental database.

Input	**Spoken query sentence**
Output	Ranking of spoken database sentences
Acoustical environment	In-door environment
Sampling rate	8 kHz
Quantization	16 bits
Frame size	256 samples (32 ms)
Frame overlapping size	64 samples (8 ms)
Speech feature	10-order LPCCs
DTW local path constraint	Type 1
FPU size	22 frames
IDW	$1/X^8$

Table 6. Characteristics of experimental environments.

Data set	**Data set A**			**Data set B**			**Data set C**		
Phase	Parameter setting phase			Evaluation phase					
Number of database sentence	50 Mandarin			50 Mandarin			50 Mandarin + 50 English		
Number of query sentence	15			15			30		
Percentage of common words among queries and their relevant database sentences	46.2			42.9			51.3		
Statistics type	Min	Max	Mean	Min	Max	Mean	Min	Max	Mean
Frame number of database sentence length	68	120	90.2	63	114	88	50	192	92
Frame number of query sentence length	65	89.1	73.8	62	85	71.6	66	208	76
Number of relevant database sentence per query	3	7	3.21	2	7	3.47	2	6	3.86

Table 7. Database statistics.

Platform	Data set	# database sentences	#query sentences	mAP	Response time for one query (sec.)
PC (Pentium 4 3.0GHz with 512Mb RAM)	B	50 Mandarin	15	0.887	<0.5
	C	50 Mandarin +50 English	30	0.763	<1.0
iPAQ H5550 PocketPC	B	50 Mandarin	15	0.799	<1.5
	C	50 Mandarin +50 English	30	0.675	<2.5

Table 8. Experimental results.

6. Conclusion

This chapter presented various speech processing approaches for use in embedded systems, involving speech feature extraction, sound localization, speaker identification/verification, and interactive retrieval of spoken documents. To facilitate implementation, related algorithms and methods of improving them are discussed with reference to FPGA and ARM-based architectures. Experiments were also conducted using testing datasets; the results showed that proper hardware design can improve the performance of the approaches, and the efficacy of the improved algorithms was subsequently demonstrated.

7. Acknowledgment

This work was supported in part by the National Science Council of the Republic of China under Grant No. 100-2218-E-006-033. The authors would like to thank Po-Yi Shih and Jr-Siang Peng for their dedication to this chapter. Furthermore, each section is written by the following authors: Bo-Wei Chen (Sections 1, 3, and 6), Po-Yi Shih (Section 2), Jr-Siang Peng (Section 4), and Po-Chun Lin (Section 5).

8. References

Baeza-Yates, R. & Ribeiro-Neto, B. (1999). *Modern Information Retrieval* (1st edition), Addison Wesley/ACM Press, ISBN 978-020-1398-29-8, New York, NY.

Burget, L.; Matejka, P.; Schwarz, P.; Glembek, O. & Cernocky, J.-H. (2007). Analysis of Feature Extraction and Channel Compensation in a GMM Speaker Recognition System. *IEEE Transactions on Speech, Audio and Language Processing*, Vol.15, No.7, (September 2007), pp. 1979-1985.

Chen, B.-W.; Wang, J.-F. & Wang, J.-C. (2010). Improving Direction of Arrival Estimation Based on the Directivity Pattern Analysis and Adaptive Cascaded Classifiers. *Journal of the Chinese Institute of Engineers*, Vol.33, No.5, (July 2010), pp. 751-760.

Clarkson, T.-G.; Christodoulou, C.-C.; Guan, Y.; Gorse, D.; Romano-Critchley, D.-A. & Taylor, J.-G. (2001). Speaker Identification For Security Systems Using Reinforcement-Trained pRAM Neural Network Architectures. *IEEE Transactions on Systems, Man, and Cybernetics (SMC)—Part C: Applications and Reviews*, Vol.31, No.1, (February 2001), pp. 65-76.

Cortes, C. & Vapnik, V. (1995). Support Vector Networks. *Machine Learning*, Vol.20, (1995), pp. 273-297.

Furui, S. (2004). Fifty Years of Progress in Speech and Speaker Recognition. *Acoustical Society of America Journal*, Vol.116, No.4, (2004), pp. 2497-2498.

Itoh, Y. (2001). A Matching Algorithm between Arbitrary Sections of Two Speech Data Sets for Speech Retrieval, *Proceedings of ICASSP 2001 IEEE International Conference on Acoustics,*

Speech, and Signal Processing, pp. 593-596, Salt Lake City, Utah, USA, May 07-11, 2001.

Itoh, Y. & Tanaka, K. (2002). Speech Labeling and the Most Frequent Phrase Extraction Using Same Section in a Presentation Speech, *Proceedings of ICASSP 2002 IEEE International Conference on Acoustics, Speech, and Signal Processing*, pp. I737-I740, Orlando, Florida, USA, May 13-17, 2002.

Kuan, T.-W.; Wang, J.-F.; Wang, J.-C.; Lin, P.-C. & Gu, G.-H. (2010). VLSI Design of an SVM Learning Core on Sequential Minimal Optimization Algorithm. *IEEE Transactions on Very Large Scale Integration Systems*, Vol.PP, No.99, (December 2010), pp. 1-11.

Lin, P.-C. & Wang, J.-F. (2007). Speaker Change Detection and Spoken Sentence Retrieval for Automatic Minute Taking. Doctoral dissertation, National Cheng Kung University, Taiwan.

Lo, W. K., Meng, H. & Ching, P. C. (2002). Multi-Scale and Multi-Model Integration for Improved Performance in Chinese Spoken Document Retrieval, *Proceedings of ICSLP2002 7th International Conference on Spoken Language Processing*, pp. 1513-1516, Denver, Colorado, USA, September 16-20, 2002.

Ng, K., & Victor W. Z. (2000). Subword-Based Approaches for Spoken Document Retrieval. *Speech Communication*, Vol.32, No.3, (October 2000), pp. 157-186.

Platt, J.-C. (1998). Fast Training of Support Vector Machines Using Sequential Minimal Optimization, In: *Advances in Kernel Methods: Support Vector Machines*, Schölkopf, B.; Burges, C. & Smola, A., (Eds.), MIT Press, ISBN 978-026-2194-16-7, Cambridge, MA.

Tomczak, M. (1998). Spatial Interpolation and Its Uncertainty Using Automated Anisotropic Inverse Distance Weighting (IDW) Cross-Validation/Jackknife Approach. *Journal of Geographic Information and Decision Analysis*, Vol.2, No.2, (May 1998), pp. 18-30.

Vergin, R.; O'Shaughnessy, D. & Gupta, V. (1996). Compensated Mel Frequency Cepstrum Coefficients, *Proceedings of ICASSP 1996 IEEE International Conference on Acoustics, Speech, and Signal Processing*, pp. 323–326, Atlanta, Georgia, USA, May 07-10, 1996.

Wang, J.-C.; Wang, J.-F. & Weng, Y.-S. (1998). The Chip Design of Mel Frequency Cepstrum Coefficient for HMM Speech Recognition, *Proceedings of the 9th VLSI Design/CAD Symposium*, pp. 439-442, Nangtou, Taiwan, August 20-22, 1998.

Wang, J.-C.; Wang, J.-F. & Weng, Y.-S. (2003). Chip Design of MFCC Extraction for Speech Recognition. *VLSI Journal on Integration*, Vol.32 No.1-3, (November 2002), pp. 111-131.

Wang, J.-F.; Chou, C.-H.; Huang, Y.-J.; Lin, P.-C. & Chen, B.-W. (2011). An Improvement of Chip Design for Auditory Source Localization Awareness, *Proceedings of 3rd International Conference on Awareness Science and Technology*, pp. 362-365, Dalian, China, September 27-30, 2011.

Wang, J.-F.; Jiang, Y.-C. & Sun, Z.-W. (2009). FPGA Implementation of a Novel Far-Field Sound Localization System, *Proceedings of TENCON 2000 IEEE Region 10 Conference*, pp. 1-4, Singapore, November 23-26, 2009.

Wang, J.-F.; Wang, J.-C. & Weng, Y.-S. (2000). Chip Design of Mel Frequency Cepstral Coefficients for Speech Recognition, *Proceedings of ICASSP 2000 IEEE International Conference on Acoustics, Speech, and Signal Processing*, pp. 3658-3661, Istanbul, Turkey, June 05-09, 2000.

Wang, J.-F.; Wang, J.-C.; Chen, B.-W. & Sun, Z.-W. (2008a). A Long-Distance Time Domain Sound Localization, *Proceedings of UIC 2008 5th International Conference on Ubiquitous Intelligence and Computing*, pp. 616–625, Oslo, Norway, June 23-25, 2008.

Wang, J.-F.; Wang, J.-C.; Mo, M.-H.; Tu, C.-I; & Lin, S.-C. (2008b). The Design of a Speech Interactivity Embedded Module and Its Applications for Mobile Consumer Devices. *IEEE Transactions on Consumer Electronics*, Vol.54, No.2, (May 2008), pp. 870-876.

Part 3

Project and Practice

10

Implementing Reconfigurable Wireless Sensor Networks: The Embedded Operating System Approach

Sanjay Misra and Emmanuel Eronu
Department of Computer Engineering , Federal University of Technology, Minna Nigeria

1. Introduction

Remote monitoring and control are vital in ensuring the efficiency and safety of entities beneficial to man and his environment. These entities cut across oil and gas, biomedical, healthcare, manufacturing, transportation, security, the Armed forces (Military, Navy, and Air force) etc. Wireless Sensor Networks (WSNs) are being used to effectively carry out the aforementioned task. Implementing WSN application might involve the deployment of hundreds or sometimes thousands of wireless sensor nodes to remote and inaccessible locations. A few examples of theses scenario can be related to the following: surveillance (e.g. international Border Monitoring, Littoral operations), environmental monitoring (e.g. Dam collapsing and flooding, earthquake early warning, avoiding Forest fire disaster), liquid (oil and water) and gas pipeline monitoring, etc. When operational needs changes or new functionalities are required in such scenario, reconfiguration of either the entire network or individual sensor nodes becomes inevitable. The inability to effect these changes could pose a serious challenge to the continued operation of the entire system. Other issues that could warrant the need for a reconfigurable WSN are bug fixes, regular code updates, update in response to security challenges, flexibility in adopting energy and performance efficient RF communication link or interface, efficient energy management, etc.

Several ways of carrying out dynamic reconfiguration exist, however employing a well-designed embedded operating system allows for a platform-independent implementation. The focus of discussion is what constitutes a well-designed platform-independent operating system for the wireless sensor network. These findings and other open research issues will form the bases of our presentation in this chapter. We also intend to highlight and discuss various research approaches adopted so far in realizing fully reconfigurable WSNs under severe size, limited processing capabilities and power consumption constraints within the context of embedded operating system.

The remainder of this chapter is organized as follows. Section 2 discusses key principles and implementation techniques of embedded operating Systems (EOS). The aim is to provide some form of background information on EOS and its advanced close relative: the real time operating system (REOS). Section 3 by extension further presents details of driving factors behind the need for a reconfigurable WSN. Some of the approaches adopted in implementing reconfigurable WSN in notable operating systems as well as on going researches in this area are discussed in section 4. Design issues of reconfigurable EOS are discussed in section 5. Section 6 concludes the chapter.

2. The embedded operating system

An embedded operating system can be viewed as a collection of software modules meant to enhance an embedded system's efficiency, flexibility and robustness (Gomaa, 1993; Labroasse, 2002). To the designer and user it appears more like an extended machine and to the system, an indispensible resource manager. An extension of EOS, the real time embedded operating system (RTOS) is characterized by its ability to implement the aforementioned goals in real time. Hence its operational paradigms are deterministic and have guaranteed worst-case interrupt latency and context switching times (Barr, 1999).

RTOS is implemented around a multi-tasking kernel. The kernel controls when each task is to be executed. And it does this by allocating a time slice to each task (Walls, 1996). The key parts of an RTOS are: the scheduler, RTOS services, synchronization and messaging tools (Ibrahim, 2008). The scheduler which forms the heart of all RTOS is responsible for the selection of tasks to be executed. It does so by implementing any of the following known scheduling algorithms: cooperative (First in First Out), Round-robin, Earliest deadline First (EDF) and fixed priority scheduling (usually rate-monotonic scheduling (RM)). The RTOS services provide some support to the kernel in the likes of Interrupt handling, memory management, input-output services, device management and timing. The essence is to ensure that the RTOS runs efficiently. Whereas, synchronization and messaging tools are used to synchronize access to shared resources and inter tasks activities. Examples of these services and tools are: semaphores, event flags, mailboxes, pipes, message queues etc.

Reconfiguring WSNs can be achieved in two ways. One is a direct method where application tasks can easily be replaced or altered during design time and the other option is to remotely effect a replacement of the application tasks or alter its functions during runtime. In one case, the entire system will have to be put on hold, if not shut down completely while the other method, the system remains active while the changes are effected in real-time. Whichever method is adopted, an abstraction of the WSN's node hardware via EOS or REOS makes the reconfiguration process much easier to implement. In section 4, we briefly introduce the Processing Elements approach, however considering programming constraints; it is evident that the EOS approach is the most effective.

3. Factors behind the need for reconfigurable WSNs

In this section, we discuss some of the driving factors that are necessitating reconfigurability in WSNs. In our survey we categorize the factors in this respect: The need to achieve an Efficient Energy management sub system, Flexible All-Standard-Communication implementable subsystem and implementing dynamic and more secured security features.

3.1 Efficient energy management sub system

The need to manage the limited energy available to Wireless sensor node efficiently constitutes the majority of reason behind the demand for reconfigurable WSN. Energy harvesting techniques have been proposed (solar, vibration etc.) and in some cases implemented (Kompis & Sureka, 2010). However not all WSN applications are deployed in environments where they can take advantage of this option. For example, solar powered nodes will be difficult to sustain in locations where sunlight intensity and duration of availability are relatively low or non-existing (for example the arctic region or under the ocean). The solution, in most cases is to look inwards by adopting appropriate RF communication standards or routing protocol that will allow for long duration of system sustenance and operation.

In (Kompis & Sureka, 2010), energy consumption in nodes has been traced to three basic components namely: Sensing energy, Communication energy and Computation energy. The Sensing energy is dissipated when activating sensing circuitry in order to obtain data from the environment being monitored. The amount of energy consumed in this respect is proportional to the application requirement. Communication energy has to do with the energy consumed while relaying data or control commands either to neighboring nodes or base stations within the network. Similarly the Computational energy refers to that energy dissipated whenever the nodes' processing element (microprocessor / microcontroller/ system on chip) implements computational and logical operations.

Taking cognizance of these components especially the Communication energy and Computation energy components, a number of research works (Muralidhar & Rao, 2008; Kompis & Sureka, 2010) have devise ways of proffering solution by means of reconfiguring related sections of the wireless sensor nodes. Easily reconfigurable sub components or processes as identified in (Kompis & Sureka, 2010) are listed in table 1.0.

3.2 All-standard-communication implementable subsystem

Use of a particular communication standard from a range of many others in wireless sensor networks can be attributed to a number of factors (as depicted in figure 1) notably energy demand, transmission range, data rates, throughput etc. Adopting a particular standard is a function of the intended application's objectives. However when there are changes in application scenarios (context-prone), to use the same WSN node can only be possible if its communication interface can be adjusted accordingly. This important requirement constitutes one of the key issues in WSN reconfigurability demands.

A review of the work done in (Ramamurthy et al., 2004; Ramamurthy et al., 2005) depicts efforts geared towards realizing a generic reconfigurable wireless interface for the WSN node. They argue that realizing such an interface will allow for the deployment of the same WSN node in two distinct application scenarios namely: an Automotive Monitoring system and a Chemical Process control system (Ramamurthy et al., 2005). Exemplifying the second scenario, they proffer the use of RFID or Zigbee wireless communication standards (cheap and power efficient low-performance wireless technologies) in conveying sensed tire pressure, liquid level and corrosion data while the conveyance of highly active sensed data from encoder and Gyro would be better handled using high performance wireless technologies like Bluetooth or Wi-Fi.

Energy Consuming Component	Identified Sub Components/Processes	Proposed/Adopted Reconfiguration Paradigms
Computation	**Supply voltage/Operating frequencies** Implementing scaling of voltage and frequency thereby avoiding use of external oscillators	Reducing the operating supply voltage by changing the architecture of the system, for example through the use of pipelining. Implementing better algorithms and software optimization (e.g. Digital Signal Processing algorithms) that require fewer numbers of operations to perform a task such as filtering.
	ADC sampling rate Conversion of an analogue output from the sensor to digital equivalent which is proportional to the magnitude of voltage or current. Low efficiency factors can result in energy loss during conversion. Whenever voltage level across battery terminals decreases, conversion process draws increasing amount of increasing amounts of current from battery in order to maintain constant supply to the sensor component. Thereby leading to fast depletion of battery life (Kompis & Sureka, 2010; Khan & Vemuri, 2005).	Varying ADC sampling rate depending on the sensitivity or accuracy of data required.
	Peripheral utilization Operating certain peripheral (sensor interface, RF communication interface, etc.) when not needed has the tendency of depleting energy sources faster	Use of operating systems or middleware in isolating or switching off sub circuits that are not needed within at certain times
Communication	**Modulation scheme –** Various modulation schemes exist. A lot of computational power is always required when Implementing these schemes, depending on the algorithm employed. This normally translates to energy consumption within the nodes. Whenever there are cases of incessant retransmission, the energy source available to the nodes gets depleted easily. **Data rate -** Higher data rates results in high power consumptions. **Transmission range –** the transmission range to a very large extend depends on the power level of the transmitter which invariably is a function of energy consumption.	Techniques to reduce the number of retransmission necessary due to packet losses from faulty wireless links are being developed and implemented in various modulation schemes. However, having a reconfigurable RF communication interface can greatly assist in selecting the most appropriate energy friendly modulation scheme. Variation of data rates as much as implementing desired transmission range is also possible.

Table 1. Identified energy consuming components in WSN.

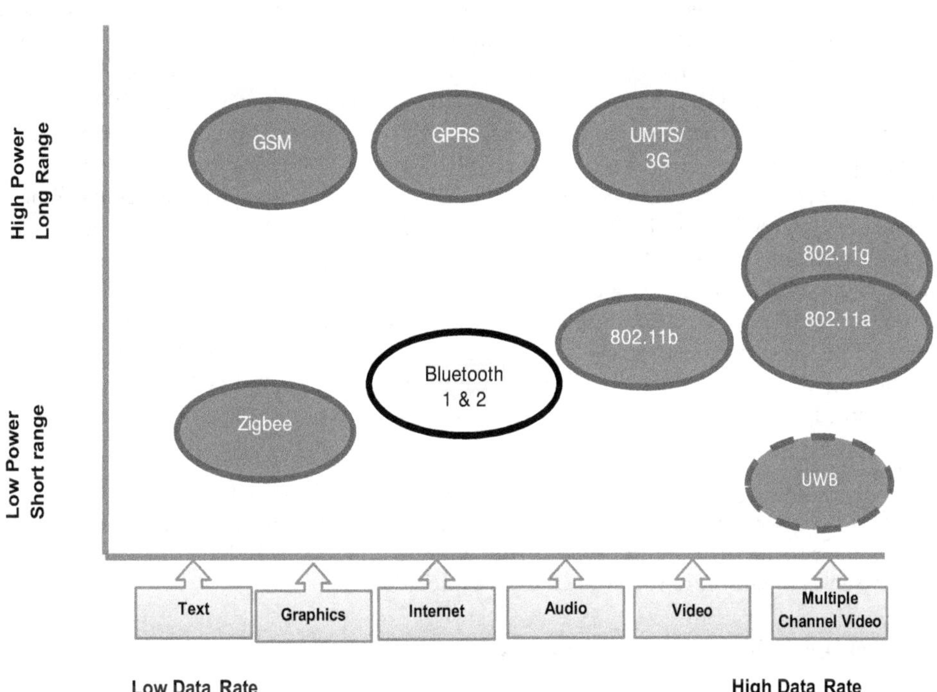

Fig. 1. Wireless communication standards (Muralidhar & Rao, 2008).

3.3 Implementing dynamic and more secured security feature

WSN by virtue of its mode of relaying messages wirelessly is open to attacks and risk. A sensor node in both isolated and non-isolated location can easily have its data or message compromised. Several attack scheme exist, among which are eavesdropping the message, injecting false messages, denial of service, data flooding, RF jamming etc. (Carpenter & Barrett, 2008; Moerschel et al., 2007). To a large extend, security requirements for WSN depends on the application where they are used. We must also recognize that providing security in sensor network can be very demanding. WSNs are resource constrained systems, having low power, less memory and limited computational abilities.

A number of security protocols have being developed for WSNs, notably among others are TinySec (Karloff et al, 2004), MiniSec (Luk et al., 2007), and SPINS (Perrig et al., 2001). SPINS, MinSec and TinySec link layer security architecture implementation are based on secret key cryptography. They are designed to provide authenticated streaming broadcast, ensured data confidentiality, data authentication based on RC5 algorithm. Using smaller key sizes for transmission of less sensitive information translates into less energy consumption. The reverse is the case when highly sensitive information is to be relayed. Varying key sizes can only be possible when the system itself is reconfigurable. A number of today's cryptographic implementations are not disposed to key varying capabilities even for the most optimized hardware-based cryptographic accelerator platforms. Examples of theses platforms are those realized on ASICS, intended to improve performance and minimize energy consumption (Portilla et al., 2010). These places restriction on scalability as predictions about future distribution have to be done before the distribution takes place. These limitations inhibit the adoption of public-key algorithms and architectures, like digital signature or session key distribution, which has being effectively used in traditional networks (Portilla et al., 2010). Public key encryption schemes allows for established private keys to be used between nodes after deployment (Portilla et al., 2010). The benefits of employing asymmetric algorithms with variable key length in WSN technologies are enormous. However the challenge can be surmounted by using a reconfigurable hardware resource.

Secure protocols currently in use are for the network layer and data link layer (Yick et al., 2008). However no layer is exempted from attacks, hence the need to have a platform that allows for real time reconfiguration of the entire set of layers (physical to application), thereby ensuring a secure WSNs need to be explored.

4. WSN reconfiguration approaches

In this section, we explore the role of Processing Elements and Embedded Operating Systems (EOS) technologies as enablers and in some cases expediters in realizing reconfigurable WSNs. In the course of our discussion, we will highlight the features, prospects and challenges associated with these role players accordingly.

4.1 The processing element approach

Processing elements by definition refer to the component in the Wireless sensor node or mote that performs the actual data processing operations and controls the entire system activities. A typical example of processing elements employed in Wireless sensor nodes are microcontrollers, digital signal processors and Field programmable gate arrays, etc. It can be argued that the degree or extend of WSN reconfigurability depends largely on the nature of the processing elements they integrate (Portilla et al., 2010; Leligou et al., 2008). Using this criterion, (Portilla et al., 2010) classified WSN reconfigurable platforms into the following categories: single microprocessor, Field Programmable Gate Array (FPGA), a combination of both microcontroller and FPGA, System on Programmable Chip (SoPC) and finally configurable hardware and microprocessor. There are basically three of these platforms: those built around Microcontrollers with detachable sensor and RF communication modules, Software based processor running on Field Programmable Gate Arrays (FPGA) and System on Programmable Chip (SoPC).

4.2 The embedded operating system approach

Traditionally operating systems were designed to provide virtual hardware platforms of processing elements in order to ease the design, development and deployment of application programs (Chen et al., 2010). The aim is to export virtual machines resembling hardware to user programs, thereby enhancing portability and flexibility.

Major issues facilitating WSN reconfiguration via Embedded Operating Systems (EOS) are the Programming Model, Communication Protocol Support and Resource sharing. We review three EOS (TinyOS, Contriki and AmbientRT) and discuss the various reconfiguration paradigms adopted as well as their associated challenges. Some of these findings are summarized in table 2 below.

4.2.1 TinyOS

TinyOS (Ramamurthy et al., 2005; Sugihara & Gupta, 2008; Omer & Kunz, 2011) originally developed by the University of California, Berkeley and Intel is one of the most popular operating systems for Wireless Sensor Networks(WSNs). Its programming model is characterized by its use of component modularization. The model is composed of monolithic abstraction layers which are broken-up into smaller, self-contained building blocks that interact with each other via interfaces. The use of distinct interfaces preserves the modularity of the solution and promotes reuse (Chen et al., 2010). TinyOS is implemented using nesC, an extension of C programming language. nesC is a flexible programming language that allows the EOS to tune every parameter for special application needs such as energy efficiency (Sugihara & Gupta, 2008).

Its support for reconfigurability can be attributed to the Encapsulation-by-modules feature in nesC that provides a unified interface. This provision frees the programmer from being conscious of whether any proposed functionality is being implemented in hardware or software (Mallikarjuna et al., 2009; Barr, 1999). More also, the introduction of Hardware Abstraction Architecture (HAA), a three-layer architecture supports WSN platform flexibility in several ways. First the bottom layer, Hardware Presentation layer (HPL) provides access to basic resources such as registers, interrupts and pins via nesC interfaces. the middle layer referred to as Hardware Abstraction Layer provides abstractions of the full capabilities of the underlying hardware. The top layer Hardware Independent Layer (HIL) presents abstractions that are hardware independent and therefore cross-platform.

4.2.2 Contriki

Contriki OS developed at SICS, is an open source, highly portable, networked, multi-tasking operating system for resource constrained systems like WSN node (Ramamurthy et al., 2004). It employs advanced reprogramming support in the form of Loadable modules as

Embedded Operating System	Example of Wireless Sensor Nodes where applicable	Reconfigurable features	Reconfigurable Implementation strategy	Reconfiguration Implementation Constraints
TinyOS	Mica, TmoteSky, BTnode, EYES	Reconfiguration is supported by accessing the boot loader found in the Atmel processor residing in the motes flash memory Provides thin abstraction over the external microcontroller pins using micros that enable setting and clearing of input/output pins as well as changing the pin's direction and function	Use is made of events programming paradigm to change the behavior of code running on a node. Supports platform flexibility through three layers of abstractions (Hardware Abstraction Architecture(HAA)) : these are Hardware Presentation Layer(HPL) , Hardware Abstraction Layer(HAL) and Hardware Independent Layer(HIL)	Exported hardware abstraction interface are strongly biased by features of the Atmel AVR microcontroller. Thereby hampering porting of the EOS to new platforms. Event-driven concurrency limits explicit state machine implementation
Contriki	ESB/2, TmoteSky	Advanced reprogramming support in the form of Loadable modules Uses Convergecast routing service to separation of communication services and implementation of various network protocols.	It provides an abstract programming interface that applications can use to perform actual transmission and routing of data message	Not Available
AmbientRT	μnode	Provides online reconfiguration and support for a modular data driven architecture. Employs Data Centric Entities (DCE) and Dynamic Loadable Module (DLM) paradigm to effect reconfiguration during runtime.	Where other embedded operating systems offer configuration only during compile time, AmbientRT dynamically adapts its functionality to create the most efficient configuration n for every situation.	Not Available

Table 2. Various reconfiguration paradigms employed by EOS.

well as an abstract programming interface that applications can use to perform actual transmission and routing of data message.

4.2.3 AmbientRT

AmbientRT is a real time operating system with the following capabilities, online reconfiguration, support for modular data driven architecture and real time scheduling. The data driven architecture enables it to dynamically reconfigure its functionalities. Its kernel can load and run modules dynamically. Modules are blocks of application software meant to achieve the application's goal.

The EOS implements dynamic reconfiguration via the concepts of Dynamic Loadable Module (DLM). This implies that the DLM can be loaded and executed anywhere in the program memory. With the module support, changes to an application can be done more efficiently. The implications are that only a section of the application software meant to perform a particular task has to be changed and not the complete application itself. This results in less traffic and thus less energy consumption. The DLM can easily be transferred to target WSN node through RF communication links where on arrival it is written to the program memory for subsequent execution.

5. Design issues and challenges

The EOS approach highlighted in section 4.2 is however without challenges. These challenges are attributed to WSNs' operational overhead and jitter. The overhead and jitter can be traced to among others the duration it takes the RTOS to execute its inherent basic system services and those of the application it is required to manage (Lee et al., 2003; Mooney & Blough, 2002). Relieving the processing unit execution time and resources by migrating some of the RTOS services to reconfigurable hardware platforms is one way of removing the overheard. These had being implemented in several research works (Stankovic & Ramamritham, 1989; Burleson et al.,1993; Lee et al., 2003; Mooney & Blough, 2002; Argon et al., 2006). The use of field programmable gate array (FPGA) in implementing some key EOS/RTOS services as system on programmable chip (SoPC) has been demonstrated (Adomat et al., 1996; Heron et al., 2001; Andrews et al., 2004). Argon et al., for example, designed and implemented a priority scheduler module as part of a multithread RTOS kernel (Argon et al., 2006). Their aim was to provide a modular and modifiable RTOS scheduling component that could perform all scheduling processing using little or no CPU processing time.

Another research work worth mentioning is that of Kohourt et al, as presented in (Kohourt et al., 2003). They were able to realize a Real-Time Task Manager (RTM) - much of a processor extension, that can reduce the performance drawbacks associated with RTOS bottlenecks (Task scheduling, time management and event management).

It is also of note that the tasks to be implemented by EOS/RTOS in WSNs are always an integral part of the application code. Hence effecting any change as a result of varying application needs, one is constrained to either directly or remotely replace the entire firmware image. However, envisioning a fully reconfigurable WSN, one should expect the changes to be effected at runtime and not design time. In comparison to operating systems run on much larger systems like the desktop or enterprise networks, it is hoped that future research work will be able to address this issue.

6. Conclusion

In this chapter we have been able to highlight and discuss various research approaches adopted towards realizing fully reconfigurable WSNs under severe constrained resources. A critical look at the EOS approach suggests a more convenient and efficient paradigm however challenges posed by overheads and jitter has raised some concern. However, we have equally shown that implementing an EOS or RTOS as a function of a reconfigurable hardware (SoPC implemented using FPGAs) in conjunction with the traditional EOS services can greatly enhance the efficiency and flexibility of WSNs

7. References

Adomat, J., Furunäs, J., Lindh, L., & Stärner. J., (1996). Real-Time Kernel in Hardware RTU: A step towards deterministic and high performance real-time systems. *In Proceedings of Eighth Euromicro Workshop on Real-Time Systems,* pp. 164-168, 'Aquila, Italy.

Andrews, D., Niehaus, D., & Ashenden, P., (2004). Programming Models for Hybrid FPGA/CPU computational Components , IEEE Computer, 2004(1) : 118-120.

Barr, M. (1999). *Programming Embedded Systems in C and C++", First Edition,* O' Reilly.

Burleson et al., (1993). The Spring Scheduling Co-Processor: A Scheduling Accelerator, *Proceedings of the International Conference on Computer Design (ICCD),* pp. 140-144..

Carpenter, T. & Barrett, J. (2008). *CWNA Certified Wireless Network Administrator Official Study Guide, Fourth Edition,* McGraw-Hill.

Chen, Y., Chein, T. & Chou, P. (2010). Enix: A Lightweight Dynamic Operating System for Tightly Constrained Wireless Sensor platforms, *In SenSys '10* , Zurich, Switzland.-

Chong, C. & Kumar, S.P. (2003). Sensor Networks: Evolution, Opportunities and Challenges, *Proceedings of the IEEE,* 91(8).

Gomaa, H., (1993). Software Design Methods for Concurrent and Real-time Systems, First edition, Addison-Wesley.

Heron, J.P., Woods, R., Sezer, S. & Turner R.H., (2001). Development of a Run-Time Reconfiguration System with Low Reconfiguration Overhead, *Journal of VLSI Signal Processing,* vol. 28, pp 97-113.

Hill, J., Horton, M., Kling, R. & Krishnamurthy, L. (2004). The Platforms Enabling Wireless Sensor Networks, *Communications of the ACM,* 47(6)

Ibrahim,D.,(2008). Advanced PIC Microcontroller projects in C, *Newness*

Karloff, C., Sastry, N. & Wagner, D. (2004). TinySec: A link Layer Security Architecture for Wireless Sensor Networks, *Proceedings of the 2nd ACM Conference on Embedded Networked Sensor Systems (Sensys 2004)*, Baltimore, MD.

Khan J. & Vemuri, R., (2005). Energy management in battery powered sensor networks with reconfigurable computing nodes, *in Proceedings of the International Conference on Field Programmable Logic and Applications (FPL '05)*, vol. 2005, pp. 543–546, Tampere, Finland.

Kohout, P., Ganesh, B. & Bruse, J. (2003). Hardware Support for Real-time Operating Systems. *CODES-ISSS'03*, California, USA.

Kompis, C. & Sureka, P. (2010). Power Management Technologies to Enable Remote and Wireless Sensing, *Cyber Security White Paper*, Available from: www.libelium.com/libelium.../libelium-ktn-power_management.pdf.

Kulkarni, K., Sanyal, S., Al-Qaheri, H. & Sanyal, S. (2009). Dynamic Reconfiguration of Wireless Sensor Networks. *International Journal of Computer Science and Applications*: 6(4),pp 16-42.

Labroasse, J., (2002) MicroC/OS-II The Real Time Kernel, *Newnes*.

Lee, J., Mooney, V., Instrom, K., Daleby, T., Klevin, T., & Lindh, L., (2003). A comparison of the RTU Hardware RTOS with a Hardware/Software RTOS, *Proceedings of Asia and South Pacific Design Automation Conference*, Asia.

Leligou, H.C., Redondo, L., Zahariads, T., Retamosa, D.R., Karkazis, P., Papaefstathiou, I. & Voliotis, S., (2008). Reconfiguration in Wireless Sensor Networks. *ARTEMIS-2008-100032, SMART 2008.*

Luk, M., Mezzour, G., Perri, A., & Gligor, V. (2007). MiniSec: A Secure Sensor Network Communication Architecture, *IPSN'07*, Cambridge, Massachusetts, U.S.A.

Mallikarjuna A., Reddy V., Kumar, P., Janakiram, D. & Kumar, G .A. (2009). Operating Systems for Wireless Sensor Networks: A Survey Technical Report, International *Journal of Sensor Networks (IJSNet)*, 5(4) : 236 - 255.

Moerschel, G., Dreger, R., Carpenter, T. (2007). *CWSP Certified Wireless Security Professional Official Study Guide, Second Edition* , McGraw-Hill.

Mooney, V., & Blough D.M.,(2002). A Hardware-Software Real-Time Operating System Framework for SOC's, *IEEE design and Test of Computers*, 2002(11):44-51.

Muralidhar, P. & Rao, C. (2008). Reconfigurable Wireless sensor network node based on NIOS core, *Processings of the 4th International Conference on Wireless Communication and Sensor Networks(WCSN'08),* Allahabad, India pp 67-72.

Omer, M. & Kunz, T. (2011). Operating Systems for Wireless Sensor Networks: A survey", *Sensors (an open access Journal)* , 11 (2011) : 5900-5930.

Perrig, A., Szewczyk, R., Wen, V., Cullerand D., Tygar, J.D. (2001). SPINS: Security Protocols for Sensor Networks, *Proceedings of 7th Annual International Conference on Mobile Computing and Networks*, Rome, Italy.

Portilla, J., Otero, A., Torre, Riesgo, T., Stecklina, O., Peter, S. & Langendorfer. P. (2010). Adaptable Security in Wireless Sensor Networks by using Reconfigurable ECC Hardware Coprocessors. *International Journal of Distributed Sensor Networks.*

Ramamurthy, H., Prabhu, B.S. & Gadh, R. (2004). Reconfigurable Wireless Interface for Networking Sensors (ReWINS), *Proceedings of IFIP TC6 , 9th International Conference on Personal Wireless Communication*. Netherlands.

Ramamurthy, H., Lal, D., Prabhu, B.S., & Gadh R. (2005). ReWINS: A Distributed Multi-RF Sensor Control Network for Industrial Automation, *IEEE wireless Telecommunication Symposium WTS 2005*, Pomona, California.

Stankovic, J.A. & Ramamritham, K, (1989). The Spring Kernel: A New Paradigm for Hard Realtime Operating Systems, *ACM Operating Systems Review*, 23(3), pp. 54-71.

Sugihara, R. & Gupta, R.K. (2008). Programming Models for Sensors Networks: A Survey, *ACM Transactions on Sensor Networks*, 4(2).

Walls, C., (1996). RTOS for Microcontroller Applications, *Electronic Engineering*, 68(831): 57-61.

Yick, J., Mukherjee B., & Ghosal, D. (2008). Wireless sensor network survey, *Journal of Computer Networks*, 52(2008):2292-2330.

Zuberi, K.M. & Shin, K.G, (1996). EMERALDS: A Microkernel for Embedded Real-Time Systems, *Proceedings of RTAS*, pp.241-249.

11

Hardware Design of Embedded Systems for Security Applications

Camel Tanougast, Abbas Dandache,
Mohamed Salah Azzaz and Said Sadoudi
University Lorraine of Metz
France

1. Introduction

Embedded systems are electronic computer systems designed for dedicated operating functions, often while respecting several constraints like real-time computing, power consumption, size and cost, etc. Embedded systems control many devices in common use today such as *smartphones, GPS, codec GSM, decoders, MP3, MPEG62, MPEG4, PDAs, RFIDs, smart cards* and *networked sensors* etc. Generally, they are controlled by one or more main processing cores that are typically either *Microcontrollers, Digital Signal Processors* (*DSPs*) or *Field Programmable Gate Arrays* (*FPGAs*). These systems are embedded as part of a complete electronic system, often including software, hardware, and communication and sensor parts. By contrast, a general-purpose computer - such as a *Personal Computer* (*PC*) - is designed to be flexible and to meet a wide range of end-user needs. The key characteristic of an embedded system is that it is dedicated to the handling of a particular task. They may require very powerful processors and extensive communications. Ideally, these embedded systems are completely self-contained and will typically run off a battery source for many years before the batteries need to be changed or charged. Since such systems are embedded and dedicated to specific tasks, design engineers search to optimise them by reducing their size (miniaturisation made possible by advanced *IC* design in order to couple full communication subsystems to sophisticated sensors) and cost in terms of energy consumption, memory and logic resources, while increasing their reliability and performance. Consequently, embedded systems are especially suited for use in transportation, medical applications, safety and security. Indeed, in dealing with security, embedded systems can be self-sufficient and should be able to deal with communication systems. Considering these specific conditions, in the fields of information and communication technology, embedded systems designers are faced with many challenges in terms of both the trade-off between cost/performance/power and architecture design. This is especially true for embedded systems designs, which often operate in non-secure environments, while at the same time being constrained by such factors as computational capacity, memory size and - in particular - power consumption. One challenge is in the design of hardware architecture able to meet the appropriate level of security and – consequently – the best trade-off between hardware resources and the best throughput rates for real-time embedded applications.

A digital implementation of chaotic generators presents certain advantages and provides accuracy and a significant hope for integration in embedded applications, especially for data encryption and secure communications between embedded systems. Unlike analogue implementations, which exhibit various practical difficulties in ensuring information recovery and dealing with the problem of chaotic synchronisation (since the component values vary with age and temperature, etc.), a digital implementation avoids the parameter mismatch between transmitter and receiver. Indeed, a programmable hardware fabric like a *FPGA* (*Field Programmable Logic Array*) is taking an increasingly important place in the design of embedded digital systems. This is due to the excellent trade-off between computational power and the flexibility of processing which it provides.

This chapter is organised as follows: In Section 2, the related embedded design approaches suitable for embedded secure application (encryption) are briefly described. Section 3 explores the architecture of a hardware implementation for helping system designers who are faced with many challenges with regards to the trade-off between *cost/performance/power/security* and architecture design. Section 4 gives an overview, namely a characterisation of three dimensional (*3-D*) continuous chaotic systems used for embedded encryption applications. In this section, the background of the digital design based on a numerical resolution method of the *3D* chaotic systems is given. Section 5 presents and discusses in detail the various steps involved in the design of a chaotic system as well as the design of its programmable hardware technology, and it illustrates this with the *Genesio*'s chaotic system designed in a *FPGA*. Finally, Section 6 summarises and concludes the chapter.

2. Overview of the hardware design of embedded systems

The electronic computing architecture of embedded systems is often composed of embedded blocks as parts of a complete device, often including hardware, an interface and mechanical parts. Usually, these systems are designed digitally in order to be flexible and to meet a wide range of application constraints. Therefore, embedded systems contain processing cores (*CPUs*) associated with several peripherals (integrated peripherals like *Analogue-to-Digital Converters* (*ADCs*), *Digital-to-Analogue Converters* (*DACs*), analogue signal conditioning blocks allowing them to operate as a *System-on-Chip*) that typically consist of *Microcontrollers, Digital Signal Processors* (*DSPs*) or else *hardware specific cores* tailored for dedicated tasks. These embedded architectures allow a good trade-off between performance, cost and application constraints (real-time processing, power consumption, etc.). Usually, these embedded systems are defined as *Systems on Chip* (*SoC*) and presented in a hand-format. Figure 1 provides an overview of one embedded *System on Chip* (a *Bluetooth System on Chip*).

However, the significant requirements and different constraints for an embedded application and the characteristics of the embedded system dedicated to handling a particular task must be taken into account. Their requirements often lead to the design of a specific embedded system for application in just one field. In this context, a methodological approach based on embedded design flow and available technologies must be considered by taking into account the advantages and main drawbacks for meeting the application constraints of the embedded application under consideration. Since embedded systems are dedicated to certain specific tasks, design engineers can optimise them in order to reduce their size and their cost, as well as increasing their reliability and performance by considering the following hardware design approach.

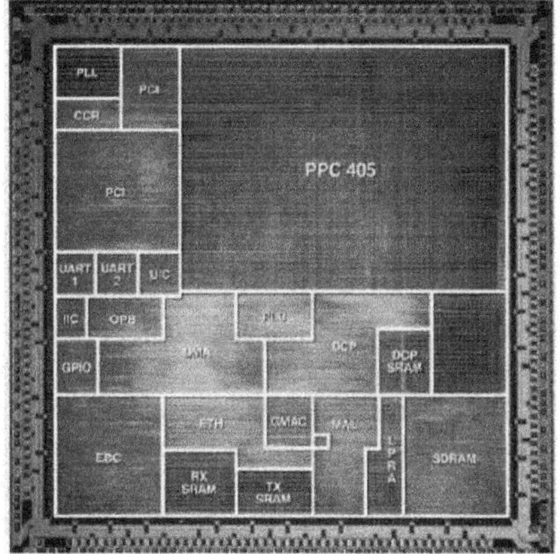

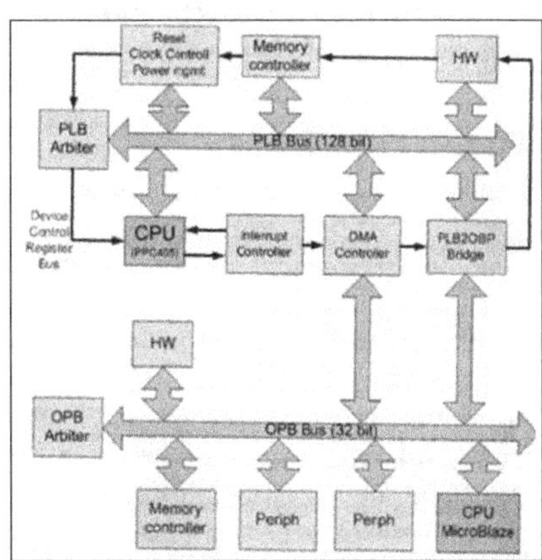

Fig. 1. Bluetooth embedded System on Chip.

The embedded system design specification stage includes successive analysis steps which will impact on the performance of the system - depending on the choice of technology used - which must comply with the application constraints. Thus, we adopt a definition of a system's specifications (the required functions, environment, input/output system, etc.) which focuses on the selection of the available technology. In this context - and depending, for example, of the system timing requirements or other timing constraints, limitations of size or the logic area and memory requirements - the development of new embedded systems products is not trivial for electronics designers. Therefore, depending on the choice of the technology used, the application requirements may not be respected.

Among the technology available for the design of embedded systems, we find:

- The processor or microcontroller (corresponding to one core processor associated with a peripheral), often defined as a software solution.
- The specific integrated circuit and the programmable circuit, such as a *CPLD* (*Complex Programmable Logic Device*) or now a *FPGA*, often defined as a hardware solution.

All of these present specific advantages and drawbacks. Thus, an *Application-Specific Integrated Circuit* (*ASIC*) - which is an integrated circuit customised for particular tasks - is not intended for general-purpose use. Similarly, an *Application-Specific Standard Product* (*ASSP*) - which is a custom product for a specific application designed for use by more than one customer - is not adapted. Indeed, the flexibility of the embedded system is required, where changes continue even after the embedded system was designed. Moreover, although the *ASIC* presents the best performance with low power consumption, the main drawbacks of an *Integrated Circuit* (*IC*) are its very high cost (which is always increasing) and lengthened development time, which is unsuitable for the design of an embedded system where evolution occurs quickly.

Software solutions based on a micro-programmed system, such as a *CPU*, a *Microcontroller* or a *DSP*, present the very best flexibility since they are only based on the change of instructions in the memory. However, their main drawback is that their computation is weakly intensive, especially for some embedded applications where the process requires a long computation time. Therefore, for most applications the computation time will be prohibitive if a software solution is adopted. This effect is directly related to the nature of *Von Neumann*'s architecture of a *CPU* which cannot operate in a parallel fashion.

FPGAs have been taking an increasingly significant place in the design of embedded digital systems thanks to their excellent trade-off between computing power and the flexibility of processing that they provides [Tanougast et al., 2003]. This is particularly true for embedded system design, which can be used for quality evaluation or protocol communication in a network of data diffusion [Compton & Hauck, 2002]. Thus, *FPGAs* are increasingly used in conventional high performance computing applications where computations are performed on the *FPGA* instead of on a microprocessor. Indeed, the logic implementation based on *FPGAs* offers performance improvements an order of magnitude over microprocessors. For example, take the implementation of the *Advanced Encryption Standard* (*AES*) encryption on a *Xilinx Virtex5 FPGA* [Xilinx, 2008], which runs at 100MHz - this is 10 times faster than a highly optimised AES encryption running on the latest *CPU* [Burr, 2003; Liu, 2005]. Other benefits are in terms of the power used, where a *FPGA* implementation of applications is expected to consume less power than a microprocessor. Low-power usage is due to a lower clock rate and the absence of wasted cycles for the fetch/decode instruction in *FPGAs*. In this context, the use of *FPGA* technology makes it possible to optimise the hardware resources required while allowing for real-time computing. Moreover, an alternate approach based on a *FPGA* is to use soft processor cores that are implemented within the *FPGA* logic. *MicroBlaze* and *Nios II* are the most popular softcore examples provided by the main *FPGA* companies (*Altera* and *Xilinx*) [Xilinx1, 2008; Altera, 2011]. Figure 2 presents comparisons in terms of flexibility versus performance between the available technologies dedicated for embedded system design.

Usually, designs implemented on *FPGAs* require on average 18 times as much logic area, 7 times as much dynamic power and are 3 times slower than the corresponding *ASIC* implementations. Although *FPGAs* have been slower, less energy efficient and have generally achieved less functionality than their *ASIC* counterparts, their main advantages lie in their ability to reprogram in order to fix bugs, their shorter design time and the lower non-recurring engineering costs suitable for a faster embedded system design. Therefore, one solution for embedded designers is in reconfigurable systems based on *FPGAs* that can be reprogrammed to accommodate changing standards and protocols in the design process. Moreover, *FPGA* technology allows the designer to control all the phases of the design from the prototype.

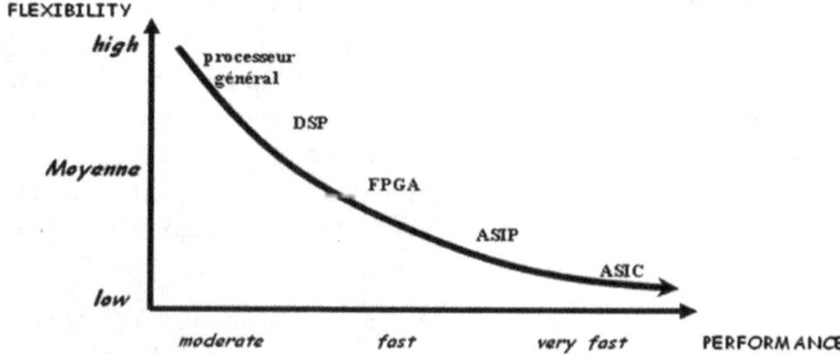

Fig. 2. Flexibility versus performance of the main technologies suitable for an embedded digital system.

A recent trend has been to take a coarse-grained architectural approach by combining the logic blocks and interconnections of traditional *FPGAs* with embedded microprocessors and related peripherals. The goal is to form a complete "System on a Programmable Chip" suitable for a large performing embedded system. In this context, advances in *Very-large-Scale Integration* (*VLSI*) technology have been employed to the manufacturing of reconfigurable logic for *FPGA* chips; and helped with their rapid growth in logic capacity, performance and popularity. In summary, a *FPGA*-based architecture is suitable for efficient computing of embedded applications with high data rate to compute. It is an excellent alternative to performing fast processing in order to reduce the total processing time, while maintaining a good level of flexibility in allowing any modifications in the run time required for current embedded systems.

3. Architecture exploration

The objective of an architecture exploration is to find an efficient matching between an algorithm and the architecture. The aim is to realise an optimal implementation that satisfies the various constraints (real-time, logic area, etc.). Therefore, digital hardware techniques can be used to implement efficiency in embedded applications like chaotic generators for embedded encryption by using digital devices such as *microcontrollers, DSPs, ASICs, processors* and *FPGA* technologies. The choice of implementation in a digital system is driven by many criteria and is heavily dependent on the application area. Table 1 gives the main contrasting features of current digital technologies for the design of embedded systems.

Features	**Processors / DSP / Microcontroller (Software)**	**FPGA (Hardware programmable)**	**ASICs (Hardware)**
Silicon area	Fixed	Variable	Fixed and low
Speed	Moderate	Fast	Very fast
Consumption	Moderate	High	Weak
Cost	Low	Moderate	High
Prototyping	Yes	Yes	No

Table 1. Features of the main technologies available for the design of embedded systems.

As mentioned previously, the designer can realise any embedded system (based on either the logic design and/or software design thanks to the embedded *softcore* processor) by utilising programmable logic devices in the form of *FPGAs* and *CPLDs* [Brown & Rose, 1996]. In the design context, the objective of *Algorithm/Architecture Adequation* (architecture exploration based on A^3 methodology [Sorel, 1994]) is to realise an optimal implementation which satisfies the constraints (real-time, logic area, etc.). In this Section, we illustrate an analysis of the costs and benefits of the use of reconfigurable technology such as *FPGAs*.

In practice, the actual embedded system is composed inside the chip of a high coupled processor with a *Programmable Array* (*FPGA, CPLD*, etc). Indeed, such a hardware structure allows the combination of the advantages of these two technologies inside the same circuit. Consequently, coupling can reduce the main drawbacks of these technologies when they are used individually. Figure 3 illustrated one such embedded programmable hardware core which is usually associated with peripheral modules.

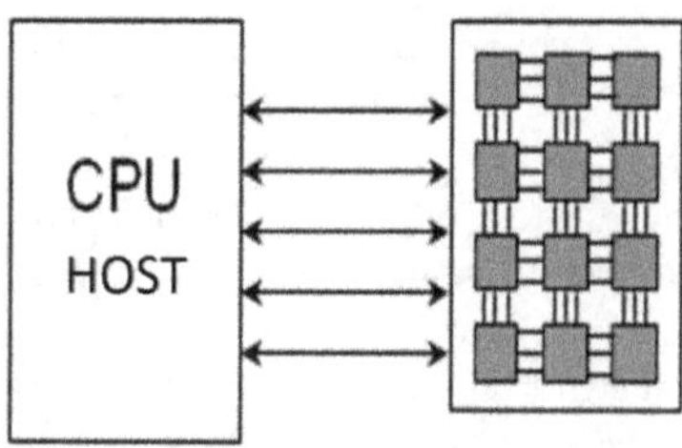

Fig. 3. High coupled processor - *FPGA* - on a chip core of a current embedded programmable hardware system.

With regard to the task of implementing an algorithm on a similar embedded programmable hardware system, we can distinguish two approaches [Tanougast et al., 2003]. The most common is what we call *the application development approach* and the other is what we call *the system design approach*. In the first case, we have to fit an algorithm with an optional time constraint in an existing system made from a host *CPU* connected to a reconfigurable logic array. In this case, the goal of an optimal implementation is to minimise one or more of the following criteria: processing time, memory bandwidth and power consumption. In the second case, we have to implement an algorithm with a required time constraint on a system which is still in the design exploration phase. The design parameter is the size of the logic array, which is used to implement the data path part of the algorithm. Here, an optimal implementation is that which leads to the minimal logic area of the reconfigurable array, memory resources and input/output port number. Figure 4 depicts an overview of the hardware design approaches of embedded systems.

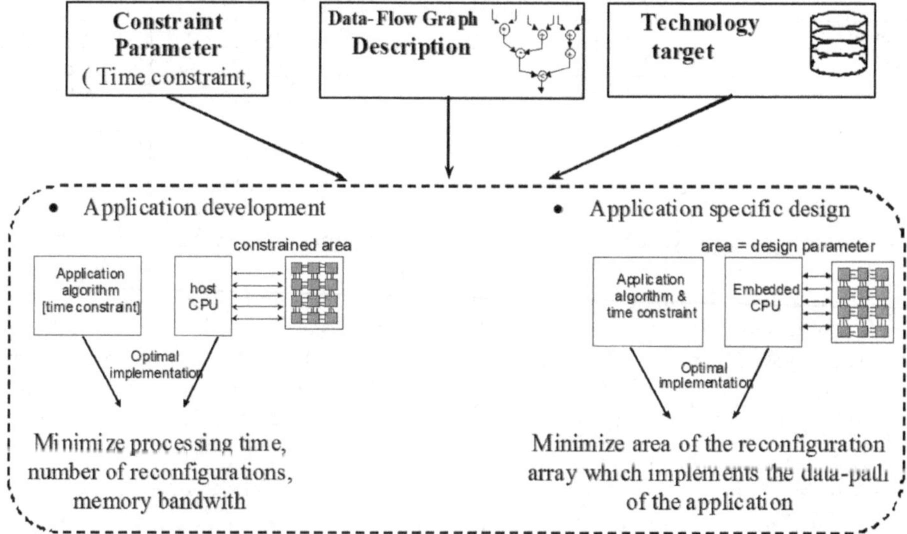

Fig. 4. The two approaches used to implement an algorithm on reconfigurable hardware.

Embedded systems exhibit several advantages through the use of *FPGAs*. The most obvious is the possibility for frequently updating the digital hardware functions. However, we can also use the dynamic resources allocation feature in order to instantiate each operator for the strict required time. This permits the enhancement of silicon efficiency by reducing the reconfigurable array's area. Consequently, the goal of the embedded system designers in architectural design flow is to minimise the *FPGA* resources needed for the implementation of a time constrained algorithm. So, the challenge is twofold. Firstly, to find a trade-off between flexibility and algorithm implementation efficiency through the programmable logic-array coupled with a *CPU* host (processor, *DSP*, etc.). Secondly, to obtain an optimal architecture synthesis allowing the best hardware implementation trade-off required for embedded applications.

In the rest of this chapter, we describe the main steps in the hardware design of embedded systems for security applications. We will consider an encryption process based on key chaotic generators and a mechanism for mixing the key with plaintext (*encryption/decryption* process).

4. Embedded digital chaotic cryptosystem

Chaos-based encryption suggests a new and efficient way of dealing with the problem of fast and highly secure data encryption. To implement the chaotic behaviour generators and the chaotic attractors associated with certain practical applications, many methods based on analogue circuits are used, such as switched capacitors or analogue *Complementary Metal Oxide Semiconductor* (*CMOS*) technology [Matsumoto, 1987; Giannakopoulos et al., 2007; Ozoguz et al., 2005; Cha & Lee, 2005]. However, these methods exhibit some practical difficulties since the component values vary with age and temperature, etc. [Aseeri et al., 2002; Sobhy et al., 1999]. To overcome this problem, a digital implementation of chaotic generators can be used, since the problem of parameter mismatch does not exist and it provides accuracy and a significant possibility of integration in the embedded system, allowing many possibilities for embedded applications. The originality of this cipher scheme is that it allows for low cost data encryption for embedded systems while still providing a good trade-off between performance and hardware resources. The experimental results have demonstrated the feasibility and efficiency of this secure solution for *FPGA* technology. In the rest of this chapter, thorough experimental tests are presented with detailed analysis, demonstrating the high security and fast encryption speed suitable for embedded cryptosystems where resource optimisation is required in the field of embedded applications.

4.1 Chaotic generators-based encryption

In recent years, a variety of encryption schemes have been proposed for real-time secure data transmission over the Internet and through wireless networks by embedded systems. Among them, chaos-based algorithms have shown some attractive properties in terms of security, complexity, speed, computing power and computational overheads, etc. More precisely, although chaotic systems are characterised by specific attractors, their generated chaotic signals are non-periodic, uncorrelated and appear random in the time domain. These properties increase the complexity of a cryptanalysis attack in terms of the visualisation and identification of the signals used for key generation through a key space analysis. Hence, embedded cryptosystems for secure communications based on chaos theory have been proposed and developed while showing that these embedded systems can be controlled

[Lorenz, 1963; Yang, 2004]. Indeed, the synchronisation between two identical chaotic embedded systems corresponding to the data encryption transmission module and the decryption reception module has been reported [Carroll & Pecora, 1990]. Consequently, it was concluded that a key generator based on chaos theory could be useful with regard to secure communication systems because chaos is extremely sensitive to initial conditions and parameters [Azzaz et al., 2011].

Usually, the embedded cryptosystems are based on the design of a real-time secure symmetric encryption scheme. According to the basic principles of cryptology, a cryptosystem should be sensitive to the key - i.e., the cipher-text should have a close correlation with the key. To accomplish this requirement, we can use an efficient (ideally, genuinely random) key generation mechanism and then mix the key thoroughly into the plain-text through the encryption process. One data encryption scheme is based on embedded chaotic key generators. Therefore, the complete *encryption/decryption* scheme consists of two operational steps, as shown for example by the Figure 5 for real time image encryption scheme.

Step 1. *Chaotic key generation and selection.* A key is generated from the previous key and one sequence of word-length bits as the key is selected in a chaotic manner.

Step 2. *Cipher operations are performed.* For example, the basic cipher that is performed is the *XOR* or *NXOR* operation.

According to the key binary sequence generated, each section of data is then operated on with the selected key. For instance, in an image encryption stream (see figure 5), each data image pixel is then *XORed* with the selected key. The decipher procedure is similar to that of the encipher process illustrated above, but with a reverse operation sequence to that described in *Steps 1* and *2* above. Since both the decipher and encipher procedures have similar structures, they have essentially the same algorithmic complexity and duration of operation.

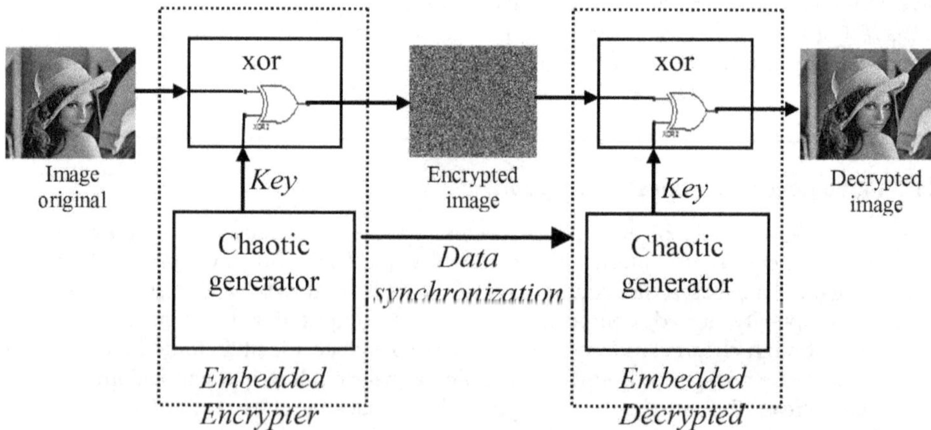

Fig. 5. Example of an embedded encryption scheme: real time image encryption based a chaotic key generator.

4.2 Tri-dimensional chaotic systems: chaos behavioural modelling and software simulation

Among chaotic systems, we find the continuous chaotic systems characterised by a system of differential equation systems. Most of the continuous chaotic systems can be expressed by an equivalent form of a three-dimensional system. Among them, we cite the tri-dimensional (*3D*) chaotic system, exemplified by such as *Lorenz*'s, *Chen*'s, *Lü*'s, *Colpitts, Chua*'s, *Rössler*'s, *Linz* and/or *Sprott*'s systems, etc. [Kvarda, 2002; Chen et al., 2007; Lü & Chen, 2002; Kennedy, 1994; Indrusiak, 2005; Genesio, 1993; Genesio & Tesi, 1992; Park, 2007]. These *3D* systems provide chaotic behaviours which depend on the initial conditions and parameter values characterising them. In particular, the *Lorenz* system is a famous example of a chaotic system [Lorenz, 1963]. It is represented by the following simplified nonlinear equation system [Cuomo, 1993] which can be understood in terms of chaotic behaviour, depending of the parameter values:

$$\begin{cases} \dfrac{dx}{dt} = \sigma(y\text{-}x) & \text{(1a)} \\ \dfrac{dy}{dt} = \text{-}xz + rx\text{-}y & \text{(1b)} \\ \dfrac{dz}{dt} = xy\text{-}bz & \text{(1c)} \end{cases}$$

The solution of this nonlinear equation system depends mainly on the initial conditions specified by the initial values of $x = x_0$, $y = y_0$ and $z = z_0$. For instance, a numerical solution to this system with Lorenz's parameters' values (σ = 10, r = 28 and b = 8/3) and initial conditions ($x_0 = 0$, $y_0 = 5$, $z_0 = 25$) gives the corresponding chaotic signals x, y and z, and the two different attractors of the chaotic system are shown in Figure 6 (obtained under the *MatLab* simulation environment tool [Mathworks, 2006]).

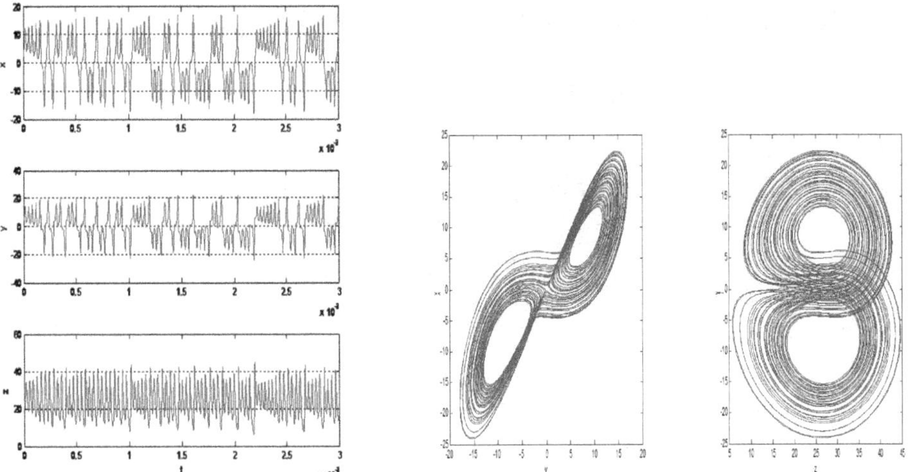

Fig. 6. *MatLab* simulation results of *Lorenz's* chaotic signals and attractors in a phase plane: (x-y) and (y-z).

4.3 Digital implementation based on the numerical resolution of 3D chaotic systems

One efficient and optimised solution for implementing a *3D* chaotic embedded system is to design a specific logic hardware architecture tailored for a digital numerical resolution method. Among these, we can cite both *Euler*'s and *Runge-Kutta*'s numerical resolution methods [Yang et al., 2005; Cartwright & Piro, 1992]. Unlike the *Euler* method - a numerical procedure for solving the simplest approximation by the first-order differential equations with initial conditions - the *Runge-Kutta* method allows for the most accurate solutions. Indeed, in numerical analysis, the *Runge–Kutta* method characterises an important family of implicit and explicit iterative methods for the approximation of solutions for *Ordinary Differential Equations* (*ODEs*) [Cartwright & Piro, 1992]. These numerical methods are based on the principle of iteration, which is to say that the first estimate of the solution is used to calculate a second estimate, more precisely, and so on. One member of the family of *Runge–Kutta* methods used is the fourth-order *Runge-Kutta* equation method, often referred to as the "classical *Runge-Kutta* method" or simply "*RK-4*". Hereafter, we focus here on the *RK-4* method.

Let us consider the following first-order nonlinear differential equation system modelling the behaviour of a *3D* chaotic system:

$$\begin{cases} \dfrac{dx}{dt} = F(x,y,z) \\ \dfrac{dy}{dt} = G(x,y,z) \\ \dfrac{dz}{dt} = Q(x,y,z) \end{cases} \tag{2}$$

where $x(t_0)= x_0$, $y(t0)= y_0$ et $z(t_0)= z_0$ and *F, G, Q* are nonlinear functions. The *RK-4* method uses several intermediate points to calculate the next value, starting from the initial value and the step length *h* in *t*, as specified by the following equations:

$$x_{n+1} = x_n + \frac{h}{6}\left(k_0 + 2k_1 + 2k_2 + k_3\right) \tag{3}$$

$$y_{n+1} = y_n + \frac{h}{6}(m_0 + 2m_1 + 2m_2 + m_3) \tag{4}$$

$$z_{n+1} = z_n + \frac{h}{6}(n_0 + 2n_1 + 2n_2 + n_3) \tag{5}$$

where at the initial t_0 instant:

$$k_0 = F(t_n, x_n) \tag{6}$$

$$m_0 = G(t_n, y_n) \tag{7}$$

$$n_0 = Q(t_n, z_n) \tag{8}$$

at $t_0 + h/2$ instant:

$$k_1 = F(t_n + \frac{h}{2}, x_n + \frac{h}{2}k_0) \tag{9}$$

$$m_1 = G(t_n + \frac{h}{2}, y_n + \frac{h}{2}m_0) \tag{10}$$

$$n_1 = Q(t_n + \frac{h}{2}, z_n + \frac{h}{2}n_0) \tag{11}$$

$$k_2 = F(t_n + \frac{h}{2}, x_n + \frac{h}{2}k_1) \tag{12}$$

$$m_2 = G(t_n + \frac{h}{2}, y_n + \frac{h}{2}m_1) \tag{13}$$

$$n_2 = Q(t_n + \frac{h}{2}, z_n + \frac{h}{2}n_1) \tag{14}$$

and at $t_0 + h$ instant:

$$k_3 = F(t_n + h, x_n + hk_2) \tag{15}$$

$$m_3 = G(t_n + h, y_n + hm_2) \tag{16}$$

$$n_3 = Q(t_n + h, z_n + hn_2) \tag{17}$$

5. Digital programmable hardware implementation

Since the introduction of *FPGAs*, the process of digital systems design has changed radically [Hauck, 1998]. This technology allows the appearance of hardware that is as flexible as the programming paradigm in the realisation of real-time applications. In the case of the implementation of a digital chaotic system, most approaches based on *FPGA* are designed using a non-optimal description embedded architecture by using automatic code generation tools as in [Aseeri et al., 2002; Sobhy et al., 1999]. However, the *"high level"* aspect of these methods keeps the user far away from the realities of the physical implementation (the low level corresponding to the *Register Transfer Level* (*RTL*)) required for the performance of a design analysis allowing the best hardware implementation. Consequently, in terms of performance and density of resources used, the result remains out of the designer's reach, which cannot be accepted by embedded electronic designers, where optimisation and efficient implementation form a primary purpose.

In the rest of this section, we present a case study of the specific design implementation of one chaotic embedded cryptosystem based on the *RTL* architecture described as structural *VHDL* (*VHSIC - Very High Speed Integrated Circuits - Hardware Description Language*) suitable for a high data encryption rate.

5.1 Case study: *Genesio-Tesi's* system

The *Genesio-Tesi* system, proposed by *Genesio* and *Tesi* [Sadoudi et al., 2010], is one of paradigms of chaos since it captures many of the features of chaotic systems. The *Genesio-Tesi* chaotic oscillator is one of the most famous and well-studied continuous nonlinear and non-autonomous chaotic systems, exhibiting various dynamic behaviours, including chaos and bifurcations [Genesio, 1993; Genesio & Tesi, 1992]. The chaotic system includes a simple square part and three simple *ODE*s that depend on three positive parameters [Park, 2007]. The nonlinear dynamic equations of the system are as follows:

$$\begin{cases} \dfrac{dx}{dt} = y & \text{(a)} \\ \dfrac{dy}{dt} = z & \text{(b)} \\ \dfrac{dz}{dt} = -az - by + x^2 - cx & \text{(c)} \end{cases} \tag{18}$$

where x, y and z are the state variables, and a, b and c are the positive real constants satisfying $ab < c$. The chaotic regime of the equation (18) is obtained by the following bifurcation parameter values $a = 1.2$, $b = 2.92$ and $c = 6$ with the initial conditions $x_0 = 0.2$, $y_0 = 0.2$ and $z_0 = 0$ [Sadoudi et al., 2010]. The *MatLab* [Mathworks, 2006] simulation results of this chaotic system are given by Figures 7 and 8 where the chaotic signals x, y and z and the three-dimensional (*3D*) chaotic attractors (x-y and x-z chaotic attractors) are presented, respectively. These results will be useful as references for the implementation of the hardware results detailed in Section 5.8.

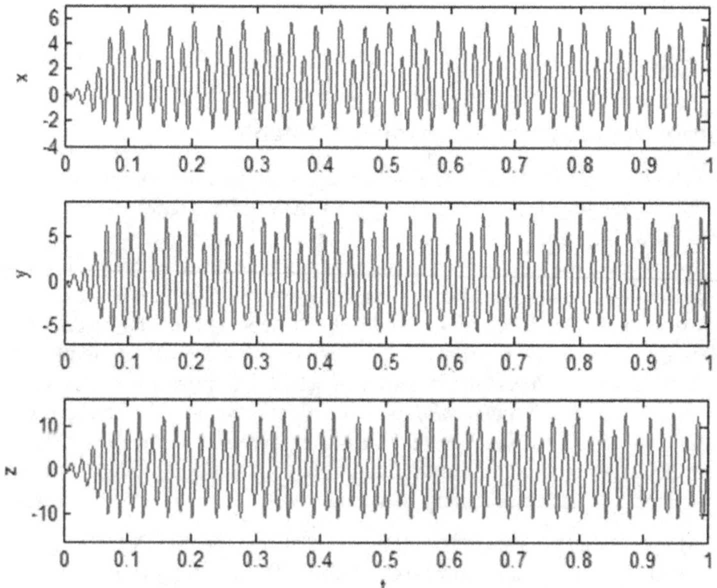

Fig. 7. *MatLab* simulation results of the x, y and z chaotic signals.

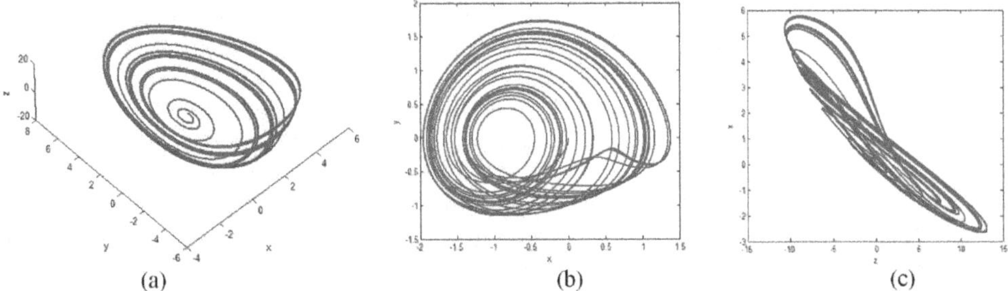

Fig. 8. *MatLab* simulation results: (a) the *3D* chaotic attractor; (b) the *x-y* chaotic attractor; (c) the *x-z* chaotic attractor.

5.2 FPGA technology

FPGA is an integrated circuit designed to be configured by the customer or the designer. Embedded systems design can have several advantages for our approach based on *FPGAs* [Tanougast et al., 2003; Compton & Hauck, 2002; Hauck, 1998]. The most obvious is the possibility of frequently updating the digital hardware's functions. The challenge is then to find trade-offs between flexibility and algorithm implementation efficiency through the programmable logic-array. They are used in various applications requiring digital electronic functions (signal processing, telecommunications, embedded systems, etc.). They are generally slower, more expensive by unit and consume more energy than their equivalents in *ASIC* (*IC* dedicated to an application) technology. However, as mentioned in the previous section, the reconfigurable embedded systems based on *FPGA* are interesting for embedded chaotic generators in the way that they ensure better computing performance in comparison with a *CPU* core and in the way that they allow the flexibility necessary for multi-standard encryption applications. Indeed, with such embedded systems, it is easy to update a suitable cipher encryption at a lower cost as compared with silicon *IP* (*Intellectual Property*) corresponding to one specific *ASIC* encryption bloc. More precisely, suppose that we have to implement a cryptosystem design requiring *P* equivalent gates and taking an area S_{area} of silicon in the case of a full custom *ASIC* design. We will need about 100 x S_{area} if we decide to use a *FPGA*. However, the significant advantage of the *FPGA* is, of course, its high flexibility and the speed of the associated design flow. This is probably the main reason for including a *FPGA* array on an embedded *System on Chip*. In summary, *FPGAs* present several advantages:

- The time to market is shorter because they are standard components.
- They have a shorter development and design period because they reuse basic functions and their circuit configuration is made on site.
- They present a lower cost for small quantities (less than 10,000 units). With technological evolution, this quantity tends to increase. Indeed, the cost of a chip is proportional to its logic area, which decreases with fine engraving, while the initial costs of producing an ASIC (design, testing and etching masks) are rapidly increasing.

Physically, a *FPGA* is a programmable logic device which can be programmed once or several times, depending on the technology used (*SRAM, EPROM, and ANTIFUSE*). Generally, one *FPGA* contains an array of *Programmable or Configurable Logic Blocks* (often called "*Logic Blocks*" and depending on a vendor denoted by *CLB - Configurable Logic Block* - by the *Xilinx* company, or by *LAB - Logic Array Block* - by the *Altera* company) and a hierarchy of reconfigurable interconnects through "*Router Matrix Blocks*" that allow the *Logic Blocks* to be inter-wired in different configurations (routing channels). Locally around the periphery of the device, the input and output cells (*I/O* pads) allow the logical connection interfaces between the design inside the *FPGA* and off-chip modules external to the device. These *I/O* components can be configured as an input, output or bidirectional interface pin. The resulting structure is vendor-dependant (*Altera, Actel, Xilinx* companies, etc.). According to the arrangement of the *Logic Blocks* and their interconnections on the device, *FPGAs* can be classified according to several categories, such as a *symmetrical array*, a *hierarchy-based array* and a *row-based array*, etc. Figure 9 describes an overview of a *symmetrical array* based the FPGA currently used (*Xilinx's Virtex FPGA* technology) [Xilinx2, 2007].

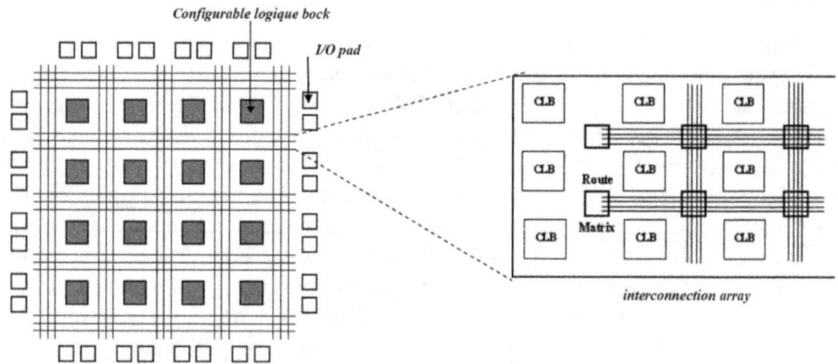

Fig. 9. Overview of the inner architecture of a FPGA.

Currently, *Logic Blocks* (*CLB* or *LAB*) consist of *logical cells* (denoted *LEs*, *Slices*, etc.) which are typically cells based on an *n-inputs function generator* (usually denoted as *Look-Up Tables* (*LUTs*)) associated with registers through local select interconnects. An *LUT* is generally made up of 4 to 6 inputs - according to the manufacturer or the *FPGA* family - and one output, which is used to implement logic equations by the combination of input values. One *LUT* acts as a truth table and then specifies its output based on its inputs and the contents of the table. The advantage of such a logic structure is in replacing a tree of logic operators with an easier consultation operation. Consequently, the speed gain increases and can be significant because one read logic value is often faster than one logic operation. Figure 10 illustrates the principle of a four-input *LUT*.

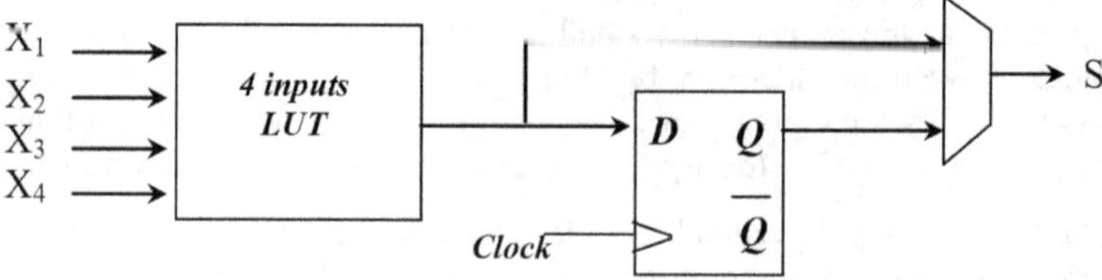

Fig. 10. Generic overview of a 4-input *Look-Up Table*.

Thanks to programmable *LUTs*, *Logic blocks* can be configured to perform complex combinational functions, or merely simple logic gates such as *AND* and *XOR*. In most *FPGAs*, the logic blocks also include memory elements, which may be simple flip-flops or more complete blocks of memory. Therefore, depending of the *FPGA* technology and family, the logical cells can also include other logic functions. For instance, Figure 11 describes one *Logic Block* involving *Virtex* technology [Xilinx3, 2000] which consists of two *3-input LUTs*, a *Full Adder* (*FA*) and a *D-type flip-flop*. In this example, depending of the mode of the cell, there are several possible configurations. In normal mode, the two *3-input LUTs* are combined into a *4-input LUT* through one multiplexer operator [Xilinx3, 2000] (*Mux* operator block in Figure 11) while in the arithmetic mode, their outputs are fed to the *FA* block. The selection of the mode is programmed thanks to one multiplexer (the middle *Mux*). Similarly, the output of the LUT can be either synchronous or asynchronous, depending on the programming of one of the multiplexers at the output cell. In practice, entire or parts of the *FA* are placed as functions into the *LUTs* in order to save on the costs of the logic area.

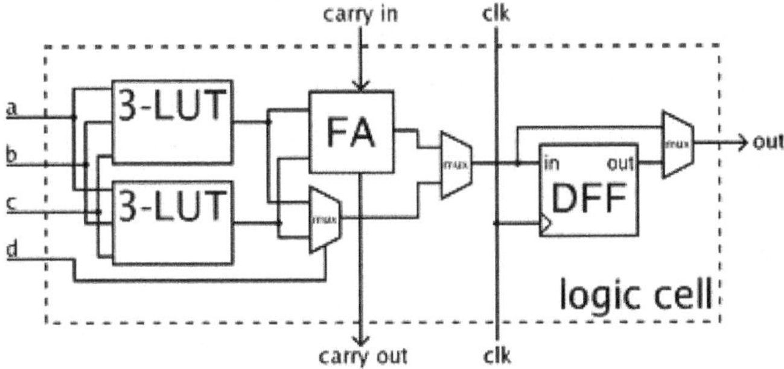

Fig. 11. Structure one *Programmable Logic Component* based on two *3-input LUTs* involving *Virtex FPGA* technology [Xilinx3, 2000].

In the current trend, modern *FPGAs* contain embedded components such as memory blocks, multipliers and even processors cores. These *FPGA* families expand upon the above capabilities to include higher level functionality fixed into the silicon. Having these common functions embedded into the silicon reduces the area required and gives those functions increased speed when compared with building them from primitives. Thus, the *Virtex II* technology includes two *IBM 405 PowerPC* processor cores in the *Xilinx Virtex II Pro device*, as described by Figure 12, which gives an overview of this *FPGA* chip [Xilinx2, 2007]. By including one or more hardcore processor cores on the *FPGA* chip, this allows the preservation of the configurable logic resources.

Similarly, some *Logic Blocks* can include complex arithmetic and logic units, such as embedded processors, depending on the type or family of the *FPGA* technology used (commonly referred to as the size granularity of the *Logic Cells*). Examples of these include *multipliers*, generic *DSP* (*digital signal processing*) blocks, high speed *I/O* logics and *embedded memories*. For example, a number of complex operations are performed using a specific arithmetic *FPGA* block called a *DSP*-Block. This type of arithmetic structure is frequently implemented onto a *Virtex FPGA* chip in order to implement digital signal processing operations. One *DSP*-block contains a multiplier of 18 × 25 bits and one accumulator to store

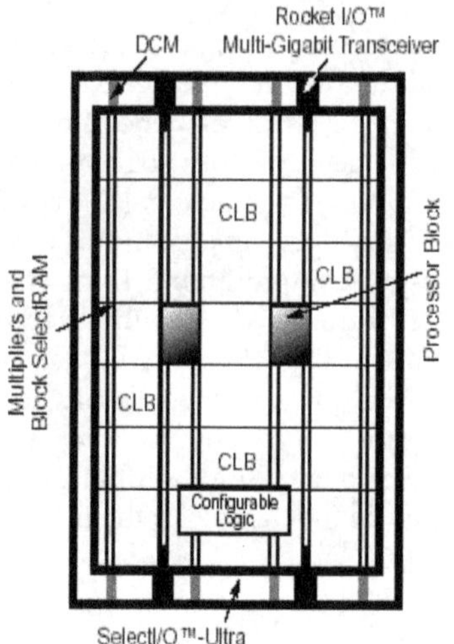

Fig. 12. Overview of the *Xilinx Virtex II FPGA* chip [Xilinx2, 2007].

the operational results [Xilinx2, 2007; Xilinx3, 2000; Xilinx, 2008]. Figure 13 presents one *DSP*-block.

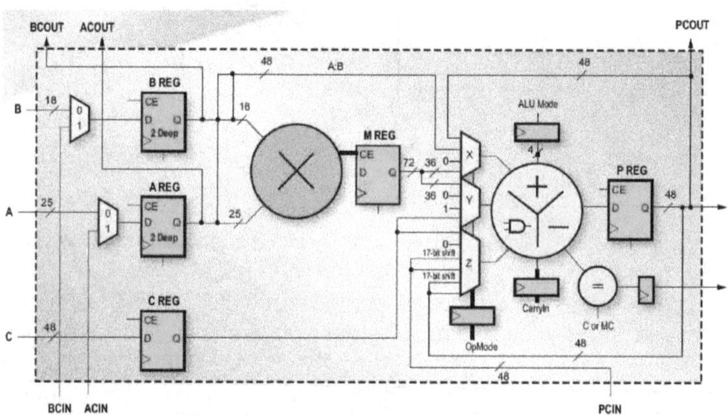

Fig. 13. Overview of the data-path of one *DSP*-Bloc using the *Xilinx Virtex II* and *V* technologies [Xilinx2, 2007; Xilinx3, 2000; Xilinx, 2008].

In fact, modern *FPGAs* are large enough and contain enough memory to be configured with either a generic or specific processor in order to execute software code. These configured processor units are called *softcore* processors as opposed to *hardcore* processors, which are buried in the silicon of the *FPGA*. As an example of such a *softcore* processor, we can cite the *MicroBlaze* or *Nios* processors of the *Xilinx* and *Altera* companies, respectively [Xilinx1, 2008; Altera, 2011]. Of course, this trend does not preclude the use of *softcore* processors in addition to the already embedded hardcore processors. However, it tends increase the integration complexity of systems in the *FPGA* silicon chip.

To define the behaviour and configuration of the *FPGA*, the user provides a *Hardware Description Language* (*HDL*) or a schematic design. Generally, the designers of digital embedded applications use a *HDL* - such as *Verilog* or *VHDL* (*VHSIC - Very High Speed Integrated Circuits - Hardware Description Language*) - to describe the functionality of *FPGAs*. Indeed, in the field of electronic design, *HDL* acts as specification and modelling languages for the description and design of electronic logic circuits. Therefore, designers can describe the operations, design and organisation of their digital circuit, and test it to verify their operation by means of simulation. In a typical design flow, a *FPGA* application developer will describe and simulate the design at multiple stages throughout the design process. The *FPGA* design flow comprises of several steps, namely design entry, design synthesis, design implementation (mapping place and route) and device programming. Figure 14 gives an overview of the *FPGA* design flow carried out by specific automation tools.

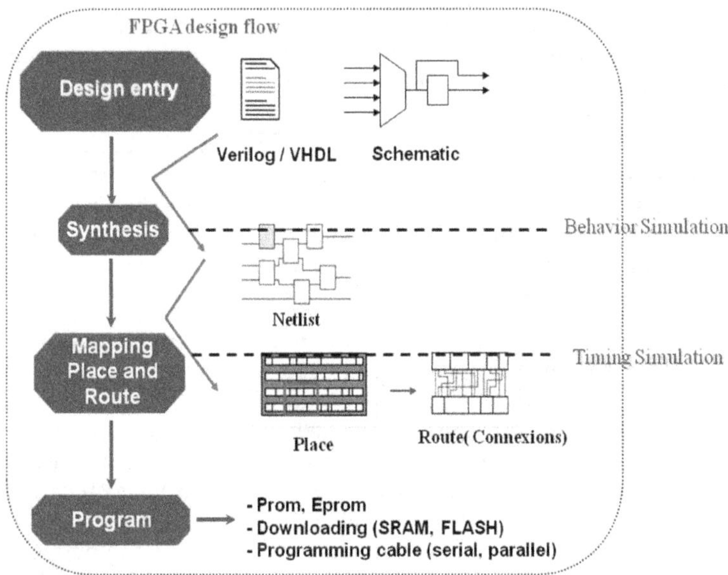

Fig. 14. *FPGA* design flow overview.

During every step of design flow, and by using an automation tool, a technology-mapped netlist is generated. The netlist can be fitted to the *FPGA* architecture using a process called *place-and-route*. Usually these steps are performed by the *FPGA* company's proprietary place-and-route software, such as the *ISE* and *Quartus* tools of the *Xilinx* and *Altera* companies, respectively [Altera2, 2011; Xilinx4, 2008].

The embedded digital system's designers will validate the map, place and route results via simulations for verification and timing analysis obtained during the design process. Furthermore, design verification - which includes both functional verification and timing verification - takes places at different points in the design flow. As mentioned in Figure 14, the functional verification of the design is done before synthesis, corresponding to the running of a behavioural simulation (*RTL* simulation), and after synthesis translation, corresponding at the running of a functional simulation (*gate-level* simulation). Thus, the

RTL description in *VHDL* or *Verilog* is initially simulated by creating test benches to simulate the system and observe the results. Next, the synthesis engine maps the design to a netlist. This netlist is translated to a gate-level description where simulation is repeated to confirm that the synthesis has proceeded without errors. Finally, the design is laid out in the *FPGA*, at which point propagation delays can be added and the simulation then runs again with these values back-annotated into the netlist. Once the design and validation process is complete, a binary file called *bitstream* is generated (also using the *FPGA* company's proprietary software) in order to (re)configure the *FPGA*. Therefore, the programming of the device is made from this programming file, containing the bits to program the specific *FPGA* by using a programming cable or by downloading into the device one memory file containing the *bitstream*. More precisely, the *bitstream* is transferred to the *FPGA/CPLD* via a serial interface (*JTAG - Joint Test Action Group* - standard support) or to an external memory device, such as an *EEPROM* or a *PROM*. Generally, after the device's programming, a circuit verification is done in order to verify the real and final functionality of the design. This final step allows for the specification of real performance in terms of power consumption, work frequency and the required logic, as well as memory hardware resources. Furthermore, in order to simplify the design of complex systems in *FPGAs*, there exist libraries of predefined complex functions and circuits that have been tested and optimised so as to speed up the design process. These predefined circuits are commonly called *IP cores*, and are available from *FPGA* vendors and third-party *IP* suppliers (under proprietary licenses). These modules are available for targeting and programming *FPGA* hardware. Other predefined circuits are also available from developer communities, such as the *OpenCores* site (typically released under free and open-source licenses) [Opencores].

Thanks to such structures, a *FPGA* can be used to implement any logical function that an *ASIC* could perform. The ability to update their functionality after shipping (defined as total or partial chip reconfiguration of a portion of the design and the low non-recurring engineering costs relative to an *ASIC* design) offers advantages for many embedded applications. Thus, the *FPGA* allows for even higher performance by trading off precision and an increased number of parallel arithmetic units. Indeed, the inherent parallelism of the logic resources on a *FPGA* allows for considerable computational throughput, even at low MHz clock-rates. The adoption of *FPGAs* in high performance computing is currently limited by the complexity of *FPGA* design compared with conventional software. Indeed, the *place and route* steps for a complex design may take a long time to succeed.

In the case of the implementation of an embedded chaotic system, an optimised hardware design coded into a *VHDL* with a structural description logic is required. Indeed, the *"high level"* aspect of one non-optimal *VHDL* code generation keeps the embedded designer far removed from the realities of physical implementation, which does not allow for the optimised performance of the design. Consequently, a result in terms of performance and the density of resources used remains out of the designer's reach. Therefore, the designers of embedded system based on *FPGAs* must find applications in any area or with any algorithm which can make use of the massive parallelism offered by the architecture. One such area is to design one cryptosystem allowing the avoidance of the breaking of the code - in particular brute-force attacks - of cryptographic algorithms carried out by the digital circuit. In this context, and in considering our embedded ciphering application, hardware implementation is designed and coded in *VHDL* with a structural description logic. This *low level* form of design seeks for resolving the *Genesio-Tesi* differential equation (18) through the

RK-4 numerical resolution method in order to produce a more accurate estimate of the solution [Cartwright & Piro, 1992].

The FPGA implementation presented in the remainder of this section will simulate the correct operation with test vectors returned by the software's implementation.

5.3 *RTL* architecture

As to logic exploration architecture, one proposed *RTL* architecture of the *Genesio-Tesi* chaotic system is depicted by Figure 15. Note that the architecture depends on the three bifurcation parameters *a*, *b* and *c* and is based on the structural feedback of three main blocks: *F*, *G* and *Q*. These three functional units realise the nonlinear functions of the equations (18.a), (18.b) and (18.c), respectively. These units are composed by an adder, a subtractor and multiplier logic arithmetic operators. Consequently, the *F* and *G* units correspond to logic assignments while the *Q* unit is simply composed of an adder, a subtractor and multiplier logic arithmetic operators in accordance with the set of equations (18) and the *RK-4* resolution method. The data-path processing architecture of the *Q* units is depicted by Figure 16.

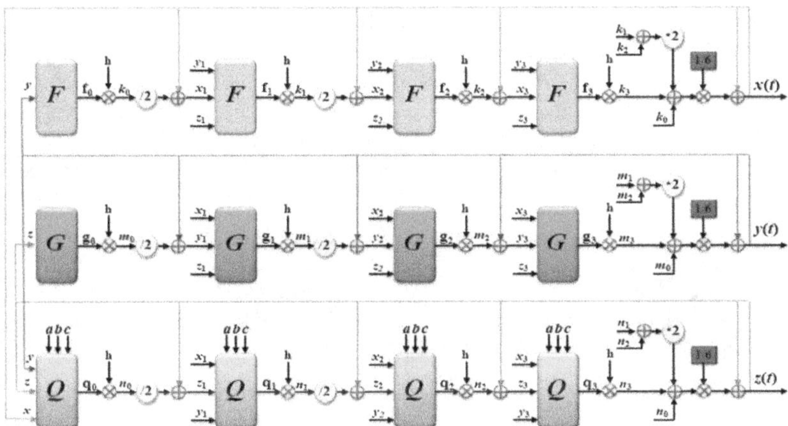

Fig. 15. *RTL* architecture of the *Genesio-Tesi* chaotic system.

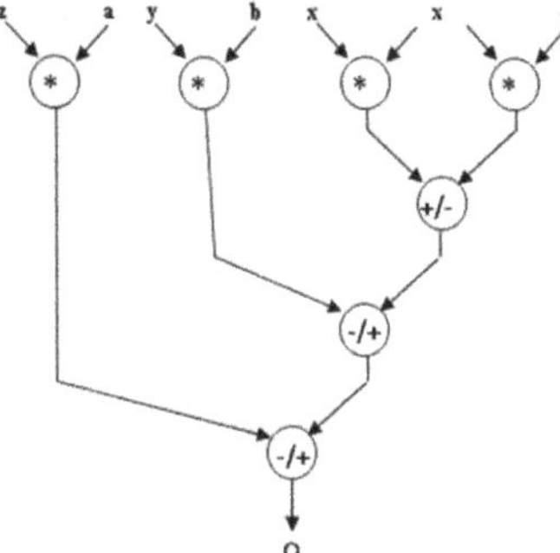

Fig. 16. *RTL* architecture of the *Q* functional units.

5.4 Logic hardware modelling and simulation

To test the effectiveness of this microelectronic solution, the *RTL* architecture of the *Genesio-Tesi* generator has been simulated with the *ModelSim* simulator tool [Mentor Graphics, 2008]. Unlike the use of *VHDL* automatic code generation [Aseeri et al., 2002; Sobhy et al., 1999], the data-path processing architecture has been implemented in the structural description in the manner depicted by Figure 15. It should be noted that the continuous chaotic signals are real, which is why the embedded proposed architecture treats a finite resolution of numbers using a binary representation. Indeed, in embedded electronic design, a fixed-point number representation is a real data-type for a number that has a fixed number of digits after the radix point. Fixed-point formats are useful for representing fractional values - usually in base 2 or base 10 - when the executing processor has no *floating point unit* (*FPU*), or else if the fixed-point provides improved performance or accuracy for the application. Moreover, most low-cost embedded systems do not have an *FPU*.

In the case study, the data-path architecture adopted one hardware implementation based on a finite solution of numbers with a fixed point representation of the real data in 32 bits (*16Q16*) - i.e., all the data is in a fixed-point format with 16 bits for the integer and fraction parts. This fixed-point arithmetic format allows for a very useful and attractive trade off between high speed and low area cost because the presentation on 32 bits (*16Q16*) provides greater precision for the representation of the real data while preserving the dynamic of the generated chaotic signals. The obtained results are shown by Figure 17, where the chaotic signals x, y and z of the *Genesio-Tesi* generator are presented. Note that all of these results are represented with 32 bits using the bifurcation parameter values as defined in Section 5.1. It can be seen that the *ModelSim* simulation results are very similar to those obtained with the *MatLab* simulations shown in Figure 7.

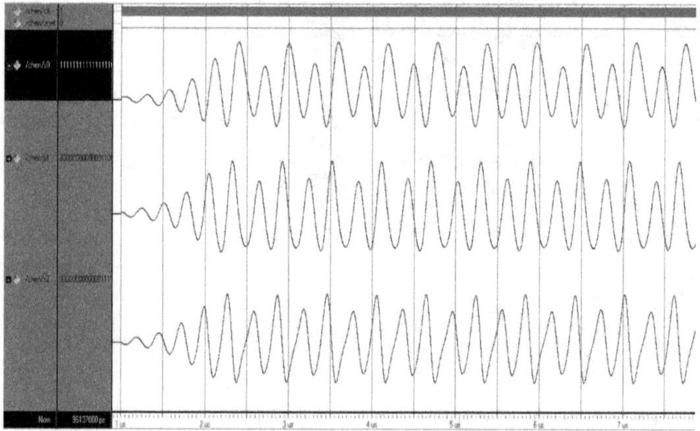

Fig. 17. *ModelSim* simulation results of the chaotic signals x, y and z.

5.5 Logic synthesis results

The *FPGA* synthesis results (after the *place* and *route* steps) in terms of logic resources and performance analysis of the implementation of the architecture inside the *FPGA* are detailed in Table 2. The maximum frequency and hardware resources consumption in terms of the slices and multipliers required are specified there. The results demonstrate that the proposed *Genesio-Tesi* chaotic generator can be efficiently implemented through *FPGA* technology by providing real-time chaotic signals. It can be seen that an attractive trade-off between high speed and low logic resources has been achieved. Indeed, their implementation on a Xilinx *Virtex-II* device uses only 1359 *CLB-Slices* (9% of the circuit size), 22 multipliers (16%) and no block *RAMs*. This justifies the advantages of the weak nonlinearity of the *Genesio-Tesi* chaotic system. To evaluate the behaviour of the proposed hardware implementation, we use certain evaluation metrics. The metrics are the *Throughput rate* and the *Time latency*. The *throughput rate* is defined as the number of bits by unit of time. In our case, this rate corresponds to 32 bits wordlength during one operating clock frequency. From the performance results (see Table 2) we achieved a maximal throughput of 806.62 Mbps. This throughput rate is computed after the initialisation phase at the output of the *FPGA* circuit. Meanwhile, at the input of the *DAC*, the rate corresponds to 18 bits wordlength during one operating clock frequency, and the maximum throughput achieved is 454.64 Mbps. *Latency* is defined as the time necessary to generate one single wordlength signal after the start of the generator. The optimised implementation of the *Genesio-Tesi* chaotic system requires 8 clock cycles to generate one wordlength chaotic signal. In this case, we obtain a time latency of 316.73 ns. These results are very attractive for the security of communications between embedded systems.

Device utilization summary ***Selected Device : 2vp30ff896-7***	
Number of Slices:	1359 out of 13696 9%
Number of Slice Flip Flops:	865 out of 27392 3%
Number of 4 input LUTs:	2591 out of 27392 9%
Number of bonded IOBs:	98 out of 556 17%
Number of MULT18X18s:	22 out of 136 16%
Number of GCLKs:	1 out of 16 6%
Maximum Frequency:	25.258MHz

Table 2. Synthesis results.

5.6 Physical hardware implementation

In this section, we consider the *XUP Xilinx Virtex-II Pro* Development embedded platform for physical hardware implementation [Xilinx4, 2008]. The *XUP* System consists of a high performance *Virtex-II Pro* FPGA (XCV2PFF896-7) surrounded by peripheral components that can be used to create a complex hardware system. Figure 18 displays a photo of the XUP *Xilinx Virtex-II Pro* platform. Note that an audio *CODEC* (*AC97*) and stereo power amplifier are included on the *XUP* platform so as to provide complete analogue functionality, allowing the external generation of chaotic signals in analogue form for real measurements [Analog Device, 2000].

An overview of the hardware architecture of the key data chaotic generator - implemented on the *XUP Virtex-II Pro* development system - is depicted by Figure 19. The *RTL* architecture has been implemented on *Xilinx Virtex-II Pro* XC2VP30 FPGA [Xilinx2, 2007]. This hardware description was designed with the *ISE 10.1 Xilinx* tools [Xilinx4, 2008].

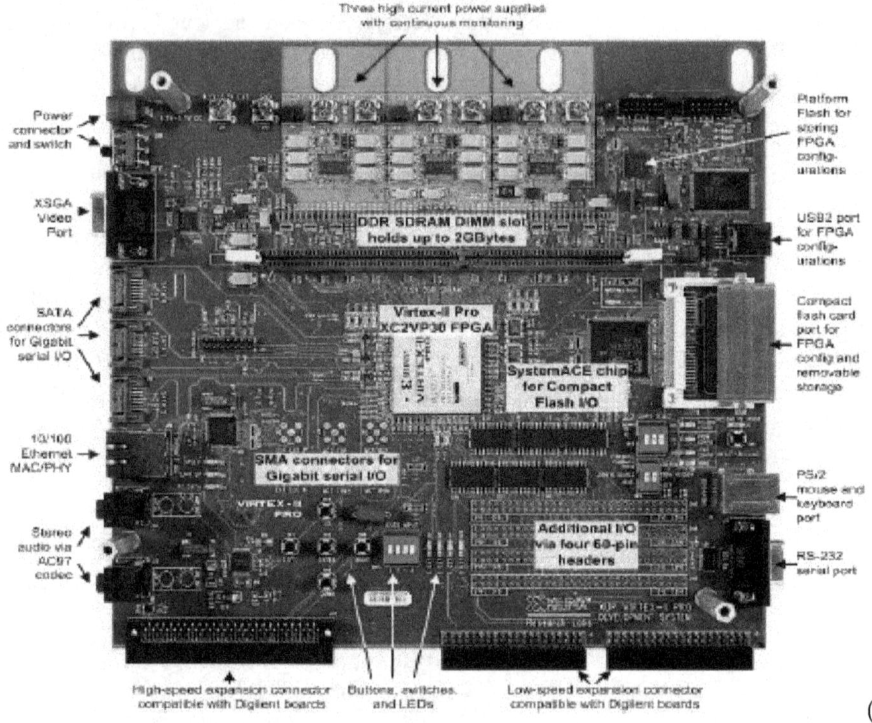

(4pt)

Fig. 18. *XUP Xilinx Virtex-II Pro* embedded platform.

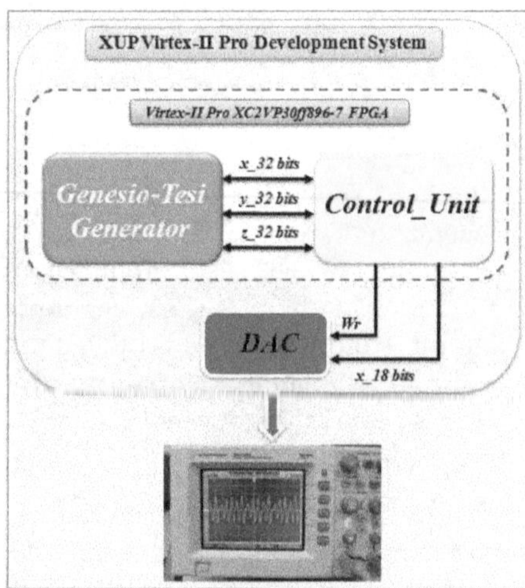

Fig. 19. Digital hardware architecture of the *Genesio-Tesi* chaotic system.

The architecture system consists of two main modules: the *Control_Unit* and the *Genesio-Tesi-Generator* module. The *Control_Unit* module is a *Moore*-state machine which manages and schedules the different operations and functions of the chaotic system. The *Genesio-Tesi-Generator* module generates the chaotic signals as described in Section 5.4. Once the chaotic signals (x, y and z) with 32 bits wordlength are obtained, they are truncated to 18 bits and converted to an analogue format using a *Digital-to-Analogue Converter* (*DAC*), and this process is then repeated. Next, the real-time chaotic signals obtained at the output of the *DAC* are visualised via a digital oscilloscope [Agilent, 2007]. Note that this proposed architecture offers two different means for using the obtained real-time chaotic signals. Indeed, it permits the use of them in their analogue form at the output of the *DAC* or their use in their digital form directly at the output of the *FPGA* circuit. This will permit the easy exploitation of the richness of the dynamical behaviour of the embedded *Genesio-Tesi* chaotic generator for such embedded applications as communications security.

To view the real-time chaotic signals generated by the *Genesio* system, we implemented the proposed digital architecture in the *FPGA* Chip of the *XUP Virtex-II Pro FPGA* platform development, and prototyping was then performed. The functional Blocks implemented in the *FPGA* chip are shown by Figure 20. This architecture is mainly composed of three modules, the *clk_generator*, the *genesio_generator* and a digital interface (*BASIC_AC97_INTERFACE*) of the *DAC* available on the *XUP Virtex-II* platform. The functions of each module are:

- *clk_generator*: it generates and distributes the clock and reset signals required for all of the modules. Thus, the signal *clk_AC97* drives the *AC97* codec at 12.5 MHz while the signal *clk_genesio* cadences the *Genesio_generator* module at 25,254 MHz. These signals are generated from the 100 MHz clock embedded on the board system.
- *Genesio_generator*: it generates the chaotic signals x, y and z of 32 wordlength bits and controls the DAC operations with a specific control signal (*cmd*).
- *BASIC_AC97_INTERFACE*: this block - after analogue conversion - transmits signals to a chaotic oscillator for digital real-time display.

Note that no block of *RAM* is used in this hardware architecture.

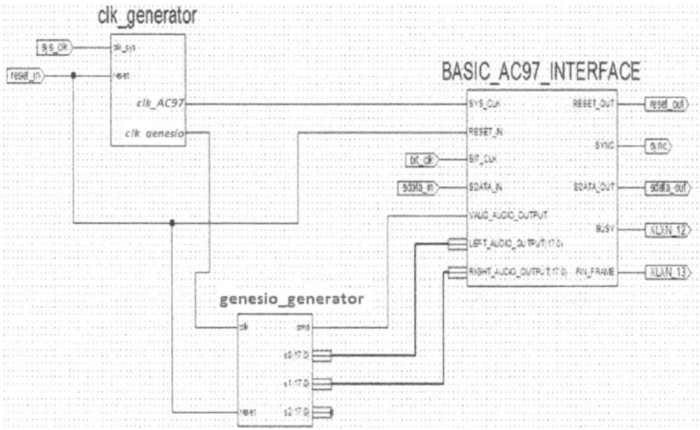

Fig. 20. Functional blocks implemented in the *FPGA* chip.

5.7 Real time measurements

Figures 21 and 22 show the real time measurements of the chaotic signals x, y and z and the strange attractors obtained in the plans (x-y) and (x-z), respectively, which were obtained simultaneously with the presented hardware system. These snapshots are provided by a digital oscilloscope (*Tektronix* oscilloscope [Agilent, 2007]) at the output of the *DAC*. The x, y and z real-time chaotic signal measurements of the embedded generator, obtained by the direct implementation of the *RTL*-optimised architecture, are given by Figures 21.a, 21.b and 21.c, respectively. The measured real-time attractors (x-z) and (x-y) are presented by Figures 22.a and 22.b, respectively. We can compare these real results with those obtained using the *MatLab* and *ModelSim* simulation tools presented in Sections 5.1 and 5.4 in order to ascertain whether or not these results are similar. These results clearly confirm that the implemented chaotic system works well in the chaotic mode. In addition, these measurements show that the proposed approach provides an efficient chaotic generator. Consequently, the hardware implementation validates this approach for the development of embedded chaotic generators based on chaotic nonlinear systems.

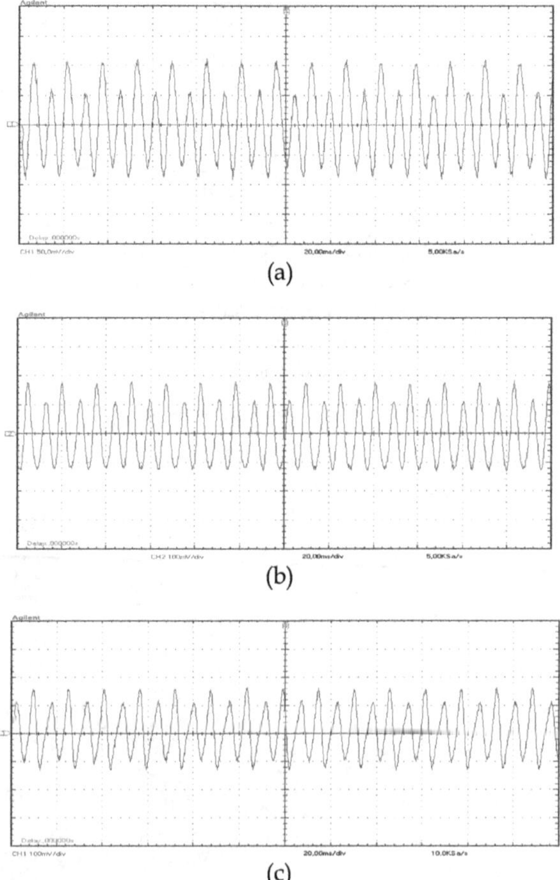

Fig. 21. Real-time measurement results of the chaotic signals x (a), y (b) and z (c).

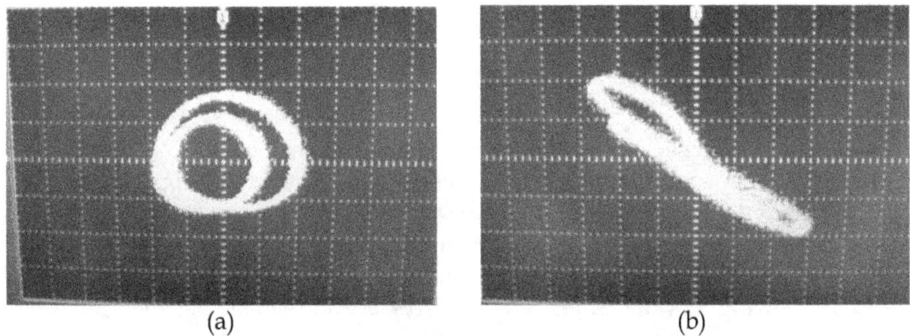

(a) (b)

Fig. 22. Real-time measurement results of (a) the (x-y) chaotic attractor, and (b) the (x-z) chaotic attractor.

Figure 23 provides a view of the experimental hardware implementation and measurements of the *Genesio* x-y chaotic attractor. Real-time measurements and digital acquisition can be made.

Fig. 23. Photo of the experimental hardware implementation and measurements of the *Genesio-Tesi* x-y chaotic attractor.

6. Conclusion

Following a general overview of the embedded digital system design based on programmable technology and its associated tools, this chapter presents a hardware design of the embedded system for security applications. One *FPGA* implementation of an embedded chaotic cryptosystem has already been detailed. The implemented embedded system is based on a *3D* chaotic key generator for a high data stream encryption rate suitable for real-time image encryption. The proposed case study provides an efficient approach for conceiving an embedded *Genesio-Tesi* chaotic generator based on the implementation of reconfigurable technology. The hardware implementation of this embedded generator gave attractive performances. More precisely, the implementation requires only 1359 *CLB*-slices, 22 multipliers and no blocks of *RAM*, and achieves a throughput rate of 808.26 Mbps at the output of the *FPGA* circuit and 454.64 Mbps at the input of the *DAC*, with a clock frequency of 25.258 MHz and with a low latency time of 316.73 ns. Thus, the signal generator performs well for embedded applications, such as secure communications based on chaos approach. The random key generator architecture that was presented is particularly attractive, since it provides low-cost secure communications solutions for embedded systems. This approach at hardware design is validated by showing that the real-time *Genesio-Tesi* chaotic signals obtained with the *RTL* architecture are similar to the software simulations as its counterparts. Moreover, embedded cipher systems can have several advantages over the use of *FPGAs*. Indeed, the experimental results using the *Xilinx Virtex* technology have demonstrated that the design approach presented can lead to designs with a small logic area, satisfactory throughput rates and low latency for embedded applications.

7. References

Agilent, (2007). 3000 Series Oscilloscopes data Sheet, Agilent Technologies, 5989-2235.

Altera. (2011). Nios II Processor, *Reference Handbook*; Available from http://www. altera.com

Altera2, (2011). Quartus II Handbook Version 11.1. Available from http://www.altera.com/literature/hb/qts/quartusii_handbook.pdf

Analog Device, (2000), AC'97 SoundMAX Codec, *AD1881A Datasheet.*

Aseeri, M. A.; Sobhy, M. I.; Lee, P. (2002). Lorenz Chaotic Model Using Field Programmable Gate Array (FPGA), *Midwest Symposium on Circuit and Systems*, pp. 686-699.

Azzaz, M. S.; Tanougast, C.; Sadoudi, S.; Dandache, A. (2011). Robust Chaotic Key Stream Generator for Real Time Images Encryption, *Journal of Real-Time Image Processing, Springer Verlag*, Vol. 6.

Brown, S.; Rose, J. (1996). FPGA and CPLD architectures: a tutorial, *IEEE Design and Test of Computers*, 13 (2), pp. 42–57.

Burr, W. E. (2003). Selecting the advanced Encryption Standard, *IEEE Security & Privacy, IEEE Computer Society*, pp. 43-52.

Carroll, P. L.; Pecora, L. M. (1990). Synchronization in chaotic systems, *Phy. Rev. Lett.*, 64 (8), pp. 821-824.

Cartwright, J. H. E.; Piro, O. (1992). The Dynamics of *Runge-Kutta* Methods, *Int. J. Bifurcation and Chaos*, Vol. 2, pp. 427-449.

Cha, C. Y.; Lee, S. G. (2005). Complementary Colpitts Oscillator in CMOS Technology', *IEEE Transaction on microwave theory and techniques*, 53 (3).

Chen, H. H ; Chiang, J S ; Lin, Y. L. ; Lee, C. I. (2007). Chaos synchronization of general Lorenz, Lü, and Chen systems, *HSIUPING Journal*, Vol. 15, pp. 159-166.

Compton, K.; Hauck, S. (2002). Reconfigurable computing : a survey of systems and software, *ACM Comput. Surv.*, 34 (2), pp. 171 - 210.

Cuomo, K. M.; Oppenheim, A. V.; Strogatz, S. H. (1993). Synchronization of Lorenz-Based Chaotic Circuits with Applications to Communications, *IEEE transactions on circuits and systems-11: analog and digital signal processing*, 40 (1), pp. 626-633.

Genesio, R.; Tesi, A.; Villoresi, F. (1993). A frequency approach for analyzing and controlling chaos in nonlinear circuits, *IEEE Trans. on Circuits Systems I: Fundamental Theory and Applications*. Vol. 40, pp. 819-828.

Genesio, R; Tesi, A. (1992). Harmonic balance methods for the analysis of chaotic dynamics in nonlinear systems, *Automatica*, Vol. 28, pp. 531–548.

Giannakopoulos, K.; Souliotis, G.; Fragoulis, N. (2007). An integratable chaotic oscillator with Current Amplifiers, *IEEE Int Symp. on Signals, Circuits and Systems*, Vol. 1, pp. 1-4.

Hauck, S. (1998). The role of FPGA in reprogrammable systems, Proceedings of IEEE, Vol. 86 (4), pp. 615–638.

Indrusiak, L. S.; Dutra Silva Junior, E.C. ; Glesner, M. (2005). Advantages of the Linz-Sprott weak nonlinearity on the FPGA implementation of chaotic systems: a comparative analysis, *Proc. Int. Symp. Signals, Circuits and Sys. 2*, pp. 753 – 756.

Kennedy, M. P. (1994). Chaos in the Colpitts oscillator, *IEEE Trans. Circuits Syst. I*, Vol. 41, pp. 771-774.

Kvarda, P. (2002). Investigating the Rössler attractor using Lorenz plot and Lyapunov exponents, *Radio Engineering*. 11 (3), pp. 22-23.

Liu, T.; Tanougast, C.; Brunet, P.; Berviller, Y.; Rabah H.; Weber, S. (2005). An Optimized FPGA Implementation of an AES Algorithm for Embedded Applications, *The International Workshop on Applied Reconfigurable Computing*, pp. 111-118.

Lorenz, T E.N. (1963). Deterministic nonperiodic flow, *Journal of the Atmospheric Sciences*, 20 (2), pp. 130-141.

Lü, J.; Chen, G. (2002). A new chaotic attractor coined, *Int. Journal of Bifurcation and Chaos*, 12 (3), pp. 659-661.

Mathworks (2006), MatLab Software, Version 7.3, *Mathworks*.

Matsumoto, T. (1987). Chaos in electronic circuits, *Proc of the IEEE*, Vol. 75 (8), pp. 1033-1046.

Mentor Graphics, (2008). Modelsim SE User's Manuel, Software, Version 6. 4, Mentor Graphics.

Opencores, Available from http://opencores.org.

Ozoguz, S. ; Ates, O.; Elwakil, A. S. O. (2005). An integrated circuit chaotic oscillator and its application for high speed random bit generation, *ISCAS 2005*, Vol. 5, pp. 4345-4348.

Park, J. H. (2007). Exponential Synchronization of the Genesio-Tesi Chaotic System via a Novel Feedback Control," *Phys.Scr.*, Vol. 76, pp. 617-622.

Sadoudi, S.; Tanougast, C.; Azzaz, M.; Bouridane, A. Dandache, A. (2010). Embedded Genesio-Tesi Chaotic Generator for cipher communications, *7th IEEE, IET International Symposium on Communication Systems, Networks and Digital Signal Processing*, pp. 234 - 238.

Sobhy, M. I.; Aseeri, M. A.; Shehata, A. E. R. (1999). Real Time Implementation Of Continuous (Chua And Lorenz) Chaotic Generator Models Using Digital Hardware, *Proc. of the Third International Symposium on Communication Systems Networks and Digital Processing*, pp. 38-41.

Sorel, Y. (1994). Massively parallel systems with real time constraints, the algorithm architecture adequation methodology, *In Proceedings of Conference on Massively Parallel Computing Systems*, May 1994, pp. 44 - 53.

Tanougast, C.; Berviller, Y.; Weber, S.; Brunet, P. (2003). A partitioning methodology that optimises the area on reconfigurable real-time embedded systems, *EURASIP Journal On Applied Signal Processing, Special Issue on Rapid Prototyping of DSP Systems*, Vol. (6), pp. 494-501.

Tanougast, C.; Berviller, Y.; Brunet, P.; Weber, S.; Rabah, H. (2003). Temporal partitioning methodology optimizing FPGA resources for dynamically reconfigurable embedded real-time system, *Microprocessors and Microsystems, Elsevier*, 27 (3), pp. 115-130.

Yang, T. (2004). A survey of chaotic secure communication systems, *International Journal of Computational Cognition*, 2 (2), pp. 81-130.

Yang, Cao, Chung and Morris, (2005). Applied Numerical Methods Using MATLAB, *John Wiley, and Sons, Inc.*

Xilinx1. (2008). MicroBlaze Processor, *Reference Guide Embedded Development Kit EDK 10.1i*, UG081 (v9.0). Available from http://www.xilinx.com/support/documentation/sw_manuals/mb_ref_guide.pdf

Xilinx2, (2007). VirtexII complete Datasheet. Available from http://www.xilinx.com/support/documentation/data_sheets/ds031.pdf.

Xilinx3, (2000). Xilinx Data Sheet DS003 (v.2.2).

Xilinx, (2008). Virtex5 FPGA Data Sheet, 2008. Available from http://www.xilinx.com/support/documentation/data_sheets/ds202.pdf.

Xilinx4, (2008). Integrated Software Environment (ISE), Version 10.1, Available from http://www.xilinx.com/support/documentation

Xilinx4, (2008). Xilinx University Program Virtex-II Pro Development System, *Xilinx, UG069 (v1.1).*

12

Native Mobile Agents for Embedded Systems

Mohamed Ali Ibrahim and Philippe Mabilleau
University of Sherbrooke
Canada

1. Introduction

Mobile agent technology can be viewed as an extension, refinement, or replacement of the traditional client-server paradigm (Dilyana & Petya, 2002). Client-server technology relies on remote procedure calls running across a network. Taking advantage of local interactions, the mobile agent can at any time decide to migrate from host to host in a network and to which location. In this way, several benefits can be obtained, such as decreasing network traffic, reducing dependency on network availability, and an increasing flexibility and autonomy.

Since the emergence of the concept of mobile agent, many platforms have been developed to facilitate the programming of mobile agent applications. Noteworthy is that these platforms exclusively use an interpreted language (virtual machine) to support the heterogeneous systems. The first language supporting the paradigm of mobile agents was Telescript (Domel, 1996) followed by many others such Obliq (Cardelli, 1995), Safe-Tcl (Borenstein, 1994), etc. Because it is a widespread virtual machine, Java has become the language of choice for distributed applications programming in diverse environments by allowing independence from networks and operating systems.

Java provides a mechanism for serialization and dynamic class loading which are directly used to implement agent migration in the platform such as JADE (Bellifemine et al., 2007), and Aglets (Lange & Mitsru, 1998). The conceptual model of a Java-based mobile-agent platform is shown in Fig. 1. However, Java and languages using virtual machines are too big in terms of required memory space for many embedded systems. A key feature of embedded systems is that they run on machines with limited resources. This limitation is generally spatial (limited size) and energetic (restricted consumption). In order to solve this problem, we propose a mobile agent platform conceived for homogeneous embedded systems. Embedded systems perform predefined tasks and constraints that have to be respected:

- Embedded systems addressing the strict need to avoid an additional cost;
- Computing power required just to meet the predefined task avoiding an additional cost of the device and an excess consumption of energy;
- Keeping energy consumption as low as possible.

In order to meet the constraints mentioned above, we propose a mobile agent platform for homogeneous embedded systems, called *μC/MAS (Microcontroller/Mobile Agent System)*. In a homogeneous environment, not only the type of the operating system needs to be identical, but also the processor type has to match. To our knowledge, this is the first attempt to engineer a mobile agent platform on microcontrollers with memories (both RAM and ROM) as small as one megabyte.

The applications targeted by this platform pertain to the field of pervasive computing and, more particularly, to the "smart space" paradigm. In this context, mobile agents can move between embedded systems implanted in physical objects of the smart space by taking into account limited resources (memory, power consumption, bandwidth, and so on). Each agent uses a native code and operates on homogeneous platforms. Thus, an agent can move only towards a microcontroller having the same physical architecture and supported by the same operating system.

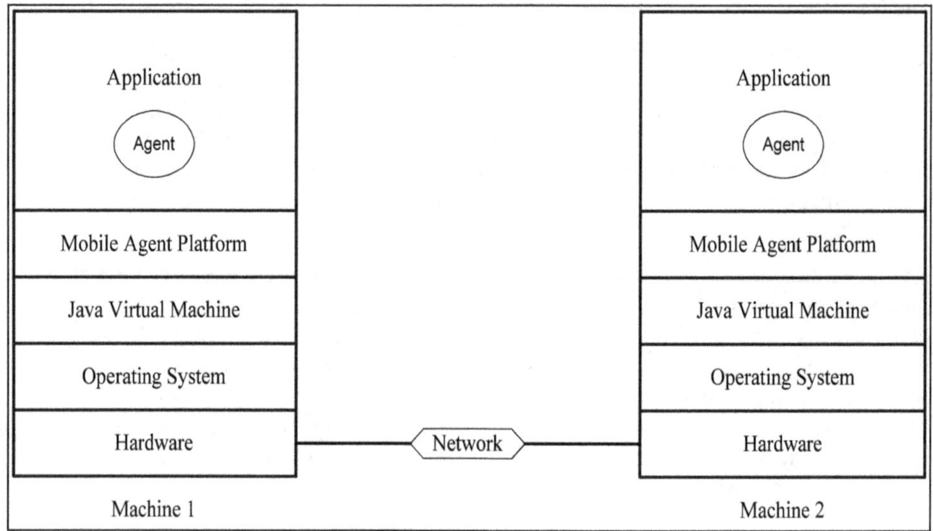

Fig. 1. Java-Based Mobile-Agent Platform.

2. Concept agents

The definition of an agent raises numerous debates in both fundamental and applied research. By simplifying as much as possible, there are on the one hand those who view agents almost like human beings, and on the other hand are those who assimilate agents to simple software. Ferber (Ferber, 1999) defines an agent as a physical or virtual entity which has the following properties:

- is capable of acting in an environment;
- can communicate directly with other agents;
- is driven by a set of tendencies (in the form of individual objective or of a satisfaction/survival function which it tries to optimize);
- possesses resources of its own;
- is capable of perceiving its environment (but to a limited extent);
- has only a partial representation of this environment (and perhaps none at all);

- possesses skills and can offer services;
- may be able to reproduce itself;
- behavior tends towards satisfying its objective, taking account of the resources and skills available to it and depending of its perception, its representation and the communication it receives.

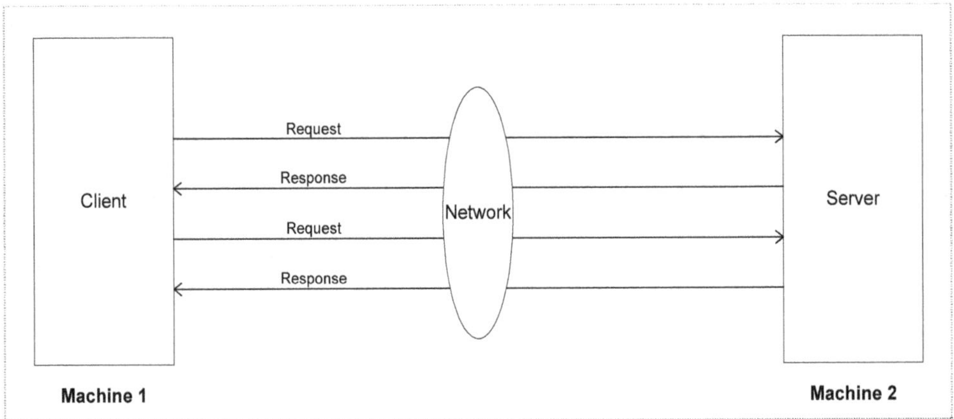

Fig. 2. Client-Server Model.

In contrast, many people consider an agent as an "entity authorized to act on behalf of someone else." According to such a definition an intelligent agent, a police officer, a security guard or a sales agent belong to the same category. As a result, the distinction between an intelligent agent and simple software is very fuzzy. Despite its limitations, this view is a starting point for a definition that is realistic enough without being simplistic. We can thus assert that an intelligent agent is a software entity that has specific attributes and acts in order to perform certain tasks on behalf of another entity (another agent or person). The problem now is to define the attributes appropriate for an agent and, on this point, the debates are ferocious. The main characteristics of an agent are:

- Autonomy: agents operate without the direct intervention of humans or others, and have some kind of control over their actions and internal state.
- Interactivity: agents interact with other agents and with humans.
- Responsiveness: agents perceive their environment which can be either the physical world, a user via a GUI or the Internet or even all at once, and respond to changes that occur.
- Intentional behavior: agents do not simply act in response to their environment, they are able to perform goal-directed behavior and take initiatives where appropriate.
- Ability to learn: the agent is able to adapt to the needs of its user by analyzing its past actions.
- Flexibility: the actions of an agent are not entirely predetermined; the agent is indeed able to choose what actions it will choose and what order, depending on the external environment.
- Self-starting: unlike traditional software, an agent can decide, according to the external environment, when to initiate a specific action.

- Mobility: some agents may be stationary as the traditional client-server shown in Fig. 2. Agents reside either on the user's machine or on the server. Other agents may be mobile, as shown in Fig. 3, i.e., they travel on the network. They can move from one machine to another during their execution, carrying with them their execution environment. These agents may meet other agents that can provide certain services, or serve as a meeting point between different agents.

For some researchers, particularly those working in the field of artificial intelligence (AI), the term "agent" has a stronger and more specific meaning. To these researchers, an agent is a computer system that, in addition to the above properties, is conceived as having properties that are most commonly attributed to humans. For example, it is common in artificial intelligence to characterize an agent by purely mental concepts such as knowledge, belief, intent or obligation. Some researchers have gone further and talk about emotional agents. But at what point can one speak of intelligent an agent? Should it have some or all of these attributes? The debate is endless, perhaps insoluble, and certainly without much interest for the end user.

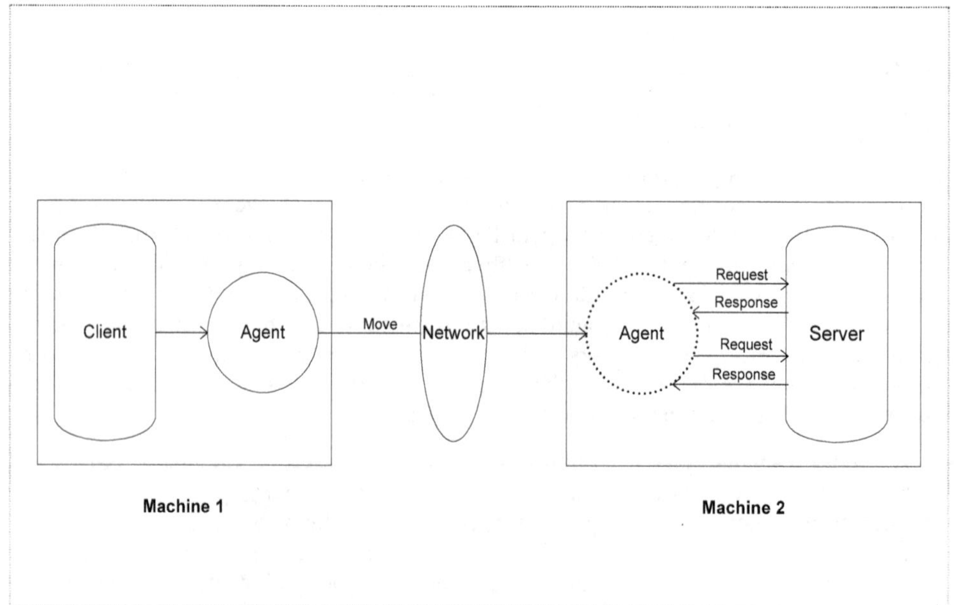

Fig. 3. Mobile Agent Model.

A mobile agent is generally defined as a computer entity capable of reasoning, use the network infrastructure to run in remote locations, search and gather results, cooperate with other agents and return to its original site after completing the assigned task. Its main feature is the ability to travel in an autonomous way between multiple machines such as presented in Fig. 4. In most systems, by virtue of the principle of autonomy, the agent decides when and where to go. This agent can interact with other agents; provide services and use of local resources.

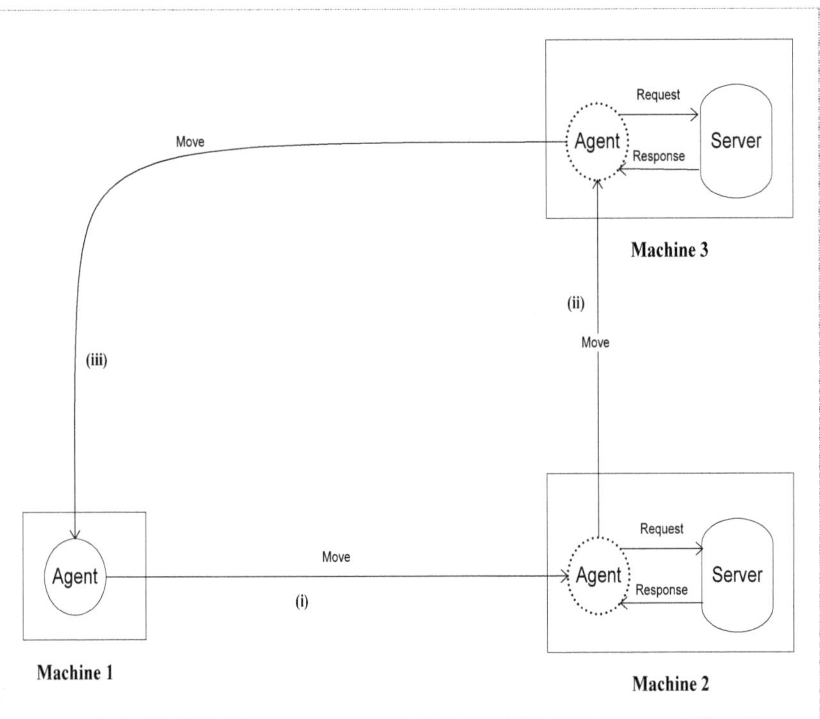

Fig. 4. Model of an Agent visiting two Servers.

2.1 Taxonomy of mobility

There are two degrees of mobility as shown in Fig. 5:

- Weak migration: code + current data.
- Strong migration: code + data + current execution state.

Weak migration is transferring the execution of the application from the source machine to a destination machine, through interruption of the execution of the application on the source site. Then the code and the current data from the application of the source site are transferred to the destination site. Finally, arriving at the destination host, the mobile application resumes execution from the beginning, while having the updated values of its data.

In addition to information taken into account by weak migration (code + current data), strong migration also takes into account the current execution state of the application. Thus, an application with strong mobility that moves during its execution from a source site to a destination site can resume its execution from the point where it left off on the start site. The mobility of an application results in the interruption of the execution of the application on the source site. Then the code, the current data used and the current state of the application running on the source are transferred to the destination site. Finally, arriving at the destination site, the mobile application continues execution where it left off on the start site.

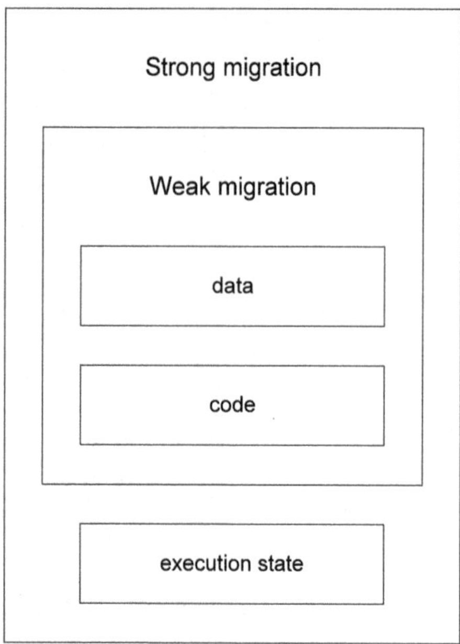

Fig. 5. Degrees of mobility.

3. Architecture of μC/MAS

In order to deploy an application based on mobile agents, it is necessary to have an appropriate platform. There are three approaches for designing and implementing a platform for mobile agents. The first is using a programming language that includes instructions for mobile agents. The second approach is implementing mobile agents as extensions of the operating system. Finally, the last approach builds the platform as a specialized application that runs on top of an operating system.

μC/MAS is based on the extension of a real-time kernel by exploiting the similarity between the tasks' context switching and the agents' mobility. The Fig. 6 shows a context switching and a task migration from one node to another. The concept of task is fundamental in a real-time kernel. The task execution is done sequentially: the instructions that compose it are loaded into the processor and executed one after the other. A task is characterized at a given time by the data, the stack, the heap, the value of the program counter, register contents, etc. A program is a static entity like the contents of a file stored on a disk while a task is an active entity with a program counter specifying the address of the next instruction to execute and related resources. A task is dynamic as opposed to a program that is static.

A task is typically an infinite loop that must necessarily be in one of the following five basic states as shown in Fig. 7 (Labrosse, 2002):

1. Dormant: the task resides in memory but is not available for scheduling
2. Ready: the task is waiting to be assigned to the CPU
3. Running: the task is one whose instructions are being executed by the CPU

4. Waiting: the task is waiting for a signal or a resource to continue its execution.
5. Interrupted: the task is interrupted when an interrupt has occurred and the CPU is in the process of servicing the interrupt.

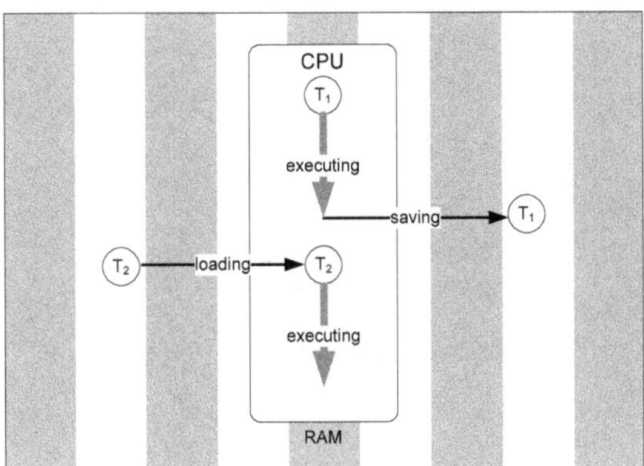

a) CPU switch from task T_1 to task T_2.

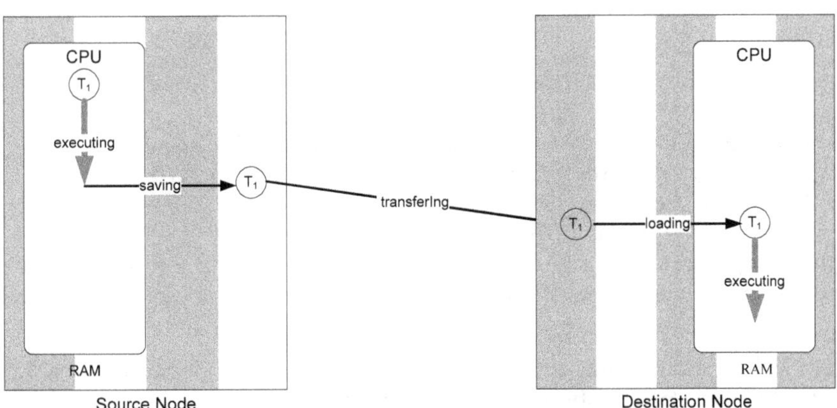

b) Migration of the task T_1 from the source node to the destination node

Fig. 6. a) Context switching and b) a task migration from one node to another.

In the context of the μC/MAS, an agent is a task that is able to migrate from one node to another. When an agent decides to migrate, it suspends execution of the current node, the source node. Then, if the agent code is not already at the destination, it will be loaded from a server. Next, the data representing the state of the agent are transferred from source node to destination node. Once the agent reaches the destination node, it resumes execution where it left off on the source node. The Fig. 8 shows the migration of various components of a mobile agent.

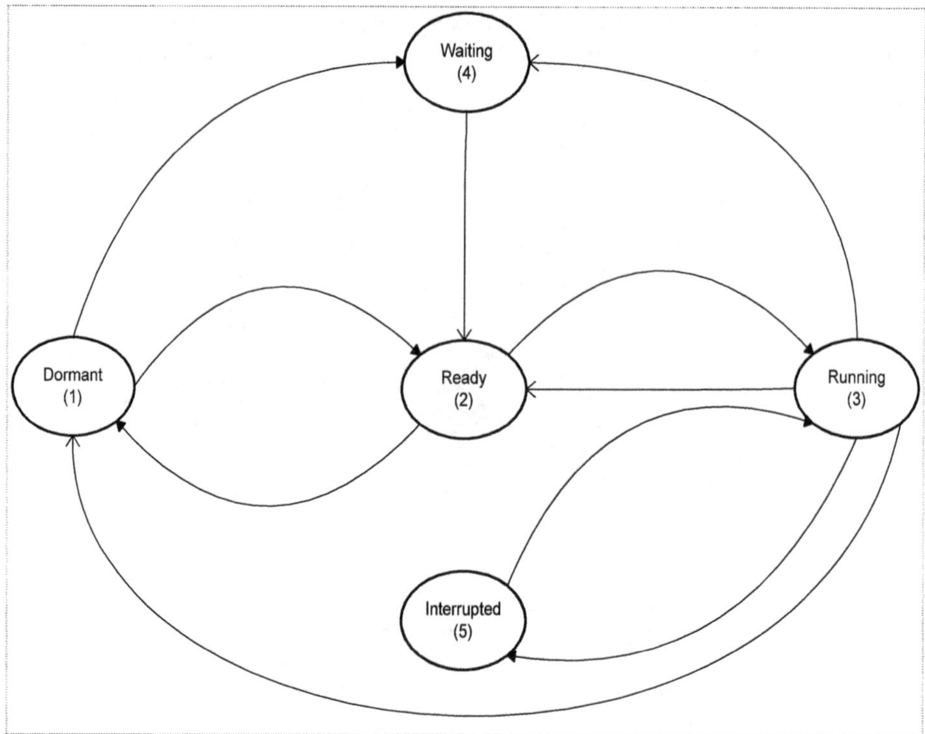

Fig. 7. Task states.

A real-time kernel provides two main functions: scheduling and context switching of tasks. Scheduling determines the ready task having the highest priority. When a task of highest priority is ready, the kernel saves the context of the current task (CPU registers) on the stack to allow a possible resumption. The context of the new task is retrieved from the memory area (the storage area, its stack) and execution resumes where it left off. Note that in a multitasking environment as a real-time kernel, each task has its own stack as shown in Fig. 9.

The μC/MAS is based on the extension of context switching mechanism (suspension and resumption) that exists in multitasking systems and especially in real-time kernels. From the context switching to the agent migration, we exploit the similarity between the CPU preemption by the real-time kernel and the agent mobility. This mechanism is integrated into the features of a real-time kernel allowing mobile agent based software to be implemented in the homogeneous embedded systems. The Fig. 10 shows the structure of the μC/MAS.

The mobile agent system differs from the migration process system in the sense that the agent moves at the time it chooses by means of a primitive while in a migration process, the system will decides when and where to go. The agents of the μC/MAS use a native code (C and Assembler) and can move as well in a wired network as in a wireless network. The agents operate on homogeneous platforms. Consequently, a mobile agent can move only towards a microcontroller of same physical architecture as well as the same environment of execution.

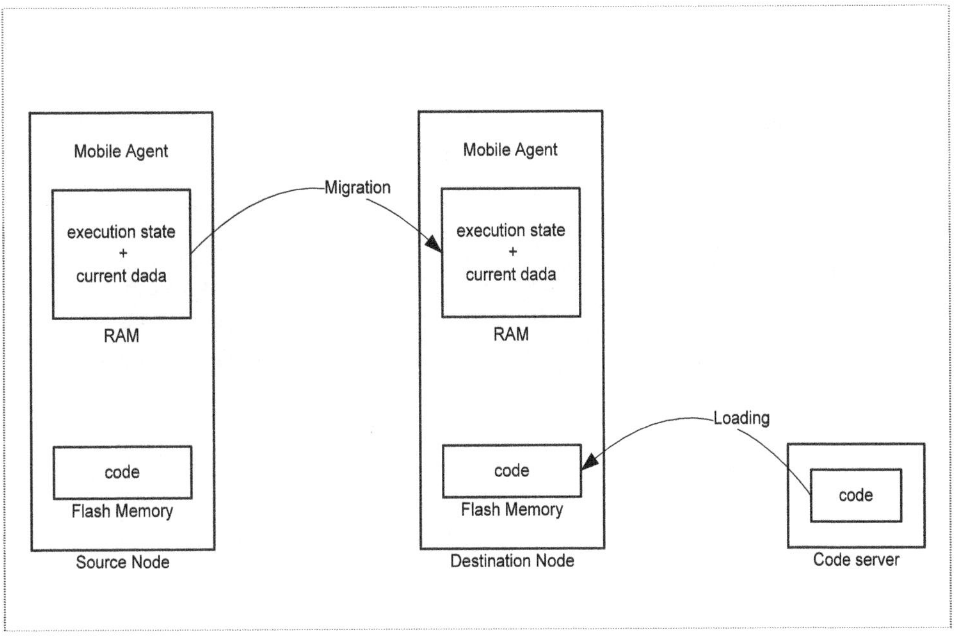

Fig. 8. Migration of various components of a mobile agent.

From the conceptual point of view, a mobile agent is a task that can autonomously migrate from one machine to another. As described above, there are two types of migration: strong migration and weak migration. The μC/MAS supports strong migration. There are very few agents platforms which support the strong mobility. These platforms do not use a native code. These platforms allow only weak migration: the mobile agent resumes execution from the beginning when it reaches the destination.

3.1 Migration of agent

Migration allows the transfer of a running agent from one node to another through a network. A platform supporting strong mobility must be able to capture and restore the structure of the agent in memory. As shown in Fig. 11, this structure consists of the following segments:

1. *Stack*: stores the function calls with their parameters and local variables. When a function return, parameters and variables are popped.
2. *Heap*: reserved for dynamic memory allocation.
3. *BSS (Block Started by Symbol)*: contains all global variables and static variables that are initialized to zero.
4. *Data*: contains global and static variables used by the program that are initialized
5. *Text*: contains executable instructions.

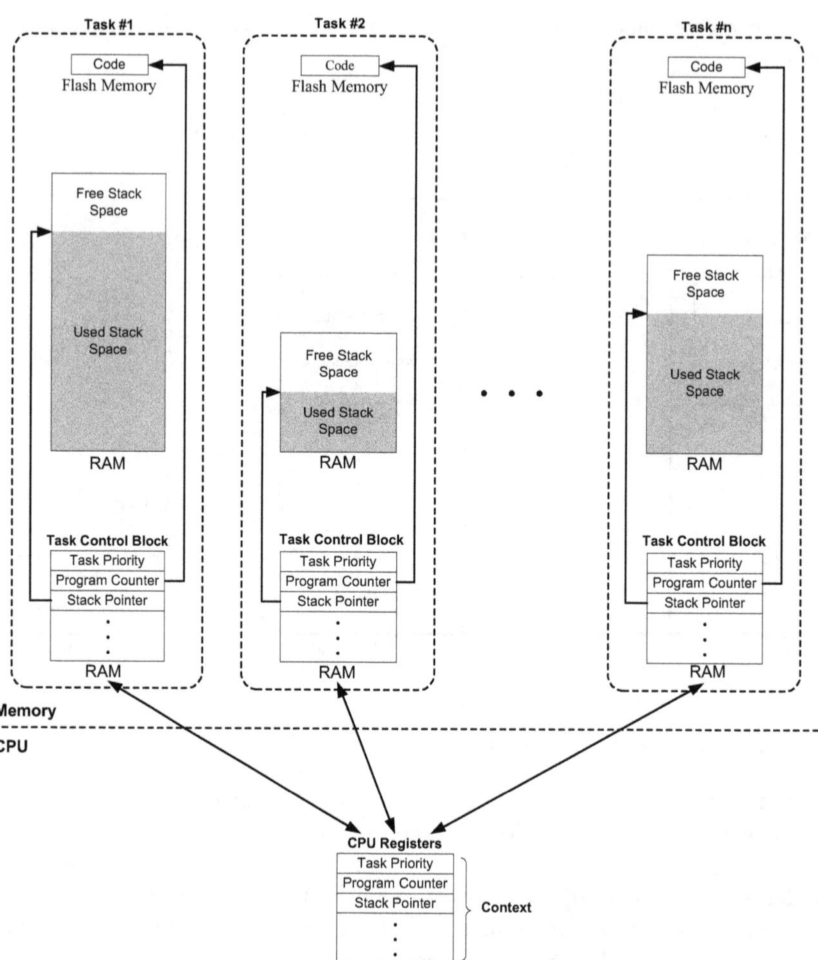

Fig. 9. Multiple tasks.

During migration in the source node, the task *agent* sends a transfer request containing its name and the address of the destination where it wants to go. Once the destination system accepts, the source system makes the following steps:

1. Capture of the current data. These are classified in two categories: the migrant data and the non-migrant data. The captured migrant data are formatted to transport used. Then, they are transferred towards the destination node.
2. Interruption of the task *agent* by generating a context switching. This saves the execution context of the task *agent* on the stack.
3. Capture of the stack and the task control block (TCB). The latter is a data structure that maintains the state of the task when it is preempted. When the task *agent* arrives at the destination node, the task control block allows the task to resume execution exactly where it left off.

4. Format the stack and the task control block to transport used.
5. Transfer of the stack and the task control block.

Before an agent is accepted into a destination system, it must be authenticated. In µC/MAS platform, the source node and destination node mutually authenticate by using passwords. Once mutual authentication is performed, the destination system makes the following steps:

1. Receiving, decoding and restoring of migrant data.
2. Receiving of the stack and the task control block.
3. Decoding the stack and the task control block.
4. Restoration of the stack and the task control block.
5. Resume execution of the task *agent*.

The Fig. 12 shows the algorithm of task *agent* migration.

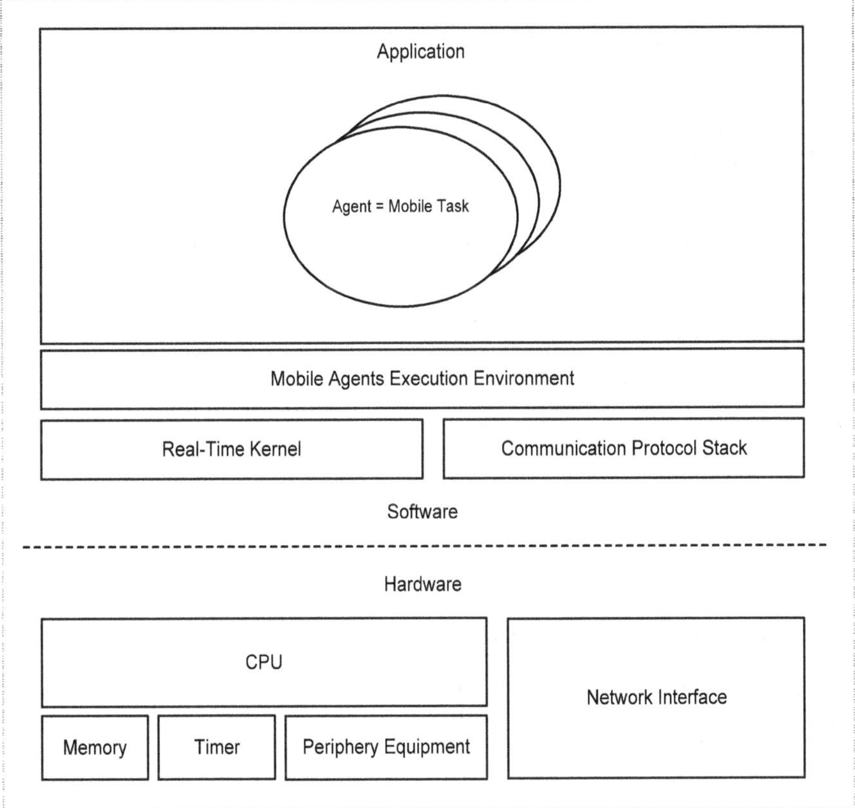

Fig. 10. Structure of the µC/MAS.

3.1.1 Directive migration and data types

Such as defined previously, an agent is a migrant task which could use local and/or global variables. This raises the following question: is it necessary migrating all the variables with the task that it used in the source node? The answer is no because some variables could be used by other tasks because they are not specific to the agent. In its life cycle, an agent uses different data types. In order to manage migration, we classify the data into different categories based on the classification of existing variables in C/C++. We may also apply this classification to other languages. In C/C++, the variables are classified into different categories according to how they are created and how they may be used. The different aspects that can take variables constitute what is called their storage class. The storage class of a variable allows specifying its life cycle and its place in memory.

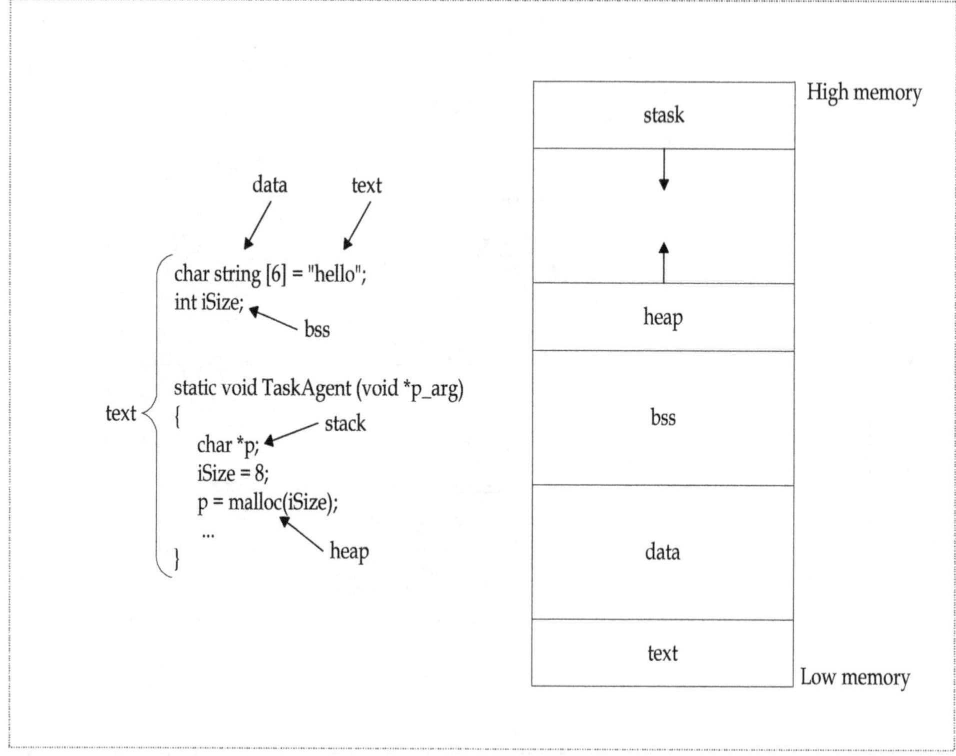

Fig. 11. Structure of the task *agent* in memory.

In order to identify the data that migrate with the agent, we first classify local and global variables. The local variables are created inside a block of instructions, in the case of the µC/MAS in the task *agent*. However, global variables are declared outside of any block of instructions in the zone of global declaration of the program. The local and global variables have different life cycles and different scopes according to their locations in memory. The variable scope is the program area in which it is accessible. The scope of global variables is the program while the scope of local variables is the block of instructions in which they were created.

The C/C++ has a range of storage classes for specifying the type of variables that you want to use:

- *auto*: the scope of an *auto* (automatic) variable is the function or block in which it is defined. The variable exists in memory during execution of the function or block in which it is defined. When all the instructions of the block are executed, the variable is removed from memory and its value is automatically lost. If the block is executed again, the variable is recreated. An *auto* variable has no initial default value.
- *static*: this storage class is used to create variables whose scope is the function or block of instructions in progress, but, unlike the *auto*, the *static* variables are not destroyed when the exit of this block. Every time that we enter this function or this block of instructions, the *static* variables exist and have value to those they had before we left. Their life cycle is that of the program, and they retain their values. If it is initialized at its declaration, it will not be reset by a subsequent call. A file can be viewed as a block. Thus, a *static* variable of a file cannot be accessed from another file. This is useful to separate compilation.
- *register* variables obey the same rules as *auto* variables, but they are not always stored in working memory. If the compiler can, it stores them in registers i.e. in memory areas included in the processor. If no register is available, the variable will receive the *auto* class. The & operator cannot be used on register variables. The advantage of having a variable stored in a register is the reduction of access time to this variable compared to the access time to a variable located in RAM. This can be useful when a variable is often requested.
- *volatile*: this class of variable is used in the programming system. It indicates that a variable can be changed in the background by another program (for example an interruption by a thread, by another process, the operating system or by another processor in a parallel machine). This requires reloading the variable every time the system refers to a processor register, even if the variable is already stored in one of these registers (which can happen if the compiler is asked to optimize the program).
- *extern*: this class is used to indicate that the variable can be defined in another file. It is used in the context of separate compilation.

There are also modifiers that may apply to a variable in order to specify its constancy:

- *const*: this keyword is used to make the contents of a variable unchangeable. In a way, the variable becomes a read-only variable. Warning, this variable is not necessarily a constant: it can be modified either through another identifier, or by an external program (such as volatile variables). When this keyword is applied to a structure, no structure field is writable.
- *mutable*: only available in C++, this keyword is used only for members of structures. It helps overcome the constancy of a possible structure for this member. Thus, a structure field declared mutable can be modified even if the structure is declared *const*.

In order to declare a particular storage class, it is sufficient to place one of the following keywords: *auto, static, register, etc.*, before or after the variable. You can only use the not contradictory storage classes. For example, *register* and *extern* are incompatible, as well as *register* and *volatile*, and *const* and *mutable*. On the other hand, *static* and *const*, as well as *const* and *volatile*, can be simultaneously used. Global variables that are defined without the *const* keyword is processed by the compiler as variables of *extern* storage class by default. These variables are accessible from any program files. However, this rule is not valid for the variables defined with the *const* keyword. These variables are automatically declared *static* by the compiler, which means they are only available in the file in which they were declared. In order to make them accessible to other files, it is imperative to declare the extern keyword before defining them.

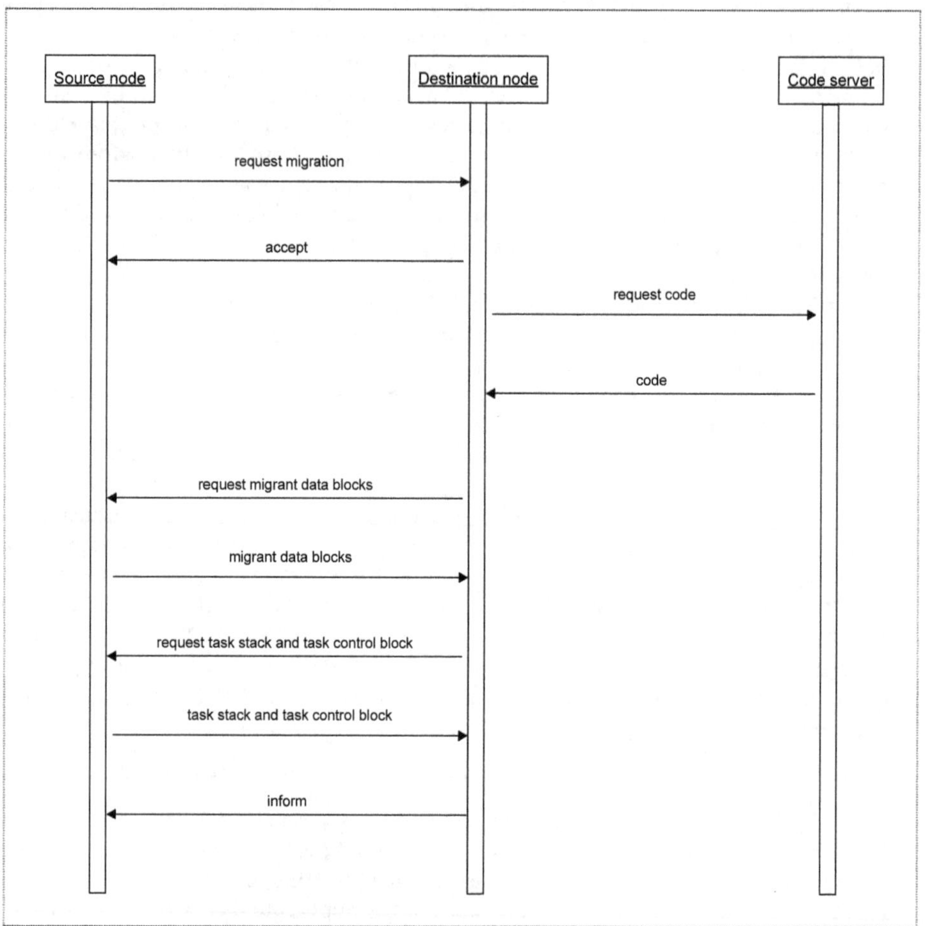

Fig. 12. Algorithm of task *agent* migration.

Second, we classify the local variables in automatic or dynamic. The area containing automatic variables is managed by the stack. For dynamic variables, we must first allocate memory using *malloc()* and subsequently liberate memory by using *free()*. The use of these functions in a real-time embedded system is dangerous because it is not always possible to obtain an area of contiguous memory due to the inherent fragmentation. The mechanism of memory partition proposed by the real-time kernels such as μC/OS-II (Labrosse, 2002) and μC/OS-III (Labrosse, 2010) provides alternatives to *malloc()* and *free()*. This mechanism allows obtaining fixed-sized memory blocks from a partition made of a contiguous memory area as illustrated in Fig. 13. Allocation and de-allocation of these memory blocks are done in constant time and is deterministic. The partition is usually allocated statically (as an array), but can also be dynamically allocated without being freed (never used the *free()* function). In an application, there may be multiple memory partitions as shown in Fig. 14. However, each specific memory block must always be returned to the partition where it originated. This type of memory management is not subject to fragmentation. Before using a partition of memory blocks, you must first create it. This allows the kernel to get the partition of memory blocks in order to manage their allocation and de-allocation. These containing blocks of the dynamic variables of the tasks *agent*, we call migrant blocks of data.

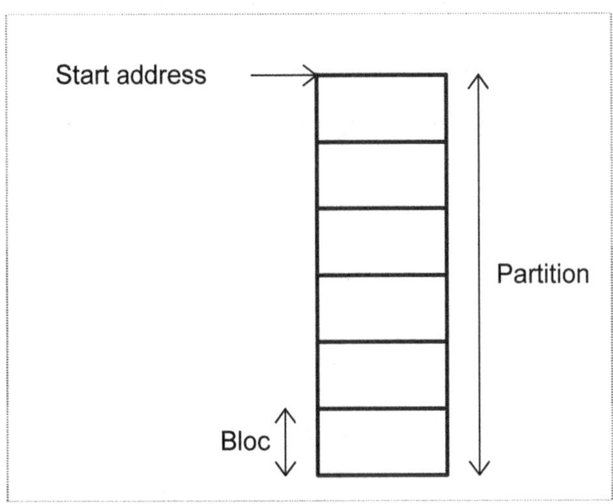

Fig. 13. Memory partition (Labrosse, 2002).

The Fig. 15 presents a classification of data as a binary tree in which each branch indicates the migration or not of these data with the agent:

1. *Automatic local variables* automatically migrate with the agent.
2. *Dynamically allocated local variables* migrate if the agent plans to use them during its travel. In the source node, the memory blocks containing these variables must be returned to their partition after use. The *dynamically allocated local variables* are stored in the stack but the spaces pointed by these variables are stored in heap.
3. *Dynamically allocated local variables* do not migrate when the agent does not use in its route. In the source node, the memory blocks containing these variables must be returned to their partition after use.
4. *Non-dynamically allocated global variables* do not migrate with the agent because the system has been designed to that effect in order to avoid that these variables would be used by other tasks.
5. *Dynamically allocated non-shared global variables* migrate if the agent plans to use during its travel. As in (2), the memory blocks containing these variables must be returned to their partition once the migration is performed.
6. *Dynamically allocated non-shared global variables* do not migrate when the agent does not use in its route. As in (3), the memory blocks containing these variables must be returned to their partition once the migration is performed.
7. *Dynamically allocated shared global variables* do not migrate with the agent.

3.1.2 Transfer format of the agent

The XML format in combination with the Intel HEX is used to transfer the task *agent* from one node to another. As shown in Fig. 8, a mobile agent consists of a code, execution state and current data. Note that the executable code of the agent does not undergo any transformation. It is loaded into the flash memory as produced by the compiler. The compiler used in this project produces an Intel HEX format object file.

The execution state of the agent is composed of the stack and task *agent* control block (Task Control Block, TCB). The stack contains the local variables of the task *agent*. The Current data are global variables specific to the task *agent*. The TCB is a data structure that is used by the real-time kernel to maintain the execution state of the task *agent* when it is preempted (Labrosse, 2002). The TCB contains the stack pointer, the priority of the task *agent*, the stack size, etc.

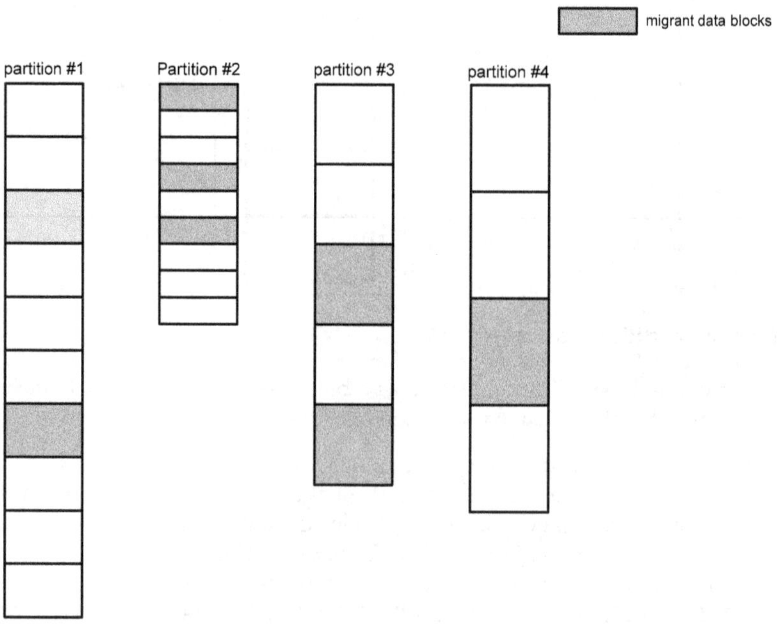

Fig. 14. Multiple memory partitions (Labrosse, 2002).

During migration of a task *agent*, the memory space used by the stack of the source node is not always available at the destination. We must therefore relocate the stack of each task as it appears at the destination. For the same reasons as previously mentioned, we use again the mechanism of the partitions to allocate the stack a memory space. In µC/MAS, we opt for static allocations. This consists in fixing the number and size of partitions of memory blocks. This approach has advantages in the context of embedded systems. Indeed, the use of fixed blocks of memory allows the allocation and de-allocation of this in a unitary manner, thus avoiding memory fragmentation. The number of memory blocks is directly dependent on the number of agents on the node at any given time. The memory requirements can be determined in advance depending on the structure and the number of agents circulating in the network. Thus, it becomes possible to produce a reliable mobile agent platform for homogeneous embedded systems. The Fig. 16 shows the relocation of a stack of tasks from one node to another.

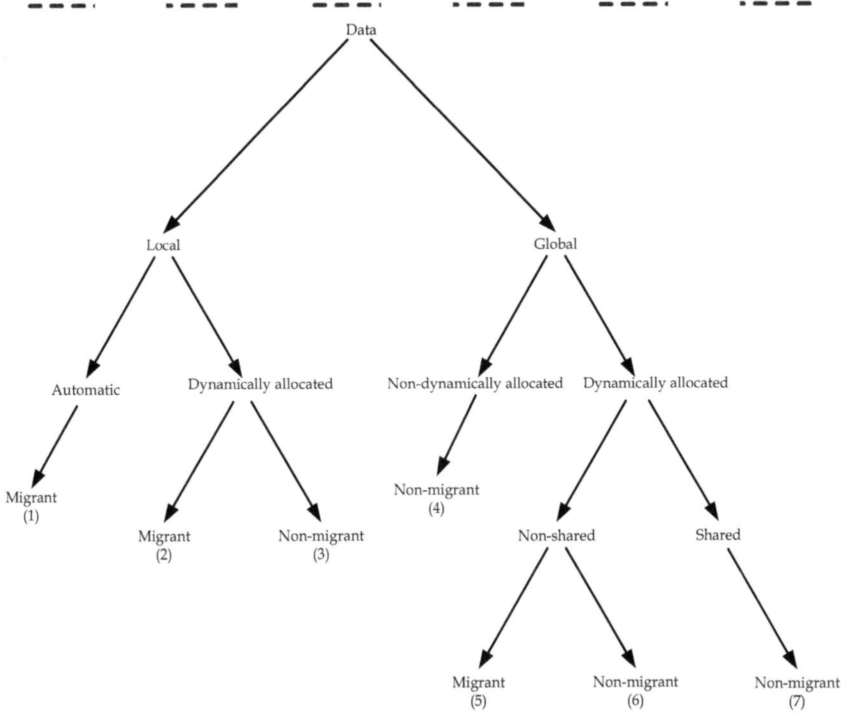

Fig. 15. Classification of data interacting with the agent.

XML presents the task *agent* (execution state and current data) as a document, and XML parser manages this document. The parser structures the document and the way the document is accessed and manipulated. It provides the following functionality: build documents, navigate, add, modify, or delete elements and their content. Unlike the TCB, the stack and the current data are first encoded in Intel HEX format before being incorporated into the XML document. As described in [Intel Corporation, 1988], the Intel Hex file is an ASCII text file that encodes and represents a binary file. Each line in an Intel HEX file contains one HEX record. These HEX records are made up of hexadecimal numbers. Data records appear as follows:

:10800000140000EA34F09FE534F09FE534F09FE57A. As shown in Fig. 17, the record is decoded as follows:

1. starts every Intel HEX record.
2. is the number of data bytes in the record.
3. is the address where the data are to be located in memory.
4. is the record type 00 (a data record).

5. is the data.
6. is the checksum of the record.

An Intel HEX file must end with the following record:

:00000001FF

The Fig. 18 shows a model of interconnection between a source node and destination node.

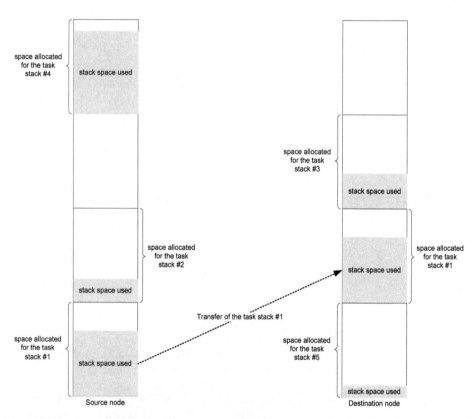

Fig. 16 Relocation of a task stack from one node to another.

Fig. 17 Intel HEX record.

4. Implementation of μC/MAS

μC/MAS platform is based on the extension of a real-time kernel called μC/OS-II Kernel. μC/OS-II is a portable, ROMable, scalable, preemptive, real-time deterministic multitasking kernel for microprocessors, microcontrollers and DSPs. μC/OS-II manages up to 250 application tasks and provides the following services (Labrosse, 2002): semaphores, event flags, mutual-exclusion semaphores that eliminate unbounded priority inversions, message mailboxes and queues; task, time and timer management; and fixed sized memory block management. μC/OS-II's footprint can be scaled (between 5 Kbytes to 24 Kbytes) to only contain the features required for a specific application. The execution time for most services provided by μC/OS-II is both constant and deterministic; execution times do not depend on the number of tasks running in the application. μC/OS-II comes with all the source code, written in portable ANSI C. However, this kernel cannot support mobile agents without modifications.

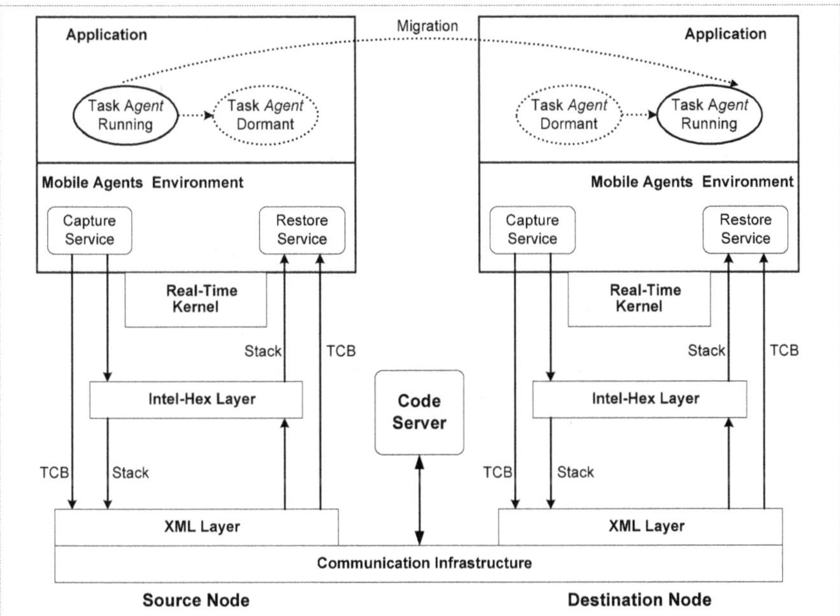

Fig. 18. Mobile Agents Platform Interconnection.

The choice of μC/OS-II is motivated by the need to use a small real-time kernel, because of the limitations incurred by the computing resource constraints of the embedded system. μC/OS-II has two major advantages: it requires not only a small memory but also it is open-source software. Thus, we can extend its code to implement a mechanism to capture and restore the task's state.

4.1 μC/MAS API

μC/MAS platform is implemented as an API. μC/MAS API is designed to integrate the features of an existing real-time kernel, in the case of this platform, μC/OS-II but also of other similar types such as μC/OS-III and μClinux. It is primarily intended for very small environments built around microcontrollers. Choice of kernel, i.e. μ/COS-II, should be written in ANSI C and its source code must be available to allow access to mechanisms for capturing and restoring the execution context that will be used by the mobile agents' platform. While most of μC/OS-II is written in C, for portability, it is still necessary to write some code in assembly language. For example, code for the context switching is written in assembly language, as it is not possible to access CPU registers directly from C. The device driver, code which initializes the hardware, also needs to be written in assembly language. The platform API is built on a modular architecture that allows integration with other services using a real-time kernel and different means of transport for agents. It includes the following modules at the base of its integrability with these services:

- Capturing/restoring module that interfaces with the real-time kernel;
- Encoding/decoding that allows formatting the agent (data + current execution state) according to the transport service;
- Module offers various transport services (TCP/IP, ZigBee, RFID, etc.) that provide the interface with the means of transport. Transport can be used synchronously as in the case of TCP/IP or ZigBee or asynchronously as in the case of using smart card storage (RFID).


```
<Doc>
        <TCB>
                <OSTCBStkPtr            INT32U="8105A760" />
                <OSTCBStkBottom         INT32U="81050A0C" />
                <OSTCBStkSize           INT32U="2800" />
                <OSTCBOpt               INT32U="03" />
                <OSTCBId                INT32U="0A" />
                <OSTCBPrio              INT32U="0A" />
                <OSTCBTaskName          string="TaskAgent" />
        </TCB>
        <Stack string=":10A76000200000D3200000130000000800000007B4
                      :10A770008105AE1404040404050505050606060655
                      :10A7800007070707080808080909090910101010 29
                      :10A790008105A7B48105A7B88000C6608000C660A7
                      :10A7A0000100F0BC200000138105A7D48105A7B8E3
                      :10A7B0008000A8EC8000C5808105A7F00000000A99
                      :10A7C0000100000260000013810 5AA088105A7D8D6
                      :10A7D00080008CCC8000A7E80000000000A21300DD
                      :10A7E0005E093E4013005E353E4000A2973B59098A
                      :10A7F00000A21300A22F0A401300686D0A4000A2B5
                      :10A80000FAB9B42F2065685469626F6D6120656C78
                      :10A81000746E6567207369206E2074612065646FB3
                      :10A820006F6E20340D0A2E7700000000000000003B
                      :10A830000000000000685400006F6D2065656C69625F
                                        ⋮
                      :10AA00008105AA0C1414141480008964000000014C
                      :00000001FF" />
</Doc>
```


Fig. 19. Transfer format of the execution state.

The mechanism of migration of the agents takes place in the following way: When the agent decides to migrate to another node, the execution thread (data and current state) of the task is saved. The execution thread is transported to the destination node using the means of transport (TCP/IP, ZigBee, RFID, etc.). At the destination node, a monitoring mechanism is to listen and identify the transport used to receive the agents arrive. This mechanism is implemented by a task that is part of the µC/MAS platform. The incoming agent is used by the task (for restoration) to create a new task that will host the execution thread of this agent. Note that in the source node, the task migrant is deleted.

```
<Bloc>
        <BlocSize>value</BlocSize>
        <BlocIntelHex =":XXXXXXXXXXXXXXXXXXXXXXXXXXXXXXXXXXXXXXXXXXX
                       :XXXXXXXXXXXXXXXXXXXXXXXXXXXXXXXXXXXXXXXXXXX
                              •
                              •
                              •
                       :00000001FF" />

</Bloc>
```

Fig. 20. Transfer format of migrant data blocks.

4.1.1 Capturing and restoring the execution context

In order to capture the execution context of a task *agent*, it is necessary to generate a context switching. To do so, we implemented the primitive *OSTaskMoveTo()*. The latter is called when the task *agent* decides to migrate to another node. Calling this primitive *OSTaskMoveTo()* generates the context switching of the task *agent*. *OSTaskMoveTo()* requires two additional arguments: *DestNodeAddr* and *MediumType*. The variable *DestNodeAddr* contains an address in the mechanism of transport such as an IP address, a MAC (Media Access Control address) to a Zigbee network, or an identifier of an RFID chip. The variable *MediumType* is the type of transport protocol used: TCP/IP, Zigbee, RFID, etc. After the context switching is done, the function *OSTaskContextCapture()* captures and encodes the stack and task control block (TCB) of the agent in a suitable for transport format. In order to capture the stack, the platform uses the value stored in the TCB *(stack pointer)* which is the pointer to the top of the stack and the starting address of the stack. From this information we can identify the stack space used to extract the addresses and data. Then, the addresses and data from the stack and task control block are encoded in a format suitable for transfer. For example, you can use a combination of two standards for data exchange: the Intel Hex format for binary elements as the content of the stack and XML for structured data such as the TCB. The Fig. 19 shows the transfer format of the execution state.

Once the execution context of the agent is encoded, *OSTaskContextTransfert()* is called for the transfer to the destination node. This transfer is transparent to the user. However, to check the status of the agent's transfer, the user can use *OSTaskTransfertStatus()* which return one of the following:

- *OS_NO_ERR* : the transfer of the agent is successful;
- *OS_PRIO_INVALID*: the priority associated with the agent is not available on the destination node;
- *OS_ADDR_INVALID*: the destination address is not valid;
- *OS_TASK_TIME_OUT*: the destination node does not respond;
- *OS_MIGR_ERR*: An error occurred during the transfer operation.

In cases where the migration fails, the agent continues to run in the node where it is located.

```
Static void TaskAgent (void *p_arg)
{
    ... // The Instructions before moving data
    OSMemBlocMove(DataBlocPtr, DestNodeAddr, DestDataBlocAddr, err);
    if(err == OS_NO_ERR)
    {
        // The data blocks transfert is successful, execution continues HERE
        OSTaskMoveTo(DestNodeAddr, MediumType);
        if(OSTaskTransfertStatus())
        {
            // The task agent transfert is successful, execution continues HERE
            ...
        }
        else
        {
            //The task agent transfert is failed, execution continues HERE
            ...
        }
    }
    else
    {
        //The data blocks transfert is  failed, execution continues HERE
        ...
    }
}
```

Fig. 21. Sequence using primitive *OSMemBlocMove()* and *OSTaskMoveTo()*.

In the destination node, the data representing the execution context of the agent are received by a monitoring task that acts as an agents' server for the node. This task decodes and restores the context of agents received and starts executing. The received data is decoded to extract the stack and the task control block, and is restored to a new task to the destination node. To do so, we modified *OSTaskCreate()* that is the task creation function of the real-time kernel μC/OS-II in order to implement *OSTaskAgentCreate()*. This function uses *OSTaskContextRestore()* that we designed to restore the execution context of the task *agent*. The task of running the agent is recreated under the same conditions as the source node, especially with the same memory card and the same executable code. The data in the stack of the task *agent* are identical to those that were present on the source node. The task *agent* then resumes execution where it left off on the source node.

Note that a task *agent* consists of an execution context and current data. For migration of current data other than the stack, partitions of memory blocks offered by the μC/OS-II can be extended to design transfer mechanisms. The Fig. 20 shows the transfer format of migrant data blocks. When migrating a data block, the task *agent* uses the function *OSMemBlocMove()*. This allows extracting data from the memory block to save and then encode into a suitable transport format. The parameters of the function *OSMemBlocMove()* are:

- *DataBlocPtr* pointing the data block to be transferred to the destination node;
- *DestNodeAddr* that contains the network address of the destination node;
- *DestDataBlocAddr* that returns the address of the data block in the destination node;

- *err* that returns one of the following:
    - OS_NO_ERR: the transfer of data block is successful migrants;
    - OS_ADDR_INVALID: the destination address is not valid;
    - OS_TASK_TIME_OUT: the destination node does not respond;
    - OS_MIGR_ERR: An error occurred during the transfer operation.

The primitive *OSMemBlocMove()* calls the function *OSMemBlocCapture()*. This captures and encodes the data block. Then, the data block must be deleted from the source node if the transfer is successful. In the destination node, the block of migrant data is received by the task that acts as an agents' server for the node. This task decodes and restores the data block in the same memory partition than the source node. To do so, it implements the function *OSMemBlocRestore()* that we designed to restore the data blocks of the task *agent*. Restoring a data block takes place according to the following sequence: (a) a data block of the same type and same size as the source node is created in the destination node, (b) the data received from the source node are copied to the newly created block, (c) the address of the block and a code indicating that the restoration is successful are sent in the source node, (d) the source node, the address of the received data block is copied to a local variable, in this case in *DestDataBlocAddr* for later use in a possible migration of the task *agent*. The Fig. 21 shows a sequence of primitives using *OSMemBlocMove()* and *OSTaskMoveTo()*.

5. Evaluation of µC/MAS

In order to ensure the proper functioning of µC/MAS, we made certain numbers of the tests on various networks.

5.1 Wired network

In order to build the wired network, we set up a system composed of two ARM7-based microcontrollers (LPC-H2214/LPC-H2294) each one being connected with a PC. Each PC serves as a code server as well as an interface displaying the results. As shown in Fig. 22, the communication between PCs and microcontrollers is done via UART0 using the serial communication protocol. The UART1 of the source node is connected directly to the UART1 of the destination node to communicate between the two microcontrollers.

In order to test µC/MAS platform on a wired network, we implemented a sample application of a mobile agent that performs the following steps to test the platform on the wired network:

1. The agent initializes a number of variables of different types (char, short, int, float, double) in a node 1;
2. It performs operations on these variables and displays their contents, and then it moves to a node 2.
3. The agent continues operations, displays the contents of variables and returns to the starting node, node 1;

In this experiment, the agent performs different operations. For example, the agent performs arithmetic operations such as addition, subtraction, etc. It also performs concatenation of strings contained in variables from a remote node.

This experience has allowed us to validate the strong migration. The agent interrupts its own execution on the source node, and then the code is transferred from the server to the destination node. Then, the data representing the state of the agent is transferred from the source node to the destination node. Finally, when the agent arrived at the destination node, it continues to run where it left off on the source node. The execution thread of this experiment is displayed on the screen of the PC that is connected to the microcontroller of each node.

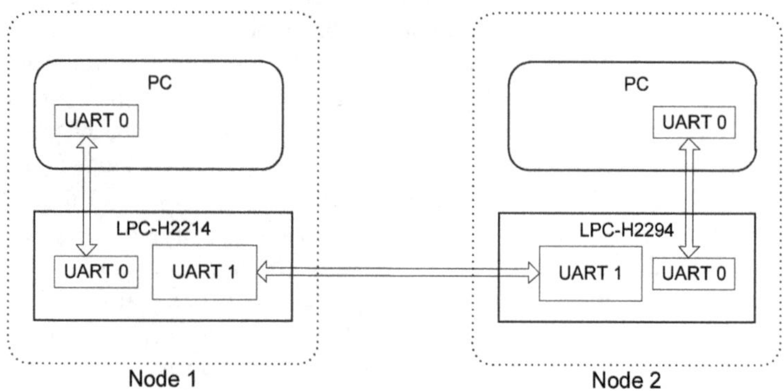

Fig. 22 Model of the wired network.

5.2 Zigbee network

In order to build the Zigbee network, we set up a system composed of six nodes. Each network node consists of:

1. ARM7-based microcontrollers (LPC-H2214/LPC-H2294);
2. Module X-bee;
3. PC to follow the thread of execution.

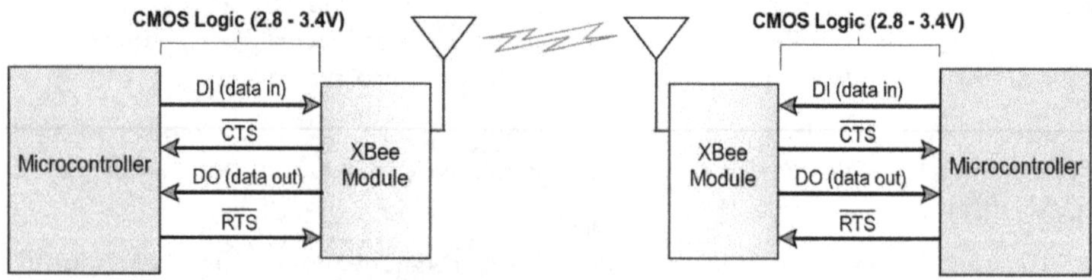

Fig. 23 Interconnection between XBee module and microcontroller (Digi International, 2009)

In order to test μC/MAS platform on the Zigbee network, we conducted a sample application of mobile agent similar to the wired network. The difference between the two experiences is the network communication infrastructure, the number of nodes used and the number of laps completed by the agent. In this experiment, as previously mentioned, we used six nodes. As shown in Fig. 23, the XBee module has a serial interface that connects directly to a microcontroller.

Furthermore, contrary to the previous experiment where the agent makes only a single iteration, in this one the agent makes five times the tour of the six nodes. As the previous experiment, this one allowed us to validate the strong mobility supported by this platform of mobile agents. The Fig. 24 illustrates the model of the Zigbee network where a mobile agent makes the tour of six nodes by beginning his route of the node 1.

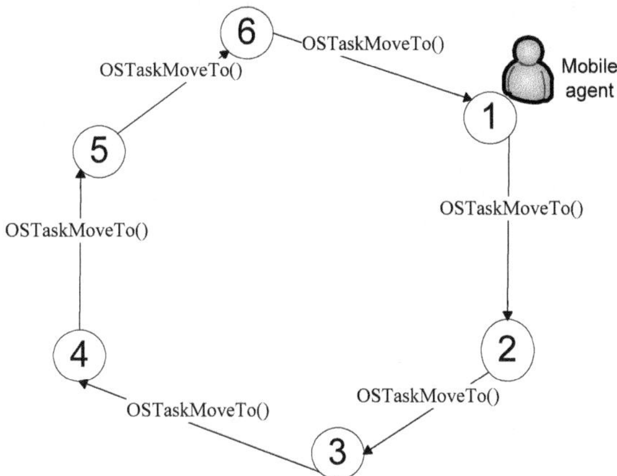

Fig. 24 Mobile Agent on Zigbee network.

In both networks we have experimented, the transfer speed of the agent depends on the communication link between the nodes. The Table 1 summarizes the quantitative evaluation of the experience we have done on the wired network and the Zigbee network. In order to calculate the transfer speed of a frame, we calculate the transfer rate of a bit. A frame is composed of 8 bit data, 1 stop bit and 1 start bit. The LPC-H2214/ LPC-H2294 can operate up to 60 MHz CPU frequency. For baud rate of 115,200 bps and CPU frequency of 60 MHz, the calculation of the constant C is as follows: C = frequency / (baud rate x 16) = 60 x 10^6/(115200 x 16) = 32.552. This can be approximated to C = 32. The actual baud rate = 60 x 10^6/ (32 x 16) = 117187.5 bps. This gives a period of 8.53 microseconds. The transfer time of a frame can be calculated as follows: the transfer time of a frame is 10 bits x 8.53 microseconds = 85.3 microseconds. Thus, we can calculate the transfer time of the execution state in the wired network like this: 34309 bytes x 85.3 microseconds = 2.926 seconds. This calculation does not take into account a possible loss of frames.

	Wired network	Zigbee network
Baud rate (bps)	115200	115200
CPU frequency (in MHz)	60	60
Used stack size (bytes)	1024	1024
Size of execution state in transfer format (in bytes)	3011	3011
Transfer time of execution state in transfer format (in seconds)	1.41	2.88

Table 1. Quantitative evaluation of wired and Zigbee network.

6. Conclusion

In this chapter, we presented the stages of the development of a mobile agent platform for embedded systems. By utilizing a context switch mechanism which already exists in the multitasking system, we have designed a mobile agent migration method and implemented it inside a real-time kernel. We have also designed and implemented a transfer format and a communication protocol stack for mobile agents' migration on a wired or wireless network. For the wireless network, the code of the agent was not transferred because of limited bandwidth.

The advantage of our mobile agent migration method, in regard to the other projects, is that it can be implemented in any multitask system, because we employ mechanisms that exist in these systems. The main advantage of our platform of mobile agents is its small size, which allows it to run on machines having a memory as small as one megabyte.

7. References

Bellifemine, F., Caire, G. & Greenwood, D. (2007) *Developing Multi-Agent Systems with JADE* In: John Wiley & Sons Ltd, ISBN 978-0-470-05747-6, Chichester, England.

Borenstein, N. S. (1994) *E-mail with a mind of its own: The Safe-Tcl language for enabled mail,* IFIP Transactions C (25):389–402.

Cardelli, L. (1995) *A language with distributed scope,* Annual Symposium on Principles of Programming Languages, Proc. 22nd ACM SIGPLAN-SIGACT symposium on Principles of programming languages, San Francisco, CA, pp. 286 - 297.

Digi International (2009) *Product Manual v1.xEx - 802.15.4 Protocol, XBee®/XBee-PRO® RF Modules* http://ftp1.digi.com/support/documentation/90000982_B.pdf (The last time accessed, November 18, 2011)

Dilyana, S. & Petya, G. (2002) *Building distributed applications with Java mobile agents,* International workshop NGNT, pp. 103 - 109

Domel, P. (1996) *Mobile Telescript agents and the Web,* In Digest of Papers, COMPCON '96, Technologies for the Information Superhighway, 41st IEEE Computer Society International Conference, pp. 52–57, IEEE Computer Society Press.

Ferber, J. (1999) *Multi-Agent Systems: An Introduction to Distributed Artificial Intelligence,* In: Addison Wesley Professional, ISBN 9780201360486.

Intel Corporation (1988) *Hexadecimal Object File Format Specification,* http://microsym.com/editor/assets/intelhex.pdf (The last time accessed, October 26, 2011).

Lange, D. B. & Mitsru, O. (1998) *Programming and Deploying Java Mobile Agents Aglets, 1st edition,* In: Addison-Wesley Longman Publishing Co., Inc., ISBN 0201325829 Boston, MA, USA.

Lange, D. B. & Mitsru, O. (1998) *Programming and Deploying Java Mobile Agents Aglets, 1st edition,* In: Addison-Wesley Longman Publishing Co., Inc., ISBN 0201325829 Boston, MA, USA.

Labrosse, J. J. (2002) *Micro/OS-II The Real-Time Kernel, Second Edition,* In: CMP Books, ISBN 1578201039, San Francisco, CA, USA.

http://micrium.com/page/products/rtos/os-ii (Last time accessed, October 26, 2011)

Labrosse, J. J. (2010) *µC/OS-III: The Real-Time Kernel and the NXP LPC1700,* In: Micriµm Press, ISBN 9780982337554, Weston, FL, USA.

13

Dynamic Control in Embedded Systems

Javier Vásquez-Morera[1], José L. Vásquez-Núñez[2] and Carlos Manuel Travieso-González[3]

[1]*University of Costa Rica, Computer Science Deparment, San José,*
[2]*University of Costa Rica, Sede del Atlántico, Cartago,*
[3]*University of Las Palmas de Gran Canaria, Signals and Communications Department, Institute for Technological Development and Innovation in Communications, Campus University of Tafira, Las Palmas de Gran Canaria,*
[1,2]*Costa Rica*
[3]*Spain*

1. Introduction

Nowadays, different advances in technology have reduced the cost of micro-controllers and devices, such as sensors and actuators. In addition, the proliferation of Internet connections has led to the appearance of digital system controllers (DSC) that are designed to monitor and control equipment distributed by remote human intervention.

These DSC consists of a series of sensors controlled commonly by a local micro-controller, device capable of performing one or more tasks related to control (hardware - software) such as:

- View and control of physical variables.
- Schedule activities.
- Message service (e-mail, mobile phone).

While devices (DSC) may work in a distributed manner, it is usual to have the control intelligence permanently associated with one of the interconnected devices. In this work control means the attempt to impose predictability to unreliable entities that react to events. We also understand control policy as the predefined set of events that activate when control devices so dictate.

To carry out the distribution of control, we propose a distributed control model (DCM) that keeps separate control rules from control devices, hence any change in such policies do not necessarily alter the hardware or software used in a DSC. This method allows the incremental construction of longer useful life and more sophisticated control devices, whose flexible policies can be managed according to the user requirements.

It is the objective of this chapter to propose a strategy for the development of embedded systems, that incorporate aspects of computing interest as an abstraction of the behaviour and component-based design which allows embedded systems to have a number of features such as:

- Easy to scale up and adapt
- Easy to use
- Easy to maintain
- Reusable sensors and actuators

The structure of the chapter is divided in 4 sections:

The first section describes the Dynamic Control Model (DCM) as well as its main components, functionality and features.

The DCM in (Vásquez, 2010) permits the partial separation of the control in embedded systems allowing some of the rules (the basic ones) to be stored in the DSC and other rules in a central server which notifies each participant about the rules it manages and also the changes in the policies every time the user modifies any of them. Additionally, this section also explains the use of DCM in the development of monitoring and control applications that include embedded systems.

The second section explores in greater detail the issue of control rules managing the behaviour of an embedded system.

The third section deals with the use of software engineering techniques in the design of embedded systems. The Component Based Design (CBD) is introduced as a class reusing mechanism and the Contract-Based Design (CrBD) leads to the construction of robust components, easier to be reused than those created without CrBD.

The last section shows how to integrate the concepts mentioned above. The example proposed in this section serves as induction for those interested in the management of dynamics control rules.

2. Architecture of the Dynamic Distributed Control Model (DCM)

In the field of software engineering, the n-tier architecture is a term used to describe a methodology for designing and deploying applications. The methodology divides the functionality of an application into logical layers that interact to form a complete system.

The basic separation of an application proposes to divide the functionality of the system into three logical parts; the first one abstracts the interface (user services), the second one abstracts the rules of business services (business logic), and the third one functions as a data repository.

Nowadays, the development of distributed control systems is based on Internet technologies which include not only Web applications, but also the use of high-level languages, design and object-oriented programming, open protocols among others. Hence, the features and advantages of the methodology of n-layers are appropriate to the design and implementation of these systems.

Generally, in a DSC the control policies are set at the construction stage, which makes the device less flexible and not to respond adequately to changes in the requirements that users experience. The use of three-tier architecture allows the dynamic modification of composition and behaviour of both the abstract control policies and the DSC.

Figure 1 shows the 3-tier architecture used in the proposed model for distributed dynamic control (DCM). In the client layer one can find monitoring devices (Device Sensor) implemented through logic circuits. In the business layer the user finds Web services containing dynamic control rules that detect and process events. In the server layer is the database that can store data of users, devices, policies and events.

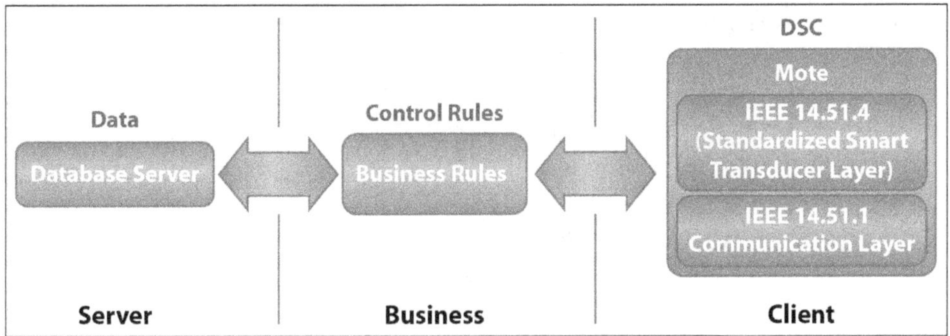

Fig. 1. Architecture for the control scheme with distributed intelligence.

2.1 Control device characterization

Figure 2 shows that control devices can be designed using the Model View Controller pattern, allowing abstract interface for managing devices. The distributed controller and the generic device model created by adding persistent components are grouped in 3 categories:

1. The sensors that conform the set of artefacts that are permanently recording the occurrence of events.
2. The actuators that are the set of artefacts reacting to determined rules, instructed to do so by a driver.
3. The microprocessors that can be microcontrollers or even personal computers.

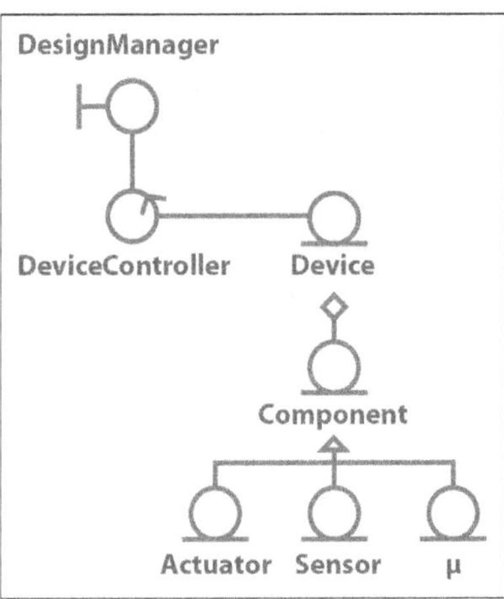

Fig. 2. Device design using reusable components.

From that abstract point of view, any device in the DCM is modelled as an object that has a number of attributes and that exhibits a behaviour which can be implemented in hardware or in software as shown in Figure 3. In this context, the components of a device are seen as the attributes of the same. Additionally, the behaviour of the object in the DCM is determined by its operations, and in the case of a device, the most common operations are related to the query and management of sensors and actuators, providing a service and setting its mode of operation.

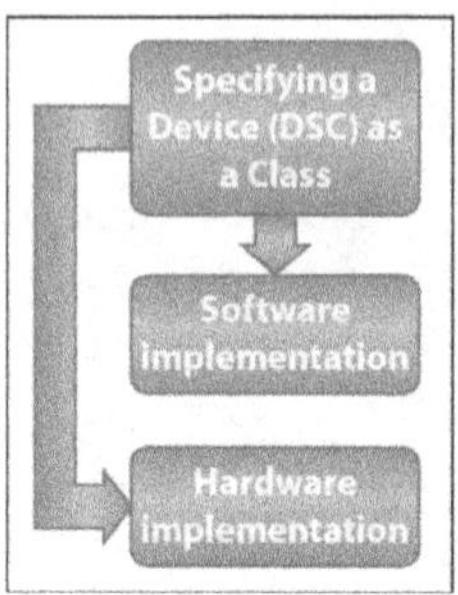

Fig. 3. Device implementation choice.

In designing a device as an object, encapsulation property allows hiding the construction details of the device. As a result, using this device requires only the knowledge of the set of operations or commands to interact with it. By using encapsulation in the device design, the control system obtains increased flexibility and better adaptability to the changes experienced by the devices as well as to changes in the user requirements. Figure 4 shows a specification of a DSC using a class diagram.

To integrate a device into the system, besides its activation, it is required to obtain participating control policies from a database. Once the device is operational, it can be accessed and managed remotely.

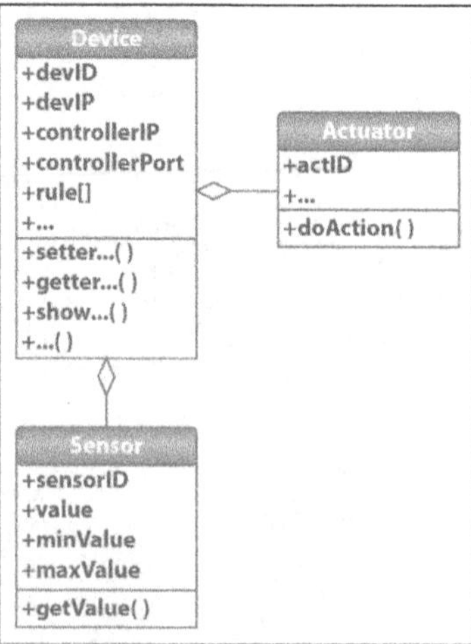

Fig. 4. DSC Diagram Class Specification.

2.2 DCM implementation using free software tools

Free software tools were used for the implementation of the DCM. The DSC device is composed by a general purpose microcontroller with an Ethernet interface built into the chip, making easier their connection to the network. Other components of the DSC are temperature sensors, humidity sensors, and electrical switches. The Events Controller is a Java application. The database, implemented with MySQL, contains the entities and relationships needed to show the performance characteristics of the model. The database was populated with data from users, devices, log of events and control rules. Finally, Tomcat was used as web application container, consisting of XHTML pages, EJB, JSP, and Servlets. This application provides the user a platform to search and specify control rules in the database, and to communicate directly with the DSC.

Once DCM is developed and implemented, there have been three important results:

1. Ability to alter the runtime behaviour of a DSC
2. Integration of open source technologies in the design and implementation of embedded systems
3. DCM_NIST model (Schneeman, 1999) was increased to enable distribution of dynamic control.

As Figure 5 shows, the use of DCM procures to obtain the following advantages:

- Adequacy, each manager can change the response that actuators must take after an event. This response is so flexible that in the future the manager can modify the actions.
- Automation, with this model it is possible to decide what sensing variables are needed to control in an automatic way.
- Scalability, the type and quantity of sensors and actuators can change in the future without discarding the old ones.
- Simplicity, the web interface allows interacting with the system in an easy way.
- Remote access, a user with an internet access point (mobile or not) may control the system and program the response of the actuators.

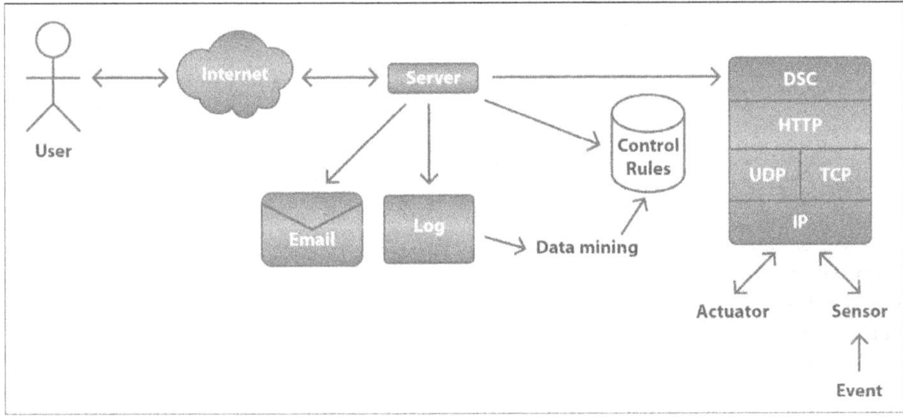

Fig. 5. DCM Implementation.

3. Management of control rules for the DCM

A control rule consists of one or more events and a series of actions that respond to the events. Any event generated by the sensors is recorded in a log, is evaluated against the control rules and if the necessary conditions are fulfilled, the controller executes the respective actions.

The MCD allows devices to record the occurrence of control events and take appropriate actions such as to activate some of the control actuators and communicate with other devices to delegate the monitoring of other rules and to enable its respective reaction, or notify by mail or messages to mobile devices.

As stated, the MCD provides three basic components:

- a set of sensors (e.g. 1,..,4)
- a set of dynamic rules of control ($Rule_a$ ... $Rule_p$)
- a set of actuators ($Actuator_1$ ... $Actuator_n$)

The microprocessor monitors the activation events from the sensors and communicates these events to the control rules engine, which is responsible for verifying those rules and triggers the respective actuators, see Figure 6.

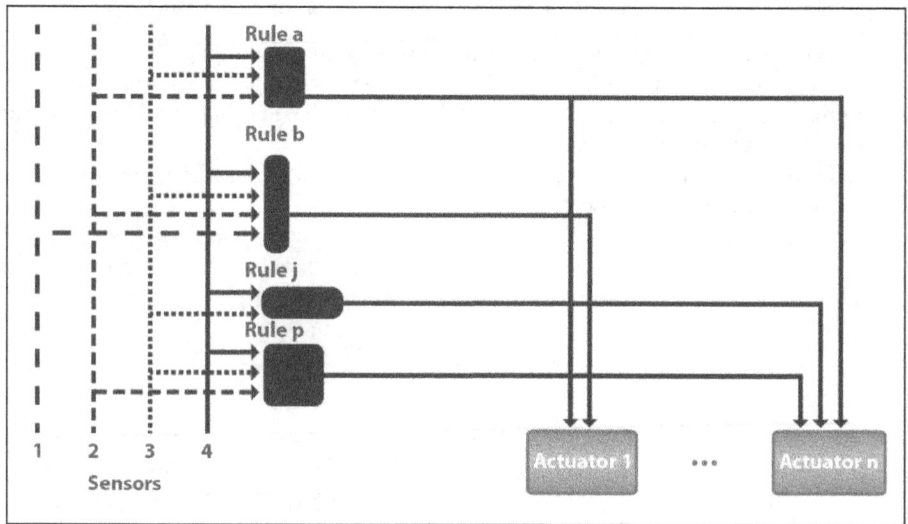

Fig. 6. Trigger mechanism of control rules.

The activation of a set of sensors could trigger different rules simultaneously, which leads to the necessity to define a strategy to trigger the rules. In the figure 6, the sensor S4 causes the activation of the rules a, b, j and p at the same time. Different rules may operate on the same actuator, which can generate an antagonising effect on the actuator, so it is necessary to recognize such situations.

The control rules management consists mainly of two phases, one to allow dynamic specification of the control rules and the other its activation:

Specification of control rules phase: The DCM allows remote users to edit a set of policies on devices if they have the security rights to do it. These devices have a longest life and can be reusable, because its control rules are persistent in a table of the database, allowing an adjustment in line with the interests and capabilities of the administrator. Control rules can be edited by the DSC manager, which allows distinguishing two instances to manage them:

1. As part of the assembly of components, default behaviour is defined and stored in persistent memory in the form of policies. Thereafter the administrator can define a set of control rules, which modify its behaviour. Rules should be evaluated and approved by the security administrator.

2. Whenever the DSC comes into operation, as a first step it checks for updates to the set of rules. In this case, new rules can be added or replace those predefined in the persistent memory and will be effective until a new set of rules is determined. The predefined rules are necessary to ensure a minimum performance in case the device cannot communicate with the business layer.

Activation of the control rules phase: when a device controller detects an event, the event is registered in the database. If there is a control rule associated to the event the commands are extracted from the database and the corresponding devices will receive instructions to perform the indicated actions.

As part of the activation mechanism of control rules, we define a server-type computer program called Events Controller whose fundamental role is to verify and apply existing control policies.

Figure 7 describes the protocol of activation of rules within DCM:

- The DSC communicates to the Events Controller the fulfilling of any condition.
- The Events Controller records in the database the received message.
- The Events Controller searches into the database to determine if there is associated a control rule, if so, obtains from the database the actions to be performed.
- The Events Controller could notify the user via a message system.
- The Events Controller orders the different actors to perform the corresponding actions that can be conceptualized as a chain of events.

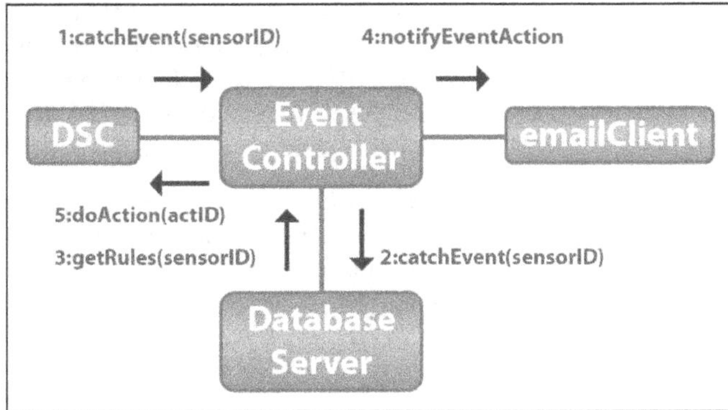

Fig. 7. Control rules implementation.

A device only performs the actions associated with an event when these are indicated by the Events Controller. However sometimes the device can perform an operation on its own initiative, a case is when the device loses communication with the controller.

There are two special cases identified in the rule triggering mechanism.

a. An event may trigger several rules at a time. There are two options to manage this situation:
   - To use the priority scheme within the rules as attributes, so if a set of rules can be selected, the choice of the rule will be according to the priority.
   - If a subset of eligible rules is still maintained, the mechanism can use a random activation sequence.
b. Many events interacting at the same time may run into contradictory actions, for example an event causes that an actuator is turned on and other event turns it off. A proposed solution to this case is to assign a priority scheme to events -according to a cost function-. These events are processed in accordance to the control rules management as follows:

Specification of control rules phase

- Identify rules for the same actuator
- Ask the user to classify them as contradictory or not
- If contradiction happens: the user must assign priority to events

Activation of the control rules phase

The actuator is empowered by the higher priority event when and if the event is in force.

4. Component-based design (CBD) used for embedded system design

To use the DCM in an embedded system, it is important to abide by the principles of component-based design, design contracts and resolve the problem of platform independence.

According to (Szyperski, 2002), a component must be understood as an executable unit, allowing the deployment and the composition at run time. This definition has been expanded from the one given in (Booch et al, 1999), where the component was conceived as the physical part of a system that meets and implements a series of interfaces. The definition also formalizes the idea given in (McIlroy, 1969). McIlroy first proposed the design of reusable component-based software, and also identified the need for catalogues of components, which are categorized according to different aspects.

Since McIllroy introduced this concept, efforts have been made to bring to the software industry, specific aspects of the culture of hardware production, but almost 40 years later there is still much to do. However, several evidences clearly show the convenience of using component-based design, both isolated in the software industry, as in embedded systems.

The component based design seeks to achieve the following benefits:

1. Reduce design and development time (using certified components).
2. Ensure the proper operation and performance of component-based software.

3. Simplify the evaluation of new components.
4. Increase the longevity of the investment associated with the design and construction of components.

Although the use of components is performed for a long time in the hardware industry, this situation does not occur in the software industry because there are conceptual differences about the use of components.

For example, they are product's catalogues which make possible the use of hardware components, and also international standards to assess the appropriateness of those components. In counterpart for using software components, catalogues are less available than those used in the hardware industry, and there are also various "universes search", where each universe corresponds to the programming language or platform used.

On the other hand while the control in the field of hardware can be sequential or parallel, and commonly there is no feedback about the success of the operation, in the field of software the control can be sequential or parallel, but almost always required to get feedback about the success of the operation.

In the field of embedded systems, they have a set of techniques that analyses the use of component-based design, for example Combest (Component-Based Embedded Systems Design Techniques) (Combest, 2007) states that to use the design based components within the field of embedded systems the following qualities are required:

- To allow heterogeneous components, combining the inherent capabilities that hardware has to work in parallel, with the usual capabilities of the software to work point to point, which should allow the existence of subsystems with execution and interaction semantics different.
- To have the ability to predict the basic properties of the designed system.

The authors of this chapter suggest that to achieve the correct composition of products in embedded systems is also required:

- Producers that are subject to rules to standardize parts.
- Clients that have access to similar parts catalogues.
- If required, the parts of a product can be transparently replaced by similar ones.
- Equivalent parts can be evaluated against other with similar properties and in function of the price.
- Time for the assembly of parts should be short.
- Predictability of the reliable performance of a component when assembled to others.

In the field of software engineering it is considered that the use of components promotes the simplification of processes, encapsulation, reusability, functionality, maintainability, efficiency, reliability and portability.

Under this strategy, all components communicate with its environment using two types of interfaces, an interface that describes the services provided (outgoing interface) and the other services required (incoming interface). However, the authors of this chapter consider that to design embedded systems based on components besides having a description of services, requires to have a description and parameterisation of the algorithms available and the data to be used.

4.1 Service description

The description of services is a common feature in software engineering issued in the software components and popularized by the use of Unified Modelling Language (UML) (Booch et al, 1999a), which although originally did not handle components, always described the amount and type of parameters and the type of return value (Booch et al, 1999b).

4.2 Algorithm description

Using software components allows to know both the services provided and required by a component, but it is not uncommon to find components that implement different algorithms, selectable by the user. As a black box a component hides commonly the implementation details of the methods. In this chapter it is stated that components should expose at least the name of the algorithms implemented and allow its parameterisation by the user.

4.3 Description of the data or signals that are sent and received

By merging the design of hardware and software it is important that the components used in embedded systems allow defining and configuring the physical layer, for example:

- meaning of the pins,
- domain and range of values in each pin,
- semantics of the value transferred
- transfer rate,
- representation of the data and
- ability to initialize variables

Other qualities of the components that the authors of this chapter consider desirable are:

1. to have a quick release of components on the market
2. to be able to certify the operation of the component
3. to have programming language independence
4. to establish, as part of deployment, the range of values on the signals to be handled, the encryption mechanism and the modulation of the signal to use.

The following features complement those mentioned by (Kopetz, 2007) as obligatory in embedded systems:

- to provide an efficient use of energy in devices that use batteries
- to have a low cost and time to market
- to have timely availability
- to have a dependable operation in safety-relevant scenarios

The authors of this document have identified some desirable qualities and other indispensable in embedded systems. Some of them are already present and others are missing, but despite this, the component-based design is now an option to the problem of designing embedded systems. Some identified solutions couple both disciplines, including:

1. Functional separation between inputs and outputs of the components.
2. Component models proposed by the software industry.
3. Standardized architectures for data migration between platforms.
4. Specialized programming languages, platform-independent, such as some based on IEC63131 standard (IEC, 2003), which despite its good intentions, has not yet reached its intended purpose.

One could also say that the evaluation of the implementation of new components via FPGA[1], to avoid the production of pieces of hardware in the initial phase of testing, allows prototyping the designs based on both technologies.

It should be noted that in designing embedded systems based on components, one must keep in mind the Principle of Compositionality, which states that the semantics of any component is determined by the semantics of the subcomponents, as well as the rules used to combine them. This is a fact to keep in mind when developing collaborative components and nested components.

4.4 Taking advantage of the component-based design into the DCM

The proposed model of distributed dynamic control (DCM) allows the separation of rules into two subsets as described in the previous section. This quality increases the longevity of embedded systems by allowing to partially modify their behaviour according to the user's requirements, to provide greater flexibility and adaptation.

The DCM allows dynamic creation of devices, taking advantage of the component-based design and the contract-based design. Rules within the DCM allow reaching cooperating devices, whose existence and location is dynamic, allowing modularity of devices. Nevertheless, the former does not ensure their compositionality. (Szabó, 2008; Zwiers, 1985) As a consequence there is a need to attend the embedded systems design with alternative arrangements to ensure the quality of the component, for example as in the contract-based design and the use of rigorous software testing.

The software industry is facing various problems that affect the development of embedded systems, including:

- To produce systems and component, which are highly efficient and robust.
- To ensure the quality of the applications and components developed.
- To eliminate side effects if software is reused.
- To facilitate the ability to leverage components and applications developed in a distributed manner, regardless of programming language and operating system for which they were developed.

To solve such problems various technologies of renowned quality have been proposed and have been using contract-based design (Meyer, 1992), software testing, component-based design (UML) and the interface definition language (OMG).

---

[1] A FPGA is a programmable logical device, of general purpose and configurable logic elements, making easy the prototyping of embedded systems, enabling to the user the design and testing of hardware components associated with software components already created.

Combining these technologies with FPGA allows achieving an environment for production of systems and devices of high quality that are easy to use and great capability to be reused.

4.5 Classes

To define an adequate functioning of a class and to increase its robustness, it is recommended to specify their behaviour and their status by using Contract-Based Design that defines pre-and post-conditions and invariant conditions defined in the classes. The control of these properties should be performed using software testing.

Although the individual quality of a class can be defined and ensured, in the context of interacting classes it is necessary to design and ensure the quality of these interactions. There are different practices and standards that divide business logic from the interfaces; this fact is reflected in several ways:

- Using the MVC pattern (Krasner et al, 1988).
- Using APIs to communicate developments made through time by various providers follows a set of specific standards, which would correspond to using the Bridge pattern (Gamma et al, 1995).
- Using Contract-Based Design (CrBD), which formalizes the provision of services between classes. All classes can define the pre and post conditions under which it can be provided a service, and also it can set some restrictions on its inner values.

4.6 Software components

Once the quality of a set of cooperating classes is assured, the set can be formalized to be reused later, giving rise to the software components.

The component-based design allows publishing the services that a component offers and also the services it requires, leaving all those hidden details of their operation, which in the best case facilitate the coupling of components and the replacement of any of them in a transparent way.

4.7 Interconnection between components

The need to combine software artefacts (whether packages, components or classes) that develop through a particular programming language for a specific operating system, led to the Object Managing Group to define the interface definition language (IDL) as a standard to regulate the definition of interfaces. Thus the IDL was created to solve the problem of the independence of programming language and operating system, allowing the definition of interfaces including embedded systems and wireless. Its implementation uses mapping between the IDL and the respective roles in different programming languages such as C, C + +, Java, Smalltalk, COBOL, Ada, Lisp, PL / 1, Python, Ruby and IDLscript.

Figure 8 shows the collaboration between components, where the weather station is responsible for providing information about weather conditions, which in turn are required by the device driver for a greenhouse. Once processed the signals and based on a set of rules, the controller may, for example, apply the irrigation of plants, opening windows to reduce temperature.

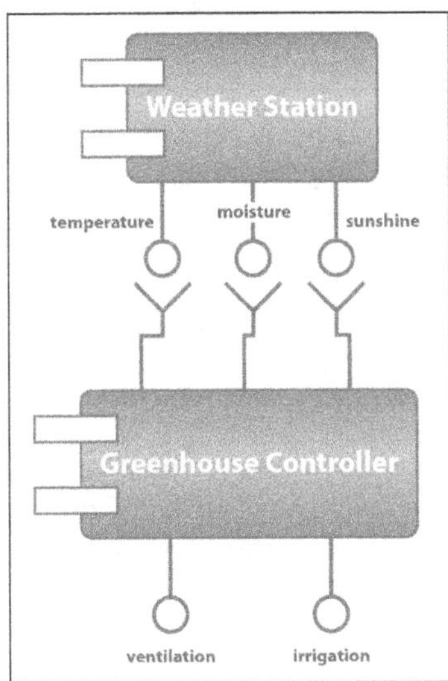

Fig. 8. Collaborating components.

From the implementation point of view, it could be a set of interacting classes used to monitor compliance with rules. For example list 1 shows one possible implementation of a unit that handles an invariant condition, and also shows the use of pre and post conditions.

```
public class Device{
 float lowValue_Warning;
 float topValue_Warning;
 float value;
 /** invariant value >=0 */

 public void setMaxValue(float v) throws UpperLimitError{
  /* require v>0; value<=topValue_Warning   */
  value+=v;
  if (value >= topValue_Warning)
   throw UpperLimitError;
 }

 public void setMinValue(float v) throws LowerLimitError{
 ...
    /* ensure v>0; value>=lowValue_Warning   */
 }
}
```

List 1. Using Contract-based design.

The code in list 1 might be associated with an IDL definition as shown in the list 2.

```
module DeviceApp {
  interface Device
  {
    // Under level exception
    exception LowerLimitError {};

    // Over level exception
    exception UpperLimitError {};

    // Record a new upper level
     void setMaxValue(in float v) raises (UpperLimitError);
     void setMinValue(in float v) raises (LowerLimitError);;
  };
};
```

List 2. IDL definition.

5. Case studies: MCD support in greenhouse management

The control rules shown below illustrate the relationship between configuring and monitoring various sensors and actuators in the production of flowers and foliage. To exemplify the control rules in the cultivation of flowers we take common concepts in the orchid's production of Phalaenopsis type. To propose control rules in the foliage production, we use examples about the coriander (Eryngium foetidum).

The example consists of three phases:

1. Definition and parameterisation of variables
2. Simple rules supported by MCD
3. Associated rules with production process supported by MCD.

5.1 Phase 1: Definition and parameterization of variables

The variables definition and initial values for temperature control, humidity and the period of lifetime of a process are described below.

5.2 Humidity

Since the low or high humidity levels impact the plant growth, the humidity control is very important. High humidity inhibits leaf transpiration, which restricts the movement of nutrients in the plant, producing a fungal infection and also the death by malnutrition. On the other hand, low humidity reduces water absorption by roots. In the examples, the values assigned to humidity are between acceptable ranges. For example

```
hum_max = value2;
hum_min = value1;
```

5.3 Temperature

Temperature is a relevant variable to which plants react. The temperature is controlled by a range defined by a maximum and a minimum value, and the interval in Celsius degrees required to warn of extreme conditions.

E.g.

```
temp_max      = 28; //Maximum limit acceptable for temperature
temp_min      = 20; //Minimum limit acceptable for temperature
delta_Temp    = 3; //range to alert the proximity to the temperature limit
```

5.4 Time

The timer has great relevance because planting, care and production is given in accordance with specific deadlines for each crop. E.g.

```
startDate     = setDate("yy1/mm1/dd1");
endDate       = setDate("yy2/mm2/dd2");
today         = getDate().getDay();
hour          = getDate().getHour();
day           = (hour > 6) && (hour<17:30)?true:false;
night         = (day)?false:true;
nsec          = # of second that activate the actuator
```

5.5 Phase 2: Simple rules supported by MCD

To describe simple rules supported by the MCD, we use the experiences of diverse researches, who have studied the Eryngium foetidum crop (Alvarado-Sanabria & Villalobos, 1999; Morales, 1995; Santiago-Santos & Cedeño-Maldonado, 1991), and we have adapted some of their experiences in the form of rules, that we describe in Table 1.

Notice in these examples that the rules are described by the combination of 4 attributes that handle: type of sensor that is controlled (in this study we have used wireless sensors connected via ZigBee protocol), the control rule (condition of interest with respect to the sensor at any given time), actions to be taken when the value reported by the sensor allow the condition to be controlled, and a message that can be mailed to an e-mail address, or mobile device.

Sensor	Control rule	Action	Message
temp	temp<=15ºC	lighting system(on)	
soil humidity	hum == 50%"	message system(send)	"hum_min=50%"
humidity	h<60%	irrigation_drip system(on, nseg)	
light	luminosity >80%	curtain system(close)	
timer	day=HARVEST_DAY	message system(send)	" time to harvest"

Table 1. Examples of simple rules to control the Eryngium foetidum crop.

5.6 Phase 3: Associated rules with production process supported by MCD.

Phase 2 described the support that the MDC gives to management the simple control rules; this section describes how the MCD also allows rules to obey production strategies, where the iterative processes specified in the pseudo-code are defined in the MCD with respect to time.

The following examples show how in the MCD is defined a production strategy according to expected demand. Here are some basic processes of interest to the owner of the greenhouse.

Controlling temperature fluctuations between day and night

The Phalaenopsis orchids can be forced to flourish when the temperature is reduced by more than 5 degrees at night for a period of 2 to 4 consecutive weeks, but if the flowering of the orchids needs to be inhibited, it is necessary to maintain a constant temperature of 29 Celsius degrees during the same period of time (Blanchard & Runkle, 2006). In the example above it is assumed that to control the temperature the glasshouse required to have windows, ceiling fans, lighting system and messages system.

```
if (temp >= (temp_max(day) - delta_Temp)) { // Temperature approaches its maximun
   fan(on)
   window(open)
}
if (temp <= (temp_min(night) - delta_Temp)) { //Temperature approaches its minimun
   send_message("abnormal temperature reduction ")
   window(close)
}
if (temp == (temp_min(night))) {              //Temperature temperature reaches its
                                              // minimum level
   light (on)
}
```

Check the average temperature over a period of several days

Control the harmony in temperature can lead to better results in the production of some flowers; hence the following pseudo-code would monitor this condition:

```
while ((startDate<today) && (endDate>today)){
   controlTempMax(temp_max);
   controlTempMin(temp_min);
}
```

Subjecting a crop to water stress or temperature stress produces alterations in the production cycle of flowers. In that case, the MCD contributes to maintain the desired conditions. E.g.:

```
for (int i=startDate;i <=endDate;i++){
   temp_maxeratura [i] = temp_max;
   temp_mineratura [i] = temp_min;
}
```

```
while ((startDate<today) && (endDate>today)){
    controlTempMax(temp_maxeratura[today]);
    controlTempMin(temp_mineratura[today]);
}
```

Other methods that could be implemented include:

- A temperature plan to establish the desired colour of the flowers.
- A temperature plan to produce more flowers a particular day of the week.

6. Acknowledgment

This work has been supported by Spanish Government, in particular by "Agencia Española de Cooperación Internacional para el Desarrollo"under funds from D/027406/09 for 2010, D/033858/10 for 2011, and A1/039089/11 for 2012 and by the Laboratory in Automate and Intelligent Systems in Biodiversity of the University of Costa Rica.

7. References

Alvarado-Sanabria, C. & Villalobos, J. (1999) El culantro de coyote (Eryngium foetidum cursiva) para exportación. Ministerio de Agricultura y Ganadería, Costa Rica. 1999

Blanchard, Mathew & Runkle, Erik. (2006) Temperature during the day, but not during the night, controls flowering of Phalaenopsis orchids. Journal of Experimental Botany. Vol 57. Issue 15, pp4043-4049.

Booch, G., Rumbaugh J. & Jacobson, I. (1999a) The Unified Modeling Language User Guide. Addison-Wesley, Reading, MA

Booch, G., Rumbaugh J. & Jacobson, I. (1999b) The Unified Modeling Language for Object-Oriented Development. Documentation Set Version 0.9a Addendum. Retrieved from: http://www.ccs.neu.edu/research/demeter/course/f96/readings/uml9.pdf

Combest. (2007) Ist Strep COMponent-Based Embedded Systems design Techniques. Scientific Foundations for Component-based Design, and their Limitations Component-based Design for Embedded Systems. Seventh Framework Programme for Research and Technological Development (2007-2013). Retrieved from: http://www.combest.eu/home/?link=CBDforESMcIlroy, Malcolm Douglas (1969). "Mass produced software components". Software Engineering: Report of a conference sponsored by the NATO Science Committee, Garmisch, Germany, 7-11 Oct. 1968. Scientific Affairs Division, NATO. p. 79.

Gamma, Erich; Helm, Richard; Johnson, Ralph & Vlissides, John. (1995) Design Patterns: Elements of Reusable Object-Oriented *Software*. Pearson Ed. Madrid. 1995

IEC International Electrotechnical Commission. (2003) IEC 61131. Programmable controllers. Retrieved from: *http://webstore.iec.ch/preview/info_iec61131-1{ed2.0}en.pdf*

Krasner, Glenn & Pope, Stephen. (1988) A cookbook for using the model-view controller user interface paradigm in Smalltalk-80. Journal of Object Oriented Programming, 1(3):26-49, August -September 1988.

Kopetz, Hermann. (2007) The Complexity Challenge in Embedded System Design. Research Report 55/2007. Retrieved from:

http://www.vmars.tuwien.ac.at/courses/dse/papers/complexity.pdf

Meyer, Bertrand. Applying Design By Contract. (1992). IEEE Computer, Vol. 25, No. 10, pp 40-51.

Morales, José Pablo. Cultivo del cilantro, cilantro ancho y perejil. (1995) Fundación de desarrollo agropecuario, Inc. Serie Cultivos. Boletín Técnico #25. Santo Domingo.

Santiago-Santos, Luis R. & Cedeño-Maldonado, Arturo. (1991) Efecto de la intensidad de la luz sobre la floración y crecimiento del culantro, Eryngium foetidum. Journal of Agricultura of the University of Puerto Rico. Oct 1991, v 75(4) p. 383-389

Schneeman, R.D. (1999). Implementing a Standards-based Distributed Measurement and Control Application on the Internet. In : U.S. Department of Commerce.

Szabó, Zoltán Gendler, "Compositionality" (2008), *The Stanford Encyclopedia of Philosophy (Winter 2008 Edition)*, Edward N. Zalta (ed.). Retrieved from: http://plato.stanford.edu/archives/win2008/entries/compositionality/.

Szyperski. Clement. Gruntz, Dominik & Murer, Stephan. (2002) Component Software - Beyond Object-Oriented Programming. Addison-Wesley

Vásquez Morera, Javier; Vásquez, Núñez, José Luis & Travieso González, Carlos M. (2010) Changing control rules dynamically in embedded digital control systems. WSEAS Transactions on Systems and Control. Issue 3, Volume 5, March 2010

Zwiers, Job; de Roever, Wilhem Paul & vam Ende Boas, Peter. (1985) Compositionality and concurrent networks: soundness and completeness of a proof system in Proc. of 12th colloquium on Automata, Languages and Programming, W. Brauer (ed.), LNCS 194, Springer-Verlag, 1985.

Permissions

The contributors of this book come from diverse backgrounds, making this book a truly international effort. This book will bring forth new frontiers with its revolutionizing research information and detailed analysis of the nascent developments around the world.

We would like to thank Kiyofumi Tanaka, for lending his expertise to make the book truly unique. He has played a crucial role in the development of this book. Without his invaluable contribution this book wouldn't have been possible. He has made vital efforts to compile up to date information on the varied aspects of this subject to make this book a valuable addition to the collection of many professionals and students.

This book was conceptualized with the vision of imparting up-to-date information and advanced data in this field. To ensure the same, a matchless editorial board was set up. Every individual on the board went through rigorous rounds of assessment to prove their worth. After which they invested a large part of their time researching and compiling the most relevant data for our readers. Conferences and sessions were held from time to time between the editorial board and the contributing authors to present the data in the most comprehensible form. The editorial team has worked tirelessly to provide valuable and valid information to help people across the globe.

Every chapter published in this book has been scrutinized by our experts. Their significance has been extensively debated. The topics covered herein carry significant findings which will fuel the growth of the discipline. They may even be implemented as practical applications or may be referred to as a beginning point for another development.

The editorial board has been involved in producing this book since its inception. They have spent rigorous hours researching and exploring the diverse topics which have resulted in the successful publishing of this book. They have passed on their knowledge of decades through this book. To expedite this challenging task, the publisher supported the team at every step. A small team of assistant editors was also appointed to further simplify the editing procedure and attain best results for the readers.

Our editorial team has been hand-picked from every corner of the world. Their multi-ethnicity adds dynamic inputs to the discussions which result in innovative outcomes. These outcomes are then further discussed with the researchers and contributors who give their valuable feedback and opinion regarding the same. The feedback is then collaborated with the researches and they are edited in a comprehensive manner to aid the understanding of the subject.

Apart from the editorial board, the designing team has also invested a significant amount of their time in understanding the subject and creating the most relevant covers. They scrutinized every image to scout for the most suitable representation of the subject and create an appropriate cover for the book.

The publishing team has been involved in this book since its early stages. They were actively engaged in every process, be it collecting the data, connecting with the contributors or procuring relevant information. The team has been an ardent support to the editorial, designing and production team. Their endless efforts to recruit the best for this project, has resulted in the accomplishment of this book. They are a veteran in the field of academics and their pool of knowledge is as vast as their experience in printing. Their expertise and guidance has proved useful at every step. Their uncompromising quality standards have made this book an exceptional effort. Their encouragement from time to time has been an inspiration for everyone.

The publisher and the editorial board hope that this book will prove to be a valuable piece of knowledge for researchers, students, practitioners and scholars across the globe.

List of Contributors

Michael Schmidt, Dietmar Fey and Marc Reichenbach
Embedded Systems Institute, Friedrich-Alexander-University Erlangen-Nuremberg, Germany

Kenn R. Luecke
The Boeing Company, USA

Jan Chudzikiewicz and Zbigniew Zieliński
Military University of Technology, Poland

David Antonio-Torres
Tecnologico de Monterrey Campus Puebla, Mexico

Inácio Fonseca
Instituto Superior de Engenharia de Coimbra, Portugal

Fernando Lopes
Instituto Superior de Engenharia de Coimbra, Portugal
Telecommunication Institute, Portugal

Yu-Cheng Chou, Bo-Shiun Huang and Bo-Jia Peng
Chung Yuan Christian University, Taiwan

Kazuhiro Nakamura, Ryo Shimazaki and Masatoshi Yamamoto
Nagoya University, Japan

Kazuyoshi Takagi and Naofumi Takagi
Kyoto University, Japan

David de la Fuente, Jesús Barba, Fernando Rincón, Julio Daniel Dondo and Juan Carlos López
School of Computer Engineering Department of Technology and Information Systems, University of Castilla-La Mancha, Ciudad Real, Spain

Jhing-Fa Wang and Bo-Wei Chen
National Cheng Kung University, Taiwan

Po-Chun Lin
Tung Fang Design University, Taiwan

Sanjay Misra and Emmanuel Eronu
Department of Computer Engineering, Federal University of Technology, Minna, Nigeria

Camel Tanougast, Abbas Dandache, Mohamed Salah Azzaz and Said Sadoudi
University Lorraine of Metz, France

Mohamed Ali Ibrahim and Philippe Mabilleau
University of Sherbrooke, Canada

Javier Vásquez-Morera
University of Costa Rica, Computer Science Deparment, San José, Costa Rica

José L. Vásquez-Núñez
University of Costa Rica, Sede del Atlántico, Cartago, Costa Rica

Carlos Manuel Travieso-González
University of Las Palmas de Gran Canaria, Signals and Communications Department, Institute for Technological Development and Innovation in Communications, Campus, University of Tafira, Las Palmas de Gran Canaria, Spain

Printed in the USA
CPSIA information can be obtained
at www.ICGtesting.com
JSHW011456221024
72173JS00005B/1093

9 781632 401694